TREASURES
⊙LD AND NEW
Images in the Lectionary

GAIL RAMSHAW

FORTRESS PRESS
MINNEAPOLIS

Treasures Old and New: Images in the Lectionary

Copyright © 2002 Augsburg Fortress. All rights reserved.
Except brief quotations in critical articles or reviews, no part of this book may be reproduced in any manner without prior written permission from the publisher. Write to: Permissions, Augsburg Fortress, Box 1209, Minneapolis, MN 55440-1209. Or visit www.augsburgfortress.org/copyrights

Scripture quotations, unless otherwise noted, are from the New Revised Standard Version (NRSV) Bible, copyright © 1989 Division of Christian Education of the National Council of Churches of Christ in the United States of America. Used by permission.

Other quoted materials are acknowledged on pp. 455–466.

Cover art: "So Close" by Daniel Nevins. © Daniel Nevins. Used by permission.
Cover and jacket design: Lecy Design, Inc.
Interior design: Becky Lowe

Library of Congress Cataloging-in-Publication Data
Ramshaw, Gail, 1947–
    Treasures old and new: images in the lectionary / Gail Ramshaw.
        p. c.m.
    Includes bibliographical references and index.
    ISBN 0-8006-3189-7
        1. Bible—Language, style. 2. Common lectionary (1992) 3. Figures of
        speech. 1. Title.
    BS537.R36 2002
    220.6'4—DC21   2002071741

Manufactured in the U.S.A.   ISBN 0-8006-3189-7
09 08 07 06 05 04 03 02   1 2 3 4 5 6 7 8 9 10

Contents

FOR MANY YEARS the images that recur in the Sunday liturgy have been filling up my head. I recall as a child in the 1950s being puzzled by the King James translation of Psalm 22 as printed in *The Lutheran Hymnal*. In it we prayed to be delivered from the horns of the unicorns, but fairy tales told me that the unicorn was a wondrous beast with a horn that granted wishes. The translation in the current *Lutheran Book of Worship* clarifies the image: it is the horns of wild bulls that we hope to avoid. So here is one question before us: how should we translate the biblical images for liturgical use?

Teaching literary classics in college, I encountered the current biblical illiteracy. Students reading Charles Dickens's *Hard Times* saw no significance in a chapter entitled "The One Thing Needful" or a protagonist named Stephen who is martyred for the cause. So here is a second question: how can liturgical language function for a biblically illiterate assembly?

And when lecturing at a pastoral conference I was asked by a clergyman, "Since we know that angels were invented by Babylonian art, how can we sing the Sanctus any more?" I realized a third issue: even when our translation is accurate and our knowledge of the Bible impressive, the church's liturgical purpose in using biblical images remains inaccessible to many worshipers.

My training in the interpretation of symbolic language made it clear to me that I needed to continue to write on the meaning of the biblical images that recur in the liturgy. When at a baptism Christians who are not biblical literalists ask God to recall Noah's flood, what are they saying? What does the liturgy intend by citing dozens of biblical images each Sunday?

I am a passionate defender of the lectionary. As a layperson, I like to prepare for the Sunday liturgy by checking the readings

5

beforehand. I delight in the complexities possible in the interpretation of three readings each Sunday. I am pleased to think of Christians of many denominations all around the world reading from the three-year lectionary. I know the lectionary may be studied in many ways. We might codify its theology, trace its themes, compare its selections with the entire biblical message or with the speculations of the Jesus Seminar. But when a Swedish feminist protested to me that the lectionary used in her church was prohibitively androcentric, I decided that my next task would be to undertake a systematic analysis of the imagery in the three-year lectionary.

In this volume I apply the three general concerns of biblical imagery—translation, familiarity, liturgical hermeneutics—to the increasingly popular three-year lectionaries. Here are some of my questions: Which images recur most often in the lectionary? What is the history of meaning of these images, before, within, and outside the Bible? What has been their usage during the centuries of Christian liturgical use? In a culture far distant from that in which they arose, can these images still speak of mercy and challenge to God's people? I recall the participants at a pastoral conference in 1997 asking me to teach them how to recognize in the Markan parable of the mustard seed the ancient Near Eastern myth of the tree of life. This book seeks to do that, and more.

I began by deciding that attention to the Psalms will require another entire book. Focusing on the three readings for each Sunday and feast, I read and reread all the lectionary's selections. I identified the images that lie through and underneath each selection, and then grouped the images into families. In deciding how many images to focus on, I considered twelve, for the gates of Jerusalem, or twenty-four, for the elders around the throne. But even twenty-four was not enough. It seemed that forty was right. If it rained on the ark for forty days and forty nights, if during Lent we struggle for forty days in the wilderness, and if strengthened by God's bread we walk for forty days to the mountain of God, we will need at least one image for each of the forty days to bring us through. To this task I bring literary training in finding images and analyzing them, continuing study of biblical imagery, knowledge of Christian liturgical speech, and dedication to, even affection for, the three-year lectionary.

I see the three readings of each Sunday and festival as treasure that we, like the householder in Matthew 13, take from our storehouse, treasures that, although old, are able to be new each week. The woman in the cover art: Is she Wisdom protecting the house she has built? Is that the tree of life behind her? Is she journeying on the Spirit's breath? She is Matthew's householder, offering us her precious treasures old and new. Each week we show these treasures to each other, and say, Ah, yes!

There once was a family that read aloud each evening from literary classics. One book the family plowed through was James Fenimore Cooper's *The Deerslayer*, a book so alien to contemporary taste that the family members were sure they were the only people alive who had actually read the whole of it. Yet its strong images found their place in the family's imagination, and "poor Hetty" in their speech. Then a daughter, off at college, encountered one other student who had read *The Deerslayer*, and she phoned home to say how the two of them had found the book to be a bridge between them. Cooper, everyone who has read *The Deerslayer*, the four family members, and the new college friend are bonded by Cooper's images. And if you have read *The Deerslayer*, you are smiling now, for you, too, remember poor Hetty and those incredible Cooper Indians. And as with *The Deerslayer*, so with the lectionary: The Sunday images bond together the Christian community. We hear the images, we incorporate them into our speech, we share them over the centuries and miles.

I thank Frank Stoldt and Martin Seltz of Ausgburg Fortress, Publishers for their continual encouragement throughout this project. I am indebted to David Efroymson and Robert Bornemann, who read the first draft of the manuscript and offered helpful comments and corrections. I am grateful to the editors of various anthologies, from M.F. Toal to Shawn Madigan, c.s.i., whose scholarship assisted my searches for quotations from the fathers and the mothers. I express once again my gratitude to Gordon Lathrop for weekly conversation, as Sunday after Sunday we together receive and hold before us these biblical images, and I am glad that this volume allows me to share these treasures with you.

Abbreviations

A	year A
ABC	years A, B, and C
Ad	Advent
Asc	Ascension
AshW	Ash Wednesday
B	year B
Bap	Baptism of the Lord
C	year C
Ch	Christmas
ChE	Christmas eve
ChDn	Christmas dawn
ChDy	Christmas day
Ea	Easter
Ep	Epiphany
GFr	Good Friday
Last	Last Sunday of each cycle
Le	Lent
MTh	Maundy or Holy Thursday
Pas	Passion Sunday
Pent	Pentecost
Pr	proper
RCL	Revised Common Lectionary
RL	Roman Lectionary
Trans	Transfiguration
Trin	Trinity
Vigil	Easter (Paschal) Vigil

Introduction

The Three-Year Lectionary

At the seventh hour all the people go up to the church on the Mount of Olives. And there hymns and antiphons proper to the day and place are sung, interspersed with appropriate readings from the Scriptures and prayers.

EGERIA, CA. 410[1]

THE BIBLE

When Christians assemble on the first day of the week to celebrate and embody the resurrection of Christ, they read aloud from the Bible. This practice came naturally to the early Christians from Jewish worship patterns, in which at each sabbath assembly, passages from the Hebrew holy books were read aloud and interpreted by various teachers. The people of Israel honored the Hebrew Scriptures as the word of God, and one of the primary purposes of the sabbath assembly was for the community of faith to hear what God was saying through the word. The writings judged to be appropriate for public reading in the sabbath assembly were the books that came to be compiled into what we call the Hebrew Bible. At their weekly meals, and perhaps at other gatherings, Christians continued the Jewish practice of reading from the Hebrew Scriptures, utilizing its most widely used Greek translation, called the Septuagint. By the second century, Christians were deciding which other writings should be read at the weekly meeting. The books that came to be identified as the New Testament were written by Christians over several generations and were selected as being appropriate for public proclamation at the Christian weekly assembly.

Thus it was not by chance or historic accident that the church came to read the Bible in public on Sunday. Rather, the Christian Bible was compiled for this very purpose: to be read in the Christian assembly on each day of the resurrection. It seems safe to say that if Christians had not been meeting together each week, there would be no Christian Bible. Christians believe that the Bible read aloud in the Sunday assembly contains and conveys the word of God. Ritually, the community acknowledges this belief by standing to hear the reading from the gospel. The scripture reading brings the Word who is Christ into our midst. Christ spoke not only in the past, but speaks also here, in this assembly. We do not go back in history, to some holy time in the first century. Rather, the Spirit of God whom the church encounters in Jesus is now in this very room, and we stand to honor that presence of Christ.

It is instructive for anyone interested in lectionary issues to read in some of those many books (such as Jubilees, or the Gospel according to Thomas) that did not make the liturgical cut, and to speculate concerning the factors that may have figured in the decisions of those first lectionary committees. For example, the creation account in the book of Jubilees attends with far greater interest to an elaborate priestly calendar than to the mighty power of God. We know of Christian criteria such as apostolicity, but because we do not have minutes of their meetings, we cannot review how the second-century church authorities came to their decisions. Currently, knowledge about and interest in the noncanonical books is growing. Postmodern thought and the literary practice of deconstruction both serve to free readers to evaluate the history and quality of the sacred books in the world's religious traditions, and some Christians, doubting the wisdom and suspecting the prejudices of those early committees, suggest that the contemporary church ought to read from some of those noncanonical books during worship. The position of the three-year lectionary, however, is the traditional Christian view that the canonical scriptures, in all their magnificence and muddle, their clarity and complexity, constitute the primary word to which the church attends.

Christians have explained in various ways what they mean by calling the Bible the word of God. Most users of the lectionary, like most theologians throughout the history of the church, not being fundamentalists, do not entertain a blanket-like acceptance of the entire Bible as an inerrant dictation from God. Rather, the dominant understanding in the contemporary Western church is that in this motley collection of texts we hear the Spirit of God speaking to us. Among other voices, Lutherans have stressed that the mercy of God proclaimed in the Bible is the Word itself, that is, Christ. In some parts of the Bible, that voice is heard loud and clear, while in other parts so dimly, so obliquely, that over the ages the church chose not to read those passages aloud on Sunday morning. It should be noted that despite the formation of the canon in the early centuries of the church, not all Christian communions agree on which books are of the highest religious significance. This disagreement explains the fact that the Bible as published and used by Roman Catholics contains some books that Protestants call *apocryphal* and that the Roman Catholic lectionary appoints readings from these deuterocanonical books for Sunday reading.

The Bible serves many differing purposes, even for believers. Christian scholars contrast this great book with the writings of the other religions of the world. They trace the historical evolution of monotheism from an earlier henotheism. Christian thinkers contrast the biblical worldviews with those of our time. Students of myth compare prehistoric, ancient Near Eastern, and Greco-Roman myths to those found in the Bible. Christian historians use the biblical books to study the development of the Jewish nation and the early Christian church. They compare the biblical record with archaeological evidence found in the Near East. They examine the Bible's socioeconomic practices, consider the record of women's oppression, and examine the notion of slavery as morally acceptable. Christians in personal trouble and sorrow search the Bible's profound poetry for individual comfort.

During the liturgy, however, the church uses the Bible for especially this purpose: to hear the saving voice of God for all. The lectionary is constructed to serve this liturgical purpose. Lectionary advocates like to remind believers that whenever Christians read from the Bible in private devotion or academic study, they are using the Bible in a secondary way, for a secondary purpose, and that any nonliturgical use of the Bible ought to acknowledge the Bible's primary purpose as a text compiled for public proclamation in the religious community. Christians interested in any of the many other reasons to read the Bible will find the lectionary's selections less than satisfactory.

THE DEVELOPMENT OF THE THREE-YEAR LECTIONARY

The Bible is, as Augustine wrote, "of mountainous difficulty and enveloped in mysteries."[2] It is also a long book for our short lives. So, which parts of the Bible should be read on Sunday? During the Reformation period, Ulrich Zwingli advocated that Christian assemblies start at Genesis 1 and read one chapter each week right through to the close of Revelation. That ideal collided with the reality that most Christians see little meaning in, for example, passages delineating the menstrual taboo, patrilineal descent, or the proper slaughtering of sacrificial animals. Zwingli's principle devolved into the practice of the preacher's choosing which chapters to skip and which to proclaim. Still today, in some Protestant churches, a primary obligation for the preacher is the selection of the biblical text for the day. Yet it is difficult for those who choose texts to ensure that their proclamation will be broader and deeper than their own training and preference. So it came about in the late twentieth century that even some of the denominations that previously prac-ticed such free choice joined with other denominations to publish a lec-tionary and to encourage its use. Note that the word *lectionary* has two mean-ings: (1) the list of biblical citations selected for public proclamation in the assembly, and (2) the bound book, sometimes mammoth and elegant, in which these Bible selections are printed out. This volume attends only to the first definition of *lectionary*.

Increasingly, the lectionary of choice for Western Christians around the world is the three-year lectionary. More and more Christian communions, either convinced by the excellence or popularity of this lectionary or awed by the excessive amount of work required to construct a lectionary of their own, are choosing as their lectionary one of several variants of the three-year lec-tionary. Several studies of the three-year lectionary explain how this lec-tionary system came into being, what its variants are, and what are its logic and hermeneutic.[3] Here we will only summarize this complex picture.[4]

Some evidence indicates that our selections for feast days are as old as the fourth century. During the medieval centuries, the Western church used a one-year lectionary that appointed two readings for each Sunday and feast day. The second reading, the most highly honored, came from the gospels—24 taken from Matthew, 4 from Mark, 21 from Luke, and 15 from John—and the first reading, taken from the epistles, was meant to complement the gospel.[5] As part of the liturgical reforms instituted at the Second Vatican Council, the Roman Catholic church assembled eighteen persons to design a new lectionary that opened up more lavishly the riches of the scriptures for liturgical use. The committee, influenced by both earlier lectionary patterns and modern biblical exegesis, designed a three-year Sunday lectionary, which was later mandated for use by all Roman Catholics around the world. The Roman Lectionary has been slightly revised over the decades, and some Roman Catholics call for further revisions. This lectionary is known as either the Revised Lectionary or Lectionary for Mass.[6] In this volume, reference to the Roman Lectionary will be with the abbreviation RL.

Even after the Reformation, several Protestant churches continued to use a variant of the one-year medieval lectionary, and after the reforms of Vati-can II, especially parts of Anglicanism and North American Lutherans were impressed by Rome's new three-year plan. These churches borrowed the three-year Roman Lectionary, made some changes, and adopted their own versions for use in their churches.[7] Other Protestants proposed their own variants, after which an English-speaking ecumenical committee of liturgical reformers known as the Consultation on Common Texts collaborated on a single ecumenical version, which they termed the Common Lectionary.[8]

Finally, in the 1980s, the Consultation on Common Texts committee undertook to reconcile some of the denominational differences and hermeneutical perspectives that were apparent in the growing number of three-year lectionaries. The result was the Revised Common Lectionary, and it is this version of the three-year lectionary that is gaining in usage among Protestants around the world.[9] In this volume, reference to the Revised Common Lectionary will be with the abbreviation RCL. A characteristic difference between the Revised Common Lectionary and the Roman Lectionary is that the Protestant version stipulates longer—sometimes considerably longer—readings. In addition, the committee that compiled the Revised Common Lectionary sought to amend what it judged were inadequacies in the Roman Lectionary, such as its inattention to women's issues.

To summarize: In the mid-twentieth century, several Western churches used variants of the medieval one-year lectionary, while many Protestant churches allowed free choice of Sunday texts. Fifty years later, at the beginning of the twenty-first century, the situation is changed. Roman Catholics are expected to use their Revised Lectionary. Some Protestant churches require or recommend use of the Revised Common Lectionary. An increasing number of Protestant churches offer the Revised Common Lectionary as a helpful option for parish use. Christians in free churches are becoming acquainted with this lectionary, thanks both to ecumenical conversation and to the creative catechetical and supportive lectionary materials pouring out of church publishing houses.

The Logic of the Calendar

To understand the plan of the three-year lectionary, we begin with calendar.

1. The primary unit of the Christian calendar is Sunday. The New Testament suggests that soon after the resurrection, believers were assembling on the first day of the week to share a meal with the risen Christ. Every Sunday celebrates the resurrection of Christ.

2. The central annual festival of the Christian year is Resurrection Sunday, called in English Easter, a day set in the Northern Hemisphere to be the first Sunday after the first full moon after the spring equinox. The Easter celebration lasts fifty days and culminates at Pentecost. The Easter preparation called Lent, according to a common way of reckoning its days, begins with Ash Wednesday and lasts forty weekdays: Sundays are not included in the count of the forty days of Lent.

3. The second annual festival of importance is Christmas, originally set to coincide with the Northern Hemisphere's winter solstice celebration.

Christmas can be said to last twelve days, culminating at Epiphany, or forty days, culminating at Presentation. Christmas is preceded by Advent, which includes four Sundays.

4. The several churches dedicate other Sundays to favored celebrations and observances. For example, All Saints is an ecumenically popular Sunday festival; Body and Blood of Christ is kept by Roman Catholics; Reformation is kept by some Lutherans.

5. The remaining Sundays of the year are counted off in succession. The Revised Common Lectionary conceives of these Sundays in two different units: one is an Epiphany season, having its own integrity, including the Sundays between Epiphany and Lent; and the second unit lasts from Trinity Sunday until Advent. The Roman Lectionary has one annual numbering system that includes the time between Epiphany and Lent, as well as the time between Pentecost Sunday and Advent. The Roman Lectionary's Latin designation for nonfestival Sundays, *per annum*, has unfortunately been rendered in English as *ordinary time*. Perhaps *normative*, *regular*, or *standard* would have been a better adjective than *ordinary* with which to title the regularly recurring celebration of Christ's resurrection. The English word *ordinary* connotes the prosaic or humdrum, and no Sunday is prosaic or humdrum. Users of the Revised Common Lectionary simply say *Epiphany X* or *Proper X* but, influenced by Roman Catholic terminology, sometimes refer to *ordinary time*.

The Logic of the Readings

The readings of the lectionary are designed to fit the calendar. It is important at the outset, however, to recognize that as with the Bible, so also with the lectionary: no minutes are available that chronicle the various committees' countless hours of conversation, debate, and decision that went into the formation of the several versions of the three-year lectionary. Thus while the general pattern of the readings in relation to the calendar is apparent, any detailed proposal of the logic must be suggested in a spirit of humility.[10]

1. The gospel reading, chosen to tell the story of Jesus Christ as celebrated by the calendar, is assumed to be the focal reading. The lectionary is centered in John, which is read at the major Christian festivals and at other significant times of the year. The selections from John are central to the church's teachings about christology.

2. Around John are readings from Matthew in year A, Mark in year B, and Luke in year C. The synoptic gospels are read semicontinuously throughout each year. This pattern, born of historical-critical studies of the Bible

and recognizing the integrity of each separate gospel, is radically different from an amalgamation of the gospels that was assumed in the medieval church.

3. During the festival half of the year, from Advent 1 through Trinity Sunday, both the first reading, taken usually from the Old Testament, and the second reading, taken usually from the epistles of the New Testament, complement the gospel reading. This complementarity is of various sorts: the readings may provide necessary background; they may employ parallel language or incorporate a similar theme; they may present a contrast that thus heightens the gospel message.[11]

4. During the nonfestival parts of the year, the second reading provides semicontinuous selections from one epistle after another.

5. Concerning the first reading during the nonfestival half of the year, we encounter a complication. In the Roman Lectionary, the first reading throughout the entire year complements the gospel. Following this pattern, the Revised Common Lectionary also appoints, throughout the Epiphany season, a first reading that complements the gospel.

After Trinity Sunday, however, the Revised Common Lectionary provides a choice between two patterns. In the one more traditional, the first reading complements the gospel reading. In this volume, these Old Testament readings appointed to complement the gospel are designated with this symbol (†). In the other choice, following the Reformed tradition of biblical usage, the books from the Hebrew Scriptures are read semicontinuously, just as are the second readings from the epistles. In this volume, the Old Testament readings appointed in the semicontinuous pattern are designated with this symbol (°). Because many church bodies and denominational publishers choose to recommend or publish only one of these two patterns, many users of the RCL, whose knowledge of the lectionary comes solely from their denominational resources, are unaware that two sets of first readings are given for the summer and fall.

The three-year lectionary presents its biblical selections always as interrelating with at least some other biblical readings.[12] Depending on the variant used and the Sunday in question, this interrelationship may be between two or three of the other readings, as well as with the readings of the prior and future Sundays. Even when the readings for a particular Sunday minimize interrelationship (for example in the nonfestival half of the year in the semicontinuous series of the Revised Common Lectionary), the human mind will attempt to find coherence in an event such as a morning liturgy. Paul Ricoeur speaks of this tendency as the human synchronic memory, that is, the attempt to synchronize pieces into the whole.[13] Meaning goes from one moment to another, from one reading to another, and makes a whole of disparate parts. The human mind seeks to tape stray pieces together, to assemble the puzzle. Pieces that do not fit together will either be disregarded or distorted, to force a fit. One liturgical scholar likened the elaborate inter-relationships set out within the three-year lectionary to a chess set that, unfortunately, many people play as if it were only checkers.[14] Among the various ways that the readings in the lectionary are interrelated, it is the images within the readings that this volume considers.

As with any lectionary scheme, the three-year lectionary selects out parts of the complex Bible as more appropriate for proclamation in the Christian assembly than are other parts of the Bible. Some Christians are so conscious of what any lectionary omits that they resist using one, preferring instead to make their own decisions about biblical readings. This procedure only replaces the selections made by a committee over several decades with their own personal and immediate preferences. We are back to the definition of *lectionary*: the lectionary is by definition a list of choices. Such a list implies that some biblical texts are more important for Christian proclamation, some less, and others not significant enough for the baptized life to be included in the Sunday liturgy.

The biblical canon is the set of books that the church judged appropriate for proclamation during Sunday worship, and the lectionary is a canon within a canon, those parts of those books judged especially appropriate for the Sunday assembly in our time and place. Bluntly put, the lectionary edits the Bible. Christians, celebrating the mystery of Christ on Sunday morning, stress some aspects of the Bible, remember some others, and yet choose to lay aside some of its pages for the theologian or the Tuesday evening Bible study group to pick up. What should Christians do with the legend in Genesis 6 that sin was occasioned by sexual intercourse between male angels and female humans? The church has decided: ignore it. We choose not to read Genesis 6:1-4 on Sunday. Many famous biblical stories—for example, the narrative of the destruction of Sodom and Gomorrah or the tales of Samson and Delilah—are not included in the lectionary. The question is always: is this part of the Bible essential for Sunday proclamation? It is not so much that the church reads the Bible in its worship. Rather, it reads from the Bible the gospel, as Christians have come to understand that good news. We follow the Jewish tradition in this practice. An Exodus passage (34:7) reads that God will not clear the guilty. Yet Jews believed that, contrary to this particular passage, God does indeed forgive. And so when this passage was incorporated into Jewish liturgical worship, its grammar was altered to omit the negative.[15] It is as if, with the continuing inspiration of the Spirit of God, the community of worshipers clarifies the Bible.

CHRISTIAN USE OF THE HEBREW SCRIPTURES

The Revised Common Lectionary provides two sets of Old Testament readings for the nonfestival half of the year. This decision represented not some creative generosity on the part of the committee, but rather its unresolved internal conflicts over the issues raised by the Christian use of the Hebrew Scriptures. Christians do not agree about why the church should know the Hebrew Scriptures, how the church should learn them, what their meaning is for Christians, and how Christians can interpret the Hebrew Bible without offense to whichever group of contemporary Jews is being envisioned. The two sets of Old Testament readings demonstrate our inability to agree, or even to compromise, on some of these issues.

In the second century, church leaders debated whether Christians ought to continue to read from the Hebrew Bible. Marcion thought not. The dominant Christian tradition, however, became ascendant: Christians not only could, but were required to continue proclamation of the Hebrew Scriptures. Some Christian imagery did arise from within the Greco-Roman world. Examples include the philosophical image of the emanation of the divine and the mythic tales of divine virgin births. Yet by far the majority of Christian terms and images derive from the church's Jewish past. Christian history contains three distinct attitudes toward the Hebrew Scriptures, and each response suggests its own lectionary leanings.

Early in its life the church understood itself as the only true development of its Jewish past. In its appropriation of the Hebrew Scriptures, the church condemned the Jews, seeing a christological reading of the Hebrew Scriptures as the only valid reading, its own version of salvation as negating the other. Undoubtedly the Roman destruction of the temple intensified this movement by suggesting that biblical Judaism was over. A classic early example of this hermeneutic is the Easter sermon of Melito of Sardis.[16] The first half of this metaphoric tour de force appropriates persons and events in the Old Testament as images of the salvation wrought by Christ. The second half of the sermon castigates the Jews in a fiercely acerbic tone. A somewhat less offensive example of this hermeneutic is what has been termed *replacement theology*, the idea that Christ has replaced the Torah as the vehicle to God.[17] Replacement theology tends to view the Hebrew Scriptures as a puzzle, which discovered its shape in Christ, and focuses on only those Old Testament passages that find a fulfillment in Christ. The term *typology* usually refers to this method of interpreting aspects of the Old Testament only as types, or prefigurings, of Christ.[18]

In the second half of the twentieth century, probably in response to the

Holocaust and in keeping with scholarly interest in the original intent of the ancient writers, many Christians began to rethink their use of the Hebrew Bible. Was it appropriate for Christians to read the Old Testament as if it were promising Christ, when scholars tell us that the writers had no such intention? Some Christians came to advocate that our respect for Judaism requires us to read the Hebrew Scriptures only in their original meaning; a phrase often heard was "in their own right." Many Christians, judging medieval typological exegesis to have presented quite bizarre interpretations of Hebrew texts, hoped to distance the contemporary church from such classical typology. This critical hermeneutic views the Hebrew Bible as an ancient religious text with its own integrity to be respected and replaces the term *Old Testament* with *First Testament* or *Hebrew Scriptures*.[19] Christians convinced of this hermeneutic resist the habit of finding parallels between Old and New Testament passages.

A third position acknowledges two separate trajectories of the Hebrew Scriptures.[20] The Judaism that developed after Rome's destruction of the temple adapted the historic Israelite texts in a manner befitting its new situation, and in contemporary Judaism diverse interpretations of the ancient texts are promulgated. The Christianity that developed simultaneous to the formation of post-biblical Judaism interpreted the historic Israelite texts in light of the resurrection of Christ and within the life of the eucharistic community. Neither trajectory negates the other. A hermeneutic derived from this position rejects replacement theology as being not only potentially anti-Semitic, but also nonbiblical, because the Bible promises God's continuing covenant with the Jews. Yet it requires the church to continue proclamation of the Hebrew sources, from which the church received not only its God but also most of its religious imagery. Christians can speak few sentences without reliance on their Jewish roots. Saying "Jesus Christ is Lord" reuses an Old Testament name Joshua, cites a Hebrew title for a national savior, and translates into English a Greek circumlocution for the Hebrew name of God (LORD, for *kyrios*, for YHWH). A lectionary useful for this hermeneutic of continuity stresses the perpetuation of God's mercy and the usefulness of the Hebrew stories and images in proclaiming the resurrection of Christ.

Unquestionably, Christians have a poor record in their conduct with regard to the sacred scriptures of the Jews. Extant from the thirteenth century is a massive manuscript, the Bible Moralisee.[21] Probably drawn up for the French court, this incomplete picture Bible contains hundreds of sets of pictures: the first roundel of each set depicts Old Testament narratives from Genesis 1 to 2 Kings 4, and the second roundel depicts some Christian parallel to the

Hebrew biblical story. The parallels are by our standards highly anti-Semitic. For example, the evil characters in the Old Testament stories are shown as parallel to thirteenth-century Jews, who are drawn with pointed hats and money-bags. Such highly problematic typology encourages some contemporary Christians to resist any complementarity.

Yet the third hermeneutical position sees Christian proclamation as one of the descendants of the Hebrew tradition. In the Bible Moralisee, one roundel shows the baby Moses lying in his basket in the bulrushes. In the parallel picture, the child Jesus is lying in the church's open Bible. God saves the people through Moses, and through Jesus; the container is the basket, and is the Bible. This interpretation is not suggesting that Moses is bad and Jesus good, or that Moses' basket is literally a prefiguring of the New Testament. Yet the parallel pictures offer to our imagination the image of the Bible as the cradle that holds the savior. This third hermeneutic undergirds much of the interrelationship between the Old and New Testaments as presented by the three-year lectionary.

The debate between the various hermeneutical positions explains why the Revised Common Lectionary provides two sets of Old Testament readings for the nonfestival half of the year. The complementary set of readings (marked †) attempts a critical continuation of the Christian pattern of reading the Old Testament in terms of the New. The semicontinuous set of readings (marked °), reading the books of Moses in year A, the court narratives in year B, and the prophets in year C, presents for half the year the Hebrew Scriptures without Christian parallel. Yet it has been argued that the semicontinuous set presents its own Christian complementarity in a wider fashion. By reading the Mosaic tradition with Matthew, the Davidic tradition with Mark, and the prophetic tradition with Luke, each gospel is heard alongside an especially appropriate voice from the Hebrew tradition.[22]

Scripture Interprets Scripture

During the thirteenth to the fifteenth centuries there circulated throughout the Western church a remarkable devotional guide that we know as the Biblia Pauperum.[23] Manuscript and blockbook copies are extant in Latin, Old French, and Old German, and images from the scheme are painted on the walls and carved into the furniture of churches from Sweden to Italy, Britain to Austria. At the center of each of its forty pages is a depiction of an event in the life of Christ. Flanking the representation of this gospel story are depictions of two complementary stories from the Old Testament, and in the four corners of the page are applicable citations from the psalms and the prophets. Finally, a summarizing phrase holds all these passages together as one unit. The art itself varies: the depictions in the books, stained glass windows, and wall paintings are crafted by local artists of differing ability. Yet the pattern is identical throughout Europe and over three centuries.

Like the three-year lectionary, this biblical list must have fascinated many Christians, who carried it with them as they traveled throughout the West. The connections made on each page of the Biblia Pauperum are not always to contemporary taste and are often distant from scholarly exegesis. For example, the psalms are considered to be prophecy from the prophet David. Yet the idea that six biblical passages surround each gospel story and interpret it exemplifies the principle that scripture interprets scripture.

The origin of this central Christian principle lies in the New Testament itself. For example, in Mark (14:28), Jesus is accused of threatening to destroy the temple. By the time the Gospel of John was written, the method of scripture interpreting scripture had led to the author's comment (John 2:21): "but he was speaking of the temple of his body." The author of John claims that what was said about the temple is now said by Christians of Christ. Christians used the imagery in the Hebrew Bible—for example, the image of the temple—to articulate their encounter with Christ. In Matthew 12:40 Jesus likens his coming death and resurrection to Jonah's stay in the belly of the fish. Here again, an Old Testament story—that of Jonah—is presented as an image of Christ, that is, a picture to help the disciples to understand and interpret the resurrection. In Luke 24:27 Jesus proclaims the resurrection to the disciples on the walk to Emmaus by interpreting to them stories and images from the Hebrew Bible. Paul writes (1 Corinthians 15:3) that Christ was raised "in accordance with the scriptures," that is, of course, the Hebrew Scriptures, the New Testament not having been written yet.

These examples illustrate the Christian practice of using one part of the Bible to illumine another part. Each verse stands interrelated to other verses. Because of this fundamental Christian interpretive principle, the fact that three readings are appointed by the three-year lectionary for each Christian assembly can be seen not as burden, but as gift.[24] The lectionary, by listing several interrelated texts and by connecting each week to the surrounding weeks, assists the church in probing the meanings of any given reading. When a reading appears twice in the lectionary, at different times of the liturgical year and surrounded by different corresponding texts, its meaning for the Christian assembly will shift. The three-year lectionary makes sense only when one accepts that the liturgical setting, its christocentric calendar and sacramental focus, provides the framework for the Christian community's interpretation of the Bible.

Images

The Lord sitteth on the Father's right hand in endless rest and peace. By this is not meant that the Son sitteth on the right hand beside his Father as one man sitteth by another, in this life: for there is no such sitting, as I understand it, in the Trinity. But he sitteth on the Father's right hand: that is to say, right in the highest nobility of the Father's joy.

JULIAN OF NORWICH, CA. 1410[25]

COMPLEMENTARY HERMENEUTICAL PATTERNS

Throughout the history of the church, various techniques have been used to interpret the biblical readings proclaimed in the liturgy. During the third century a noticeable difference developed between the Alexandrians and the Antiochians. The Alexandrian school, which came to be more important in the Eastern church, sought to allegorize biblical passages to find their meaning within the contemporary believers. So Gregory of Nyssa preached that the three dousings of water that Elijah poured over the sacrifice during the contest with the prophets of Baal signified the three dousings of water at Christian baptism.[26] The Antiochian school, more influential in the Western church, interpreted the Bible in a more historical and linear fashion. Moses, Elijah, and Jesus all fasted for forty days, Augustine argued, and so to follow the law, the prophets, and the gospel, Christians also fast for forty days during Lent.[27] It was as if the East thought more in layered and trinitarian circles, and the West more in a chronological and christological line. With these different patterns of thought, it is not surprising that the liturgy of the Eastern church immerses itself into a sense of timelessness, while the worship services of Western churches are usually out in about an hour.

In the West during the Middle Ages, the attempt of theologians to synchronize faith with secular knowledge led to scholarly approaches to interpretation in which the biblical texts were dissected and analyzed just as a text from Aristotle might have been. To counteract this heavily intellectual emphasis, medieval mystics interiorized all meaning, interpreting the scriptural passages as poetic descriptions of God's action within the individual soul. Following this era, Reformation preachers railed against what they saw as excessive emotional subjectivity and stressed the communal experiential interpretation: God acts in the church, and the text speaks to the world now in judgment and mercy. Some Reformation traditions instituted a new literalism, by teaching, for example, that some Israelite regulations such as the sabbath were to be revived among Christians and that the Bible's apocalyptic poetry contained accurate descriptions of the world's future.

This volume does not intend to provide a detailed history of the church's hermeneutical patterns and practices.[28] But even this brief overview demonstrates how the pendulum swings back and forth, the church trying one method of interpretation, and then once again its opposite, exploring the many ways that God speaks to the church through the Bible. It is not surprising that the church's various techniques lean toward either the literalist or the symbolic, for the church has always claimed both these two complementary truths. On the literal side is a more or less factual history to the faith. A people named Israel really experienced a covenant with God; the preacher and healer Jesus of Nazareth was really executed in the first century; and the church really spread around the world proclaiming the word. Meanwhile, on the symbolic side, the word continues to come alive within us with a meaning new to each generation. If Christ is not born within the community, it does not much matter that Christ was born long ago; faith is not about accepting facts of ancient history, but about a transformation of ourselves and the world in our contemporary experience.

Often the two techniques are interwoven. For example, even though we can assume that preachers in the early church understood the biblical stories of Jesus' miracles to be factually true, their sermons did not place significance in this literal meaning. Consider Augustine's sermon on the three miracles of Jesus in raising the dead. Although his sermon makes clear that Augustine accepted the stories as factual, the point of his sermon was that we sinners, just like Jairus's daughter, the young man of Nain, and Lazarus, are already dead. He urged his congregation "in whichever of these three deaths they find themselves, let them act at once, to rise here and now from the dead."[29] For Augustine, the point was not that Jesus was an amazing first-century miracle worker, but that God will give new life to all of us who are now already lying dead in our sin.

The Problems with Literalism

For the church's proclamation in the twenty-first century, the extreme to avoid is literalism. Particularly in the American church, literalism has been the dominant tendency since the nineteenth century. Perhaps this historic Western focus on literalism was intensified by the experience of Christians on the American prairie. Oftentimes on the frontier, the faith of the church was sustained by laypeople reading their Bibles. Most of these persons had minimal education, little theological training, no knowledge of Hebrew and Greek, and general distrust of scholarly expertise. They had not read the church fathers explaining the symbolic meaning of the Genesis creation account. The scientific movement, central to American education and worldview during the twentieth century, suggested that truth resides in facts and that whatever cannot be scientifically verified is not worth our attention. Furthermore, the thriving of fundamentalist churches suggests that in an increasingly complex world, at least once a week people seek the simple answers that literalist interpretation provides.

However, the practice of literalism in biblical interpretation collides with two quite different contemporary phenomena. The first is the historical-critical method of biblical study. Except in the strictest fundamentalist churches, learned studies of the Bible conducted in parishes, universities, and seminaries assume critical biblical study. This practice presumes that the Bible is a collection of various genres of texts written after the event by persons of faith, believers who saw in the history of their people the extraordinary acts of God. Even about Jesus we know few facts. All we have are the sometimes conflicting memories from a number of communities of faith. Already in the Bible the historical record has been shaped by communal memory, the facts interpreted by faith.

An example is Exodus 14:21. Moses stretched out his hand, and an east wind blew all night long, and the LORD drove the sea back. What actually was the more powerful, Moses' hand or an extraordinary wind? Both together? In either case, it was the LORD. Faith interpreted history. Few of the biblical writers resemble in any way the objective eyewitnesses that contemporary journalism leads us to expect. Sometimes the records vary in small ways: what was more significant for the people's salvation, the patriarchal authority of Moses or the natural might of the wind? The faith may be strong, but the record ambiguous.

Increasingly, scholarship suggests that entire sweeps of the Bible are more mythic memory than accurate record. Thus while popular fundamentalism may try to explain exactly how the waters of the Red Sea effected the destruction of Pharaoh's army, critical biblical studies suggest that nothing resembling the exodus of Israelites from Egypt ever occurred. These studies often conclude that the Israelites were a later assemblage of Semitic nomads and resident Canaanites whose faith in God led them to construct a fascinating religious history for their people. The book of Exodus presents us not with the Congressional Record of a past people, but with a tradition of belief into which we are invited. According to the great preachers of both West and East, the only Red Sea that matters to Christians is our baptism.

To the extent that historical-critical studies of the Bible reflect accurate scholarship, and to the extent that the Bible is more a document of faith than a chronicle of history, literalist interpretation of the Bible is not only a misguided or ill-educated technique. It is a dangerous habit that threatens the continued life of an intellectually responsible Christian church. Fundamentalist interpretation claims as facts what careful study has shown to be unfactual and thus fuels the notion that religion is no more than a fantasy about an alternative reality. If the church is recognized as wrong about its facts, it is unlikely that it will be trusted when it tries to proclaim its truth. The medieval mystic Julian realized the need to explain what "the right hand of the Father" meant, and Augustine writes that the commonplace literal interpretation of the Scriptures had kept him from taking Christianity seriously, and that it was Ambrose's preaching of the spirit of the biblical text that Augustine credits with having converted him to the faith.[30]

If fundamentalism itself must be rejected, then patterns of literalist interpretation must also be avoided. For example, we ought not assume that the Davidic court history embodies divine intent just because the text says it does, since we know that much of that record is nationalist propaganda. Sermons that speculate on exactly what Jesus was feeling or thinking when he walked down the street suggest a naive literalism that in conversation the preacher probably would deny. The fundamentalist tendency is so ubiquitous that we fall into literalism unawares. Some Christians claim that the fact of twelve male disciples requires a male-only clergy, while other Christians counter that the fact of Jesus' extraordinary interaction with the woman at the well authorizes women's preaching. Both groups are using biblical narrative as if it contains the factual foundation on which religious truth is built.

A second contemporary phenomenon that collides with literalism is postmodernism. In its liturgical proclamation, the church needs to take seriously the challenge of this late twentieth-century worldview. Postmodernism interprets everything as relative. All systems crash and burn. "Things fall apart; the centre cannot hold," wrote the poet W. B. Yeats when anticipating the turn of the millennium.[31] In postmodernism, history is untrustworthy, tradition unimportant, authority rejected, diversity the norm, reason subservient to the senses, truth no more than someone's personal preference. For the postmodernist, what has been taught by anyone in the past has little or no power in the present. What matters is not what Jesus did, but whether I am personally caught up by my experience in the community of Jesus.

A biblical hermeneutic that places considerable value on the historicity of the text will not be persuasive for persons who are more or less dismissive of anything that presents itself as historic. To the extent that preachers rely on the authority of the text or the institution of the church, postmodernists will remain unconnected. Yet postmodernists are eager to find themselves personally engaged by the individual stories and images of scripture as celebrated within a community of care. Thus it may be that, given symbolic interpretation, the lectionary's selections will serve well the postmodernist attitude, as long as the liturgy can engage each individual beyond the self and with the wider communal meaning.

The Possibilities with Images

The word *image* is used in many contexts and with a variety of meanings. In this volume, *image* refers to a mental picture, a literary detail or a graphic representation of some entity. The entity that is imaged is not physically present. However, thanks to the image in the mind, or in the text, or in the art, that entity is made present to the community. Those talented with a pen could draw that shape and show it to others, and one would hope that the depiction of the image could convey to another person one's idea or memory or concept.

Images are bowls filled with meaning. One bowl, a cut-glass treasure that your grandmother received for a wedding gift nearly a century ago, you use each Thanksgiving for the cranberry relish. Another is a wooden salad bowl that you bought last vacation at the artist's craft shop. Yet another is the large stainless steel bowl that your parish used last year for the footwashing on Maundy Thursday. Each bowl has a history and a special use. Each bowl can carry into each subsequent use our memories of the last time it was used. When the bowl waits on the shelf, it is holding for us its meaning.

Or: Images are the glue that holds human life together. Who am I? The images of our past days and years remind us of our identity. When college seniors replace the image of themselves in jeans with an image of themselves in business clothes, their identity shifts. Images hold together not only the self, but the community as well. A family's memories, a city's history, a community's symbols: these images bind human life together. Our increasingly polyglot society has fewer and fewer such alabaster jars of glue binding our common life into one. When the monastery at Taizé, France, needed some glue to bind together the thousands of pilgrims speaking a dozen different languages who arrived for retreats and festivals, the monks introduced a unique kind of music, and now Taizé's music glues together not only the guests, but friends of the monastery around the world.

Or: Images are more like trees than like furniture. Images do not merely sit there, bulky Victorian bureaus taking up space in our crowded psyches. Like trees, they grow. New branches appear. Images must be nurtured to remain fruitful. If I ignore a set of images for decades, those images may well atrophy, to make space for new growth, for trees newly planted, for images more carefully attended.

The last three paragraphs described images by means of images—the bowl on the shelf, the glue, living trees. That we liken an image to a treasured bowl suggests that we honor images. That we think of images as glue shows their power in the psyche and the community. When we admit that images grow and change, we liken images to trees. People who revere images employ them, not only because they effectively convey information and emotion, but also because images are often more memorable than discursive prose. We go home from the lecture having forgotten much, but with several images stuck in our head.

Cameras help us to recall and share our mental images by objectifying them. We want to remember our wondrous vacations at the Maine cabin. So we stick a photo of the seaside on the refrigerator to bring that place to mind, and we show others the photo, hoping that the picture of the shore will convey to them our impression of the place. A photograph is an objective image that assists the subjective image in memory. As we all know, the subjective mental image can change, and grow, and shrink, as the idea or memory or concept gets reconfigured in the personal or communal mind. The church utilizes many objective images. The cross hanging on the sanctuary wall evokes for Christians specific Christian meaning: meaning that can deepen with one's age, life experience, and religious study; meaning that may well be partly or wholly misunderstood by the stranger.

What we wish to examine with this volume, however, is not concrete images, such as a framed photograph or a cross on the wall. Rather, this volume attends to the Bible's textual images, pictures that animate the lectionary's readings and so come to reside in Christian minds. Use of the lectionary assumes that these images are in the church's mind as if on a hard drive, ready to appear onto the screen whenever we need them. What is, unfortunately, all too common is that when the readings expect us to click on *clothing* or *journey* or *wisdom*, nothing connects. The screen is blank. Much catechesis is required for us to catch biblical images and access their many meanings.

Some people protest that they do not think in images or respond to images. Perhaps what they mean is that they did not enjoy studying poetry in school. In fact, it is unlikely that our society includes many persons who are immune to the power of images. Can any of us see the image of an arch without thinking of fast food? Think of the depiction of *beautiful woman* we have in our heads, thanks to the magazine covers at the grocery store's check-out line. The illustrations of what the magazine presents as a beautiful woman have imbedded themselves in the imagination of the culture. That image exerts enormous power in dictating what both women and men imagine beauty to be. The family of an anorexic teenager knows all too well the power of images.

Culturally shared images evoke meaning and value inside the individual psyche and within the community. The persons in a society share images, sometimes willingly, sometimes not. We may be exceedingly weary of those fast-food arches, but they are in our minds just the same. Just as some images denote a society, other images are banned: the swastika, for example, in our country, or the bikini-clad female, in conservative Islamic societies. Show me your images, and I will know much about you, your history, your ideas, and your values.

The desire in some Christian communities to make Sunday morning worship totally accessible to the stranger by eliminating Christian images from walls and rhetoric underestimates the function of image within human society. If two or three (or two or three billion) are gathered together for two or three years (or two or three millennia), of course there will be images that mark their journey in the past, contain the meaning of their present, and chart their future. The community has its treasured bowls, its favorite glue, its trees now beloved and mighty. The Christian evangelistic effort must not resort to eliminating the images. Rather, the church must make members more conscious of the meanings of its images and must welcome the newcomers into those meanings. If we see no images, we doubt the presence of a human community of thought and value. Even the Quaker meeting house, with its scarcity of images, harbors the image of no-image. Abundant light, unadorned space, and pregnant silence for the gathered community are themselves persuasive images, especially in our cluttered world, for conveying Quaker values.

Some images are so central to Christian identity that they become concretized into ritual practice. That as mortals we are made of soil and will return to soil, that as sinners our actions are often only dirt and dust: these beliefs are ritualized annually with the Ash Wednesday rite. The number of minimally practicing Christians who crowd into church on Ash Wednesday to be marked with the image of death and sin attests to the human desire for images of belief. Perhaps the image of ashes is so accessible that it needs little catechesis. Yet understanding the narrative of Jesus washing his disciples' feet requires that we know about both the manners of a first-century host and the New Testament language of servanthood. We are then surprised that Jesus, the lord of the meal, is acting as the servant. An increasing number of Christian assemblies are enacting this image with a symbolic footwashing on Maundy Thursday, in which everyone who participates practices being both the one who is served—your feet are washed—and the one who serves—you wash the next person's feet. The image has become a ritual in order to intensify the image: the people in church do not literally need to have their dirty feet washed.

IMAGES OF LAW AND GOSPEL

One way of thinking about the biblical message, a way that has been prominent in Lutheran tradition, is the distinction between law and gospel. Although some use of these categories has contributed to anti-Semitic interpretation, as if law characterizes the Old Testament and is bad, and gospel marks the New and is good, a far more nuanced use of these categories can offer one useful way to think about biblical images.

The term *law* can refer to the harsh reality of the human condition. Law is the revelation of everything that restricts us, that limits our hopes and potential, that separates us from one another, that makes us fear the future, that leads us to death. The reality of human existence is that life is hard, that social organizations—including religions—confine us, that people are prone to evil and that death is our end. Despite our limitless dreams, humans, *adam*, are made of humus, *adamah*. We need to hear and face the truth that human life is bounded by limitation. The Bible provides us with many images of those limits. In Genesis 2–3, the man and the woman come to know many of these realities of human existence: that deceit takes place, that human judgment errs, that sexuality gets linked with shame, that humans are distant from God, that pain and subjugation will occur, that we must work for food, that we will die. So the serpent, the fruit, the bushes, the fig leaves, male and female labor, the angel with the fire sword, the tree of life cordoned off: each of these is an image for the realities of human limitation. We might call them images of law.

Gospel is the promise of divine mercy, the gift of God's life within and beyond our limitations. The term *gospel* can mean the revelation of the unceasing outpouring of God's forgiveness that opens up each person to God and to one another. This divine peace is pictured in many biblical images, described in many narratives. In Genesis 1 are images of such mercy: divine order, a perfect creation well designed for human life, sexual goodness, regular rest, the divine image (whatever that means) in humankind. Even sea monsters fit peacefully into a world marked by divine goodness. The Bible is filled with stories of good news: God affords solutions for our problems, food for our hunger, release from bonds, healing for leprosy, life to replace death. These stories, whether historically grounded or not, contain images for us of the gospel.

IMAGES THAT ARE METAPHORS

Many of the lectionary's images are metaphors. We use the term *metaphor* to name a figure of speech that to signify A says B. Metaphor fills the need that arises when we realize that calling A A will not convey everything we need to say about A. Perhaps A conveys only one side of the reality we mean to express. And so we say B. By calling A B, we add a second layer of meaning to our conversation. The hearer, knowing that A is not B, is surprised to discover that B actually conveys the truth of A amazingly well. The hearer encounters A in a new way because of the linguistic surprise of our calling it B, and maybe C and D as well. Our initial No turns into a Yes.[32] Jerusalem is called not only Jerusalem, but also Zion, the navel of the world, the bride of God. The more metaphors in a sentence, the slower we read, because we need time for our mind to process all the layering of B over A, D over C, to play with the interactions, to experience the new values.

We can think of the metaphors the church uses to name and illumine Jesus of Nazareth. He is the anointed one, the king, the bread of life, the new creation, light, lamb, shepherd, mother, husband, water, tree of life. To each of these images we could say, No, that is not what Jesus of Nazareth is. Yet metaphor calls us into the Yes. Each metaphor adds another layer to the church's understanding of Jesus. For history books, the name Jesus of Nazareth is enough. For believers, the many images help to contain mystery and to convey faith. Each metaphor is another beam of light illuminating the faith of the church.

During the twentieth century, linguistic philosophers wrote extensive analyses of the metaphoric process. George Lakoff and Mark Johnson argued that the ordinary conceptual system of the human being is fundamentally metaphoric.[33] For example, we think that up is better than down, and not only our speech, but also our cultural patterns of living correspond to that metaphor. Paul Ricoeur wrote about the phrase used by Majorca storytellers: "It was and it was not."[34] Metaphor creates meaning "by suddenly combining elements that have not been put together before."[35] Ricoeur argues that it is this *seeing as* that constitutes the creativity of the human mind. Since we cannot speak of God in any accurate divine language, all speech about God requires considerable metaphor. We can say only what God is like, and as the medieval theologians stated at the Fourth Lateran Council, when we speak of God, what is unlike is always more than what is like. Metaphor illumines and intensifies, but does not define.

The twentieth-century anthropologist Roy Rappaport devoted considerable thought to religious metaphor.[36] He suggested that the lowest and simplest level of meaning was that of literal information. For such literal information, we use a common noun to designate an object. The middle level of meaning is metaphor. Here connotations overlay the denotative meaning. Humans see similarities, add emotionality, and make of a thing more than it is. Metaphor adds human subjectivity to the objective task of designation. Rappaport writes, "Metaphor seems to enrich the world's meaningfulness, for the significance of every term that participates in a metaphor is magnified into something more than itself, that is, an icon of other things as well."[37] Finally, Rappaport sets out a third and highest level of meaning: communal participation in the metaphoric word. He cites art, ritual, religion, and lovemaking as examples of situations in which human beings enter together into the meaning of the metaphor. By together appropriating the metaphor, we come together with one another. The metaphor provides not only layered meaning in one's own mind; the metaphor brings together the community. It is this communal participation in metaphoric images that occurs during the liturgy.

The Problems with Images

Often Christians focus excessive attention on images that are only secondary or tertiary. It may be that a carnation presented to each mother on Mother's Day is more significant than the fire of Pentecost, the anecdotes from the preacher's autobiography more memorable than the biblical images in the readings. If lighting the candles receives more honor than sharing the cup, lesser images are taking over. Thus the first task is for the church to recognize which of its images are central to its identity and proclamation.

A fundamental problem with our reception of biblical images is that biblical authors thought and wrote in a more metaphorical manner than most contemporary persons do. Paul Minear illustrates this difference by discussing the map of Amsterdam, a city in which the streets are like the spokes of the wheel and the canals like concentric circles around the hub.[38] Our culture trains us to take the straight streets directly into the central city. Biblical writers, on the other hand, wander around on the canals. That Hebrew speakers always heard the word *soil* underneath the word *human*— we need to think of our word *humus*—exemplifies this metaphoric thinking. Metaphors are notoriously difficult to translate, because their meaning moves between layers of perception.

An obstacle to a reliance on images is that the hearers may not know the referents. Too many Christians know little about biblical images, the sacred stories in which these images arise, and the religious response they mean to evoke. Few contemporary Western Christians practice the discipline of daily Bible reading. Many churches have replaced weekly Bible study with group discussions of contemporary issues. When some Christians began incorporating the Sophia image into their prayers and hymns, it was in part the lack of acquaintance with the biblical image of Wise Woman that accounted for the fury of the conservative rage that ensued. Teachers of literature report that it is increasingly difficult for young people to read the literary classics, because they do not recognize the countless biblical references incorporated into the text.

Into this lack of familiarity with the Bible comes the three-year lectionary, which separates out the four gospel accounts, drops down here and there in the Hebrew Scriptures, and skims through first-century correspondence, all as if the hearers knew what was going on. Users of the three-year lectionary find themselves in a paradoxical situation: the Sunday readings value, even to some degree assume, enormous biblical knowledge, and yet our society is marked by increasing biblical illiteracy.

Even when we acquaint ourselves with the Bible, many of its images are alien to our lives and worldview. These images arose within a certain cultural context and find their original meaning within that context. "The sea is no more," says the description of paradise in Revelation 22, and only if we, who adore the life-renewing qualities of the sea and lake, know that in the ancient Near East the sea was understood to be the place of the monster of chaos, can this image have any meaning for us. To contemporary urban dwellers whose only contact with sheep is at a petting zoo, sheep are mainly dirty and dumb. To an ancient pastoral economy, however, sheep were God's gift for the life of the people. The shepherd Abel is remembered as a more true believer than the farmer Cain, and both the greatest prophet Moses and the greatest king David were at first shepherds. To keep from misinterpreting the imagery of sheep, we must know something of how sheep functioned in the culture within which the texts originated.

Even God talks in ways that strike us as alien. In Isaiah 7, God speaks to Ahaz about Sheol. Contemporary Christians do not accept a cosmological view that imagines the dead as residing in an underground world called Sheol. Yet God speaks to the prophet as if there were a Sheol. That is, in the Bible God speaks using the categories of the people being addressed. The Bible is full of ancient language and archaic images, and for these to have meaning in contemporary proclamation and spirituality, Christians must both understand the original meaning of the imagery and find effective ways to render this imagery today. We need to be able to get behind the biblical text before we can stand together in faith in front of the text.[39]

Some biblical images are not only alien, but for one reason or another objectionable. Contemporary citizens of democratic countries may find the Bible's continual use of the image of kingdom archaic, even unjust. The idea that justice will be secured for all when the right king is acclaimed on the throne may be distasteful to contemporary people. Feminists may find tiresome, even offensive, the ancient assumption that the monarch must be male. If we receive the image of kingship that pervades the scriptures as hierarchical, authoritarian, and androcentric, the term *the kingdom* will not readily depict divine life communally shared. Thus while we might recognize an image, we may wish we had not.

Some Christians question whether certain biblical images must be judged inappropriate for the current situation. The image of divinely sanctioned warfare would function quite differently for a small state precariously poised between military aggressors than it might for the citizens of a contemporary nuclear superpower. Another example is the biblical image of the divine marriage, in which the divine is always the active, independent male and the human always the passive, dependent female. We might know a biblical image all too well, but reject it as harmful for our time.

Sometimes the image is hidden away in a word or two. Think of the line from Joel that is proclaimed on Pentecost, "I will pour out my spirit." This phrase, going by so quickly, incorporates the image of flowing water, the water within which we are born and without which we cannot live, in its description of the arrival of God's Spirit. To grasp this image, we will want to recall God's Spirit hovering over the creation, the divine Spirit poured as oil over the head of the priest and the king, and baptismal water pouring God's Spirit on the catechumen. It is helpful for us on Pentecost if at Maundy Thursday, only seven weeks earlier, our community poured out water over one another's feet, enacting in the community that lively Spirit of God. One verb—pour out—can be a mighty flood, but it might trickle by unnoticed.

LEARNING FROM THE PSALMS

Yet these difficulties with our engagement with biblical images must not suggest that we can hide in literalism, retreat into private interpretation, or discard the images altogether. Challenges notwithstanding, images are often the hermeneutical key to biblical passages, and images hold the power to convey meaning to and through the community. We do well to be instructed by the psalter, which is not only a primer, but something of an encyclopedia of biblical imagery.

Presumably, once long ago, an individual poet crafted what we know as the 23rd Psalm. The talented poet, who seems to have known well the lives of shepherds and sheep, appropriated the ancient Near Eastern practice of describing the king as if he were the shepherd of the people in a poem to God as shepherd. Some centuries later, when the Jews compiled their collection of temple songs, the poem acquired yet another layer of meaning: the speaker was no longer an individual poet, but the people of Israel, and the images gained a communal dimension. Urban Jews were able to sing metaphorically the images of rural herders. Still later, Christians prayed this psalm and gave it baptismal interpretation. Catechists taught that the pastures of verse 2 are like prebaptismal catechesis, the rod and staff of verse 4 like the outpouring of the Spirit that guides the believer into truth.[40] In the present, the interpretation of the psalm's images is all too often flattened, limited by and to the personal.

The psalms are replete with images. Praying the psalms can train us how more fully to appropriate for ourselves the realm of imagery. But praying even so familiar a psalm as the 23rd ought also to impel us to more study, of prebiblical patterns of thought, of Hebrew images, of Christian developments with those images, and especially of the communal possibilities of these images. Without such constant and communal care, the vast treasury of biblical images, like broken pottery in a museum case, might be observed only occasionally by the enthusiast and used by nobody.

The Images in the Lectionary

In your light we come to know
that you are this matchless eternal garden,
and you hold enclosed within yourself
both the flowers and the fruits—
O gentle gatekeeper!
O humble Lamb!
you are the gardener. . . .
   CATHERINE OF SIENA, 1379[41]
   RESPONDING TO THE EASTER GOSPEL, JOHN 20:1-18

IDENTIFYING THE IMAGES IN LECTIONARY READINGS

In John 10, the Johannine Jesus uses images familiar to the biblical world—
the sheepfold, the gatekeeper, the shepherd, the gate—to talk about himself
(year A, the fourth Sunday of Easter, hereafter Ea4A). Yet even about these
relatively accessible images, the evangelist writes, "Jesus used this figure of
speech with them, but they did not understand what he was saying to them."
We smile at these words, knowing how often we also do not grasp the figures
of speech we find in the Bible.

   Our first step toward understanding is to learn how to identify the images.
Let us begin with Matthew 13:31-33, 44-52, the gospel for proper 12 in year
A (Pr12A), from which the title for this volume is taken. The readings of the
previous weeks present from Jesus' teachings a series of images: a cup of cold
water (Pr8A), wisdom and the yoke (Pr9A), the sowing of seed (Pr10A), and an
infestation of weeds (Pr11A). Now on proper 12 Jesus presents the images of
the mustard seed, the yeast, the hidden treasure, the fishing net, the pearl of
great price, and the final judgment by the angels, all of which serve to illumine a reality that he names with yet another image, the kingdom of heaven.
Each image is set off next to the others. At the conclusion of these parables,
Jesus says that the scribe is like a householder "who brings out of the household treasure what is new and what is old." Grammarians refer to this simple

form of comparison, A is like B, as a simile. The sentence makes it clear that we are being presented with a comparison. The image is highlighted by the use of the phrase *is like*.

Yet the straightforward character of the simile ought not fool us into thinking that the image is simplistic. "The household treasure" must refer to a cupboard or chest full of either dinnerware or jewelry; some of the treasure is old and some new. Treasure that is old is often of more value than that which is new, just as old images might be layered with more meaning for the self and the community than new images. Jesus is suggesting that the scriptures are such a treasure, protected property, value passed down to us from our ancestors in the faith. So it is that, just as many young people do not yet value old family treasures, some Christians newly come to liturgy undervalue the treasures of the church's past. Yet new treasures are also a part of the household store. Over the centuries Christians have elaborated on the biblical images, seeing new facets of them, layering on additional meaning, and surrounding the familiar with innovative images. Christians who think that only old treasures are valuable forget that God's Spirit continues each week to offer our world signs of divine mercy.

Some biblical readings present us with a single strong image that is relatively accessible to us. For example, our interpretation of the sermon on the mount (Ep4A) builds upon our recognizing the image of the mountain. Jesus is the second Moses, and the mountain in Matthew 5–7 is meant to parallel Mount Sinai. Jesus' words in this discourse are to be understood in light of God's giving of the law in Exodus. For the Jew, the Torah is life; for the Christian, Christ is life. Mountains still have strong appeal for contemporary urban culture. Vacations in the mountains, fascination with mountain climbers, preferences for skyscrapers, the linguistic practice that what is up is better than what is down, what is high is better than what is low: these examples illustrate that the image of the mountain is readily available to most contemporary believers.

In many biblical passages several images are layered on top of one another. The mustard seed passage from Matthew (Pr12A) illustrates such a layering of imagery. Jesus is teaching about what he calls the kingdom of heaven. The language of kingdom is of course itself imagistic speech. Whatever this kingdom of heaven is, Jesus likens it to a mustard seed. Many of us have heard an interpretation of this image that sounds as if it comes from Benjamin Franklin's *Poor Richard's Almanac*: small beginnings reap great harvests. However, this interpretation misinterprets and vastly undervalues the treasure of this parable. We must first get straight the facts behind the image: the mustard seed does not grow into a great tree. Jesus is being ironic, and his audience would have known it. The mustard bush is a scrubby annual plant, not anything like a towering tree that lives for decades. So the parable must mean something other than Poor Richard does.

Layered into this parable is a second detail, crucial for the interpretation of the image of the mustard seed: that the birds of the air will find nest in its branches. The parable assumes that the hearers know the archetypal image of the tree of life, common in the legends and iconography of the ancient Near East, found for example twice in Ezekiel. In fact, when in year B the parable of the mustard seed is read from Mark (Pr6B), the Old Testament reading that parallels this parable is the tree of life image from Ezekiel 17. A characteristic description of the mythic tree is that it provides nest for all the birds of the air (Ezekiel 17:23). So to Jesus' hearers, the parable holds a double irony: the mustard bush is likened to a tree, and that tree is likened to the mythic tree of life that gives a home to all the birds of the air. Thus a simple interpretation in the style of Benjamin Franklin is not nearly layered enough to hold all of what the parable means. What is self-evident is that the divine mystery that Jesus is proclaiming, called in Matthew "the kingdom of heaven" and in Mark "the kingdom of God," is other than we first imagined.

Some liturgical readings juxtapose images next to each other. We recall Jesus saying that we will be "salted with fire" (Pr21B). Salted with fire? Although the literature professor might complain about mixed metaphors, the liturgical scholar Daniel Stevick pointed out that liturgical language is loaded with mixed metaphors.[42] It is as if writers realize that no single image will be true enough to speak of the things of God, and so they set one image next to another, each one guiding our imagination in a slightly different direction.

The Bible's superimposition of images makes interpretation a complex task. For example, in the narrative of the presentation of the infant Jesus in the temple (Luke 2:22-40, Ch1B), several quite different images vie for our attention. We need first to be familiar with first-century Jewish birth rituals before we can consider any symbolic meaning that the evangelist gives to Jesus' presentation before God. It is helpful to recall that this ritual of buying back the firstborn son served as a substitute for child sacrifice, so prevalent in the ancient Near East. Yet we know that although Jesus survived infant death, he did in the end die, and that furthermore the church uses that ancient image of sacrifice to describe his execution. We must consider also the image of the temple, for Jewish legend held that the messiah would appear in the temple to begin the end time. And the Christian says, yes: here is Jesus, beginning the end-time. In Simeon's song is the image of light, and in his speech to Mary the image of battle. All these images—family, sacrifice, temple, the end-time, light, battle—call for our consideration.

Poetry from the prophetic books and from the book of Revelation, especially, contains many images. The images move along rapidly, like cars on a
fast-moving train, and it is unlikely that we can grasp them all in one hearing.
Consider for example Isaiah 58:9b-14 (Pr16c†). In verse 9b, the word *yoke*
evokes the image of farming and harvest; verse 10 introduces the images of
food and light; verse 11, journey, garden, and water; verse 12, battle and city;
verse 13, the week; and verse 14, mountain. The reading also includes reference to the biblical name Jacob, and in the last line is "the mouth of the
LORD," an image of God speaking. Similarly, the reading from Revelation 21
and 22 (Ea6c) includes the images of mountain, city, heaven, temple, lamb,
light, water, throne, tree of life, servant, the face of God, the name of God. In
a single reading are twelve of the forty images we examine in this volume.
Because this reading comes only once every three years, we must be experienced in identifying and appropriating images, or we will not benefit from
these dozen flowing out toward us in a grand imagistic river.

LECTIONARY IMAGES THROUGHOUT THE BIBLE

After we locate and identify the images in any particular reading, we inquire,
as would any reader of any book, into the meaning of those images within
the book itself. If we are to focus on the Isaiah 58 reading (Pr16c†), we need
to know what the author of Second Isaiah meant by *city*. How did that
author's use of *city* build on previous biblical uses of *city*? So we check out the
prior biblical uses of the image of the city. Is the city a wholesome or an evil
place? Is the city marked by divine mercy, or by foreign abominations? Does
each author's evocation of city intend a meaning more historical and factual,
or a meaning more mythic and symbolic? To the extent that the meaning is
more factual, we will want to learn the historical record of what Jerusalem,
and other cities, were like during certain decades and centuries. To the extent
that the author's intent was more metaphoric, we will need to reacquaint
ourselves with the poetry about the city—the longing for it, the praise of it,
or fear and rejection of it—remembering that the mythic view of the city
may have little to do with the historical data available to us about the actual
cities of the author's lifetime. Theological libraries offer us considerable help
in this aspect of our task. Biblical encyclopedias, studies of individual biblical books, and monographs focusing on the Bible's primary images provide
mammoth amounts of data about the lectionary's images.

Lectionary Images before and outside the Bible

The writers of the Bible were not isolated from their context, inventing wholly unique literature. Rather, they wrote in the language, with the imagery, and supported by the myths of their ancestors and neighbors. For example, attention to the biblical use of *city* must attend also to the extrabiblical history and religions of the ancient Near East, so the reader can determine where these biblical images came from and to what degree the biblical tradition altered stereotypical meanings. Archaeological museums may represent cities as wholesome centers of the best of ancient Near Eastern civilization. Yet because Israel remembered its own beginnings as a pastoral nomadic people, cities in Old Testament legend may well be described negatively. Already in Genesis 4, the city was construed as the place of the evil outsider, for it is Cain who built the first city. In Genesis 13 Lot is asking for trouble by choosing to reside near Sodom and Gomorrah. Yet by the time of David, the people of Israel had evolved a more positive view of cities. The way that David demonstrated God's support of his reign was by conquering a city and establishing it as his capital. So by 1000 B.C.E., Israel had changed its view of the city from negative to positive. In Revelation, paradise is depicted not as a garden—a typical image in ancient myth—but rather as God's city, which stands in contrast to the diabolical Rome. Our knowledge about the geopolitical situation of the biblical writers helps illumine the biblical authors' use of imagery.

One text central to our understanding of many biblical images is the ancient Near Eastern narrative myth known as the Enuma elish. This Babylonian text narrates the tale of the creation of the earth and the founding of Babylonian civilization. According to the myth, life began as the watery chaos of the sea, in which resided the terrifying sea monster herself, Tiamat. The male hero Marduk conquers Tiamat and, tearing her body in two, uses her carcass to create the earth. Humans are formed out of the blood of Tiamat's dead spouse Kingu. Marduk then builds the city of Babylon with its temple and palace. This city is lauded by the people as the center of civilization, indeed, as the center of the world, and Marduk is acclaimed the king of the gods.

Scholars have long discussed to what degree this myth lay behind Israel's sense of its own history and liturgical practice. There is no question, however, that the Old Testament images of battle, city, creation, day of the LORD, fish, kingdom, temple, and water are each in some way related to the Enuma elish. Whether we focus on isolated phrases, such as the promise in Revelation that at the end of time the sea will be no more, or on entire constructs such as the Davidic monarchy, we recognize in biblical imagery counterparts of the Marduk-Tiamat story. It follows, then, that when we consider the creation of the earth, the relative values of men versus women, God's use of warfare, the establishment of proper religion, the centrality of Jerusalem, and the hope for the messiah, we do well to be acquainted with the Enuma elish. Traces of Marduk are also evident in Christian imagery depicting Jesus as Lord.

LECTIONARY IMAGES THROUGH THE LITURGICAL YEAR

We next ask what the lectionary makes of each biblical image. How often on Sunday morning is the city an evil place, and how often the site of God's mercy? The Bible's most negative pictures of the city, for example the narrative of the destruction of Sodom and Gomorrah in Genesis and the condemnations of Babylon in Revelation, are not included in the lectionary. In the fifty days of Easter in year c, we read through only the glorious passages of Revelation, where the city is the primary image of the church's resurrected life in God.

The lectionary selects some images over others, and its valuing is somewhat different from the valuing of those images in individual biblical books or in the Bible as a whole. One example is with the biblical images that this volume groups under the category THE OUTSIDER. Although the written record undoubtedly exaggerates the community's exclusion of the outsider, considerable biblical condemnation of the alien, Babylon, Egypt, the foreigner, the leper, the prostitute, the Samaritan, the tax collector, or the uncircumcised man can be found. Even Jesus is quoted as saying that his gospel is meant only for the insider. According to much religious thinking, one's deity will help only one's own people, and too bad for the outsider. Religion often confirms xenophobia. Yet the lectionary takes its direction from a counter emphasis in the Bible, that God chooses the outsider. In the lectionary, the outsider is consistently blessed by God, placed in the center. The foreigner is included, the leper healed, the murderer welcomed into paradise. When one is exploring the images found in the lectionary readings, one cannot simply check the corresponding entries in a biblical encyclopedia, where the complete Bible will be referenced. The lectionary's annual selections give priority to some biblical emphases over others.

In the lectionary, the interpretation of the biblical selections is to some degree determined by the liturgical calendar. The logic of the lectionary's semicontinuous readings, whether of the gospels throughout most of the year or the other readings during parts of the year, implies that the meaning of this week's reading is related to that of last week and next week. Each Sunday's biblical passages stand flanked by other biblical readings that enhance its meaning, correct its leanings, show us another side of the question, say it all with different images. The year that we read Matthew we are provided with a quite different viewpoint, and different images for Christ, from the year that we read Luke. Each Holy Week, a synoptic passion account is read a few days away from the Johannine passion. Although each Sunday stands distinct, its deepest meaning comes in relation to the Sundays before and after. This aspect of the three-year lectionary is problematic in a time when many worshipers participate in the liturgy only occasionally.

The emphasis of a given biblical passage varies depending on when in the liturgical year it is read and its juxtaposition to other readings. For example, Isaiah 53 is read each year on Good Friday and in year B on proper 24. The interpretation of Isaiah 53 would not be identical during the Triduum and in the middle of October, since the different gospel readings of John 18:1—19:42 and Mark 10:35-45 pull different emphases out of Isaiah 53. The first-century hymn recorded in Philippians 2 will lean in different directions depending on when it is proclaimed, whether on Passion Sunday or during the semicontinuous readings of year A.

The lectionary readings for Advent present a good example of how in the liturgy the Bible is interpreted in light of the liturgical calendar. The secular calendar tells us that Advent is about shopping days until Christmas. However, the church is expected not to mimic the culture with some four-week focus on the manger story. Rather, the lectionary directs the church to wait until Christmas Eve and Christmas Day for proclamations from Luke 2 and John 1. During Advent, the lectionary presents a wide array of biblical images to broaden and deepen the church's understanding of Christ's incarnation. Through the ministry of John the Baptist, we hear that Christ is Noah's flood (Ad1A), the winnowing fork (Ad2A), and the miracle worker who raises the dead (Ad3A). From Isaiah comes Christ as peace and light (Ad1A), the tree of life and the waters covering the sea (Ad2A), both springtime and vengeance (Ad3A). The epistles proclaim that the coming Christ is dawn (Ad1A), servant (Ad2A), and judge (Ad3A). What all is arriving at Christmas? We look through the Bible for answers, and during Advent these many multivalent images function as pictures of God's salvation that stand prior to the story of the birth of Jesus, apart from which the manger story can too easily be sentimentalized.

LECTIONARY IMAGES AND CHRISTOLOGY

Biblical scholars tell us that the gospel writers, who apparently did not witness the execution of Jesus, appropriated language from their religious tradition to describe this event and its meaning. For example, to describe the crucifixion, which was outside their experience, with its meaning only partially understood, the evangelists used the language of their historic lament Psalm 22. Thus the poet's line (22:17) that "they divide my garments among them" became an image for the totally abandoned Christ, the child of God left finally alone in death. For Christians, the liturgical meaning of Psalm 22 is determined by the life, death, and resurrection of Christ. That the evangelists used imagery from the Hebrew Scriptures to describe the life, destiny, and purpose of Christ confirms Christians in their lectionary tradition of reading the whole Bible in the light of Christ, to form Christians.

The sermons of the church fathers and the preachers of the Reformation present many examples—some brilliant, some bizarre—of applying biblical images to Christ. This pattern naturally arose in the early church as Christian preachers sought to demonstrate that their encounter with the story of Christ was the fitting continuation of Israelite religion. Thus, taught by Matthew 12:40, early preachers presented the adventures of Jonah as an image of the resurrection. John 3:14 inspired preachers to connect the serpent on the pole in the wilderness with Christ on the cross. Still today many churches display side by side a depiction of the sacrifice of Isaac and the crucifixion of Christ. Some of the parallels commonplace in the past strike many contemporary believers as more nonsense than substance, as for example when the widow of Zarephath carrying firewood is made parallel to Christ carrying his cross. Yet even the most moderate reading of the Old Testament by Christians will call forth some christological parallels. Indeed, the very title *Christ* is the result of christological interpretation of the Old Testament's imagery of the one anointed by God to save the people.

Thus while the scholar is interested in the original meaning of biblical passages, or what contemporary Jewish believers see in them, or what an encyclopedia of ancient religion says of them, in the liturgy the church receives biblical images primarily as participating in the proclamation of Christ. So it is that Paul could say of the Israelites receiving water in the wilderness that the rock was Christ (1 Corinthians 10:4). That is, Christ gives to Christians the water of life; Christ accompanies us in our wanderings. The Israelites would not have said that, and contemporary Jews would not say it. But for his Christian proclamation, Paul used the picture of the watering rock as an image for Christ, and the lectionary continues Paul's method. The biblical scholar realizes that the story of the serpent on the pole (Numbers 21:9) was in all likelihood a memory from Israel's history of goddess worship, for we know that the serpent in the tree was a symbol of Asherah. But in the Christian liturgy, that serpent is a sign of God's mercy: God paradoxically turns death itself into life for the whole community. In the Christian liturgy, biblical images serve christology.

An example of the christological use of a biblical image is the liturgical language of calling Christ a king. One disadvantage of naming the last Sunday of the liturgical year *Christ the King* is that when a metaphor gets repeated over and over, the metaphor devolves into definition. With so much repetition, the word loses its surprising edge. We come to think that Christ actually was a king. We come to literalize the metaphor, and in a world that no longer values kingship, we must inquire whether the image has been helpful to contemporary faith.

However, the image has its strength in the might of the metaphor. Christ was not a king in any literal way. It is only in the faith of the church that we pray for the reign of Christ, using the imagery from the Hebrew Scriptures that saw in the king the beneficence of God. In the three-year lectionary, the gospel readings for the last Sunday of the year make clear the metaphoric nature of the king image. In the gospel for year A, Jesus tells a parable, that is, a wholly metaphoric story, of the judgment day; in year B, Jesus tells Pilate that he is not a king; in year C, Jesus is crucified under the inscription "The King of the Jews." Each of these gospels layers its interpretation onto the metaphor of the kingship of Christ. Yet if we are not careful with the image, our depictions of Christ wearing a crown or our triumphal hymns about lauding a king might concretize the metaphor. The consequence of literalizing an image is not to intensify it, but rather to diminish it.

In the lectionary's parallels between the first reading and the gospel, we see christological readings of the Old Testament. Take for example the Sundays in year B when the gospel reads through the bread of life chapter of John 6 (Pr12B[†], Pr13B[†], Pr14B[†], Pr15B[†]). Those who read the complementary first readings encounter Elisha feeding the crowd (2 Kings 4), the manna feeding the Israelites (Exodus 16), Elijah nourished for his walk to the mountain of God (1 Kings 19), and Wisdom serving up a meal of bread and wine (Proverbs 9). The lectionary presents these passages as images of God's nourishing the people, and as such they are parallels of Christ's feeding of the multitude and the church's meal of the eucharist. Most Jewish believers read these stories as inspirations for lives of charity to which the whole people are called. In the lectionary, Christians use these stories as images of God's food, a food Christians see as most perfect through Christ.

A problematic example from Christian history of such christological interpretation is the traditional use of Isaiah 7. Isaiah 7:10-16 narrates a conversation between Isaiah and King Ahaz. Ahaz is appropriately terrified about an approaching military engagement that threatens the continuation of the Davidic monarchy. Through the prophet Isaiah God speaks a word of hope, promising that the future will bring life to Israel and destruction to the enemy kings. This future will materialize in several years, the time that it will take for a young woman to bear a son and for that child to become a toddler.

Because the Hebrew word for *young woman* came to be translated with the Greek word for *virgin woman*, Christian preachers established the pattern of seeing in this text a prophecy for the coming of Christ. To support this inter-pretation, the church cited the gospel of Matthew, where the evangelist, in narrating the angel's appearance to Joseph, quoted Isaiah 7:14 in the Greek version with its misconstrual of the Hebrew noun. From Matthew's Greek version of the Isaiah passage, it was but a short step to claim that the woman and child Isaiah anticipated, whether he knew it or not, were Mary and Jesus. Critical biblical studies urge us to avoid such naive interpretation. Many Christians now agree that to assert that the mother in the Isaian text is Mary is to misconstrue the oracle. Yet the three-year lectionary continues this his-toric pattern by setting the Isaian oracle next to the narrative of the angel's dream to Joseph in Matthew 1 (Ad4A).

If we see the Bible as offering Christians images of Christ, we need not imagine that Isaiah was predicting Jesus' birth. Instead, we think imagisti-cally. The lectionary presents the Isaiah passage as an image of salvation. In the time of Isaiah, God promised to save Israel, to protect the people from military destruction, to nurture the people as a mother rears her child. So also Christians, who share with King Ahaz a fear of the future, hope in God's mysterious salvation, a salvation that the church encounters preemi-nently in Christ. This christological technique recurs each year on the fourth Sunday of Advent. The reading from 2 Samuel (Ad4B) says that David wished to build a temple, but God promised the king the coming of a salvation far better than might be symbolized by an impressive building. The prophet in Micah 5 (Ad4c) proclaims the coming of a shepherd-like ruler who will ensure safety and peace for all, whom Christians see as Christ. Each year the fourth Sunday of Advent offers us ancient images of the coming one: God's salvation is like a growing boy, like a people safe from enemies, like a nation that never ends, like a magnificent city, like a mythic monarchy, like a shepherd tending the flock. Each of these images stands next to the birth of the infant Jesus and sheds its own light on Christ.

LECTIONARY IMAGES AND THE TRINITARIAN COMMUNITY

When one reads Shakespeare, a glossary of sixteenth-century English is helpful. The changed meanings of certain English words since Shakespeare wrote his poems and plays complicate our current understanding of his work. When reading Shakespeare, we delete the meanings of English words developed since Shakespeare, because our more recent usage only obscures and confuses our reception of Shakespeare.

Our procedure changes, however, when we encounter the Bible in the liturgy. The Bible is God's word for Christians now, and for Christians, God is triune and their faith trinitarian. Although the liturgical calendar organizes the year around the narratives of the life of Jesus, the three-year lectionary is not finally only about Jesus. Reading the gospels, we do not set aside our trinitarian faith, which proposes that God's actions seen in the death and resurrection of Christ are made manifest through the Spirit in the life of the church. Thus Easter is not only about the resurrection of Christ; it is also the time of baptism and the renewal of baptismal vows, as the entire community embodies the Spirit of Christ's resurrection. Christmas is not only about an extraordinary birth two millennia ago; it is also about the Spirit of God continuously alive in the created world. Because God has been revealed as triune, the church does not stop with a christological interpretation of the Bible. Rather, Christianity encounters a triune God, a God who in Christ continues to create, save, and nurture the world through the Spirit. The Spirit is manifest in this earth, undoubtedly in many more places than we are aware, but at least, we believe, in the church.

A trinitarian interpretation will always attend to the Spirit of God in the community. The biblical image offers us a picture of God's mercy, or God's justice, or God's very being. This divine image, Christians believe, is also an image for Christ. And although some preachers conclude their thinking with that step, it is likely that the image can also be a picture of the life of the Spirit in the church. Since for Christians the biblical images continue to accrue meaning, an ancient Israelite image can serve Christians as a proclamation of the Trinity. The burning bush can function as an image of the mysterious God, of the cross that both destroys and purifies, and of the tongues of fire on the disciples' heads. The church is trinitarian, and so it receives all biblical revelation as of the triune God.

The use of Genesis 1 at the Easter Vigil is an example of such trinitarian reading of the Bible. Scholars remind us that when in Genesis 1, God speaks in the plural, the author was not imagining a triune God, but was either using the divine plural from prior centuries of polytheistic speech or was borrowing from contemporary court ritual the monarchical plural. Indeed, the plural form of the Hebrew noun for *god* takes a singular verb: the Hebrew scribe is thinking monotheistically. Yet the lectionary appoints Genesis 1 at the Easter Vigil as an image of the resurrection, and for Christians, it was the triune God who created the world. The Word of God, whom we call Christ, calls out divine blessing over the chaos of our world, and the Spirit of God hovers over that world, bringing it to life. In the liturgy, even in the words of an ancient Hebrew poem, Christians receive the triune God.

In Advent, the lectionary presents Noah's flood as one image of the coming messiah (AD1A). The lectionary presents the story of Noah's flood again in Lent (LE1B), a liturgical season in which we attend to the baptismal renewal of the Spirit in the community. The story of the flood provides Christians with an image of God, like the torrent of old, washing away evil and yet saving us all. Christians proclaim that Christ is our ark, the wood of the cross carrying us over the flood. The trinitarian interpreter considers then the life of the Spirit in the church. We are saved, not one by one, but in a community, the entire family and all the animals. The ancient story becomes for Christians an image of salvation by and in the Trinity.

If we stop at the first level of interpretation, we are theists, affirming belief in God. If we go to the second level, our thinking is christological. But as trinitarian believers, we include also the life of the Spirit in the church in our biblical interpretation. The God of water and ark is here in the worshiping assembly, and our care for all the persons and animals surrounding us is part of our participation in the triune God. One technique that Christians can use in examining the interrelated readings in the lectionary is a Trinity Test. Where, manifest in these readings, is an image of God, the source of life? Where is an image of the death and resurrection of Christ? Where is the Spirit, in whom the church and all creation lives? The trinitarian approach moves the lectionary through Christ and into Spirit's life in the community. We think—and interpret the Bible—trinitarianly.

LECTIONARY IMAGES AND THE SELF

After all these steps are completed, one might attend to the meaning of a biblical image in one's personal history. Of course one's personal experience is always there, surrounding one's hearing of the biblical text. Yet placing one's individual viewpoint last guards against one's life experience being the primary or even sole lens through which one receives the archetypal images of the faith. Even though it is helpful for me to be aware of whether, because of my life's experiences, I like or dislike the city, that personal inclination is perhaps the least important ingredient in my receiving the biblical language of *city*. Perhaps I hate cities: but in Revelation, the city becomes the abode of God.

A lectionary reads the Bible communally. Not only is the Bible comprised of many voices; not only does each biblical passage rely on other passages for meaning; but also the meaning of each Sunday's readings is a conversation over the centuries. In a lectionary church, believers are not free to say about the biblical texts anything that suits their fancy. My voice is only one of many voices. What is Christmas? We start with John. Add Matthew and Luke. Add Isaiah and Paul. Add Psalms 96–98. Add the hymnwriters of the past. Find echoes in the words of the liturgy itself. Listen to the men and the women of the past who loved the scriptures and who commented in their own voices on the mystery of the incarnation. Be listening for even more voices: all the worshipers together, rejoicing, mourning, those celebrating a marriage, those returning from the cemetery. Too often the English word *you* is heard in the singular. In the Bible, however, *you* is most often plural. "The body of Christ for you" is a plural you. Unlike much in our individualistic culture, the center is not the self, but is the Spirit of Christ within the community.

The Example of the Easter Vigil

Easter proclaims the deepest mystery of the Christian faith. For this proclamation the Easter Vigil sets before us the richest array of images of the entire year. Each image adds something of the truth of the resurrection. It is not that the four, or seven, or twelve Old Testament readings are a *Reader's Digest* version of the Bible. As Paul wrote in 1 Corinthians, Christ was raised according to the scriptures, that is, of course, the Hebrew Scriptures, and the Vigil readings present some of those scriptures as images to help us appropriate the mystery of the resurrection. In addition, each image illumines the baptisms celebrated at the Vigil. The resurrection is not only an event in the first century, but continues through baptism in the life of the church.

The readings begin with Genesis 1, the story of God's miraculous creation of a world that was very good and of humankind as in some way the likeness of God on earth. This opening picture presents the resurrection of Christ as a re-creation of the whole earth in accord with God's intent. In the Revised Common Lectionary, the readings continue with the flood story. The resurrection is like Noah's family and the animals surviving the flood of death, Christ our ark floating on the waters. Then: the resurrection is like Isaac's escape from sacrifice. Death is not for Isaac, nor for us, the final word.

Then: the resurrection is like the Israelites escaping from slavery and is enacted by the church, like Israel, passing through the waters of baptism. As Israel was saved, so we are saved.

Among the many readings that Christian assemblies choose for the Vigil is Isaiah 55. In this reading, the resurrection is like the feast with food for all, like a covenant with the people that will never be revoked, like rain ensuring the harvest. In Isaiah 54, the image of the resurrection is of marriage. Proverbs 8 or Baruch 3 introduces Wisdom: resurrection is like the arrival of Wise Woman, who serves up fine fruit, better than gold. The food of the resurrection meal is like the bread and wine that she prepared long ago. Ezekiel 36 suggests that the resurrection is like water cleansing all that is dirty and dead. With Ezekiel 37 the church proclaims that the resurrection of Christ is able to raise us all, who are like bones bleached in the sun, to a new life. In Zephaniah 3 are the images of city, Israel, judge, kingdom, battle, body, marriage, the outsider, and treasure.

Yet more images are available. Deuteronomy 31 speaks of the resurrected life as the land flowing with milk and honey. The Jonah reading from chapter 3 presents the picture of God forgiving the people, giving life where death was expected. In earlier centuries, the Easter Vigil selected chapter 1 from Jonah, so as to echo Jesus in Matthew 12:40 referring to the story of Jonah's three days in the belly of the fish as an image of his stay in the tomb. Thus Jonah being coughed up on the shore is an image of Christ raised from death. Repeatedly in medieval church art, a depiction of Jonah grabbing onto a tree and pulling himself up out of the fish's mouth was set parallel to a picture of Jesus, his cross become a standard of victory, arising from the tomb. Some assemblies bring the Vigil's readings to a conclusion with the grand tale from Daniel 3 of the three children in the furnace of blazing fire. In this narrative, death is a fiery furnace where, when we are thrown in, we meet Christ, who walks with us in the midst of the fire. At the conclusion of these many readings, even King Nebuchadnezzar is now worshiping our God, the pagan monarch convinced into faith by the fire of God's salvation.

The lectionary does not appoint these readings so that as an article of faith we annually affirm their historicity. Nor does the lectionary suggest that God's mercy to the Israelites was somehow less than God's mercy to the church. Rather, these biblical passages are offered to the triune community as images of the baptized life and as pictures of the resurrection of Christ. Paul, John, and the synoptic gospels offer differing descriptions of the resurrected body of Christ, and the four, or seven, or twelve Vigil readings from the Old Testament offer yet more images of what Easter is about.

Examining the Treasure

Taking its inspiration from the Easter Vigil, the three-year lectionary presents to the worshiping church a treasury of images. Some images, such as covenant, come from ancient Near Eastern culture; some, such as emanation of the divine, from Greek philosophy; some, such as the day of the Lord, from Israelite religion. Some images, such as sacrifice and temple, arise in many ancient and contemporary religions, and images such as light and tree of life appear in art as far back in history as we find evidence of art. We want to know as much as we can about what is behind the text, so that we do not misunderstand the original meaning of the text. But in the liturgy, proclamation is always about what is in front of the text: the gospel for the Christian assembly and for the contemporary world.

Some people imagine religion to be fantasy time, time out of time, as if attending the liturgy is like watching *Star Trek* on television or going to the Renaissance Faire, as if religion is an alternate reality that releases us from life's difficulties for a short time. It is the thesis of this volume that Christian religion, far from being an escape from life, is the fundamental way that the community lives. Religion is the process of sharing and incorporating the community's primary values, and the church articulates this process in its use of images.

Our images are to be deep. Human beings are complex creatures, each unique, changing week by week, some hanging back, some running ahead. We do not only wade in God's water; we swim in God's rivers, we drown in God's sea. If the images presented in the Sunday liturgy are too shallow, they will not supply enough water to quench the thirst of so many people and so complex an assembly.

Our images are to be broad. The problem with relying too much on a personal interpretation of the Bible is that no single experience is wide enough. The archetypal images in the biblical readings echo through the centuries, around and in the lives of much of humankind. The biblical stories become images for us all, enhanced by study, enlightened by the reflections of Christians through the ages, sung in beloved hymns, perhaps adorning the walls of the church building. The images are to be broad enough for the entire community.

Acknowledging the monumental role of the lectionary in shaping the Christian assembly, we can only hope that the lectionary in use is as Christian as possible, as nuanced as ecumenical cooperation can make it, as wise as two millennia of Christian development can demonstrate, as deep as the living can know about life and death, as lucid as is required for the proclamation of the mercy of God. The hope is that in each week's multivalent readings are images with which to picture pain and joy, law and gospel, human death and life in God. May it be that the lectionary offers us such treasures old and new.

Using This Volume

You will think, Sisters, that since so much has been said about this spiritual path, it will be impossible for anything more to be said. Such a thought would be very foolish. Who will finish telling of God's mercies and grandeurs? The more we know about God's communication to creatures, the more we will praise God's grandeur and make the effort to have esteem for souls in which the Lord delights so much.

TERESA OF AVILA, 1577[43]

Throughout this volume's discussion of the images in the three-year lectionary, each citation identifies the year—A, B, C, or (when all three years appoint the same reading) ABC—and the specific Sunday, festival, or remembrance to which the readings apply. The abbreviations of the day are listed in the front of the book on page 8. Throughout this volume, citations are to the Revised Common Lectionary. An appendix notes parallels to the Roman Lectionary. It is hoped that users of all three-year lectionaries will find this resource close enough to their variant to be helpful.

THE FORTY IMAGES OF THIS VOLUME

First, the 600-some biblical texts in the three-year lectionary were each studied to identify the images in and under the passage. The volume could have presented longer chapters on fewer images or shorter chapters on more images. The decision was to attend to forty, a number which itself is a biblical image suggesting prolongation. It is important to say at the outset that each of these chapters could be expanded into a full-length book. This volume is only a primer in liturgical images, getting the reader started on this method of interpretation.

The several hundred images are grouped together into categories. Sometimes the grouping is self-evident. For example, SHEPHERD includes references to flock, gate, lamb, and sheep. Sometimes the grouping is less obvious: the chapter on FIRE includes the burning bush; JOURNEY includes language of the highway and the race. MOTHER includes not only significant human mothers, such as Rachel and Mary, and mothering tasks such as nursing, but also the similes of the eagle and the hen, since the readings cite these animals as examples of mothering. RESURRECTION includes Jonah, the dry bones, the raising of Lazarus, and the empty tomb, all used by Christians to portray the life of the resurrection. The grouping titled OUTSIDER includes a wide range of biblical characters—the person with leprosy, the foreigner, the tax collector, the prostitute, an uncircumcised man, the alien, the people of Egypt, the people of Babylon—all of whom function in the readings as outsiders. WIND includes storm waves and the sky phenomena such as lightning, since these manifestations of wild weather are used to indicate the emotions of God.

This volume delineates biblical images by their current English-language translation, usually with the vocabulary choices of the New Revised Standard Version of the Bible. In some biblical passages, however, the underlying image may not be verbally present in the vocabulary of the text. For example, the Matthean parable of the last judgment (LastA) does not include the term *the poor*. Conducting a biblical word search for *the poor* will not pull up this parable. Yet those who are hungry or thirsty, the stranger, the naked, the sick, and the imprisoned are all examples of those the scriptures usually refer to as *the poor*. Thus the image upon which a passage relies may lie deeper than the specific vocabulary of the passage itself. The image may be the foundation underneath the structure that we encounter.

As much as was possible, the title of each chapter is itself some single thing that can be drawn, an image that can be pictured in the mind. For example, the idea of *word* and the concept that *God speaks* are included in the grouping titled PROPHET, the one through whom the community hears the word of a speaking God. An artist can draw a prophet: Deborah judging under her tree and John the Baptist preaching in the wilderness. Only a few of the forty chapters are titled with a category more conceptual than pictorial.

It is not envisioned that the reader would read through this volume cover to cover, but rather will attend to individual chapters as the images arise in the lectionary and throughout the liturgical year. One might read KINGDOM and TREE OF LIFE when preparing for Advent, SHEPHERD when mediating on the readings of the fourth Sunday in Easter, or DAY OF THE LORD when contemplating the apocalyptic readings at the close of each year.

The Contents of Each Chapter

Each chapter heading lists all the members of that category and suggests related chapters. For example, because the images of battle, city, creation, kingdom, and water all share parallels to the Enuma elish, each of these images illumines the others. The cosmic map that is central to many biblical stories, in this volume titled HEAVEN-EARTH-HELL, is closely related to stories about the wind, since what we popularly call *the sky* figures in both sets of images. The images of garden, harvest, and tree of life are interrelated. Ideally, one might read at the same time the chapters on all the interrelated images, for each family of images reflects on and illumines the others.

Each chapter includes a citation from the Psalms. Although not all these psalm passages are appointed in the three-year lectionary, the psalm quotations present one example of the biblical use of that image and illustrate the use of an image in the community's worship vocabulary.

These forty images also permeate the ordinary texts of the liturgy, the proper prayers for specific Sundays and the occasional services of a Christian community. For example, the image of judge occurs in the ecumenical creeds, the image of clothing in the baptismal rite, and the image of temple in prayers for the dedication of a church building. One goal of this volume is to attune us to the treasure of images that fill the regularly recurring language of our worship life. Thus each chapter presents also a citation of that image in a standard liturgical text.

Especially in the poetic form of the hymn these forty images are proclaimed and celebrated in the assembly's worship. For example, the text of the ninth-century Irish hymn "Be thou my vision" presents the images of body, light, wisdom, prophet, city, heaven, family, treasure, and kingdom. In the sixteenth century Philipp Nicolai composed what is called the Queen of Chorales, "O Morning Star." This masterpiece invokes the images of light, kingdom, marriage, body, tree of life, food, treasure, family, battle, and heaven. The twentieth-century American Easter hymn by Herbert Brokering, "Alleluia! Jesus is risen!" includes the images of the resurrection of the body, light, shepherd, heaven, journey, body, food, tree of life, clothing, city, water, and name of God.

To acknowledge the centrality of hymnody in celebrating biblical images, each chapter presents stanzas from a hymn text that highlight that particular image. Dozens of hymns employ the images of city, cross, light, kingdom, sacrifice. Yet some of these images are found in relatively few hymns. It is hoped that hymnwriters will continue in the twenty-first century the task they took up so ardently in the twentieth century, to provide hymns for the less popular images, so that Christian assemblies can sing about clothing, fish, the outsider, temple, and wisdom.

Each chapter includes a quotation from two of the church's theologians, poets, mystics, preachers, and reformers, writers who used the image in a creative or striking manner. This diverse list of authors cites from a wide array of Christian pieties from different centuries and locales. Quotations from the church fathers, Ambrose, Augustine, Gregory I, are included. Other significant male theologians through the ages add their voices, from Melito of Sardis to Thomas Merton, from Martin Luther to Martin Luther King Jr. Such lists are often overwhelmingly male; in this volume each chapter presents also a quote from a woman in the Christian tradition. The women include the martyr Perpetua, mystics like Beatrice of Nazareth and Mechthild of Magdeburg, vowed religious such as Clare of Assisi and Rose Hawthorne Lathrop, church reformers such as Catherine of Siena, social reformers such as Dorothy Day, early preachers such as Julia Foote, contemporary Christian authors such as Annie Dillard and Kathleen Norris, feminist liberation theologians like Rosemary Radford Ruether and Letty Russell. All these voices assist us in broadening and deepening our use of biblical images.

APPENDIXES AND INDEXES

The first appendix located at the conclusion of this volume is a list of three significant images found in each set of readings in both the Revised Common Lectionary and the Roman Lectionary. It is important to state that this listing is somewhat subjective. Although all readers would agree that in the readings for Easter 4 the dominant image is shepherd, other readings present many interwoven images, and which are the dominant images is a more subjective choice. What, for example, are the dominant images for John 1, the gospel for Christmas Day? The complete list would include word, creation, light, prophet, emanation of the divine, family, the name of God; the first reading adds mountain, city, and body; the second reading adds kingdom, the cosmic map of heaven-earth-hell, and clothing. On the other hand, some selections from the epistles present no governing image. Thus the list of images in this appendix is more suggestive than absolute, intending only to get the reader started on the interpretive adventure.

Because many of the authors whose texts are quoted may be unfamiliar to readers, a biographical appendix with index is included.

The endnotes function in the standard manner, to indicate the source of all citations.

A bibliography follows. This bibliography lists not only general works, such as encyclopedias of biblical imagery, but also specific resources appropriate for each chapter. These works will prove helpful to those persons who want to study any particular image further.

A final index is an alphabetical listing with page references of all images, both primary and secondary, and liturgical terms that this volume treats.

Battle

armor of God, battle, Christ, conqueror,
LORD of hosts, ransom, Satan, shield,
sword, victory

Related chapters: DAY OF THE LORD

Some biblical language of battle describes actual warfare. However, most of the lectionary's use of battle imagery is metaphoric.
Some Christians find continued use of battle imagery problematic,
even incendiary, while others believe that its archetypal power to
contrast good and evil is useful, even indispensable, in liturgical
language.

PSALM 18:35,
36, 40

You train my hands for battle
    and my arms for bending even a bow of bronze.
You have given me your shield of victory;
        your right hand also sustains me;
        your loving care makes me great.
You have girded me with strength for the battle;
        you have cast down my adversaries beneath me;
        you have put my enemies to flight.

HYMN OF PRAISE

This is the feast of victory for our God.

MARTIN LUTHER

A mighty fortress is our God,
a sword and shield victorious,
who breaks the cruel oppressor's rod
and wins salvation glorious.
The old evil foe,
sworn to work us woe,
with guile and great might
is armed to wage the fight:
on earth there is no equal.

No strength of ours can match this might!
We would be lost, rejected.
But now a champion comes to fight,
whom God for us elected.
Ask who this may be:
Lord of hosts is he!
Christ Jesus, our Lord,
God's only Son, adored,
shall hold the field victorious.

Joan said that if she was in the woods, she easily heard the voice come to her. It seemed to her a worthy voice, and she believed it was sent from God. This voice taught her to be good and to go to church often, and that she should raise the siege of Orleans, although being a poor maid, knowing nothing of riding or fighting.

JOAN OF ARC'S TRIAL TRANSCRIPT

The enemy's behavior is like that of a military leader who wishes to conquer and plunder the object of his desires. Just as the commander of an army pitches his camp, studies the strength and defenses of a fortress, and then attacks it on its weakest side, in like manner the enemy of our human nature studies from all sides our theological, cardinal and moral virtues. Wherever he finds us weakest and most in need regarding our eternal salvation he attacks and tries to take us by storm.

IGNATIUS LOYOLA, *The Spiritual Exercises*

MYTH, LITERATURE, HISTORY, and current events: all are filled with battles. Consider the widely read Christian children's classic, *The Lion, the Witch, and the Wardrobe*. The struggle of the Narnian creatures against the domination of the evil White Witch climaxes in a battle. Yet the second sentence of the book indicates that the entire adventure took place because the children "were sent away from London during the war because of the air-raids."[1] Into the reality of World War II comes a mythic story about spiritual war.

Stories about war go all the way back in the Western tradition. *The Iliad* proposes that it is the deities who are always at war with one another and that humans are merely pawns in a perpetual heavenly battle. However, in a later Greek work, *The Trojan Women*, the author Euripides refuses to blame the deities for the senseless cruelty of human warfare. According to Genesis 4, as soon as there were two brothers, there was hatred, violence, and fratricide. Whether we decide that God or humankind is responsible for warfare, we are stunned before the ceaseless cruelty of war throughout history and literature, and we wonder whether Heraclitus was correct when he wrote, "War is father of all, king of all."

Many students of the Bible are acquainted with the cosmogonic myths of the ancient Near East. According to the Babylonian epic Enuma elish, the chaos that ruled all things before time was a sea goddess named Tiamat. After a primordial battle with the storm god Marduk, she was conquered and split in two, and from her corpse and that of her lover, the earth and humankind were created. Marduk became the lord of human civilization and the king of the newly established city. The Canaanites had a similar myth, in which the god Baal conquered the goddess Yam. Psychologists might see in this archetypal myth the pattern of adult maturation: one must leave the womb waters and the mother's hold in order to rule one's own life. Evolutionists might see among the ancients the realization that although life came from the sea, it is land that is home to human civilization. Feminists recognize in these myths the pattern of male domination over the female that came to characterize Western cultures. For our purposes here, we see that these myths assume that human society arose after a battle and that violence is fundamental to the human condition. A cosmogonic myth proposing that human society emerged from warfare alleviates the need to agonize toward some rationalization for the misery of continuing warfare. Rather, there is war because there always was war. Where there is a female and a male, where there are two brothers, there is a battle.

Although Israel presented a far more benign cosmogonic myth than did Babylon and Canaan, the conquering of a sea monster is a poetic image found about half a dozen times in the Old Testament. In Psalm 74:12-17, God conquered the power of the sea and its creatures as part of creation. Psalm 77:16-20 repeats the idea that the powers of the sky, such as thunder and lightning, subdued the powers of the sea: "the very deep trembled." In Isaiah 51 the LORD cut the monster Rahab in pieces. All these passages hint of a primordial conflict.

However, it is not only in small poetic passages that Israel's poets paralleled the myth of Enuma elish. The central story of Israel's redemption, the Exodus, is a historic reshaping of the cosmogonic myth in which the tribe's land-based deity conquered the destructive power of the sea. In the Song of the Sea in Exodus 15 (VigilABC), the people are safely on the shore of what is called "the sea," while the oppressors get drowned underneath the waters. Reading the narrative carefully, we see that God's natural forces saved Israel: the east wind, the dry pathway, the mighty waters. Yet note the vocabulary that is used in both the narrative and the long poem: Israel is an "army," the Egyptians "pursued," the LORD is "fighting" against Egypt, "the LORD is a warrior," the Egyptians are "the enemy" that is threatening Israel with the "sword." The Israelites' escape is told as if it were a pitched battle. Recurring human experience of warfare so permeated the ancient imagination that Israel remembers as a battle an event that was not in fact a battle. Here battle language is not literal, but figurative.

A parallel of the Exodus is found in Judges 4–5 (Pr28A°), in which Deborah is praised for her role in Israel's escape from King Jabin of Canaan. Here what was apparently an actual military encounter came to be remembered in mythic terms. Sisera's chariots of iron were overwhelmed because of a rainstorm. Yet this miracle gets recalled as if the chaos of the sea was conquered by the god of the sky. The *tohu wabohu* was brought to order by God, yet the event was remembered as a stupendous battle. Once again, battle imagery is used to recall the salvation of God.

That the origin of the Israelite nation was recalled as a battle at sea is perhaps the most ancient level of the Bible's motif of holy war. In Exodus 14–15, God was the warrior, garnering the forces of nature so that Israel did not have to fight: no actual military engagement occurs at the Red Sea. Many stories in the books of Joshua and Judges are similar. "God has given you the city" is a recurring claim. It is the LORD who achieves victory, not, for example, Gideon's meager army of 300. Consequently, regulations applied to the spoils of war, because booty was understood as belonging to the LORD. In the wonderful tale of the battle against the Moabites and the Ammonites, as the Levites sang a psalm, "the LORD set an ambush" and conquered the enemy: Jehoshaphat's army, said to number more than a million soldiers, was unnecessary. Contemporary biblical scholars do not agree on how much genuine warfare actually took place in Israel's history, or indeed whether anything like a military conquest of Canaan was achieved. Yet the narratives of battle became central memories for the people.

A second pattern in stories of battle indicated that God the warrior fought, not instead of, but with Israel. God led the conquering armies to victory. The name of God introduced in 1 Samuel, YHWH of Sabaoth, probably means "the one who causes the divine armies to be." *Sabaoth*, traditionally translated "hosts," might have referred to the heavenly bodies, the angelic forces or the tribal armies. Contemporary worshipers encounter an echo of this idea in the weekly singing of the Sanctus. "Holy, holy, holy LORD God of Sabaoth" is the original line that is currently translated "Holy, holy, holy Lord, God of power and might." Perhaps the translation "mystery and might" would have expressed not only the ancient notion of divine military might, but also the miraculous mystery that usually characterized the narratives of the victories achieved by God for Israel.

In later history, battles involving the Jewish people were all too real. If enemies were attacking, God was a shield of protection. During the monarchy, the king was granted military power, as if he were anointed by God to wield the divinely sanctioned sword. This authorization is clear in royal psalms, such as 2, 89, and 110. The narrative in 1 Samuel 17 introduces David as first receiving acclaim through his victory over Goliath (Pr7B°). During the exile, prophets suggested that God used enemy armies to punish Israel for its disregard of the covenant. Later apocalyptic literature exploited the imagery of God as divine warrior and asserted that at the end of time, God will fight the ultimate battle, conquer evil, and free the righteous from their oppression. Now the people are threatened not by the chaos of the sea, but by the rule of the enemy nation; yet, as in the primordial past, God will win the victory.

Especially for those churches that in the summer and autumn use the semicontinuous readings of the Old Testament, the congregation's familiarity with this historical sweep is important. Otherwise, the hearers will have little context for the first readings of years B and C. For those churches that tie the first readings to the gospel, details of the role of warfare in the history of Israel are of less concern, because the readings are heard less as historic presentation, and more as accompaniments to the images in the gospels.

Whether Jesus was the expected military warrior come to free Israel is a recurring question in the gospels. It is significant that Jesus bears the name Joshua, the military leader who brought the people across the Jordan: our pronouncing Jesus' name in Greek, rather than in Hebrew or Aramaic, disguises the referent of Christ's given name. The title *Christ*, naming Jesus as the one anointed by God to save the people, reinforces the military overtones. Yet Nathan promised David a future of peace (Pr11B°). Inspired by a prophetic poem in Isaiah, Christmas hymnody calls Jesus "Prince of peace," and according to the Johannine passion narrative (GFrABC), Jesus rejected the role of military leader. Jesus' supporters did not rise up in Maccabean fashion to protect Jesus and to ensure his cause.

Yet the language of battles is found occasionally in the gospels. Like the deities of old, Jesus conquers the sea (Pr7B). By exorcising demons, Jesus was understood to be fighting against the powers of evil (Pr5B). The seventy disciples were given authority "to tread on snakes and scorpions," clearly setting them in the fight against the primordial evil serpent of Genesis 3 (Pr9C). Yet the very title *Christ* forces us to ask what Jesus was anointed to do. How is the language of battle helpful, or not, in proposing a soteriology?

The imagery of Christ as conqueror became central to early christology. How does what happened to Jesus save humankind? One second-century suggestion, proposed by Irenaeus, was cast largely in battle imagery. Human life is lived out within the battle against good and evil. Christ fought against Satan, who at the crucifixion appeared to have won. But at the resurrection Christ was shown to be victorious over the devil. The dynamism of this Christ-the-victor christology appealed to Martin Luther and can be seen in his Easter hymn "Christ Jesus lay in death's strong bands": "It was a strange and dreadful strife when life and death contended." Perhaps the most accessible way to encounter Irenaeus's theory is by rereading C. S. Lewis's *The Lion, the Witch, and the Wardrobe*. The Witch thinks she has won, but it turns out that, thanks to deeper magic from before the dawn of time, Aslan is victorious, coming back to life and routing the forces of evil.

The language of Christ as conqueror includes another motif from military imagery: evil as Satan (Pr5B). The Old Testament does not speak of a supernatural personified force of evil. The satan of the book of Job is not the Western medieval devil, but a trickster, a troublemaker, one of many anthropomorphized characters in the courts of heaven. The neighboring dualistic religions, however, exercised an increasing influence on Jewish imagination. The New Testament tells of an archenemy of God, whom Jesus confronts in the wilderness, whom believers fight against, and who will contend with God in the final battle at the end of time. Evil is mythologized as "the great dragon, . . . that ancient serpent, who is called the Devil and Satan, the deceiver of the whole world" (Revelation 12:9). The story of the war in heaven blames evil on a primordial battle between the evil angels and the good angels. The legend of the war in heaven is like *The Iliad* in that it pushes blame for human misery back onto the heavenly beings. Christian theologians seldom referred to this story, because theology sought to make humans responsible for their own failures. The story of the war in heaven parallels the Genesis 3 story: creatures made by God, wishing to be more than they are, revolt against God's order, and are condemned for their behavior.

Some Christians maintain the traditional belief in the reality of a supernatural evil being. Others view references to Satan as mythic language. Among those who judge the language metaphoric, some view it as archaic, even silly, and not useful for mature believers. Others find the mythic imagery effective, and they judge that the image of Satan encapsulates all the variations of human sin and misery in a single depiction of evil. In either case, Christians intent on remaining orthodox believers do well to take with great seriousness the power of evil and the way that evil can take over systems and persons. Christian liturgy and its inherent imagery must be able to acknowledge the horror and magnitude of evil. If the world is treating us well and everyone is basically good, salvation is unnecessary. So it is that many contemporary texts of the baptism rite include a remnant of an exorcism. The candidates and their sponsors "renounce the devil and all the devil's empty promises." As Paul wrote (Romans 16:20), "The God of peace will shortly crush Satan under your feet." The language referring to the might of the devil indicates that the Christian life is not a perpetual peaceful sabbath, but rather a continuous struggle against evil and the powers of death. Baptism joins believers to Jesus as he casts out Satan.

A related image is the biblical language of ransom (Pr20c). It is because a person was captured in battle that a ransom would be sought for the prisoner's release. One more appeal to *The Lion, the Witch, and the Wardrobe*: Because Edmund needs to be set free, Aslan offers his own life as ransom. The image of Christ as ransom occurs only three times in the New Testament. Yet early theologians found it engaging, and it occurs in many beloved Christian hymns. The idea that the devil has the authority to set terms for our ransom relies on two ancient constructs: the personification of evil, and the conventions of classical warfare. It is not clear to what degree the imagery of Christ as our ransom is helpful in the present time. In the present time, ransom language is more likely to evoke a situation of kidnapping than of warring.

Most of the battle imagery found in the lectionary comes from the metaphoric use of battle imagery in the New Testament epistles. The devil is an adversary we must resist (Ea7A); however, it is also our old self that must be fought against (Pr9A); the Christian life is spoken of as "the good fight" (Pr25C). Yet, following the pacifist attitude of the sermon on the mount (Ep7A), warfare is not to be directed against our literal earthly enemies (Pr17A). Paul describes Christ's resurrection as a victory over death (Pr3C). The passage that contains the most sustained battle image (Pr16B) speaks of strength, power, armor, struggle, enemies, forces of evil, breastplate, shield, flaming arrows, helmet, and sword. Some Christians relish the strength of this battle imagery, finding it forceful for life's struggles, while others downplay it, judging that it encourages violent patterns of thought.

The history of Christian attitudes toward war is complex and conflicted. Some evidence suggests that the early church was pacifist and that baptized Christians could not serve in the military. The most famous example is Martin of Tours, who in the fourth century claimed to be a solider only for Christ. He abandoned his military career as being incompatible with Christian beliefs. No scholarly consensus exists, however, about whether pacifism was the universal practice of Christians. Indeed, a proscription against military service probably indicates that the issue was controversial. Reports of early martyrdoms, especially those that took place in the arena, popularized language of battle as the ultimate fight against evil. Perpetua, for example, dreams of herself as a gladiator. Cyril of Jerusalem is one of several church fathers who describe the oil of chrismation as preparation for the battles against evil required in Christian life. It is fascinating that the Latin word *sacramentum*, used by theologians as the category for the most sacred rituals of the faith, originally meant the military oath required of the Roman legions, expressing their covenant service to the emperor.

After the peace of Constantine, the question became literalized: can Christians engage in, in fact lead, battle? The realists and the idealists did not, and do not, agree. Augustine represents the tradition of Christians who judge that at least some wars are just, fought in order to right egregious political wrongs. Yet killing in battle was understood to be sinful, and medieval soldiers were required to do penance when they came home from fighting, even from a just war. Many Christian emperors, however, used Augustine's categories to legitimize their military activity. The Crusades were blessed by popes as righting the wrong of non-Christian command of the Holy Land, and the conquest of the native population of the Americas was understood as punishing persons who would not accept baptism and domination by Christian monarchs.

However, Francis of Assisi stands as representative of the pacifist Christian tradition. Legend has it that while the pope was sanctioning war against the Muslims, Francis met and conferred with the sultan. Later in history, the Anabaptists maintained their position of pacifism in the face of brutal opposition by both Roman Catholics and mainstream Protestants. Especially since Hiroshima, more and more Christians are positing that just war is no longer a possibility and are listening to what are called the peace churches—Mennonites, Brethren, the Quakers—and those who advocate nonviolent resistance to oppression.

Yet for every pacifist in the church, who urges that even the imagery of battle degrades human life, there is a veteran of World War II who testifies that Christians had to conquer fascism. One thinks of Dietrich Bonhoeffer, concurring finally in a plot to assassinate Hitler. Christian ethicists continue the debate: is the New Testament record of Jesus' pacifism a prescription for personal or for communal life? We have here no consensus.

When in recent decades the committees who compiled hymns for church publications sought to delete beloved battle hymns, judging them to be incendiary and to encourage aggression, many of the faithful expressed their admiration for war hymns. "For all the saints," "Lift high the cross," and "Onward, Christian soldiers" (which, incidentally, was written for children to sing as they processed to a Sunday school rally festival) are examples of hymns based on classic battle imagery. The obvious psychological question: does singing this imagery nurture and foster warlike attitudes, or does it release primordial human emotions in a harmless way? At least churches must acknowledge that what the scriptures figuratively call "the enemies of God" are not identical with what any particular nation views as its political enemy or economic threat. It is instructive for us to know that during World War I, in the United States, patriotic Christians set up the American flag inside their worship space. This practice, suggesting that God was on the side of U.S. citizens, continues to be controversial, and contemporary liturgical reformers urge all churches to remove political flags from their sanctuaries. It is the baptismal font, not an emblem of national identity, that stands before worshipers on Sunday.

Churches need to demonstrate that they are not facilely appropriating biblical imagery about battle for their own national interest. The weekly intercessions offer a key opportunity to strike an appropriate balance. A prayer for world peace ought probably every single week to be included in the intercessions. It is important that these prayers not be solely for the victory of our allies or the protection of our soldiers in some military engagement. Were our prayers to face squarely the reality of war around the world and to beg God's protection for everyone who is either willingly or unwillingly implicated, any battle language that seems to authorize war would be mitigated.

Some critics claim that battle imagery is heard so literally that it cannot function as metaphor. Consider Egyptian Christians, praying the psalms in which the Egyptians are the enemy! Can we break the power of war by using the language of war? The lectionary proposes that as an image, battle language can function in a healthy way. The details of Israel's military history, controverted as they are, are not essential knowledge for receiving the readings in the lectionary. It is also important to remember that the battles in the Hebrew Scriptures most likely did not occur as they are described. Much of this battle talk expresses faith, not fact. The fundamental idea is that evil is a mighty power that the baptized community must not only withstand, but also attack. This idea can be expressed with various images, battle being one of them. Of course, the church must always guard against literalizing the metaphor. Yet to lay aside battle imagery as too harsh perhaps sentimentalizes the Christian life. We do wrestle against the principalities and powers, and if we are not resisting the powers of evil, actively, forcefully, we are unwittingly conceding to them. It is hoped that mainstream churches will keep in conversation with peace churches, as we continue to probe the liturgical effectiveness of the imagery of battle.

One narrative reminiscent of battle, while central to Jews, has been less significant for Christians. The origin of the name Israel is tied to the memory of Jacob's wrestling, not against evil, but with God's very being (Pr13A°, Pr24c†). This enigmatic story sanctioned the Jewish tradition to confront God, in frank acknowledgment that often it is God with whom humankind must wrestle. Yet whether God battles against the enemy or against us, *Isra-el*, that is, El, God, prevails. Perhaps in times of tragedy and grief, this ancient mysterious story of the patriarch and God doing battle against one another might be pastorally useful also for Christians.

Christians believe that in the resurrection Christ conquered the power of evil and that the baptized community now embodies Christ's Spirit of victory. All that would deprive us of life and freedom, from personal demons to political oppression, is, paradoxically, both already conquered and also a sitting duck as we attack. If we are not attacking something, we are not embodying that Spirit of victory. Yet the good news is that even when we are under attack, we can live victorious. The baptized community is around us always to help us experience and celebrate the victory.

Body

the arm, the hand of God;
the image of God;
the body of Christ, the blood of Christ;
the feet, the head, the side of Christ;
healing the sick, raising the dead

Related chapters: COVENANT, RESURRECTION OF THE BODY, SACRIFICE

To counter any religious notion that only spiritual realities matter, the Bible is full of talk about the body. God created the human body, and God became incarnate in the body of Jesus. Jesus healed many bodies, his body overcame death, and the term *the body of Christ* is the primary phrase used to describe both the church and the eucharist.

PSALM 31:10,
16

For my life is wasted with grief,
and my years with sighing;
    my strength fails because of affliction,
    and my bones are consumed.
Make your face to shine upon your servant,
    and in your lovingkindness save me.

WORDS AT
THE COMMUNION

The body of Christ, given for you.

FRED PRATT
GREEN

O Christ, the healer, we have come
to pray for health, to plead for friends.
How can we fail to be restored
when reached by love that never ends?

From every ailment flesh endures
our bodies clamor to be freed;
yet in our hearts we would confess
that wholeness is our deepest need.

In conflicts that destroy our health
we recognize the world's disease;
our common life declares our ills.
Is there no cure, O Christ, for these?

Grant that we all, made one in faith,
in your community may find
the wholeness that, enriching us,
shall reach and prosper humankind.

If you want to understand the body of Christ, listen to the apostle telling the faithful, "You, though, are the body of Christ and its members" (1 Corinthians 12:27). So if it's you that are the body of Christ and its members, it's the mystery meaning you that has been placed on the Lord's table; what you receive is the mystery that means you. It is to what you are that you reply "Amen." So be a member of the body of Christ, in order to make that "Amen" true.

AUGUSTINE,
SERMON 272

Our bodies play an enormously important role in our life in the Risen Christ. The Incarnation has given a sacramental quality to our flesh and blood, so that we can offer an unceasing prayer of the body that can begin here and never end. This prayer sanctifies not only the suffering of the body but its joys as well. The prayer of the body is preparation for the eternity when our bodies will be glorified as the risen body of Christ is glorified now.

CARYLL
HOUSELANDER,
The Risen Christ

THROUGHOUT THE MEDITERRANEAN WORLD at the time of the origins of Christianity, gnosticism was a dominant credo, and it continues to be a seductive worldview in contemporary spiritualities. Of all biblical images that carry the message of the gospel in the lectionary's readings, the image of the body is the one most antithetical to gnosticism. It will be helpful in a consideration of the body to begin by defining gnosticism.

To make sense of gnosticism, one must take evil with utmost seriousness. According to gnostics, the world is so bad that it is impossible to believe that a good God created it. The gnostic creation myth suggested that a malicious power created the world and that earthly existence, including the body we inhabit, is irretrievably flawed. The only solution is to distance oneself from the created world, as best one can. Extreme asceticism is one way: sexual abstinence is another, so as not to perpetuate within a human body any entrapment of the divine. Gnostics believed that humans have at their core a spark of divinity that seeks return to the perfect spiritual realm. Gnostic doctrine and practice conveyed to people the secret knowledge (*gnosis* = knowledge) that would assist them in liberating themselves from the prison of the body, flying away from this wretched world, and regaining the bliss of heaven. All was a struggle: good against evil, divine against human, spirit against flesh, and soul against body. Although not all contemporary Americans are as convinced as classical gnostics were concerning the evils of the world or the degrading nature of sexual activity, the idea that humans have a divine inner self that eventually returns to God from whom it came is a commonplace belief among both religious and nonreligious people today.

In the several centuries before the birth of Christ, as the Jewish people were increasingly influenced by Hellenistic ideas, this popular Greek belief edged onto the biblical landscape. Some New Testament writers held the Greek philosophical belief in the immortality of the soul, not a Hebrew idea but one central to gnosticism. For the most part, however, the biblical message is radically different from gnostic beliefs. Judaism held and continues to hold that the one good God created this world and called it good, that the created earth is good for human life, and that God visits the admittedly fallen creation and its creatures with mercy. Christians extended this goodness to include the idea of incarnation—that even God became a human person and so inhabited the earth—and they confess that the body of the faithful community is one instance of God's continual re-creation of the world. A gnostic narrative would be characterized by mysterious messages to individuals, trances, and visitations into the heavenly sphere. The gospels, on the other hand, are filled with stories of Jesus interacting with people and healing their bodies, and the epistles teach that we can see divinity most clearly in what is called "the body of Christ."

In the first place, the Bible teaches that the created world and our human bodies are good. According to Genesis 1, God called the whole creation very good. In the poem in Job 38–39, God takes credit for all the astounding creation, from the sea to the snow, from the lion to the ostrich. Psalm 104 says that even sea monsters were made by God's wisdom, and according to Genesis 2, human bodies were specially sculpted and formed by the divine artisan. According to the holiness code in Leviticus, it is only the human body gone wrong or out of control, with excretions or disease or deformity, that brings about uncleanness; the human body itself is not unclean. Similarly, Paul's negative use of *sarx*, often translated "flesh," for example in Romans 8, usually does not mean *body*, which Greek philosophy would contrast with *soul*, but something more like carnality. Yes, the body can go, and has gone, in ways other than God's design. Bodies can turn only into themselves, rather than toward God and others. But God's design of the body was perfect.

According to Hebrew religion, not only is the body good, but it is understood holistically. In fact, neither Hebrew nor Aramaic have a word *body* as one part distinct from some other part of the human person, such as *soul*, unless one is referring to a corpse. This holistic understanding of the body is evident in the intertestamental development of the idea of the resurrection of the body. Although Greeks could imagine a disembodied soul living forever in a spiritual realm, Jews needed to have a body present for there to be personal existence. The resurrected bodies would reside in a genuine new Jerusalem on a real new earth. Plato wrote that Socrates was content to face execution because he welcomed the freedom his soul would experience when it would be released from the strictures of the body. The Bible, on the other hand, says that God's life comes to this earth and to these very bodies. The Song of Songs is a canonized erotic poem, celebrating the goodness of the body and sexuality. Another biblical example: After the resurrection, Jesus still eats breakfast.

The lectionary includes a number of readings that deal with our bodies. Jesus discussed with the Pharisees the question of uncleanness: What outside forces defile the good created body? "From the human heart," says Jesus,

73

comes evil (Pr17B), speaking a line that has echoed down through Augustine's theory of original sin. Many Christian theologians joined more or less with Augustine, placing responsibility for sin on the individual and seeking to explain how the once perfect creatures, created in the image of God, are now prone to evil. As the church continues to probe the nature of evil, we must go deeper than Augustine. For example, his suggestion that sexual intercourse itself was culpable reflects his Hellenistic formation, not the Bible's understanding of sexuality.

Paul took the human body with utter seriousness (Ep2B), referring precisely to our bodies as parts of the body of Christ and a temple of the Holy Spirit. For this reason a believer should shun sexual promiscuity, which would dissipate the integrity of the body. Note that even though Paul employs the category of spirit, the body itself is honored or dishonored by one's sexual lifestyle. Any Christian distaste for the body and denunciation of its sexual functions are far more gnostic than biblical. In medieval Europe, the usual wedding ritual was not a worship service in a church, but rather the priest blessing the couple's bed, after which the community celebrated with a party. It is essential that in the twenty-first century the church work toward a credible sexual ethic for our time, one that reveres the good sexual body that God created and within which the Spirit of God resides. Paul's sexual ethic in 1 Corinthians 7 calls for our attention. Contrary to patriarchal patterns, the husband was not to have authority over the bodies of both himself and his wife; however, Paul would reject the contemporary opinion that each individual owns his or her own body. Rather, in accord with his usual corporate ethic in the body of Christ, Paul wrote that it is the married couple who is the body, each bearing responsibility for the other.

One indication in the New Testament of God's care for the human body lies in all the healing miracles of Jesus. Like other religious figures in the tradition, such as Elijah (Ep6B, Pr9c°, Pr23c†) and Peter after the resurrection (Ea4c), like countless charismatic miracle workers in many religions, Jesus radiated healing powers that brought wholeness back to broken bodies. The ancient promises of the coming reign of God said that the lame would walk, that the lepers would be cleansed. In one liturgical cycle alone we hear of the man with an unclean spirit (Ep4B), Simon's mother-in-law (Ep5B), a leper (Ep6B), a paralyzed man (Ep7B), a man with a deformed hand (Pr4B), the hemorrhaging woman (Pr8B), a daughter with an unclean spirit (Pr18B), and a deaf man (Pr18B). Even the dead were given a second chance to live (Pr8B), because Jesus also resuscitated corpses. Sometimes the narratives stress the faith of the sick person or the forgiveness God grants; other times the focus is on the compassion Jesus showed for those whose bodies were not whole.

It is important to note that a revived corpse is a healed body, not an instance of the resurrection.

Some biblical passages, particularly in the Psalms, suggest that sickness is God's punishment for sin (Le4B). This characteristic human explanation for suffering recurs repeatedly in history, for example during the European medieval plague and the early years of the AIDS infection. Only if one introduces the Hindu and Buddhist idea of reincarnation, however, can the notion that sickness is punishment account for the suffering of children; and many Christians, remembering Jesus' comment about the man born blind (Le4A), have avoided a simplistic equation between human sickness and divine displeasure. What is clear, nonetheless, is that Jesus worked to restore wholeness to human bodies, bodies not only of prominent males, but also of young girls and peasant women. It is as if Christ were recreating the world, starting with the human body.

Many parishes report that rituals of healing hold enormous pastoral significance for their members. Some congregations schedule services of communal prayer for healing with the laying on of hands. Some parishes include, at the distribution of communion, a station with a prayer of healing and the laying on of hands. The church seems to be rediscovering the Hebrew idea of the integrity of the human body, while also refuting the common ancient notion that a broken body could not approach a holy place.

If we could go far enough back in history, we might encounter ancestors of the Israelites who believed that even God had a body. Consider the ancient victory song in Exodus 15, in which the poet gives God a hand, nostrils, breath, an arm, and an abode. According to Jewish theological tradition, however, God does not have a literal body. A grammarian would call the mighty hand and outstretched arm of God, often cited in the Hebrew Scriptures, synecdoche, that is, the calling of the whole by one of its parts: so *arm* stands for the divine being. It is instructive that even though the Hebrew refers to God as *he* and repeatedly calls God King, YHWH is never given a penis. And while it may be that the Hebrew noun for divine mercy evolved from the noun for womb, by the time of the biblical writings God is never portrayed as sexually active, female or male. Poetically God may have a body, but God does not procreate: that which dies must reproduce, and God does not die. Rather, the synecdoches serve to anthropomorphize God, to make God in some way like humans so that humans can better communicate with God. Another example of poetic description in the psalms refers to God's wings, an image that Jews and Christians transferred from the being of God to angels.

A more problematic phrase for the history of theology is "the image of God" in Genesis 1. Theologians have offered many and various proposals as to what the image of God is—rationality, free will, the ability to love, creativity, maleness, even upright posture. It is not at all clear what the author of Genesis 1 meant by *image* and *likeness*. The lectionary appoints Genesis 1 as the first reading at the Easter Vigil, not to speculate about the form of God, but to celebrate the creation of the new world in the resurrection of Christ.

However, Christians believe that God became incarnate, that is, took on a body, in Jesus. When according to John's gospel the soldiers came to arrest Jesus, to take hold of his body, he identified himself with the name of God by saying, "Ego eimi," and the soldiers fall to the ground, for they have encountered God (GFrABC). To make clear that in John Jesus is claiming divine identity, we might better render his answer "Here I AM," rather than "I am he." One of the early Christian heresies rejected by orthodox theologians was the gnostic idea that God's spirit only used the body of Jesus and that Christ only seemed to die, as if God only appeared to become human. "And became truly human" is the contemporary translation of the line (old translation: "and became man") in the Nicene Creed that sought to condemn this Docetism. The resurrection accounts speak of his pierced hands, side, and feet, for Christ's body is both whole and broken. Here we see how Christianity has taken the Jewish belief of the goodness of the created body and built upon it the doctrine of the incarnation of God in Christ.

The early church continued the Jewish prohibition against depicting God in any way. But over the centuries the church experimented with various ways of drawing the divine body. At first Christians presented metaphoric depictions of Christ: Christ as a shepherd, Christ as a king. In medieval times, church walls came to be painted with depictions of God, usually as an old bearded man, and Christ's body was drawn with more realism and less metaphor: a young shepherd boy was replaced by a bleeding body on a cross. It would be a good idea for each parish to be aware of its own images on bulletin covers, Sunday school material, stained glass, and wall paintings. Is God presented as having a body? How is Christ's body drawn? Are these pictures helpful? Because such depictions can exert enormous power on the unconscious of the faithful, it is wise to bring them out into communal consciousness, shared and discussed.

What distinguishes a Christian from a person who respects Jesus as a famous healer and teacher is belief in the resurrection. Of course, what exactly the church means by the resurrection of Jesus Christ from the dead continues to be debated by theologians. A contemporary person might ask what a video camera set up at the tomb would have filmed on Easter Day. We can say at least this much: that the creative power of God was evident in the destiny of the crucified Jesus, who rose out of the finality of death to a new life with God. In keeping with the biblical honoring of the human body, the New Testament narratives stress that Jesus' life after his death was one with a genuine body. He could eat (Ea3A, Ea3B, Ea3C). Yet, while he could rather like a specter appear and disappear, his body still showed its wounds (Ea2ABC). These stories of Jesus' body reflect the biblical ideas of the unity of the human person and the goodness of the human body.

The source of the liturgical handshake of peace is the resurrection story in John 20 about the wounds of Christ. Our greeting, "The peace of Christ be with you," is other than a pleasant "Good morning," and ought not deteriorate into one. Rather, in this ritual we as the body of Christ embody the resurrection. Joining with the disciples hiding in the locked room, we are recreated into the body of Christ, and we touch the wounds of the crucified one. Passing the peace is the sign of the Spirit of the risen Christ, conveyed from one baptized person to another in a room deeply marked by the wounds of the world.

Body of Christ language continues. In the eloquent first chapter of Ephesians (AscABC, LastA), "the eyes of your heart" see the power of God, a power seen most fully in the resurrection of Christ. The metaphoric language goes on: Christ is sitting on God's right hand; Christ has feet and a head; and although this body of Christ "fills all in all," the body of Christ is also language used to describe the church. The epistles make considerable use of the metaphor of the body of Christ, Paul stressing that the church is itself the one unified body of Christ (PentA, Pr16A, Ep3C). The deutero-Pauline writings, in a more hierarchical vein, teach that Christ is the head of the church and the faithful are the rest of the body (Pr13B, Pr11C, Pr12C). That is, just as the human body of Jesus once contained the Spirit of God, now the corporate body of the church is that embodiment of the divine Spirit, "the body of Christ." The Spirit does not only blow about unseen and free, it also is embodied in and by the community of the baptized.

Most believers accept that referring to the church as the body of Christ is metaphor. Yet the biblical and liturgical use of the body of Christ as language for the bread of the eucharist has less ecclesial consensus. Many Christians were exiled or executed for explaining in some unauthorized way what the church means by calling the bread the body of Christ. This language occurs each week in the eucharist and appears in the lectionary on Maundy Thursday and in the Johannine passages in year B (Pr15B, Pr16B). Mark and

Matthew quote Jesus as speaking of "my body" and "my blood of the covenant," and Luke and Paul of "my body" and "the new covenant in my blood." To intensify the metaphor, John writes of "eating my flesh" and "drinking my blood," *flesh* and *blood* being words that a Semitic culture could use to indicate the full reality of a person's body. Thus even the biblical record demonstrates some variety in the use of this image.

The theologians' desire to confirm the sacramental reality of the eucharistic meal led the medieval church to employ language of change. What changed, according to Thomas Aquinas, was not what the bread was made out of, the ingredients or "accidents" of the bread, but rather what the bread was, the "substance" of the bread. Here is an example: The annual confection topped with lighted candles, brought with singing to the dining room table, is *made of* flour, sugar, butter, but it *is* a birthday cake. The food on the altar was still made of the ingredients of bread, but in the eucharist was by faith "the body of Christ." The church meant this language to stress the reality of the Spirit's working the sacrament. The bread was not just a symbol. An example in our time might be a swastika, which society does not view as just an ancient northern European symbol of the sun, but rather a designation of reality that can get a graffiti artist jailed.

Protestants offered several different explanations as to what the church means by calling the eucharistic bread the body of Christ. Contemporary theologians endeavor to suggest language that avoids anachronistic physics, mystifying obfuscations, or just plain nonsense. One current proposal is the term *transignification*; that is, by the thanksgiving to God, with the promise of Christ, and in the sharing of the eucharist, the significance of the bread is other than it was before the liturgy began. Some Christians stress that the body of Christ that is most paramount is not the bread itself, but the community's sharing of the bread. As Paul wrote in 1 Corinthians 11, if the community does not recognize both rich and poor members of this body, the meal is eaten unworthily. Not only the bread, but also the community is the body of Christ. Although some believers are troubled by a possible echo of cannibalism in this biblical language, others find in the widespread human ritual of consuming the body of the dead so as to ingest the power of its life a parallel for what the Christian community does in the eucharist.

In bread, that is, in the community's staple food, we see God, and in joining together to share that bread, we come to embody that God. The Eastern Orthodox tradition speaks of our realization, at the great thanksgiving of the eucharist, that in bread is God. Martin Luther taught that "in, with, and under" the bread comes forgiveness of sin, life and salvation. We are what we eat, we eat what we are: the body of Christ. The body of

Christ is always at least three things: the bread shared in eucharist, the baptized community that eats together, and the resurrected Christ who fills the whole world.

The use of this image is more extreme when we call the wine the blood of Christ. The synoptics offer two different grammatical ways to link the wine with the covenant: "my blood of the covenant" and "the new covenant in my blood." Over its history the Israelite religious tradition included various blood rituals—for example, the lamb's blood smeared on the doorposts, the ox's blood thrown on the altar and the people, the bull's blood poured out before the altar. For humankind to live, some blood must be shed. Perhaps this religious symbolism arose in ancient times out of the phenomenon of menstruation and childbirth, by which the human community realized a connection between blood and life. Perhaps the imagery expressed the reality of tribal warfare, in which some persons had to die for the people. Some anthropologists theorize that the ritual of circumcision, which many peoples practiced at a boy's puberty, mimicked menstruation by tying the shedding of blood to adulthood. In any case, blood has often been seen as symbolic of human life. As is characteristic, the author of John pushed the metaphor to its very edge, writing of "drinking blood," a particularly bizarre linguistic construction for Jews, for whom the drinking of any blood was anathema. See, for example, the words of God to Noah, "You shall not eat flesh with its life, that is, its blood" (Genesis 9:4). Here the Christian tradition follows the Greek more than the Hebrew worldview, for the church has used the words *body* and *blood* as expressions of the encounterability of the person of Christ. Some Christians temper the image by saying, not "the blood of Christ," but "the cup of life," at the distribution of communion.

Our use of biblical language of the body is always complex. Take for example Ezekiel 36:24-28 (VigilABC). In the biblical context, the prophet condemned the people's apostasy, which was likened to a woman's menstrual uncleanness. The Israelites, along with many ancient peoples, judged the flowing of menstrual blood inexplicable, thus frightening, and created social taboos to isolate the phenomenon. Such bleeding was judged by the men to be a body out of control; it extended the body beyond its borders, and so rendered the body unclean. Yet Ezekiel proclaims that clean water is on its way. God will return the body of the community to a perfect state, giving it a new heart of flesh to replace its heart of stone.

Can this biblical passage be good news also for us? Some might view the Ezekiel passage as best avoided, since its context repeats an ancient prejudice against menstruation based on prescientific ignorance about bodily functions.

Others may argue that, removed from its problematic context, the passage is an eloquent poem that we can spiritualize and individualize, stressing my heart of stone to be replaced by a heart of flesh in the coming Easter season. Still others can see the water as referring to the waters of baptism at the resurrection festival, and thus an appropriate reading for the Vigil, with its emphasis on the communal reentry into the cleansing waters. Remember, the *you* in the passage is plural: the church recognizes that the heart transplant is meant for the body of Christ. The believing community is to grow together into the full stature of Christ, the image of God, the individual bodies of its one body being the good new creation begun in the resurrection of Christ from the dead.

City

Babel, Babylon, building, citizenship,
cornerstone, foundation, gates,
Jerusalem, keys, Nineveh, Sodom, Zion

Related chapters: KINGDOM, MOUNTAIN

In both the Bible and the lectionary, the image of city evokes both
the worst and the best of human society. The contemporary challenge is to continue this tradition by allowing the image to be both
negative and positive.

PSALM 48:2, Beautiful and lofty, the joy of all the earth,
11, 12 is the hill of Zion,
　　the city of the great Sovereign
　　and the very center of the world.
Make the circuit of Zion;
walk round about it;
　　count the number of its towers.
Consider well its bulwarks;
examine its strongholds;
　　that you may tell those who come after.

PSALM 137:1, 8 By the waters of Babylon we sat down and wept,
　　when we remembered you, O Zion.
O city of Babylon, doomed to destruction,
　　happy the one who pays you back
　　for what you have done to us!

EASTER PSALM The glory of the Lord shines on the city. Alleluia.
ANTIPHON Its lamp is the Lamb. Alleluia.

ERIK ROUTLEY All who love and serve your city,
all who bear its daily stress,
all who cry for peace and justice,
all who curse and all who bless,

in your day of loss and sorrow,
in your day of helpless strife,
honor, peace, and love retreating,
seek the Lord, who is your life.

Risen Lord, shall yet the city
be the city of despair?
Come today, our judge, our glory;
be its name "The Lord is there!"

Two cities have been formed by two loves: the earthly city, by the love of self, even to the contempt of God; and the heavenly city, by the love of God, even to the contempt of self. The former city glories in itself, the latter in the Lord. The one delights in its own strength, represented in the person of its ruler; the other says to its God, "I will love you, O Lord, my strength." The wise men of the one city, living according to humankind, have sought for profit to their own bodies or souls. But in the other city there is no human wisdom, but only godliness.

AUGUSTINE, *The City of God*

It is all in the seeing, and the saying: what came as revelation to John of Patmos, that heaven is a city, and not a solitude. And what came to Thomas Merton on first seeing the Abbey of Gethsemani: "this is the only city in America," he wrote to a friend. And here is what I saw: Manhattan before me, a city made of stars, and human beings, all of whom, the physicians now tell us, were once the stuff of stars. Light. And I thought of the words of Psalm 97, which I had read distractedly on the plane: "Light is sown for the righteous, and gladness for the upright of heart" (v. 11, KJV). Light a seed, and the city Jerusalem, grounded in peace.

KATHLEEN NORRIS, *Amazing Grace*

THE CITY IS an ambivalent image. Whether one examines the Bible, religious symbolism and literature from around the world, or the daily newspaper, one sees that sometimes the city is praised as the apex of human civilization, while other times it is condemned as a locus of all that is harmful. This same ambivalence is found in the lectionary's use of the image of the city. Biblical studies explore this ambivalence, some studies concentrating on the positive religious symbolism of Jerusalem and others marked by a detailed criticism of urban life.

Around the second millennium B.C.E., human communities in various places around the world began building cities. Usually the establishment of cities followed upon, and then accelerated further, several technological advances in human life: food, goods, and services beyond the subsistence level; ready availability and storage of water; development of an alphabet; improved methods of transportation; division of labor; a single religious ideology; and a central government with policing power. What is especially religiously significant are the myths in many ancient societies that indicate that the city is divine in origin and intent.

The version of this archetypal myth that most influenced biblical authors was the Babylonian Enuma elish. Chaos was personified as a female sea monster, churning up trouble for everything. As was characteristic in these tales, a male hero overcomes the chaos and builds a city. The city is then a symbol of the divine order that the hero personified; the deity resides in a temple in the city, thus insuring continued security for the people; the monarch is the vice-regent of the deity, authorized by the deity to effect cosmic order among the human population. One recognizes this myth behind the divine right of kings, a political doctrine accepted by many in the West until 200 years ago. Since the deity has come down from the skies to live among the people, the city is a sacred place, and the physical arrangement of the city—its buildings, its streets, its reservoir—mirrors the divine world and establishes the hierarchical order deemed necessary by the rulers for the smooth running of the society. Those who live closest to the palace are the most politically powerful; those condemned to death are executed outside the city walls. As for the symbolic ambivalence of the city: Naturally, if one experiences an improvement in one's living situation from urbanization, then the city is a blessed thing; if on the other hand the enemy lives in the city, urbanization is judged to be destructive of wholesome human life.

The myth of the divine origin of the benevolent capital city underlies the language describing Jerusalem in Psalms 2, 46, 48, 87, 89, 99, and 110, among others. In Psalm 48, a thorough presentation of this ancient myth, God is credited with establishing the city of Mount Zion, which is "the joy of all the earth," even though what the NRSV translates "north" (v. 2) is the name of the Olympus-type mountain Zaphon on which Baal was long since said to inhabit. Chaos is described as the enemy; the invading kings are like women in the throes of labor or like the wild seas destroying ships. Although this psalm does not refer to a female sea monster, the images of women in childbirth and the uncontrolled seas carry the same idea: chaos is like female nature, and it must be conquered by male order. The city represents this divine order: "The towns of Judah rejoice because of your judgments." The city provides safety for the people and a good life for which the deity is praised. A particularly positive designation for the city Jerusalem used in the Bible is Mount Zion. Apparently based on a pre-Israelite name for the Jebusite city, it remained a mythic title for the city and for the social good it represented.

Because the city was said to have been founded by the deities, it became the place of the primary temple and the center of religious ceremonies. Tourists who visit the ruins of the ancient Mexican city Teotihuacan are stunned to contemplate the power of the religious rites that ordered a city of perhaps 200,000 inhabitants. Jerusalem at the time of King Solomon represents a much smaller version of this phenomenon, with the temple erected by the powerful monarch as evidence of divine authorization. Honor was directed to the deities from the city, and the populace honored the deities by honoring the city. Religious ceremonies conducted in shrines outside the city were discouraged or outlawed.

The city is a place where people work together. Sometimes the shared labor was militarily enforced by an oppressive regime. The Bible records that even Solomon instituted forced labor for his building projects. At other times cooperation was voluntary, as in the Greco-Roman city, where monarchical despotism was replaced by a government in which at least the citizens, who were the free males, participated. Aristotle described the city-state as "a common life for a noble end." Our word *city* derives from the same root as the word *civilization*. The city brought with it not only a temple, but also a reservoir, theaters, public baths, ready markets, a library—structures and opportunities that require large groups of cooperating persons for their continued maintenance. Often the city produced an ethnic mix, both for good and for ill, that stood in stark contrast to earlier communities bonded by blood ties. In Psalm 87, the dream of the mythic city suggests that even enemy peoples—Babylonians, Philistines—will some day be included as residents of God's great city.

The city was thought to be a place of communal justice. In Aeschylus' play *The Eumenides*, it is in the city Athens, blessed by the goddess Athena, that tribal retributive revenge is replaced with rational trial by jury. Justice moves beyond family pride to consider more broadly the entire community. In some Old Testament references, the Israelite city is said to embody such justice. For example, in Psalm 99, God is called a "lover of justice" who through the king in Zion has established equity and righteousness in the land.

The city was constructed as a place of protection and peace. City walls surrounded the people with arms of safety. Perhaps it was this aspect of embrace that led Hebrew, like so many linguistic systems, to refer to the city as a *she*, a great mother who protected her people. As we see in *The Iliad*, to destroy a city was to destroy the entire civilization, because the city was the symbol of the people's communal identity. In the Hebrew of Psalm 46 as well, the city is a round she in the midst of which rises up the divine he, the sexual symbolism a picture of confident protection. This female depiction of the city lies behind also the biblical terminology *Daughter Zion* as a designation of the people of God.

The city meant security not only from military attack, but also from other human dangers. In the city were cisterns or reservoirs, food storage, a system of food distribution, indeed, many cooperative endeavors that assist human survival in times of natural disaster. The availability of water from the Gihon spring functioned mythically for the residents of Jerusalem, who laud the city as insurance against thirst. As Psalm 87 says of Zion, "All my springs are in you," and the prophet Zechariah promises that from Jerusalem shall flow out living waters to water the entire land. Israel's increasing urbanization coincided with its growing sense of divine election and of military invulnerability. The prophet we call First Isaiah proclaimed that God established Jerusalem, and from it God would rule the world in peace.

The city also came to signify a greater measure of freedom for the individual. Release from the harshest of survival needs led people to increased options for their livelihood and their leisure time. The account in the Bible of cities of refuge indicates one aspect of the freedoms granted by urban life: the city creates an anonymity that is a gift to a person guilty of manslaughter.

All these positive characteristics of urban life are judged differently, however, if one is outside the city. Some contemporary New Testament scholars suggest that the primitive Christian church was a conservative peasant movement marked by staunch rejection of the city and all it stood for. For rural peasants, the plentiful water available in the city was provided by an aqueduct system that drew water away from the farmers' distant fields. Urban building projects demanded massive labor forces, which were often constituted by the young men from rural areas. Even if urbanization promised eventual improvement of the life of the poor, the women and the old men remaining in the fields cannot have appreciated such a migration or conscription of their young males.

Apparent in many stories in the Old Testament is the opposite opinion: the city is not founded by God, but stands against all that is good. Lot was foolish in choosing to live near the ungodly cities of Sodom and Gomorrah. The ethnic mix in the city meant a loss of traditional values and threatened religious purity, as Solomon's wives exemplify. The prophets condemned the injustices against the poor that were concentrated in the commerce of the city, where the tribal ties that ensure communal decency had been loosened or altogether dissolved. Increased options were available only for the rich, whose ease was built upon the backs of the struggling poor. The murderer Cain is remembered as having built the first city. The Bible contains many stories of divine judgment upon cities. Babel is remembered as a place of communal chaos, Sodom a haven for immorality, Pharaoh's building projects the occasion for human slavery, Babylon a center of paganism, Nineveh a place of unbelief, and Rome the archetypal military oppressor.

The lectionary demonstrates the same ambivalence toward the city that the entire Bible contains. Sometimes both images come to us on the same Sunday. For example, on Pentecost year c, the narrative of Babel presents urbanization as symbolic of human pride. The building project signals a loss of religious values and is halted by God. On the other hand, the epistle tells of Jerusalem, a place alive with peoples from all nations and languages, which becomes, like the mythic cities of old, the place where the God's Spirit dwells. Thus the city is both the place of human arrogance that merits destruction and the center of divine blessing for all the earth.

On some Sundays the city is wholly benevolent. The psalms of Zion that occur as responses to the first readings include many examples of the city as a positive blessing from God. In Advent, readings from Second Isaiah (Ad2B) and Zephaniah (Ad3C) look forward with joy to the restoration of God's city. Here the city is a picture of human peace and security that embodies the divine. God will dwell not in the wilderness, but in the renewed city. The stereotypical metaphor that cites the city as female nurturer occurs in Isaiah 66 (Pr9c†), where Jerusalem as a nursing mother is an image of God's loving care. The book of Hebrews includes evocation of the myth of the city, as the magnificent abode of God promised to God's people (Pr14c).

Readings from the epistles that describe church life employ the image of city positively. Citizenship is one metaphor used to denote the Christian participation in the church. *Building, cornerstone, foundation,* and the *gates of the city* are words that make the hearer think positively of urban structures. The conversation between Jesus and Peter about the structure of the church (Pr16A) relies on imagery about the city. The keys that Peter is given authorize him to grant someone entrance, perhaps through the city gates or into a prominent building: it is in cities, not in tents or villages, that people require keys.

Yet another positive use of the image of the city occurs in the glorious passages from Revelation (Ea5c, Ea6c). Although in Revelation the city of Babylon figures as the image of all that is evil, only the passages describing the new Jerusalem are heard in the lectionary. God will save us by sending down from heaven a new perfected city, which will itself be a temple, the center of the people's civic life, surrounded by protective gates, praised for its water, its abundant food, a benevolent monarch, and even the freedom provided by perpetual supernatural light.

The lectionary also includes several prophetic condemnations of the city. In a poem from Isaiah 25, God will replace the evil city with God's very self (Pr23A†, EaB). Those who read from Lamentations 1 hear a devastating description of the city that, like a piteous widow, has been abandoned by God (Pr22c°). The gospels report that it was outside the great city that Jesus was born, lived, died, and rose. Jesus wept over the city of Jerusalem (Le2c), and in the unbelieving city he was tried and convicted. The evangelists, living in the real world, realize that the city may not always be the abode of God. Yet as Jeremiah urged, even as you find yourself exiled in Babylon, pray for the welfare of that city (Pr23c°).

Care must be taken that worshipers understand the symbolic meaning of Jerusalem language. On the one hand, Christians should be regularly praying in the weekly intercessions that the actual city of Jerusalem come to a time of peace. However, usually when liturgical language evokes Jerusalem, the reference is not to the contemporary city, but in some cases to immoral human society, while in other cases to the church, in yet other cases to God's promise of perfection at the end of time. Linguistic philosophers teach that a word has no definition outside its specific context: what *Jerusalem* or *Zion* means depends on the sentence and paragraph in which the word is located.

Ambivalence about cities has continued throughout history. Cities, situated at the crossroads of highways, were home to prominent bishops and central to the spread of Christianity. Cities were also places of military might and political oppression. The literal city of Jerusalem has been a place of intense religious devotion since at least the pilgrimage of Queen Helena in the fourth century. It is also a city experiencing nearly continuous political and religious turmoil. Today's cities contain both state-of-the-art medical facilities and street corner drug sales, magnificent art museums and uncontrolled graffiti, fully stocked department stores and abandoned slums. It remains the case that the city, a symbol of enriched human life, presents graphic examples of human failure and injustice.

Despair marks also rural areas. Interpreters do neither the Bible nor contemporary life any favor by demonizing the city. Although the lectionary provides both positive and negative references to the city, the city seldom functions in the church's literature as an image of divine blessing. For example, try to locate hymn stanzas that thank God for the city, the actual contemporary city, as a place that improves human life. Our song traditions contain many hymns from especially the Romantic movement of the nineteenth century, which judged the cities of the early industrial revolution as centers of disease, dehumanization, poverty, and death. Although our hymns and church art do laud a heavenly city, a place beyond the real city, as an image for the divine, church language tends to praise the forest and the flower, rather than the library and the train line, as signs of God's beneficence.

A more biblical balance would see that the earthly city is filled with possibilities for human community and health for which God is praised. The Bible promises that God will reside in the city. The believer is not a hermit alone in a cave. Rather, believers live together, sharing the advantages and the tasks of communal existence. Even John Bunyan's lone Pilgrim is heading not toward a primordial garden, but toward the city. It is appropriate that the Pentecost story takes place in the city of Jerusalem, which becomes a picture of the church, our communal life in the Spirit of the resurrection.

Some biblical images pose difficulties to the interpreter because they are archaic or alien. Other images, however, pose the opposite danger, since we have a lifetime of personal experience with them. Do I like or dislike cities? Naturally one's personal experience figures in one's reception of a biblical image. But the lectionary asks us to moderate our reactions and to inform our experience with the centuries of stories and poems of the whole people of God, proclaiming not our personal satisfaction or dissatisfaction with life in the city, but rather the city as archetypal image.

In some world religions, the devout are expected to make pilgrimages to sacred cities, places made holy because deities or saints dwelt there. Following

Queen Helena in the fourth century, many Christians have traveled to Jerusalem or Rome as being particularly sacred cities. Yet Christianity has never required pilgrimages. The city that radiates holiness, the city with ever-flowing water and food for all, is the Sunday assembly around word and sacrament. We reside in God as in a city. Christ is the cornerstone of the city. Our communal life in the Spirit is like life in a city. We need not go to Jerusalem, for Jerusalem is here.

Clothing

clothing, garments of salvation, white robes

Related chapters: BODY

In most societies, humans cover parts of their bodies with clothing. In Genesis 3, as soon as the first woman and man realize their human condition, they make themselves clothes, and later God provides them with better clothing. The Bible speaks of God's salvation as if it were clothing, and the church symbolizes that clothing with the alb, the vestment signifying baptism.

PSALM 30:12   You have turned my wailing into dancing;
              you have put off my sackcloth and clothed me with joy.

RITE OF   Put on this robe, for in baptism you have been clothed in
BAPTISM   the righteousness of Christ, who calls you to his great feast.

JOEL W.   Now we join in celebration
LUNDEEN   at our Savior's invitation,
              dressed no more in spirit somber,
              clothed instead in joy and wonder;
              for the Lord of all existence,
              putting off divine transcendence,
              stoops again in love to meet us,
              with his very life to feed us.

As soon as you entered the baptistry, you put off your garment, and this was an image of putting off the old man with his deeds. Having stripped yourselves, you were naked; in this you were imitating Christ, who hung naked on the cross. But now, having put on these garments that are spiritually white, you must be continually robed in white. We do not mean that you must always wear white raiment, but that you must be entirely clothed in truly white and glistening and spiritual attire.

CYRIL OF
JERUSALEM,
*Mystagogical
Catechesis*

Our good Lord is our clothing that, for love, wraps us up and winds us about, embracing us, all beclosing us and hanging about us, for tender love.

JULIAN OF
NORWICH,
*Revelations of
Divine Love*

IN NEARLY ALL human communities that the contemporary world has studied or encountered, people wore clothing. Clothing adds layers to the human person, so that the interior vulnerable self can be less exposed to all that might harm. Clothing signifies one's life situation and achieves various purposes: it provides privacy for the genitals; it protects the relatively hairless human skin from the extremes of weather; it announces one's socioeconomic identity. Some tribal peoples who go naked in warm weather practice bodily ornamentation, yet another object of human dress. The dress of many contemporary Westerners achieves all these purposes at once: the first layer, underwear, covers genitals; the second is weather-appropriate protection, but its style or cost announces to everyone the socioeconomic groups with which one wishes to be associated; and on top of this layer is a wholly decorative touch, a necklace or a tie. Thus we are dressed, and ready to face the world.

In what is the Bible's most famous story involving dress, clothes function in their most basic way as protection of the human. Adam and Eve, in coming into adult consciousness, recognize their sinfulness, understand their sexuality, and fear the otherness of the divine. Trying to protect themselves from the reality of these truths, they dress themselves (Le1A). The Garden of Eden story concludes as God's mercy provides them with more substantial clothing than fig leaves. Leaf loincloths give way to leather coats. The irony is poignant: as humans become fully human, less like other animals, as they become aware of themselves and their frailties, their lives require assistance from animals without human consciousness. Adult life is no longer a paradise. We must get dressed and go to work, eating in order to live, procreating in view of death, and killing other species so that we can survive. In the Genesis story, clothing moves from a literal prop in the drama to a symbolic sign of our humanness. Yet at the conclusion of the story, clothing comes to symbolize the mercy of God, who knows human needs and meets them far beyond our own abilities.

The clothing of some people marks them as members of their group: one thinks of the Amish people or of conservative veiled Muslim women. But generally in our culture, which values individual choice and enjoys relative or excessive affluence, clothing is a more significant portrayal of the self than it was in tribal societies or in times of poverty. However, clothing that announces the self is not a new phenomenon. In several famous biblical stories about clothing, what one wears marks who one is. The coat of many colors that Jacob gives his favorite son Joseph, the eldest son of his favorite wife, is now judged by linguists to have been a long coat with sleeves, that is, an outfit distinctive because of how much fabric was used (Pr14A°). The favorite son gets more fabric, and this privileged status incites his brothers into jealousy. His clothing did distinguish him from the group, but for ill rather than for good. Exodus 28 records in meticulous detail the Israelites' priestly vestments as authorized by God. The priests' garb—breastplate, ephod, robe, tunic, turban, and sash, adorned with gold, blue, purple, and crimson yarns, twelve gems, bells, and gold filigree—indicates their unique status in the community as the ones chosen to stand between God and the rest of the community.

Several of the Bible's stories involving clothing are included in the lectionary. We read the story of Jonah (VigilABC, Ep3B), after whose preaching the people of Nineveh signify their repentance by donning sackcloth. Beloved is the parable of the prodigal son (Le4C), who is given a new robe as part of his welcome home. The gospels include the detail that sick persons tried to touch Jesus' clothing, explicitly the Jewish ritual fringes of his attire, in order to be miraculously healed (Pr5A, Pr11B). In the passion narratives, Jesus' clothing changes from one scene to another, from the dazzling white of the transfiguration, to the purple robe after the trial, to the perhaps total nakedness of the crucifixion.

In the lectionary, clothing functions not only as literal dress, but also as metaphor. In Isaiah 61 (Ad3B) the prophet describes the coming of the Spirit of God as if one is donning a garland and putting on a mantle. God will clothe the people with garments of salvation and a robe of righteousness, clothing as stunning as the jewels that adorn a bride for her wedding. The church teaches that, even though it was the Israelite priests who were gorgeously arrayed, now all the baptized have donned, like wedding garments, the salvation of God. Like the animal skins God provided for poor exposed Adam and Eve, our baptism protects us with the mercy of God, and we can survive, despite the ambiguities of sex, the harshness of living, and the reality of death.

More symbolic references to clothing occur in especially year c of the epistle readings. As baptized children of God, we are clothed in Christ (Pr7C). Our old self is stripped away, and we are clothed newly with the image of God (Pr13C). Perhaps this passage refers to a baptismal ritual in which one's clothing was removed, the naked body was washed, and then the new white robe was donned. Another reading from Colossians (Ch1C) describes our clothing as the life of loving virtue that characterizes the baptized body of Christ. The stunning passage from Revelation (E24c) describes all the baptized standing around the heavenly throne in robes made white by being washed in blood. This image involves a poetic reversal of nature, since by nature water washes away blood stains. Yet Christ's blood metaphorically turns our garment white; it reverses normalcy. A stained glass window in one of Rome's medieval churches depicts Christ's blood pouring down from the cross and filling up a spa-like pool, in which the naked faithful are dancing.

The classic white baptismal dress is supposed to recall these white robes. Too often, however, the infant's frilly outfit is too far removed from the white robes around the throne for people to see any connection. Furthermore, since in some churches only ordained people wear liturgical vestments, some Christians imagine the white alb to signify ordination. However, both the robe of the newly baptized and the white robe of those leading in the liturgy are meant to recall the clothing of those baptized into Christ. Women in the Holiness churches maintain this symbol in their Sunday practice of wearing white from head to toe. Parishes do well to make the most of this biblical image. The newly baptized, both infants and adults, should be dressed in white. Confirmation and choir robes are best modeled on albs, not on academic robes and hoods, because their meaning refers to baptism, not to intellectual achievement. Albs are the clothing of all the baptized, not of only some of the baptized.

In fourteenth-century Norwich, England, there lived a remarkable woman whom we know only as Julian, which was the name of the church next to which she lived as a solitary. She experienced a series of visions from God, the most often-cited being that of the Trinity as her father, her mother, and her spouse. She also wrote of Christ as having taken on our human tunic, "dyed with the sweat of his body, close-fitting and short and threadbare," and our having received, in a merciful exchange, the cloak of Christ, that wraps us round with endless love. Yet Julian, who wrote with a positive delight in God's mercy that is unfortunately so uncharacteristic of the medieval church, moves one step more with her image of clothing. Not only do we enjoy wearing Christ, but "we are his crown"; that is, Christ is wearing us. Not only are we wrapped round with the cloak of Christ, but Christ is arrayed with us.[1]

The New Testament calls the church *the body of Christ*, and the body requires clothing. How might we describe the clothing that we wear? We might say that it is the white tunic that covers the wet body of the newly baptized, the blood-bleached white robe of the saints around the heavenly throne, the seamless cloak of Christ, the dazzling divine clothes of Christ's transfiguration. Many medieval churches displayed an image called Our Lady's Mantle, in which Mary spreads out her arms so that her cloak provides an overarching umbrella of embrace, protecting the group of naked Christians who crowd next to her. The image can also be interpreted as the cloak of Lady Church, the mantle being the covering we are granted in our baptism.

The liturgical image of clothing calls us to reflect on the matter of our dress. It is commonplace for churches to participate in clothing drives for the poor and to run secondhand clothing sales. The church might think more deeply about how the clothing that Christians wear might signify the values of a baptized people. Through much of medieval European history, local sumptuary laws attempted to force citizens to wear only those clothes denoting their socioeconomic status. In the secular culture, clothes cost money and disclose status. How might Christians think about this issue? How much money can believers spend on clothes? How many clothes is it appropriate for Christians to own? Many sisters in religious orders of women, in adapting the classic vow of poverty into one of simplicity, now wear simple inexpensive clothing. A more essential symbol of St. Francis than birds on his arm is the poor man's robe he elected to wear. Reflection on our lives as clothed in Christ may have some effect on our participation in an affluent culture's obsession with expensive and individualistic attire.

It is unfortunate that light-skinned persons are usually called *white*. The white of baptismal identity means to recall not the skin tone of northern Europeans, but the blood-bleached robes of the saints around the throne. The good news is that the baptized become, not fair-skinned, but God-covered, Christ-attired, dressed in the communal values that arise from life in the Spirit. It might be useful to remember that the white color of baptismal robes is the spectrum's way of combining all the colors of the rainbow.

Covenant

covenant, forgiveness, new covenant

Related chapters: PROPHET, SACRIFICE

The ancient Hebrews took the idea of covenant from the political system of their world and adapted it to describe their relationship with God. Although the Old Testament contains variations of covenant, the primary idea—that God relates to the chosen people with mercy—remains central in the New Testament and undergirds the Christian understanding of eucharist.

PSALM 105:8-10   The LORD has always been mindful of the covenant,
     the promise made for a thousand generations:
the covenant made with Abraham,
     the oath sworn to Isaac,
which God established as a statute for Jacob,
     an everlasting covenant for Israel.

CANTICLE OF   Blessed are you, Lord, the God of Israel. . . .
ZECHARIAH   Through your holy prophets, you promised of old
to save us from our enemies,
     from the hands of all who hate us,
to show mercy to our forebears,
     and to remember your holy covenant.

MARTY HAUGEN   From of old you loved and sought us!
Thanks be to you forever!
Truth and justice you have taught us;
thanks be to you forever!

Strong is your faithfulness,
strong is your love,
remembering your covenant of life with us.

The gospels could not possibly be either more or less in number than they are. Since there are four zones of the world in which we live, and four principal winds, it is clear that the Word, the artificer of all things, gave to us the gospel fourfold in form but held together by one Spirit. For the cherubim have four faces, and their faces are images of the activity of the Son of God. Therefore four general covenants were given to humankind: one was that of Noah's deluge, by the rainbow; the second was Abraham's, by the sign of circumcision; the third was the giving of the law by Moses; and the fourth is that of the gospel, through our Lord Jesus Christ.

IRENAEUS,
Against Heresies

A Covenant: My present and my future possessions, in family and estate, I here solemnly yield up in everlasting covenant to Thee. I hereby covenant to trust in Thee for the needful aid of Thy Spirit. Through the power of Thy Spirit alone I have complied with the conditions laid down in Thy Word upon which thou dost promise to enter into these covenant engagements with me: and now, before angels and men, I will declare my faith in Thee as my covenant-keeping God. And I solemnly purpose that I would sooner die than break my covenant engagements with Thee. Trusting in Thee to keep me that I may never break from Thee by violating this my solemn covenant, I hereunto set my hand and seal, on the __ day of __, 18__.

PHOEBE
PALMER,
*Entire Devotion
to God*

W<small>HEN</small> <small>TRACING</small> <small>THE</small> <small>LANGUAGE</small> of covenant through the Bible, we become aware of how enduring an image can be. The ancient image of a treaty in which two unequal parties vow to perform or refrain from certain actions in a mutually beneficial arrangement has persisted for perhaps three thousand years in the Judeo-Christian tradition. Considerable scholarship continues to study and debate the origin and content of ancient Near Eastern covenants, and Old Testament scholars are by no means in agreement as to precisely which century the cultural phenomenon of covenant was taken over to become the major metaphor describing the relationship between God and the Israelites. In addition, throughout this long history, both the cultural manifestations of covenant and the theological understandings of God's covenant changed considerably. Yet all these variations got tagged onto each other under the common name of *covenant* and as such occur several dozen times in the three-year lectionary. Here we will briefly review the complex development of covenant from ancient social contract to contemporary theological concept.

Numerous Near Eastern documents dating from the Late Bronze Age indicate the cultural importance of societal covenants that were suzerainty treaties. The standard documentary pattern included the following elements: an opening that declared how the overlord gained authority; the overlord's promises, usually protection; the vassal's obligations, usually grateful fealty, sometimes goods; a list of witnesses to this oath; and a concluding section of blessings or curses directed at the vassal. The sealing of the covenant often included a ritual, sometimes an animal sacrifice: the blood sealed the covenant, and the ritual warned the vassals that disobedience would result in the shedding of their blood. Sometimes the sealed covenant was deposited in the temple, at the feet of the image of the deity. In the Iron Age, these societal covenants took on a more military tone: subjects promised loyalty, not in gratitude, but in fear of punishment. In either case, such covenants were essential social documents, regulating behavior between or within states. The underlying premise was that the rigid hierarchy marking social relations served all parties well and was approved by the deities. What is called the *if-then* construct of the covenant— if you submit, then I will protect—delineated the consequences of obedience or of disobedience and so secured the social order.

The debate among biblical scholars is whether Israelites actually spoke of such a covenant between God and the people as far back as Sinai in 1200 B.C.E., or whether this claim is an imaginative fabrication from several centuries later. Whichever is the case, it is easy to see how much these suzerainty treaties are echoed in whole in Exodus 19 and Joshua 24 and in part in dozens of biblical references to the covenant. The covenant was between the saving God and the people, who included both the Semitic tribes bound together by a memory of Egypt and those Canaanite groups who joined up with them. Exactly as with the suzerainty treaties, the covenant claims that the exodus event demonstrated God's rights; God promised continued protection; the people promised to keep the commandments; the witness was the community itself; and a concluding list of blessings and curses was incorporated. The covenant indicates that the people are to live in certain ways, maintaining strong community, in gratitude to God, who is their overlord. The sacrifice (Exodus 24:5-8) and the meal (Exodus 24:9-11) parallel the stereotypical ritual designed to seal the covenant. Whether or not the Sinai covenant was historical, memorial language about it underlies all the biblical references to covenant. A particularly biblical emphasis is that God's rights proceeded from God's mercy. God chose Israel and saved its people, and this divine love became the foundation of the covenant. The relationship was less overlord-to-vassal than liberator-to-grateful-people.

A late tradition said that the tables of the law were kept in a chest called the ark of the covenant. This sacred cabinet was described as the footstool of God (2 Kings 19:15) and was kept in the most holy place of the temple, just as other societal treaties were placed "at the feet" of the deity in other religion's temples. The ark of the covenant was a visible sign of the invisible YHWH. It was taken along to battles to ensure victory (Joshua 6:6). The ark, enshrining the covenant, stood for the power of God when, for example, it divided the Jordan River for Joshua and the people to walk through, and its capture was interpreted to mean that God had departed from Israel. The ark was remembered as a symbolic container of the Sinai covenant, a sacred symbol of the merciful agreement God had made with the people.

Other uses of covenant besides Sinai references are evident through biblical history. The Davidic covenant (2 Samuel 7) claimed that God granted one particular dynasty legitimation as the agent of a divine covenant. According to this idea, the covenant was made between God and one royal line. This divine sanction was not only an ancient idea. The notion that God establishes a covenant with the monarch, blessing the sovereign with nearly divine authority, continued in the West until the eighteenth century and is still alive in parts of the world today.

Secondly, the covenant with Abraham (Genesis 15) backdated God's treaty with the people to more than 500 years before the exodus and granted them the promised land. The ritual sealing of the covenant was male circumcision, which we know to have been a widespread cultural practice in the ancient Near East. Thirdly, the covenant with Noah (Genesis 9) was actually an elaboration of a folk tale about nature. That the language of covenant got applied to the widespread myth of a flood shows how adaptable and pervasive the image of covenant had become among biblical writers.

Covenant permutations continued. Historians view the covenants of Josiah (2 Kings 22) and Nehemiah (Nehemiah 9) as mainly political attempts to employ religious language so as to consolidate power. It was, however, the turn of the covenant idea found in Jeremiah 31:31-34 that became of central significance to Christians. The horrors of the exile caused the people to doubt God's covenant with them, the dynasty, the land, and even nature. But the prophets maintained that it was the people, not God, who had broken the covenant, and Jeremiah preached that in the future the covenant with Israel would be renewed, even perfected. Later apocalyptic literature continued to refer to the covenant. Sometimes its classic terms were reinterpreted, as when the promised land was described as a new earth.

All this background is important for understanding the centrality of *new covenant* in the New Testament. Paul referred to the covenant with Abraham mainly to describe divine mercy. Both Paul and Luke wrote of the new covenant sealed with Christ's blood and ritualized in the eucharist (1 Corinthians 11:25, Luke 22:20). Matthew urged a more profound adherence to the law as the Christian version of the covenant, and the Johannine material describes the new covenant as one of mutual abiding love. The book of Hebrews developed a lengthy comparison between the covenant's sacrifices and the sacrifice of Christ. For the author of Hebrews, the old Israelite covenant existed as a prior and less effective model of its fruition in the better covenant sealed with Christ's blood. Despite these differences, the New Testament writers seem to agree that the main benefit of the divine covenant is forgiveness and that both the blessings and the curses implicit in the covenant are to be realized mainly in the world to come.

All this condensed history notwithstanding, the lectionary does not seek to present the Sunday assembly with detailed variations of suzerainty treaties. The purpose of preaching is not to instruct the faithful in ancient Near Eastern history and myth. Yet many readings include references to one or another of these covenants. The main point for the lectionary is that covenant comes into Christianity as a dominant metaphor for salvation through Christ. The relationship between humans and God through Christ is termed *the new covenant*, and the development of the eucharist relied on considerable carry-over of covenant language and understanding. In summary: Although the historical specifics of ancient covenants are not our focus during the liturgy, the goal of those covenants—relationship between two unequal parties—is fundamental to the Christian gospel. Because of Christ, sinners can be in covenantal relationship with God. The image of covenant is like a grand chest containing pieces of history, parts of myth, and sentences of theology, and the contents of this chest figure in much Christian soteriology and sacramentology. The Christian use of the image of covenant includes several major propositions, and we will illustrate each from the lectionary.

For Christians, the image of the covenant serves to proclaim the good news that God and the people are in a committed relationship. Of course, various other options are found in religion. No deity may be recognized, as for example in Buddhism. Many deities may be acknowledged, as in polytheism, and religious exercises may attempt to cultivate a favorable relationship with at least some of the deities. *God* or *goddess* may be language that refers to an impersonal force of life, as in earth religions. New Age religion speaks of the deity within, as if the primary religious relationship is with one's own self. These religious traditions do not stress, as does Christianity, an enduring relationship with a transcendent yet personal deity.

According to the biblical covenant, the deity chooses a loving relationship with us. The interchange required of any relationship is the main idea behind some of the lectionary's readings from the Torah: the speech of Moses from Deuteronomy 31 (VigilABC), and words of Moses from Exodus 19 (Pr6A[†]) and from Deuteronomy 30 (Pr10C[†]). Similarly, the Johannine epistles speak about the interchange of love between God and Christians (Ea4B). The fact that Christians assemble weekly for a meal with God is an enactment of the covenant. The idea is that God and the people meet regularly as part of the covenantal relationship.

Christians in the Roman empire designated the eucharist with the Latin word *sacramentum*, the word for the soldier's oath of fealty to the emperor. This terminology indicates that the early church saw communion, like the soldier's vow of loyalty, as a covenant ritual. Just as society's covenants were sealed with the blood of a sacrifice, so this covenant with God was sealed with Christ's blood and shared in the meal. The weekly meeting affirms the relationship with the deity, and the meal confirms it. Throughout human history we see the pattern that when persons or groups of people meet for significant events, they mark the occasion by eating together. In the weekly Christian eucharist the church reaffirms its covenant sealed by Christ's blood and enacts that covenant with God by joining together in a meal.

Yet another inheritance from ancient Near Eastern suzerainty treaties is the emphasis in biblical covenant on gratitude. The cultural idea was that the vassal was grateful for the beneficence of the overlord. The church indicates this same gratefulness by naming its weekly meal *eucharist*, a Greek word meaning giving thanks. In the second century, the layman Justin, later martyred, wrote about the life of Christians: "We always give thanks." If our weekly worship does not express and evoke the assembly's gratitude for a loving relationship with God, liturgical reforms are called for.

The covenant image proclaims that God's part in the covenant is salvation. God saved us in the past, is saving us now, and will save us in the future. This salvation is described in many ways: we were placed in a good earth, given food, brought out from slavery, healed of diseases, released from fear, forgiven our sins, and promised life beyond this life. These gifts of life are God's part of the covenant. We see especially this aspect of covenant in God's covenant with Noah (Le1B); God's covenant with Abraham (Le2C); God's promises to David (Pr13A†); and Jeremiah's promise of God's new covenant (Le5B).

Because both the Old and New Testaments understand that what God's covenant promises us is forgiveness, we could cite here every passage that proclaims divine forgiveness. Whether one thinks of forgiveness primarily as God's part of the covenant or whether one imagines it as mercy from the judge, the church's ritualizing of the proclamation of forgiveness needs far more critical thought than many give it.

Although some persons are aware of their need for forgiveness, perhaps even neurotically, many contemporary people are not. Western society has popularized the idea that people are basically good, even though they sometimes commit errors. Too often the ritual of corporate confession and absolution is a perfunctory recitation. Even this minimalist approach is being abandoned by some congregations that judge confession of sin as too negative. Classical Christianity taught, on the other hand, that people are essentially distant from God, resisting the Spirit's covenant and breaking relationship with other people. The lectionary readings ought to impel the entire liturgy toward better covenantal resonance. Yet a prayer in which worshipers confess specific sins of which they may not actually be guilty is not an appropriate technique. Rigorous attention to the image of covenant may assist us in designing ritual that expresses our need for forgiveness from God and from one another.

The image of covenant proclaims our obligations in response to the saving God. A life of beauty and order, of care and respect, is as much a part of the good news as is God's salvation. Some of the lectionary's readings stress the believers' part of the covenant: certain selections from the Torah (Ep6A, Pr4A†, Le3B, Pr17B†, Pr26B†, Pr18c†); Joshua's call to faithfulness (Pr16B†, Pr27A°); a selection from Luke's sermon on the plain (Ep7c); a selection from the High Priestly Prayer (Ea6B); and a passage from Paul (Pr3B). Although Paul wrote harshly of the law, the best of the Jewish tradition speaks positively of the gift of the law: We know what is right, and in enacting together a covenantal community we live more fully in the peace of God. Too often when the church depicted "covenant" in art, the only image presented was a stern Moses delivering the tablets of the law. Perhaps the Israelites dancing together on the safe side of the sea is a better depiction of covenant. This part of the narrative suggests that God has mercifully saved the people, and the community has joined together in praise.

Some communities of Christians have paid particular attention to the image of the covenant. The Anglican John Wesley, whose methods for intense spiritual fellowship developed into Methodism, was especially fascinated by the covenant idea. Contemporary Methodist books of worship demonstrate this legacy in two ways: they call the rituals of baptism Services of the Baptismal Covenant, and they contain an updated version of Wesley's Covenant Prayer, which included promises spoken by the people confirming their side of the covenant. Wesley imagined this ritual as lasting several days and concluding with communion. "Jesus, I do here on bended knee accept Christ as the only new and living Way, and sincerely join myself in a covenant with him," is one sentence from the contemporary three-page ritual.[1] Methodists generally found that services on either New Year's Eve or New Year's Day were appropriate times for such a rite of covenantal renewal. The Holiness movement, which developed out of Methodism, also found the image of covenant to be helpful. Phoebe Palmer's intensification of Wesley's Covenant Prayer suggests that believers sign and date the covenant, as they would a legal document.

Whether or not other Christian denominations adopt anything like the Methodist covenant prayer, we all could use more attention to the biblical image of covenant. Western culture places continuous excessive emphasis on the self. Each individual striving for self-actualization, freedom understood mainly as personal prerogative, individual economic success: these mainstays of our society render the ancient idea of covenant foreign, if not archaic. That my well-being is thanks to the mercy of God and the graciousness of others is not a popular idea. Yet baptism suggests even more: that covenant within human community, as well as between God and the community, is good news. We cannot, we need not, live alone. We live in gracious, giving, and grateful covenant with God and with one another, and that is good news.

Perhaps the most countercultural idea behind biblical covenant language is its everlasting nature. God's covenant has been established to last forever. In a culture in which many agreements are made for the short term and in which legal contracts can be renegotiated, the ideas that God loves the chosen people forever and that the church becomes a community forever bonded in the Spirit are somewhat alien notions. An increasing body of Christian theologians acknowledges that God's covenant to the Jews also continues forever, and thus earlier talk of Christians replacing Jews in the heart of God is being rejected. Furthermore, the legend of Noah's flood proclaims that God promises a covenantal relationship with the earth itself. It is fortunate that the churches are reexamining the rituals of confirmation, hoping to replace a puberty rite with something of more covenantal significance that can express more fully a life of baptismal covenant with the whole community of the Spirit.

Creation

beginning, creation, firstborn,
new creation, virgin birth

Related chapters: EMANATION OF THE DIVINE, MOTHER, WISDOM

A cosmogony is a story about the creation of the world that expresses a people's present values and future hopes. The lectionary's several biblical cosmogonies, especially significant at Christmas and the Easter Vigil, function not as science lessons, but as affirmations of the faith that life comes from God and is renewed through Christ.

PSALM 104:5,
25

You have set the earth upon its foundations,
   so that it never shall move at any time.
O LORD, how manifold are your works!
   In wisdom you have made them all;
   the earth is full of your creatures.

NICENE CREED

We believe in one God,
   the Father, the Almighty,
   maker of heaven and earth,
   of all that is, seen and unseen.

CATHERINE
CAMERON

God, who stretched the spangled heavens
infinite in time and place,
flung the suns in burning radiance
through the silent fields of space:
We, your children in your likeness,
share inventive powers with you;
great Creator, still creating,
show us what we yet may do.

As each far horizon beckons,
may it challenge us anew:
children of creative purpose,
serving others, honoring you.
May our dreams prove rich with promise;
each endeavor well begun;
great Creator, give us guidance
till our goals and yours are one.

Glory to your mercy, glory to your power, glory to you!
because, remaining immutable and without change,
you are always completely in movement,
completely outside creation and completely
    in every creature,
you fill everything completely,
you who are completely outside everything,
    above everything.
You are not separated from the world,
for you are in everything, but above everything.

SYMEON,
*Hymns of
Divine Love*

God showed me a little thing, the size of a hazelnut, lying
in the palm of my hand. It was as round as any ball, as it
seemed to me. I looked at it with the eyes of my understanding and thought, "What can this be?" My question
was answered in general terms in this fashion: "It is everything that is made." I marveled how this could be, for it
seemed that it might suddenly fall into nothingness, it was
so small. An answer for this was given to my understanding:
"It lasts, and ever shall last, because God loves it. And in
this fashion all things have their being by the grace of
God." In this little thing, I saw three properties. The first
is that God made it. The second is that God loves it. The
third is that God keeps it. And what did I see in this? Truly,
the Maker, the Lover, and the Keeper.

JULIAN OF
NORWICH,
*Revelations of
Divine Love*

⁓

INSIDE A PEOPLE'S COSMOGONY is its cosmology. A people's religious or cultural narratives about the formation of the world and the origins of humankind indicate the people's ideas about the meaning of life. The Talmud, elaborating on Genesis 1, says that the alphabet presented itself before God, each letter wanting to be instrumental in creation. The letter B was chosen, and so it was with a Blessing that God created the earth. Here a fanciful tale about earth's origins reminded the Jewish people that the universe is full of the blessing of God. Contrast this with the famous Greek myth of Prometheus, who is punished by Zeus until the end of time for having given to humankind the fire necessary for human civilization. The cosmogonies indicate cosmology: one deity blesses human life, another deity thwarts life in the human community.

Mircea Eliade gave considerable attention to the creation stories of the world's religions. He outlined how cosmogonies explain natural phenomena (where does rain comes from? see Genesis 1:7); indicate the community's morality (how do we know right from wrong? see Genesis 2:17); chart human rituals (why do we rest on the sabbath? see Genesis 2:2); and account for evil in the world (see Genesis 3). According to Eliade, when a community retells its creation stories, the primordial time is alive once again. The creative powers are active once more, and our present time of chaos or unhappiness is reconstituted into a primal harmony and stability. Creation did not occur only once, back then; religion effects the recurring re-creation of life. Creation continues.

One might not at first classify creation as a lectionary image. The word *creation* is used in many ways, for example as a pious synonym for *the universe*. In this chapter the word *creation* means the divine process of bringing life to birth. Creation is God's way of forming life. The noun *creation* means to evoke in our imaginations the various ways that God's Spirit moves over the waters to engender life.

It is interesting to contrast the several biblical stories of creation with other religious cosmogonies. Some of the world's cosmogonies, like Genesis 1, indicate that divine power needs nothing but itself for the work of creation. Other narratives are similar to Genesis 2–3, in depicting the creator as a craftsperson, shaping human beings out of some raw material. Some cosmogonies omit a creator, suggesting instead that humans evolved naturally from a plant or another animal, usually one essential for the life of the community. Pantheist religions tell of the goddess or god lying down and being transformed into the earth. People honoring such a story will view all that lives, rather than a single deity, as holy.

The Genesis 1 story stresses the otherness of the omnipotent creator. God is before and beyond all that we can know. Although later Christian theologians taught that according to Genesis 1 God made the world *ex nihilo*, it is much more likely that the writer of Genesis 1 believed, as did many other creation storytellers, that the deity wrested a world out of watery chaos. First-century Hellenistic Jews believed that God created the world through the emanation of the Word, and later trinitarian Christian theologians interpreted Genesis to say that the Word and the Spirit were active in creation. But probably the author of the majestic poem meant to stress the omnipotence of a single divine creator. The earth may have been born from a watery womb, just as humans are, but in this relatively philosophical cosmogony, prior maternal or other anthropomorphic details have been edited out.

Divine omnipotence is the theme of several other biblical cosmogonies. In Isaiah 40, the people's despair over their current political situation leads to their retelling of the creation story. Surely, says the poem in verses 12-26, the incomparable creator will continue to bless the chosen people with life. In Proverbs 8 (VigilABC, Trinc), the creation story is nationalized in a different way. God's creation of wisdom, which guided the formation of all the earth, became resident among the wise in Israel. God's creative wisdom served up the communal meal of bread and wine, thus continuously providing life for the faithful people. Proverbs 8 exemplifies a cosmogony that focuses on life in the present, not in the primordial past. A reversal is proposed in Jeremiah 4 (Pr19c°). Because of the people's unfaithfulness, creation will work backwards, the wind returning the earth once again to a dark waste and void.

The Genesis 2–3 story presents God as an anthropomorphic artist, trying first this, then that, working to ensure a good creation, using various raw materials to form the world. God first tries to solve the man's loneliness by creating other animals, but in the end shapes a woman. Sad but true, perfection was not the final result. This cosmogony, far more important for the history of Christian doctrine and piety than it is for the three-year lectionary, tells the origin of human suffering, sin, labor, pain, and death. Genesis 1 answers how God's might created the world, while Genesis 2–3 describes how humans marred it. The two stories can fit together, each telling half of the truth of human life on earth.

The cosmogony of Job 38 (Pr7B[†], Pr24B°) addresses the conundrum of the suffering of the innocent. Human suffering is relativized in the face of divine sovereignty, for Job's lament is silenced before God's majesty. Here the recital of God's creative powers stresses the vast distance between the creator and the creation. God created the magnificent world, and humans suffer immensely: so it goes.

According to the Babylonian cosmogony, the watery chaos, described as a female monster Tiamat, was conquered by the male ruler Marduk. This story finds its way into the psalms, most clearly in Psalm 74:13-14 and 89:10-11, as well as in Isaiah 51:9-11. Here the Babylonian narrative of the divine ordering of chaos gets applied to the political realm. The Song of the Sea in Exodus 15 historicizes the primordial conflict. Pharaoh's army personifies the chaos from which God creates order. The exodus, then, is a variation of the creation story: God created the earth from chaos, God created a people out of chaos. Later Iranian dualistic myths of the continuous warfare between the good Ozmazd and the evil Ahriman influenced the Jewish intertestamental literature, which contains speculation about the original war in heaven and the final apocalyptic battle, a last battle that will recapitulate the battle at the beginning of time.

For the church, the cosmogony in John 1 (ChDyABC) is paramount. Its christology is found also in Colossians 1:15-21 (Lastc). These Christian creation accounts focus on the person of Christ and the renewal that life in Christ affords. Early Christians apparently did not find it important to repeat traditional stories that detailed the origin of the natural universe. Their interest was life renewed in Christ, a renewal of the creation described by the poem of Genesis 1.

Many religious cosmogonies are imaginative anthropocentric tales with their truth told metaphorically. Yet contemporary Westerners are all more or less scientists. We think of truth as fact. We value information to the degree that it is verifiably incontrovertible. Many modern people expect their cosmogony to be an impersonal scientific report bolstered by scholarly proof. This scientific worldview helps explain the power of biblical fundamentalism, which since the late nineteenth century has tried to apply to the Bible the same criterion for truth as is sought in a laboratory experiment. Yet the majority of Christians are not, and have not been, fundamentalists, and even in our postmodern society, in which many nonscientific images and rituals are enjoying a second life, creation narratives are readily dismissed as nonsensical myths.

Yet the doctrine that God is the creator has been rejected by premoderns for centuries. The *Madapurana*, the atheistic ninth-century document of Jainism, reads:

If God created the world by an act of his own will,
without any raw material,
then it is just his will and nothing else—
and who will believe this silly stuff?
If he is ever perfect and complete,
how could the will to create have arisen in him?
If, on the other hand, he is not perfect,
he could no more create the universe than a potter could.[1]

This millennium-old text challenged the core of religious cosmogonies. Their point is not in any prescientific and imaginative details, but in their belief that there is a divine creator, existing prior to the universe, whose power is behind all that is. According to Genesis 1, the individual person is not the ultimate reality. Neither is the mother, nor the father, nor warfare, nor any nation, nor suffering, nor death. The ultimate reality, from whom at the beginning everything comes, who will remain after the end of everything else, is God. Biblical cosmogonies do not present us with impossible tales we are expected to believe. Rather, they offer us the good news that God is God and that God, the giver of life, will be merciful. As Julian said concerning her vision of the hazelnut, God is Maker, Lover, and Keeper of all.

Biblical cosmogonies have inspired a growing list of contemporary theologians to reflect more fully on ecology than previous Christians did. The idea that Genesis 1:28 sanctions human destruction of nature has given way to an ecological theology grounded in Genesis 1:1 and 3:23. God created a good universe, and it is this universe, from which the human was formed, that humans are to tend. In Judaism, Christianity, and Islam, God was not transformed into the earth. Rather, God remains other than the created world. Yet God's power and mercy are encountered in the things of the earth. To misuse the creation is to despise the God who made it.

Christian theologians use the term *panentheism* to express the idea that God is in the universe. Pantheism teaches that the earth is divine: however, according to panentheism, the earth, citing the Christian poet Gerard Manley Hopkins, "is charged with the grandeur of God." Especially the church, with its doctrine of the incarnation, should find panentheism an amenable idea. The creator is not only beyond the universe, but also within it. Perhaps there will be literally a new creation at the end of time. But there is now the first creation, and it is already filled with the grace of God.

Genesis 1 contains the enigmatic concept of the image of God. Christians have interpreted this phrase in a great variety of ways. Some have suggested that the image of God is the ability to create. Humans, like God, are creators, co-creators in the world, through childbearing, art, and technology.

Whether God is the sole creator of life, or whether humankind cooperates with divine creativity, will be an increasingly intense debate within the church.

Anthropologists have discovered that many human societies maintained a ritual practice in which people recited their cosmogony, perhaps annually, so as, with a kind of sympathetic magic, to reinstate in nature and society the creative order that existed at the beginning of time. Although Christians do not teach that the ritual reading of the Bible is sympathetic magic, the three-year lectionary, in a pattern similar to those ancient rituals, repeats biblical cosmogonies annually.

Genesis 1 is appointed as the first reading at the Easter Vigil. All the readings of the Vigil are stories from the Hebrew Scriptures that tell the gospel of Easter: God is making all things new. So in the night of Easter, Christians gather around a small flame and acclaim that Christ is the light, that in the beginning God created light, and that now, in this community of the resurrection, light continues to shine in a dark world. God called forth light: God spoke the word over the chaos; God's spirit of life brought life to birth. So Christians saw in the ancient Near Eastern myth a picture of the life of the triune God. The Vigil's ritual superimposes several images of new life. From ancient times comes the practice of lighting of the year's new fire. Appropriate to the Northern Hemisphere, this ritual occurs at the coming of spring. It is as if during the Vigil the church is once again in the beginning, being reshaped once again by God's creative energy at the beginning of time. Whenever Christians read Genesis 1:1—2:4a (also TrinA), they meditate on the first creation by the triune God as the model of the creation of life that comes continuously from God. Medieval Christians believed so fully that Christ was the mouthpiece of the creative God that when they painted Genesis 1 on their church walls, they drew a man, Christ, as presiding over the seven days. This practice led to an acceptance of drawing God as a male, an artistic convention wholly rejected by the ancient church.

Secondly, the church proclaims a biblical cosmogony on Christmas Day (ChDyABC). Many Christian communities are now skipping the liturgy of Christmas Day, perhaps because most members are home recovering from a night of gifts, food, and midnight liturgy. Omitting the Christmas Day service at which John 1 is read is an extremely unfortunate pattern for the church to fall into. Christmas, the second most important Christian feast day, functions in many ways, in church and culture, as a new year's festival. It is a time when near the solstice of our planet, the peoples in the Northern Hemisphere counter winter by feasting, song, evergreens, and gift giving. The church's celebration of Jesus' birth at the time of the solstice reminds Christians in the north that it is God who is going to bring life back again and that we experience that nascent life in the infant Jesus. The Bible's richest statement of christology is in John 1, the gospel reading for Christmas Day: Christ, the original light of creation, is now the light shining in the darkness of our world. John 1 on Christmas Day is not a reading to be missed.

Ancient Israelite culture saw in the firstborn child of every woman a sign of God's creation. In Exodus 13:1-16 and 19:19-20, the Torah outlines the rituals that were incumbent upon the parents of the firstborn. Because the deity gives all life, the firstborn child is a primary manifestation of divine life. Thus the deity deserves to receive that first life back, in order that the deity will continue to give life. This thinking may help explain the common Canaanite practice of sacrificing the firstborn child, and perhaps also the Israelites' historicizing of such firstborn sacrifice in the story of the tenth plague. This emphasis on the firstborn as the inauguration of new life is background to the description in lectionary readings of Christ as the firstborn of all creation (ChDyABC, Pr12A, Pr22B, LastB, Ea2C, Pr11C, Lastc). It is as if Christ opens, not only Mary's womb, but also the heart of God, so that more life can come forth for all the world.

It is most likely as an elaboration of the idea of God the creator of all life that contemporary Christians can best understand the meaning of the virgin birth. The stories in Matthew and Luke (Ad4A, Ad4B, Ad4C, ChEABC) tell of Jesus' conception within a virgin woman. First-century authors did not know that a woman had ovaries. They thought that conception occurred when the male inserted into a woman's empty womb a homunculus, the entire tiny fetus. The biblical stories of Mary as virgin are best understood not as comments either on Mary's anatomy or on contemporary sexual practices. Rather, the stories in Matthew 2 and Luke 2 are narrative versions of the theology of John 1. The point of the virgin birth is that Christ came, not from "the will of a man" (John 1:13), but from God. The Christmas stories are christological cosmogonies. God is the creator of the entire creation, and Christ is the church's primary instance of God's creation. Christmas is creation-time.

The Christian belief that in Christ is the re-creation of the world is seen in other places in the lectionary. For example, the theophany of Job 38 is appointed on the same Sunday as the stilling of the tempest (Pr7B†). God created the world, and in Christ God recreates the order, bringing the sea's chaos into calm for the survival of the human race.

The readings in the three-year lectionary also present a trinitarian reflection on God's creation. Not only is God the creator, and Christ the firstborn of the new creation, but the Spirit of Christ is in the Christian community, making us into a new creation. We read a poem from Isaiah on a day when parish baptisms might well be celebrated (BapA). This poem recalls God's creation of light at the beginning of time and promises that God is now creating new things. Jesus' conversation with Nicodemus (Le2A, TrinB) is a key passage in Christian reflection on baptism into Christ as birth into God's creative life. "Can one enter a second time into the mother's womb and be born?" Yes, in the baptized community: a miraculous rebirth is one way that the New Testament talks about our entry into the Christian community.

The church celebrates and explores that new life in the community throughout the Easter season (Ea2A, Ea6A). Furthermore, the lectionary's use of the story of the miraculous birth of Isaac (Le2B, Pr6A°, Pr11C†) ought to be seen, like the story of the virgin birth, not as an example of an unlikely physiological anomaly, but as a narrative of the community's faith that all life is created by God. John Chrysostom used the story of the birth of Isaac to illustrate baptism. He posed the idea this way: "Tell me, Nicodemus, how was Isaac begotten?" For Chrysostom, the Bible's miraculous birth stories were not about extraordinary mothering, for the ancients believed that babies came solely from the father. Rather, the stories function for Christians as images of the creative might of God.

If we imagine that the biblical cosmogonies must be viewed as scientifically accurate descriptions, we will be, along with Nicodemus, perplexed. We may find ourselves embarrassed by ancient imagery, as if to be Christian is to ascribe, or to pretend to ascribe, to an archaic worldview. However, if we can read the cosmogonies of the creation of the world, the birth of Jesus, and the formation of the newly born Christian community as descriptions of God's creative power, we can, without apology, celebrate the good news that God is creator, that Christ is the key to our life, and that the Christian community is the place where the Spirit of life creates life anew.

Cross

cross, crucifixion, take up your cross

Related chapters: SACRIFICE

The symbol of the cross and various other cruciforms is found throughout time in many cultures and religions. Although the image occurs rarely in the lectionary, the cross is the most distinctive Christian symbol and is central to Christian teaching, which interprets the cross as a sign of both death and life.

PSALM 69:23,
31

They gave me gall to eat,
    and when I was thirsty, they gave me vinegar to drink.
As for me, I am afflicted and in pain;
    your help, O God, will lift me up on high.

THE GOOD
FRIDAY LITURGY

Behold, the life-giving cross
    on which was hung the salvation of the whole world.
Oh, come, let us worship him.

THOMAS KELLY

Inscribed upon the cross we see
in shining letters, "God is love."
He bears our sins upon the tree;
he brings us mercy from above.

The cross! It takes our guilt away;
it holds the fainting spirit up.
It cheers with hope the gloomy day
and sweetens every bitter cup.

It makes the coward spirit brave
and nerves the feeble arm for fight;
it takes the terror from the grave
and gilds the bed of death with light;

the balm of life, the cure of woe,
the measure and the pledge of love,
the sinner's refuge here below,
the angels' theme in heaven above.

This cross is the tree of my eternal salvation, my nourishment when I am hungry, my fountain when I am thirsty, my covering when I am stripped, my safeguard when I fear God, my support when I falter, my prize when I enter combat, my trophy when I triumph. This is my narrow path, my steep way. This is the ladder of Jacob, the way of angels, at the summit of which the Lord is truly established. This is my tree, wide as the firmament, which extends from earth to the heavens. It is the pillar of the universe, the support of the whole world, holding together the variety of human nature, and riveted by the invisible bolts of the Spirit, so that it may remain fastened to the divinity and impossible to detach.

ANONYMOUS,
*The Pasch
History*

Afua Kuma lives and works in the tropical forest of Ghana, a farmer and midwife from the Kwawu area. Afua's theology and precisely her Christology—as most of her words refer to Jesus—is one that comes from the interplay of faith and life. The cross, she says, has become the fishing net of Jesus. It is the bridge from which Christians can jump into the pool of saving blood that leads to everlasting life. Here is a perception of the cross that demands not only that we admire what Jesus has done, but that we too stand ready to jump into the pool of blood through which we shall reach the life that is life indeed.

MERCY AMBA
ODUYOYE,
*With Passion
and Compassion*

⁓

THE CROSS AND VARIOUS OTHER CRUCIFORMS have long been used by various cultures and religions as symbols of life. The cross might depict the four corners of the world, the four elements of creation (earth, air, fire, and water), the four beasts in a zodiacal scheme, the four solstices and equinoxes, the four seasons of the temperate zone, the four winds that bring rain. Ancient Egypt used the cross in the form of the ankh as a symbol for eternal life. Eastern religions see in the cruciform the balance of the opposites in one whole. Town centers and temple spaces have been set up in a cruciform so as to image perfection and order. New Age religion has popularized the image of a cross-tree, each fourth of which represents one season of the tree's annual cycle. In all these examples, the cross is a symbol of the life of nature or community.

The cruciform as a sign of unity is not part of the iconography of ancient Israel. However, the Old Testament contains several passages related to Christian focus on the cross. The first is the Deuteronomic regulation that the corpse of an executed criminal be displayed to the community by being impaled on a tree (Deuteronomy 21:22-23). Such a display of the corpse on a tree was God's ultimate curse and an Israelite's deepest horror. We need to understand this ancient interpretation—that God stipulated hanging on a tree as the worst possible punishment—in order to grasp the ambiguity of the Christian use of the cross and to fathom the shock and shame of the primitive Christian community over the manner of Jesus' execution. For Christians, the cross is not solely an image of life.

A related Old Testament image is the Tau, the last letter of the Hebrew alphabet. According to Ezekiel 9:4, the Tau marks the forehead of the faithful, who have been strengthened to persevere through the difficulties of the end time. The book of Revelation refers several times to this protective mark on the forehead of the faithful. According to Jewish tradition, the ancient Israelites marked their doors with the lamb's blood in the form of a Tau. The Tau was thus a sign of God's life, saving the people from death now and at the eschaton. Thematically the same as the Lord's Prayer, the mark of the Tau placed the believers in God's eschatological kingdom and at the service of God's will.

Some early Christian interpreters used the Tau much as later Christians used the cross. Like the mast of the Noah's ark, like the Tau, the cross protects believers from death and leads them to life. Many preachers, Ambrose and Augustine among them, taught that the Tau's numerical value recalled the 300 soldiers that Gideon chose as his army (Judges 7:4-18). Here again the Tau is a symbol of victory, not of suffering. It is unclear whether Francis of Assisi knew of this interpretation when he adopted the Tau as his personal signature.

Some New Testament scholars believe that the famous dictum in the gospels, take up your cross, refers not to an attitude toward suffering but rather to the inscription of the Tau. This teaching of Jesus is cited five times in the synoptics, four of which are included in the lectionary (Pr17A, Le2B, Pr19B, Pr18C). The repetition of this teaching might urge a quietism or even fatalism among believers, especially if interpreted to mean that the cross we are to carry is our personal suffering willingly accepted. If, however, those biblical scholars are correct who identify *take up your cross* with the Tau sign, then the Tau-cross is a sign of the end time, the protective mark of one living already in the freedom of the reign of God. The Tau, traced on our forehead at baptism, is a sign of strength on our forehead, not of a punishment borne on our back. Like the mark of Cain that protects him from retribution, the Tau is God's salvation. What we pick up and carry is our baptism, not a mode of death, but a way of life.

Important for Christian interpretation of the cross is the fascinating story in Numbers 21 of the plague of serpents (Le4B). Probably this narrative preserves an ancient memory of a time when the ancestors appealed not to YHWH, but to Asherah. Asherah was the Canaanite goddess of life, depicted as a tree of life or a pole. By appealing to the image on the pole, the people were saved. Later the memory was emended to fit the worship of YHWH, as was also done with the story of the woman and the goddess-snake in the tree in Eden, for Numbers reports the veneration not as polytheism but as obedience to YHWH's command. The writer of John's gospel found the story important as an image of the death of Christ: just as the Israelites were saved in an incongruous way, so the world will be saved in a similarly surprising way, by God's lifting Christ up on the cross (Le4B).

Much imagery from the lament psalms became important in Christian imagination as ways to describe Christ's death on the cross. An earlier hermeneutic explained these parallels by asserting that the psalmist was foretelling the future by describing the death of the ultimate sufferer, Christ. Contemporary New Testament scholars suggest, rather, that the evangelists, who were not present at Jesus' crucifixion, had the psalms in their minds and thus had recourse to traditional descriptions of the sufferer when they narrated Jesus' death. So it is that Christ, like the sufferer in Psalm 69, drank vinegar and was lifted up on high. Whether or not Jesus quoted Psalm 22 while on the cross, the gospel writer told the story of the abandoned messiah using the language of this psalm: They gloat over me, they divide my garments among them.

In the Greco-Roman world, crucifixion was used as an instrument of torture and execution for the lowest criminals. Often the victims were defeated enemies: Darius of Persia crucified 3,000 Babylonians, and Alexander the Great crucified 2,000 residents of Tyre. Sometimes the victims were internal threats. In about 100 B.C.E., the Sadducean high priest Alexander Janneus had 800 Pharisees crucified, with their wives and children slaughtered as the victims watched from their crosses. The mad emperor Caligula crucified Jews in the amphitheater as entertainment, although most crucifixions were mounted alongside major roadways to terrorize the population. In the Roman Empire, crucifixion was used especially to punish slave rebellions, for example when, in 71 B.C.E., 6,000 slaves were crucified along the Appian Way. Crucifixion was generally judged too horrible to inflict on any Roman citizen. Cicero wrote that even the very mention of crucifixion was unworthy of a Roman citizen and free man. Tradition says that Paul, a Roman citizen, was executed in a far more benign manner: beheading.

Only when we take seriously how despicable the cross was can we imagine the extreme dishonor that Jesus' followers must have experienced at the crucifixion of their leader. In the second century Justin Martyr records that non-Christians considered Christians insane for putting a crucified man in second place after the unchangeable and eternal God. Some gnostic literature sought to distance Christ from the cross by suggesting that the spiritual Christ was somehow outside of Jesus' body on the cross. Because of the overwhelming sense of shame associated with the cross in the Roman Empire, Christians during the early centuries did not draw the crucifixion. The earliest depictions that we have discovered somehow disguise the cross: either Christ is standing in an *orans* position in front of it or the cross is entwined with vines into a tree of life.

Two actions taken by the fourth-century Roman emperor Constantine changed the cross from a symbol of shame into the dominant cultural icon of power. It is said that Constantine employed a form of the cross, a Chi-Rho, on his military standard and won the battle. Later he outlawed crucifixions. With the emperor's victory, the cross became a logo for supremacy, and with crucifixions terminated, the brutality of the method of execution faded from memory. Realism made way for symbol. Horror at the violence of the punishment evolved into reverence for the instrument of redemption.

One other fourth-century event is significant in Christian consideration of the cross. The mother of Emperor Constantine, Helena, sponsored an archaeological dig in and around Jerusalem, and she excavated what she claimed was the true cross. The story says that Helena knew she had found the True Cross because, laid on top of a dead woman, it restored the corpse to life. From this legend arose the iconographical practice of picturing Adam's skull at the base of Christ's cross and the belief that the cross, at Adam's grave, marked the very center of the world. Constantine's reception and exaltation of a fragment of this cross gave rise to the festival of the Holy Cross, September 14, on which the readings deal explicitly with the image of the cross. A medieval legend explained that the cross was constructed of the wood from a tree that Seth had planted by God's command inside Adam's grave.

Helena's True Cross led to two phenomena: the wearing of the cross, ideally a fragment of the True Cross, around one's neck and the Good Friday ritual of the Adoration of the Cross. Even in the early fifth century, the bishop Paulinus of Nola remarked on the miracle that despite thousands of bits of the True Cross everywhere, the cross grew no smaller! The Good Friday ritual of the Adoration of the Cross was described by Egeria in her journal and is conducted in many Christian churches around the world to this day. Contemporary liturgical resources offer various suggestions about how to make this ritual meaningful in our time. The ritual employs metaphor; we say of whatever cross we have before us, "Behold the wood of the cross on which was hung the salvation of the whole world." The cross before us stands in the place of the wood of the true cross.

Over the centuries, the bare cross gave way to crucifixes. Only in the second millennium did western medieval spirituality popularize corpuses marked by grotesque detail. Sometimes the horrific detail had pastoral meaning: the famous Isenheim crucifixion painted by Matthias Grünewald, on which Christ's body is greenish and covered with bloody sores, was painted for a hospital chapel in which persons dying of St. Vitus' Dance came to resemble this corpus. Although Calvin preferred the bare cross, Martin Luther preferred a crucifix (one was engraved on the wedding ring he gave to Katherina von Bora). The Roman rite required a corpus on the cross only in 1746, in clear attempt to distinguish Catholicism from Protestantism. Some European towns erected standing crosses at market squares, along roadsides, and in cemeteries. Most artistic depictions of the passion show Jesus carrying his entire cross. What actually would have been carried was the transverse beam, onto which the victim was roped or nailed before being hoisted onto a stake already fixed deeply in the ground.

Twentieth-century Christian interest in enculturation led to the cross being depicted in new ways. A Christian church in Arizona's Navajo Nation depicts a dead Navajo man being removed from a cross by a Navajo woman, and in several venues are crucifixes bearing female figures. For some Christians, a nude woman on a cross is sacrilege, while for others a Christa cross proclaims God's identification with all who suffer. Some church buildings multiply the image to absurdity by placing a cross everywhere one might look, from the reredos behind the altar, to the embroidery on the vestments and paraments, to the stopper in the wine cruet. Here more is less. It might be useful for each parish to examine its crosses and crucifixes, to discuss their continuing spiritual value.

Even when the cross was not depicted, it was praised metaphorically in sermons. The second-century Epistle of Barnabas cited the story of Moses extending his arms over the battle as a precursor of the cross: Christ's extended arms saves not ancient Israel, but us all. Much preaching for the church's first millennium saw in anything wood a precursor of the cross. The wood of the fire for Isaac's sacrifice, the ladder in Jacob's dream, the cross-spits used in roasting the passover lamb, Moses' staff, the wood that made the bitter water sweet, Aaron's rod, the pole on which Moses hoisted the bronze serpent: all these articles of wood presented metaphors for preachers in their discussion of the cross. An impressive literary piece about the cross is "The Dream of the Rood," a poem written in Anglo-Saxon in perhaps the eighth century. In the poet's vision, the true cross speaks about its role in the crucifixion, which is described as a battle that the warrior, "the young hero, God almighty, strong and stouthearted," underwent. In the vision, the cross alternates between the "most brilliant of timbers," the bloody "rood" and a bejeweled processional cross, "emblazoned with gold."[1] The cross both shares the pain and humiliation of Christ the king and functions as the primary instrument of Christ's victory over his enemies.

Already in the early centuries of the church, Christians practiced the ritual of making the sign of the cross on one's body. One theory holds that, informed by the Jewish practice of inscribing a Tau for the end time or a Yod for the name of God on one's phylactery bands, Christians signed Christ's name with a Chi on their hand. Second-century churchmen write of tracing the sign of the cross on one's forehead at baptism and daily in devotion. Ambrose taught that one's fingers traced first on the forehead, for Christian profession, second over the heart, for love toward God, and last over the arms, for the work of the Christian life. In his catechism, Martin Luther counseled Christians, "In the morning, as soon as you get out of bed, you are to make the sign of the holy cross and say, 'Under the care of God, the Father, the Son, and Holy Spirit. Amen.'"[2] Eventually the cross came also to determine the floor plan for church buildings. It was as if God could look down from heaven and see the believers in the shape of the cross.

Already in the fifth century Christians used the sign of the cross in exorcisms to ward off demons. Marking the catechumen with the sign of the cross has long been one ritual component of the exorcism at baptism. When in the nineteenth century the neolithic cave paintings of France were rediscovered, one Christian, who must have been overwhelmed by the immense power of these ancient religious images, superimposed a cross over some of the cave paintings, as though even after 15,000 years the pre-Christian images needed exorcising. The continuing popularity of medieval European vampire legends in films and novels keeps alive the notion that the cross will protect people from the power of evil. Currently, Christian churches are not agreed on the usefulness or content of rites of exorcism. A recent instance of the rite was Archbishop Desmond Tutu's exorcism of a church building that had been used for a pro-apartheid rally.

Christians continue to make a ritual sign of the cross. An older liturgical practice required the presider to make a sign of the cross over the communion elements, in order for the consecration to be valid, but many liturgists suggest that this practice is no longer a useful liturgical action. In the Central American *penitentes'* presentations of Holy Week, a man volunteers to be crucified for the town's drama. The famous passion drama enacted each decade in Oberammergau has undergone recent editing to minimize the medieval interpretation that it was the Jews who were responsible for the death of Jesus. Contemporary biblical scholarship finds that this interpretation is historically untenable. As the Reproaches, the litany used by some Christians on Good Friday, makes clear, Christians are to aim toward themselves, not toward any others, the biblical condemnations of those who abandon the covenant and who crucify their Lord.

Medieval Christians knew the passion narrative through a harmonized gospel version. The situation for users of the lectionary is quite different. Over the three years of Passion Sunday, the passion in either Matthew, Mark, or Luke is read, and on Good Friday, the passion in John is read. Each of these accounts gives a different view of the cross and a distinct christology. In Mark, the cross is the paradoxical sign of the hidden messiah; in Matthew, the cross fulfills all of Jewish expectation; in Luke, the cross is the locus of God's forgiveness; and in John, the cross is the throne from which the Son of God reigns. The lectionary asks us to receive separately each passion account and focus on its unique message.

Fifty years ago mid-week Lenten services were commonplace, and it was usual over the course of these five Wednesdays for worshipers to focus on the details of the passion. As this practice fades away, and an ecumenical consensus grows that the focus of Lent should be on baptism rather than on Jesus' suffering, the challenge of teaching the faithful about the passion of Christ remains. Furthermore, due to the exceptional nature of the liturgies of Passion Sunday and Good Friday, some assemblies minimize preaching on those days. In any increasingly post-Christian society, we cannot assume any knowledge of the passion, even among those who may be present for worship.

Just as the depiction of the cross has changed through Christian history, so too has preaching concerning its meaning. Some theologians continue the interpretation that Jesus' death was a sacrifice for sin. The idea that the cross was Jesus' method of sacrifice for our salvation is found in many hymns and is commonplace among preachers. Others explain that Jesus was executed because of his passion for social justice. This interpretation calls the community into its baptism as its entry into Christ's death, and into a similar passion for justice. Another contemporary interpretation is that in the cross the world sees that God suffers with all who suffer. Liberation theology and feminist theology have criticized the church for suggesting that the cross of Christ means that suffering is a good thing: Suffering is welcome, because it is salvific in itself, or suffering is to be endured, in comparison with the suffering of Christ. It is understandable that where suffering is unavoidable, oppression omnipresent, pain inescapable, and death early, the church developed a christology grounded in suffering. Glorification of suffering affected the poor far more than it did the rich, however. One thinks of the medieval church teaching that women were not to use painkillers while in labor, for, thanks to Eve, women were supposed to suffer in childbirth. Liberation theologians remind us that Christians must avoid any suggestion that the suffering of some other people is for a religious reason laudatory.

The church continues to struggle with that earliest of Christian questions: what is the meaning of the cross? The cross holds before us the ubiquity of suffering and death: according to Christianity, even God experienced death. Yet in our society, suffering of persons and groups is recognized to be an evil we are to endeavor to alleviate. The church is the community of the resurrection, and so it brings the Spirit of life wherever it can to a world of suffering. The cross presents us always with the ambiguity of the faith: suffering is here, yet suffering is taken away by Christ. Death is before us, yet the Spirit of life upholds us.

The cross remains all around us, on church steeples, on tattoos, on hot cross buns, on w.w.j.d. bracelets. It is important to realize that in the lectionary the cross is not so much in certain readings as it is behind them all. The mystery of the cross is central to the Christian faith. That the cross is the paradox of God's life in Christ is the gospel message that we encounter especially in the lectionary's citations from 1 Corinthians, Galatians, and Philippians. Of the twelve times that the epistles speak of the cross as foolishness, stumbling block, and the emptying of the divine, the three-year lectionary includes eleven. These readings should assist us in our goal of rendering the preaching, singing, depicting, and enacting of the image of the cross as true as we can to its paradoxical meaning.

Day
of the LORD

Alpha-and-Omega, day of the LORD,
the hour, signs, Son-of-man

Related chapters: BATTLE, CREATION, JUDGE, WIND

Especially at the start and close of each liturgical year, the lectionary presents the ancient apocalyptic imagery of a cataclysmic end-time that promises to bring both reward and judgment. Although some believers maintain that apocalyptic imagery should be interpreted literally, most contemporary Christians view this language as metaphor for God's activity.

PSALM 110:1,
5, 6

The LORD said to my lord, "Sit at my right hand,
until I make your enemies your footstool."
The lord who is at God's right hand
will smite rulers in the day of his wrath;
he will rule over the nations.
He will drink from the brook beside the road
and therefore will lift high his head.

PRAYER
OF THE DAY,
PROPER 27

Lord, when the day of wrath comes we have no hope except
in your grace. Make us so to watch for the last days that the
consummation of our hope may be the joy of the marriage
feast of your Son, Jesus Christ our Lord.

WILHELM A.
WEXELS

Oh, happy day when we shall stand
in heaven with the saved;
all peoples at the Lord's right hand
shall find their names engraved.

Oh, blessed day when Christ shall come
and show himself as Lord,
and thousands meet in their new home
which Jesus has prepared.

In that hour when darkness like a cloak shall be spread over all things, may your grace, O Lord, shine on us in the place of the earthly sun. On that day when all people are called to earthly burial, make us worthy, O Lord, to rejoice in heavenly rest. In that day when all darkness shall cease, and all are freed from weariness, grant, O Lord, that we may take our delight in the joys of the life to come.

EPHRAEM,
SERMON 13

Thou art coming, we are waiting
with a hope that cannot fail;
asking not the day or hour,
resting on thy word of power,
anchored safe within the veil.
Time appointed may be long,
but the vision must be sure;
certainty shall make us strong,
joyful patience can endure.

FRANCES R.
HAVERGAL

To UNDERSTAND APOCALYPTIC IMAGERY and to receive it with any sympathy, we must imagine the historical situations during which it was developed and elaborated. In both Judaism and Christianity, believers trust that God will save them from all that threatens. Is there sickness? God will heal. Are we oppressed? God will set us free. On an eschatological day in the future, God will act. Time and again through history, however, believers suffered through injustice and persecution without any sign of God's deliverance. In these situations, the imagery of battle in which God will give the faithful people victory over the enemy, and the imagery of creation in which God will create a new and perfect world of justice and peace, combine to produce apocalyptic rhetoric. The horrors of warfare and natural disaster are the birth pangs of the wonders of a new creation: these are the two sides of apocalypticism.

During the historic periods that apocalypticism was psychologically useful, the political situation was so bad that it is as if the chaos that existed before time had returned. The situation appeared so horrible as to be irredeemable: an entirely new world would have to be created. Believers tended to assume that the situation would get worse before it got better. The future promised not only political oppression, but also natural catastrophes, such as earthquakes and fireballs. Apocalypticism revels in imagery of violence and disaster. Everything will come to a horrific climax in God's final battle of good versus evil. Only after that day will evil finally and irrevocably be defeated. What the prophets ask is which side the people will be on.

Apocalyptic imagery lives on in various forms. The political theorist Karl Marx suggested that a violent revolution and total destruction of the present world order would be required before justice could come for the poor. Although Marx was scornful of the role religion had played in securing justice for the oppressed, his predictions of the future paralleled classic religious imagery of apocalypticism. Terrorists use violence in hopes of inaugurating a new society. Currently, the film industry exploits similar violence in its disaster movies, which enjoy immense popularity, even for an audience that does not hope for political upheaval.

The other side of apocalyptic imagery expresses the promise of vindication of the righteous. In the new world order, those who lived a life of holiness will finally enjoy an idyllic communal life. If they suffered in the old world, they will enjoy peace and plenty in the new world. For many of those Christians who take apocalyptic language literally, this perfect existence will occur here on earth, in a second paradise created by God for humankind. Others speculate that the righteous will be removed from this earth in an experience of the rapture to enjoy a new world created in the heavens. For yet others, the imagery appears as mythic descriptions of heaven, an everlasting afterlife enjoyed by all the saved, the catastrophe of hell averted by the miracle of heaven.

An example of how eschatological imagery developed is seen in the word *Armageddon*. The book of Revelation uses apocalyptic language to predict the final battle between the forces of evil and the armies of God at Armageddon. The place-name is a Greek form of Mount Megiddo, an ancient battle site remembered both for its victories, for example, Deborah's defeat of Sisera, and its calamities, for example, the death of the good king Josiah. The memory of both victory and disaster weave together: when God comes at the end of time, it will mean both victory for the oppressed and disaster for the wicked. Historical memories provide the background for eschatological hope, and this hope weaves increasingly extreme imagery into what we call apocalypticism.

The numerous times that the Bible refers to this future event employ the phrases *the day of the Lord*, *that day*, *the hour*, and *at that time*. All indicate a future occurrence in human time. Each of the synoptic gospels includes a section of classic apocalypticism, in which Jesus himself describes the end-time in language reminiscent of especially the book of Daniel. A characteristic feature of this speech is the unpredictability of the timing of this event: one must be perpetually ready for the coming of the day. The synoptics claim that the day is known only by the Father, not even by the Son. The community must be aware of the signs: increased injustice, political oppression, natural disasters on earth and in the sky. It is this time of trial that the Lord's Prayer refers to as it petitions God for salvation from the woes that will inevitably arrive. Early apostolic writings also urge readiness for the coming of the end, although later epistles, by laying out rules for church governance, are settling in for the long haul and look less expectantly into the skies.

In John's gospel, the phrase *the hour* is used in a way surprising to the hearer. *The hour* is generally used to refer to the future time of judgment and vindication, yet John uses it to refer to the time of Christ's crucifixion. The end-time is already here, an idea theologians call realized eschatology. The cataclysmic overturning of the world order already occurred in the death of

Christ. If Jesus' death is Armageddon, believers are already living in the new age, and they need not fear what appear to be the threats of evil around them. The primitive church's use of the term *the eighth day* for the day of eucharistic celebration exemplifies this idea of the new age already begun, a time of grace outside and beyond old time.

Who is coming on the day is the Son-of-man. Perhaps no divine title in the scriptures is more unclear, complex, and misinterpreted. This volume hyphenates the words, *Son-of-man*, to highlight the idiosyncratic meaning of the nouns in this title. First, about the misinterpretation: Hymns such as "Beautiful Savior" that refer to Christ as the "Son of God and Son of Man" erroneously suggest to many persons that the first title refers to Christ's divine origin and the second to his human existence, as if the language points to father-God and mother-Mary. Furthermore, both the word *son* and the word *man* are male terms, which lead some Christians to argue for divine masculinity.

Nothing could be farther from the meaning of this term in the Bible. Sometimes in Old Testament usage, son of man means only human being, a descendent of the human race. Readers of the Narnia books recall the terminology "son of Adam" and "daughter of Eve" as similar designations. Later apocalyptic literature promised one like a human being who will come in the clouds to reign. This human-like one is wholly different from the beasts, creatures who represent the evil rulers of other nations. In Daniel 7, this one is identified as the people of Israel (Daniel 7:18). The term is thus a metaphor for the poet's faith that God's people will be vindicated. They will conquer the beasts who currently hold sway, rising out of their political oppression into a new day.

During the intertestamental period the idea of a unique son-of-man grew in Jewish imagination. Under the domination of the Roman empire it did not look as if the whole people would be victorious without the assistance of a superhuman champion. The end-time will come only by means of a divinely appointed human one who would bridge heaven and earth, transport the people to the holiness of God, and bring down the justice of God to the people of earth. It is this singular mysterious figure that is much discussed in the gospels, and it figures especially in the readings of Advent (Ad1A, Ad1B, Ad1C). In the minds of Jesus' contemporaries, this coming one would effect divine justice. The only question was whether Jesus was that one. Contemporary biblical scholars do not agree whether Jesus understood himself to be this Son-of-man, or whether this biblical language reflects later Christian reinterpretation of the traditional hope for the people's savior.

Interpretation of the imagery of Son-of-man is not easy. John the Baptist promised a divine avenger. The gospels stress a future deliverance promised to the faithful people. Yet John's gospel tells us that the hour took place on Good Friday. At least the language proclaims that Christians are already living after Armageddon. As the third-century eucharistic prayer of Hippolytus says it, Christ came "at this end of the ages." Now is the time of justice, the victory of God over evil, the day of the ascendance of the things of God.

Such talk can be hollow if proclaimed in a community that knows no justice and that enacts no peace. The Son-of-man birthed the new age, and the Spirit of that divine human one is bringing the new age to fullness. Our hope is for more, at least this much: that the church itself takes on the language and becomes the fruition of the image.

The complexity of this imagery strikes each year at the outset of Advent. John the Baptist preaches apocalyptic terrors (Ad2A, Ad2B, Ad3C). John was himself a prophet in the desert, having rejected the values of his culture to ready himself for the coming of the end-time. Yet Christians listen to John's threats of burning chaff as they purchase holiday gifts, for Christmas is coming. The psalms appointed for Christmas Eve and Christmas Day say that the trees and the hills are singing for joy at the arrival of the judge. The church needs to meditate more deeply the incongruity of Advent. The Bible suggests that the oppressed will hear the advent of God as good news. Thus the readings call the church to be on the side of the oppressed. If we live in palaces—and on the world's scale of wealth, many of us do—we are in trouble on *that day*.

At both the beginning and the close of the liturgical year, apocalyptic words of Jesus are read as the gospel. It is always disconcerting to listen to these dreadful threats (Ad1A, Ad1B, Pr28B, LastB, Ad1C, Pr27C, Pr28C) and to respond with a joyous, "Praise to you, O Christ." Yet it is precisely this complex ambivalence that the classic liturgy calls us to experience. All these readings are calls to justice. We have nothing to fear, unless we are the evil ones. Our awareness of sin reminds us that we are indeed the evil ones; yet, in the same ambivalence that the liturgy and its readings try to express, we are also the saved ones who have nothing to fear.

From Matthew we hear this apocalyptic message in the parables of the wise and foolish bridesmaids (Pr27A), the servants with their talents (Pr28A), and the judgment of the sheep and the goats (LastA). Although these parables do not utilize the stereotypical apocalyptic imagery of war and natural disaster, the message is the same: a day is coming in which a final division will be made between good and evil. No gray exists: all is either white or black.

Just as some believers literalize apocalyptic imagery, so too do some believers follow ethics, like Matthew's, that admit no gray. In the minds of some

Christians, certain behaviors are clearly wholly evil. For example, Christian pacifists understand all killing as always wholly evil. Many Christians, however, and Lutherans among them, see most moral decisions as choices between tones of gray, as though evil is always in, with, and under our human attempts at goodness. In fear and trembling the community must journey forward, although we do not always agree which are the good trees to preserve and which the trees to cut down and throw into the fire.

Although the phrase *the second coming* does not appear in the Bible, groups of Christians throughout the history of the church have eagerly anticipated a second coming of Christ. The pattern was that if a group took the language too literally, assembling on a mountaintop to wait for the Son-of-man, that group moved away from interaction with the wider church and became a sect. An example is the Shaker movement, which began within Protestantism and evolved into a separatist community that imagined only itself as the people of the eschaton. Other groups, such as the Seventh Day Adventists, muted their early apocalyptic emphasis and took their place alongside mainstream Christian churches.

The biblical language describing the day of the Lord recognizes the enormity of evil. Particularly the Romantic movement of the nineteenth century and the human potential movement of the twentieth century tended to minimize evil, seeing mostly in human beings a power to effect good. Classical Christian doctrine takes evil much more seriously. If evil is as pernicious as apocalyptic imagery says, it follows that much of the world's value system will have to be destroyed to make way for justice to reign. If we are on the side of the evil powers, the coming of the day will not be the happy day sung by nineteenth-century believers.

One more title for Christ is closely associated with apocalyptic imagery: Alpha-and-Omega. Christ is the beginning of all, of a perfect creation, of peaceful community, of our entry into the life of God. Christ is also the end of all, the goal to which we head, the final justice, the ultimate peace. So it is that the paschal candle each Easter Vigil is inscribed with an Alpha and an Omega, as well as with the year's date. Calling Christ Alpha-and-Omega lessens our need for either Armageddon or heaven. In the community of the body of Christ we experience the day of the LORD. The book of Revelation says that the seer's vision occurs on *the Lord's day*. A slightly different grammatical phrase than *the day of the Lord*, this phrase echoes the earlier apocalyptic image, yet applies it to new Christian use: *the day of the Lord* became a title for Sunday, the day of worship. The church is now by baptism in the Spirit practicing the justice and reward for which we all hope. On that day will be a feast on the mountain, and here we are, sharing the bread and wine:

for on the Lord's day is the hour of the Lord's supper. It is both enough, and not enough. The promise of yet another day calls us forward.

Apocalyptic language finally calls us into hope. The imagery promises that God will, in the end, bring wrong to right. The church repeats this hope in its evening prayer, as for centuries it has sung Mary's song each night. The Magnificat echoes eschatological imagery: The rulers will be overthrown, the poor will be fed. Indeed, Luke's placement of this canticle in his gospel suggests that this great day occurred in the birth and destiny of Christ. God is coming; the promise of mercy is being fulfilled now.

Emanation
of the Divine

begotten, being, emanation of the divine,
image, word

Related chapters: CREATION, LIGHT, PROPHET

The Greek philosophical idea that all life emanates from one
divine power influenced the Gospel of John and the development
of christology and trinitarian theology. Greek emanationism is
seen in those readings that refer to God as the One from whom
the being of Christ comes, and to Christ as light, word, and the
begotten one.

PSALM 104:31　　You send forth your Spirit, and they are created;
　　　　　　　　and so you renew the face of the earth.

NICENE CREED　　We believe in one Lord, Jesus Christ,
　　　　　　　　the only Son of God,
　　　　　　　　eternally begotten of the Father,
　　　　　　　　God from God, Light from Light,
　　　　　　　　true God from true God,
　　　　　　　　begotten, not made,
　　　　　　　　of one Being with the Father . . .
　　　　　　　We believe in the Holy Spirit, the Lord, the giver of life,
　　　　　　　　who proceeds from the Father and the Son.

AMBROSE　　　Not of human seed or worth,
OF MILAN　　　but from God's own mystic breath,
　　　　　　　fruit in Mary's womb begun
　　　　　　　when God breathed the Word, his Son.

　　　　　　　God the Father is his source,
　　　　　　　back to God he runs his course;
　　　　　　　down to death and hell descends,
　　　　　　　God's high throne he reascends.

Inspired by the Father, each procession of the Light spreads itself generously toward us, and, in its power to unify, it stirs us by lifting us up. It returns us back to the oneness and deifying simplicity of the Father who gathers us in. Let us call upon Jesus, the Light of the Father, the "true light enlightening every one coming into the world." We should raise our eyes to the paternally transmitted enlightenment coming from sacred scriptures, and we must lift up the immaterial and steady eyes of our minds to that outpouring of Light which comes from that source of divinity, the Father.

PSEUDO-
DIONYSIUS,
*The Celestial
Hierarchy*

As soon as she was raised aloft into ecstasy, she saw herself placed above the world, her eyes of contemplation magnetized towards the incomprehensible Essence of the Divinity, while the innermost point of her intelligence, in an admirable manner, considered the eternal and true God, the uncreated Most High, the Lord, in the majesty of his substance. She was so adequately positioned between God and humankind that, below God but higher than the whole world, she trampled upon terrestrial things, remaining inseparably united to the Divine Essence by the embrace of charity. And as if her spirit had been transferred entirely within the Divine Spirit, she thus understood that, for a short while, she was united to the Most High Deity and rendered entirely celestial.

BEATRICE OF
NAZARETH,
*Vision
of the World
as a Wheel*

OF THE FORTY IMAGES discussed in this study, emanation of the divine is perhaps the least like what we might envision as an image. It may be that the mental picture conveyed by this language is so central to much Christian theology that believers come to assume that emanation is actually, literally, how God functions. However, emanation of the divine needs to be recognized as a Greek philosophical construct that was borrowed by some early Christian writers as helpful in expressing their understanding of the faith. This philosophical idea and the varied pictures and language that expressed it pervaded several centuries of Greek philosophical thought, beginning in Platonism and continuing through Stoicism and Neoplatonism. We read it in selections from the Gospel of John that are used at Christmas, throughout the Triduum, for Lent's baptismal catechesis, and for the eucharistic focus in year B. This Greek idea moved into Christian theology and is found in much mystical reverie of the Middle Ages, and it is alive again in contemporary New Age religion. Each historic stage of Greek philosophical and religious thought adapted the notion of emanation for its own particular purposes. Yet despite this diversity in detail, one can still get a general sense of the meaning of this persistent mental image.

Emanationism presupposes a single, unified, transcendent origin of reality. Everything that is, all that we see and all that we cannot see, derives from one center of being. The One, usually understood to be an impersonal principle, sometimes imagined as the primary Idea of all, and occasionally anthropomorphized into a deity, brings the universe into being through a process something like radiation. All being—all that is—comes from the one Being. The source eternally emanates its life, producing successively lesser forms of life. Yet the source remains everlastingly undiminished. The further a thing is from the One, the less perfect it is. Fulfillment comes in returning to the One, as if by means of a tractor beam we can be brought back home to the mother spaceship.

Emanationism proposes a picture opposite to evolution. According to evolutionary development, successive life forms are more detailed and more complete than the previous ones, rather than less perfect. Nor is emanationism like biblical creation, according to which God, with conscious intent, created everything to be perfectly as it should be. The notion of emanationism rather resembles our sense of sound waves, the quality weakening as the distance from the source increases.

Early Christian theologians worked to distinguish their beliefs from that of gnostic emanationism. In gnostic belief, created matter was so far from the source that the material world was seen as wholly evil, and the religious enterprise was an attempt, one way or another, to distance oneself from this life. Against this belief, Christians preached the goodness of creation and God's love for humanity in the incarnation. The gnostic idea that only a hidden, abstruse knowledge could free us from evil was met with the gospel of the promise of God's mercy for all.

Recent scholarship suggests that Christians were more influenced by emanationism than they realized. Greek philosophical ideas already affected Palestinian Judaism in the several centuries before the rise of Christianity. The intertestamental development of a doctrine of a heavenly hierarchy containing nine degrees of angels is one example of such Hellenistic tendencies. Here Jewish thought incorporated the Greek idea of a succession of increasingly less perfect intermediary beings that stand between the One and the world. The Western belief in the immortality of the soul is another expression of the doctrine of emanation. The soul, that which is divine in the human, returns at death to its source, the One who is immortal. The importance of emanation imagery to later Christian theological reflection is apparent in Augustine's *Confessions*. Speaking to God, Augustine writes, "You brought under my eye some books of the Platonists, translated from Greek into Latin. There I read, not of course in these words, but with entirely the same sense and supported by numerous and varied reasons, 'In the beginning was the Word, and the Word was with God, and the Word was God.'"[1]

One Christian image influenced by Greek emanationism is the language of Christ as redeemer. The Hebrew faith in God's redemption developed into the hope for an extraordinary human who would arise from the people to bring about their salvation. This image became overlaid with the Greek philosophical idea of a redeemer, an emanation from the source, a power beaming out from beyond our world in order to draw us back to the One. Both ideas continue throughout the life of the church, with some Christians stressing redemption of the poor from social evils, and others envisioning redemption as a transmigration from the lower earth to the higher sphere of heaven.

John 1 (ChDyABC) presents a christianized emanationism. God is the One, the Logos Christ is the primary emanation, and one of the lesser intermediaries is the prophet John the Baptist. The darkness of our world is far from the source of life. The Word comes from the One, just as speech comes from the mouth. Life is what a philosopher might call *being*, and the created world came into being from the Being of the One. All light that shines has its source in God. Those who come to live in this light are now born of God; that is, they now come from God. The author of John 1 offers several metaphors: God shines divine light, God grants the world being, God makes us children. Each of these phrases presents a Christian version of Greek emanationism, in which the believer does not get transported outside this world to a divine sphere, but rather, because of the incarnation, is transformed to live newly within it.

The idea of emanation of the divine has been depicted in church art mostly by means of the Johannine image of light. A sky full of light, radiant angels, a bright beam descending onto the believer's shining face, a nimbus surrounding the head of the saint: these familiar symbols suggest that salvation is like light emanating from God above onto the earth and both absorbed and reflected by the baptized. The early church referred to baptism as enlightenment, because the process of becoming *of God* was likened to one's receiving the ray of light proceeding from God.

Other passages in John offer yet more pictures of the emanation of the divine. In John the Baptist's account in John 1 of the baptism of Jesus (Ep2A), the Spirit descends from heaven like a dove. Perhaps the author means that John the Baptist saw a dove. But the sentence could also mean that, descending from heaven as a dove does, the power of God came down upon Jesus. In the eucharistic chapter of John 6 (Pr13B, Pr14B, Pr15B, Pr16B), Jesus passed on to others the bread from God, accomplished the will of God, conveyed the life of God, spoke the word of God, and personified on earth the One who sent him. The language in the High Priestly Prayer (Ea7A, Ea7B, Ea7C) imagines a son who came from the father now returning to that father and bringing along with him all that he has gathered to himself. Jesus, who is the power of God on earth (Pentc), goes back to the Father (Ea5c), to draw all the world to God.

The term *begotten*, known to English-speaking Christians from the KJV translation of John 3:16 and its incorporation in the ecumenical creeds, is another biblical reflection of emanationism. The archaic word described the father's role in procreation according to the belief that the male seed contained the entire fetus. The mother only bears. It is the father who begets. From this erroneous biology came a metaphor of life's origins useful in conveying emanationism. Just as the son comes from the father, so life comes from the One. As Christian theology strove to articulate the relationship of Jesus to God, it relied increasingly on Greek emanation imagery expressed in language of the son being eternally begotten of the father. For those using the NRSV, the term *begotten* appears only in passages from Hebrews

(ChDyABC, Le5B, Pr24B), but it remains in the Nicene Creed. The Nicene Creed goes on to describe the Trinity as the one God, the Son of God begotten of the Father, and the Spirit who proceeds from the Father. This classical philosophical language is unintelligible to many contemporary worshipers. How often to appoint use of the Nicene Creed on Sundays is a question that bears our consideration.

Another way that the church presented its variation on emanationism is with the language of Christ as the image of the One. Occurring in 2 Corinthians and central to the poem in Colossians 1 (Pr11c, Lastc), the image of God is like an emanation from the One, a living representation of the power of the One, made accessible to us lower beings. As the poem in Colossians says, we now are to be transferred to the realm of the One through this emanation of the divine image, a markedly Hellenistic way of talking about the fruits of the incarnation.

Another way that Greek emanationism has come into Christian speech is in our saying that Christ is the word of God. That God speaks to humankind, conveying the divine will through direct or indirect means, was already a fundamental idea in Judaism. In John, however, the Hebrew idea that God speaks merged with the Greek idea of the Logos, the divine word emanating from the One down to earth, the mind of God brought down to humankind. Although not a primary image in the lectionary, the language became essential to many theologians for whom Word of God is a primary way to understand the being of Jesus.

When Christ pulls believers back to the being of God, they come finally to be, in a way, *in God*. The Western church, keen to maintain the absolute otherness of God and concerned lest any religious language too easily divinize humanity, has been nervous about using this language. On the other hand, the Eastern church uses it regularly, for example in referring to baptism as that which brings us into the life of the triune God, faith as the process of making us more like God, and death as our return to the being of God. For those Christians uncomfortable with anthropomorphized descriptions of heaven, the language of our return to the God from whom we came might prove useful.

The Greek imagery of emanation is only one set of metaphors borrowed from the secular culture by Christians striving to speak of their faith. The imagery of emanation is just as—but no more—susceptible than is any other image to problematic interpretations. Pushing any one set of metaphors over others will inevitably distort the gospel, and misunderstanding the original theological intent of the imagery—for example, not grasping what *begotten* meant—leads to bad theology.

However, the epoch of those believers who lived through Greek philosophy has to a great degree formed subsequent believers with the language of their worldview. Contemporary preachers can find this imagery useful in speaking the gospel, by speaking of the divine life that comes to us through Christ. The imagery can be useful also in speaking of the church. We can imagine the church as being people transformed by the power of the Spirit into children of God, made into countless emanations from God, lights shining to enlighten the world. The ranks of angels who teach us to sing the Sanctus, the prophets and evangelists of the scriptures, the martyrs and saints of history, indeed, the people standing next to us in the pew on Sunday morning, all share in the life emanating from God, and all radiate that life to the world around. We are being brought into God. The Spirit of that God is around us and among us, and the Spirit draws us together into one.

Family

Abba, adoption, brothers and sisters,
children of God, family,
Father, inheritance, Son of God

Related chapters: KINGDOM, MOTHER

The Bible both assumes the patriarchal family and criticizes it, and the lectionary presents us with a countercultural ambivalence about the image and reality of family. The church uses the language of family both about itself and for its christology. The designation of Jesus as the son of God the father brings comfort to some Christians and distress to others.

PSALM 103:13   As a father cares for his children,
           so does the LORD care for the God-fearing.

RITE
OF BAPTISM   In Holy Baptism our gracious heavenly Father liberates us from sin and death by joining us to the death and resurrection of our Lord Jesus Christ. We are born children of a fallen humanity; in the waters of Baptism we are reborn children of God and inheritors of eternal life.

F. BLAND
TUCKER   Our Father, by whose name
all parenthood is known:
In love divine you claim
each family as your own.
Bless mothers, fathers, guarding well,
with constant love as sentinel,
the homes in which your people dwell.

O Christ, yourself a child
within an earthly home,
with heart still undefiled
to full adulthood come:
Our children bless in every place
that they may all behold your face
and knowing you may grow in grace.

For the love of the most holy and beloved Child who was wrapped in the poorest of swaddling clothes and laid in a manger, and of his most holy mother, I admonish, entreat, and exhort my sisters that they always wear the poorest of garments. To preserve the unity of mutual love and peace, all who hold offices in the monastery should be chosen by the common consent of all the sisters. When the Blessed Father Francis saw that we had no fear of poverty, he wrote for us a form of life as follows: "Since by divine inspiration you have made yourselves daughters and servants of the most high king, the heavenly Father, and have taken the Holy Spirit as your spouse, I resolve and promise for myself and for my brothers always to have that same loving care and special solicitude for you as I have for them."

RULE OF
ST. CLARE

"Our Father in heaven."

What is this? With these words God wants to attract us, so that we believe he is truly our Father and we are truly his children, in order that we may ask him boldly and with complete confidence, just as loving children ask their loving father.

MARTIN
LUTHER,
*The Small
Catechism*

THE IMAGE OF FAMILY, like the family itself, is ambivalent. Despite decades of television programs in which family difficulties get resolved in a half-hour with much laughter, we know that life within family structures can be both healthy and destructive. Furthermore, scholars studying the family do not agree on a definition of family. For example, the Census Bureau's definition is far more restrictive than would be a sociologist's understanding. For some anthropologists, the family is an economic unit, a kinship group sharing a domicile and making a living together. In some periods of history, such a family could include dozens of people, persons related by blood or marriage, as well as unrelated servants or slaves. Another type of family is a biological unit, for example, the Johannine picture of the adult siblings Mary, Martha, and Lazarus residing together.

Many contemporary psychologists describe the family as an affinity group, perhaps formed by, but surely maintained by, choice as much as if not more than by birth. If we think of the married or unmarried couple as the center of the family, we are thinking of the family as an emotional affinity unit. Children bringing suit in court to be divorced from their parents present an extreme example of seeing the family as an affinity group. Historically, most economic families were not in our sense primarily emotional units. In our society, various categories of family exist side by side. A lesbian professional couple raising an adopted biracial child may live next door to an immigrant clan of a dozen siblings, spouses, cousins, and children who together run a vegetable market. The first step, then, in interpreting the lectionary's language of family is to realize that even in our society, family is a complex notion.

The myths of world religions idealize one kind of family over another. Many patriarchal traditions tell ancient stories of the father-god alone giving birth. One example is Zeus, experiencing a severe headache and forthwith bearing Athena, the goddess of wisdom, from his head. Matrifocal traditions, such as the Northeast Woodlands natives of North America, tell of the primordial woman who unassisted bore the first children. In myths like that of Persian Zoroastrianism, the sibling unit is primary, while in others, such as Genesis, the married couple is central, with the first sibling unit resulting in fratricide. The ancestor veneration important in some religious traditions, such as Confucianism, serves to sanctify bloodlines. Yet the American history of the pilgrims and the pioneers diminished the importance of bloodlines. Young people moved away from their parents and from the graves of their dead, using religious language to describe their migration away from the ancestors to a new promised land. In American tradition, the freely chosen future for a small family unit was judged more significant than the religious sites and rituals of a family's ancestral past.

The family as described in the Old Testament was to great degree the patriarchal economic unit. It extended three or four generations, and its primary relationship was the father and eldest son, who never grew away from his father, but came in time to replace his father in the ongoing economic situation. In biblical times and until the eighteenth century, the Western world thought that the male's sperm contained a homunculus, a minuscule human, and that the female functioned only as the incubator; therefore, the infant came literally from the father and was owned by the father, who had the right of life or death over the babies born into his household. The role of the woman was to produce sons and so continue the male line, and her inability to do so usually meant another woman would be introduced into the household to meet this goal. The Genesis narratives exemplify this desire of the wife to produce sons for her husband.

During New Testament times, the urbanization of Palestine meant an increasing distance between rich and poor. The urban family size shrunk, for the city could support fewer people than the nomadic or agricultural life. In the Herodian period, an estimated one percent of the population consumed fifty percent of the goods and was considered the ruling class. Ten percent made up the upper class and lived in large economic units of several conjugal groups. Seventy percent included peasants and day laborers, who lived in single-room residences. Five percent made their living as craftspersons, and as many as fifteen percent subsisted on the margins of the society, as beggars or social outcasts of one kind or another. As now, so in biblical times the actual configuration of families depended upon the people's socioeconomic conditions, and we ought not romanticize that in previous centuries family structures were uniform, healthy, and happy.

The Bible indicates significant exceptions to this patriarchal social pattern. In the Old Testament, the ancestral line of God's inherited promise follows Seth, Isaac, Jacob, Judah, David, Solomon. Despite a culture espousing primogeniture, not a single one of these was the eldest son. Numbers 27 records the story of the five daughters of Zelophehad who, because they had no brothers, won the right to inherit their father's property. The New Testament includes stories of a surprising number of persons living outside of patriarchal family units: Jesus himself, Mary of Magdala, James and John,

John the Baptist, Paul, to name a few. The New Testament also indicates that loyalty to Christ may require a rejection of natural family ties. Identity in the countercultural Christian community comes to be described in familial terms, this fictive family replacing the economic or biological family of one's origin.

The image of family functions in four different ways in the readings of the lectionary. First, in some readings the role of the patriarchal family is evident. Sometimes, such as when an entire household is baptized, the patriarchal family is an assumed social structure, accepted as God's intention for the people. The lectionary includes God's promise to Abraham that he will be father to an extensive family (Le2A, Pr5A°, Le2B, Le2C, Pr15C[†]). Some narratives stress God's promise to Sarah (Pr6A°, Pr11C[†]), but by the time the narratives were transcribed, the author's focus is on how Abraham got the son that God wanted him to have. Proverbs includes a long poem about the ideal wife (Pr20B°). Although the woman is described as an affluent mother, directing servants and managing real estate, her primary identification is as a wife. The conclusion of the book of Job (Pr25B°) indicates that the way God blesses the righteous man is by giving him plenty of children, yet in an antipatriarchal detail, only the daughters of Job are named.

Passages in the Bible that exalt unmitigated patriarchy, for example the passage in Hebrews 12 that praises the father for punishing his children, are not included in the lectionary. The household codes, which prescribe Christian adherence to the patriarchal Greco-Roman household, are included in older versions of the three-year lectionary, but were omitted from the Revised Common Lectionary. Here we see a graphic example of the fact that the lectionary is a conscious selection from the Bible meant to preach the gospel to Christians, not a condensed form of the Testaments meant to inform worshipers about ancient Near Eastern sacred texts.

Some lectionary readings indicate a challenge to the patriarchal family. The lectionary includes the tale of Jacob's and Esau's fight over primogeniture (Pr10A°); the story of Joseph forgiving his elder brothers (Pr19A[†]); and the account of Absolom's death (Pr14B°). Ruth plays a prominent role in Jewish salvation history (Pr26B°) despite the many ways her identity and her behavior run counter to patriarchal family expectations. The so-called divorce texts portray Jesus as reiterating God's primordial blessing of the married couple and thus challenging the husband's traditional patriarchal right to divorce his wife (Ep6A, Pr22B).

The infancy narratives in Matthew and Luke describe not the patriarchal family as much as the affinity group. Joseph is not in any way the authority or foundation of what has come to be called the holy family. Joseph and

Mary are to raise a child who is not naturally their own, one who will cause his mother anguish. The reading from 2 Timothy (Pr22c) that praises Timothy, his mother Lois, and his grandmother Eunice presents another nonpatriarchal family as a Christian model. These New Testament examples of how the church reconfigured cultural norms can inspire us to continue a similar critical inquiry into family in our own time.

Some readings go further to suggest that family ties must be severed for a life of genuine religious devotion. The toddler Samuel (Ch1c) leaves his mother to live at Eli's shrine. Jesus tells the questioners that patriarchal families will not persist in heaven (Pr27c). Yet despite this pericope, especially the nineteenth-century church described heaven as the place where natural families would reunite and live together forever. We are warned that the gospel will instigate family fights (Pr7a, Pr15c), and as Jesus ignored his mother and siblings at the door, he said that those who hear his preaching are his family (Pr5b). The church's monastic practice found this language of the replacement family useful among vowed members of religious communities.

The readings for the feast of the Presentation (see also Ch1b) use family in two contrasting ways. The holy family is shown participating in the expected temple ritual. The point of this patriarchal ritual was both to cleanse the wife so that she could return to her husband's bed and to buy the son from the deity, who then would not require the sacrifice of the firstborn but give him back to his natural family. Yet the second reading uses the language of family wholly metaphorically. In Hebrews 2, Jesus is described as becoming like his brothers (and sisters, NRSV), and in Galatians the believer is the child of God. Thus the lectionary juxtaposes an archaic patriarchal family and the metaphoric Christian family.

The epistle readings repeatedly use family as a metaphor for the baptized community. The language of inheritance (Pr10b) is part of the image of the patriarchal family pattern. Words with the root *adelph-* occur about a hundred times in the writings of Paul. The controversial practice of the New Revised Standard Version to render *adelphoi* as "brothers and sisters" diminishes the patriarchal overtones of the New Testament's family passages. It is ironic, however, that Paul's beloved passages enshrining family language come from someone who apparently left his natural or social family for a life of itinerant missionary travel.

Preeminent among these metaphoric passages are the second half of Romans 8 (Pr11a, Pr12a, Trinb), Galatians 1 and 4 (Pr4c, Ch1b); various selections from 1 Thessalonians, Philippians, and Ephesians; as well as readings from John (Ea6a) and 1 John (Ea3b). In the language of the metaphor,

Christians are no longer orphans or slaves (another metaphor, of course). Rather, they are adopted into God's family as heirs in God's household, descendants of the patriarch Abraham; they are siblings to one another; Christ is their brother; God is father to Christ, who is the firstborn son, and to all Christ's brothers and sisters; those adopted into God's family are privileged to pray to God as their Abba. Paul used this metaphor continuously, and scholars disagree over how much Paul hoped to replace social patriarchy with sibling-like affection in the church.

According to this metaphor God, the source of life, grants life to us in a pattern counter to cultural inheritance practice. Slaves or workers subject to the patriarch would not inherit the household's goods. Only the sons could inherit. Although we were not originally recipients of the promise, by baptism we are adopted into the household to become children of God and heirs of the divine promise. Current considerations about adoption often focus on the emotional aspects of the new relationship. First-century texts, however, stress the legal right of inheritance effected by the adoption. Scholars debate to what extent filial affection is a major aspect of the New Testament's metaphor of family. Plutarch praised a woman who preferred the life of her brother over that of her child, because a child is replaceable, but a brother is not. Perhaps for the early Christians, the image evoked, among other things, loyalty.

The American English translation of *adelph-* involves two goals for biblical translators, and often these goals suggest opposite translations. One goal is to render the Hebrew and Greek as literally as possible, so that the reader knows what the original writer actually said. This goal would argue that *adelphoi* should be translated "brothers" to maintain first-century accuracy. The second goal is to render the biblical message in as contemporary speech as possible, so that the hearer can more readily receive it as God's good news. This goal would argue that *adelphoi* should be translated "brothers and sisters," since women were also recipients of Paul's letters, although it was first-century cultural practice to address a roomful of men and women as *Brothers*. Whichever decision governs the translation used for public worship, it is important to bring both of these dimensions to our proclamation of the word. On Sunday morning, the scriptures are both a revered ancient text and the living voice of God.

As with the church's other root metaphors, *family* requires continuous, careful consideration. We need to inquire in what ways the metaphor is helpful. We are newly aware of personal or social situations in which the family metaphor can be destructive. The imagery of family might only feed our culture's unrealistic expectation that all persons are entitled to a perfect nuclear family. Scholars of language teach that when a metaphor becomes enshrined, the metaphor becomes a kind of golden calf. The idol absorbs adoration in itself, rather than serving as a vehicle for praise of the reality to which the metaphor points. Even though family language calls us into certain Christian truths, the speech might also inhibit mature growth in faith. Sometimes children language works to infantilize adult Christians. Families are both wholesome and problematic, and the church is only in metaphor a family at all.

The most doctrinally important use of family imagery is the New Testament's language of Jesus as the son of God. That in English we typically capitalize *Son* (in the Greek language, capitalization was not used to signify a word's distinctiveness or importance) indicates the extent to which this metaphoric description of Jesus functions as the church's essential christological label.

Were we to read only Paul or Mark, we would conclude that Jesus' origins were obscure. Matthew and Luke, however, narrate Jesus' miraculous conception, the theological point being that his patriarchal family line has nothing to do with his status, since he comes wholly from God. This theological description of Christ makes odd the Lucan genealogy, in which Adam's line descends to Jesus through Joseph. The focus on the particulars of Jesus' birth that has characterized centuries of Christian imagination attests far more to our perennial fascination with sex and to the church's interest in celibacy than to a serious theological proposal about the meaning of Jesus as the son of God. Some Christians argue that the virgin birth means that Mary was Jesus' mother and God Jesus' father, and necessarily proves that God is male. Such a literalist interpretation demonstrates the need for continuous reflection on the theological meaning of the language of Jesus as God's son. In John's prologue, Christ's connection to God is described primarily with the imagery of word and light.

The imagery of son-father has several antecedents. Probably the foundation was the biological notion that the father was the source of all life. Theologically, the metaphor suggested that God chose and adopted humans into a divine inheritance. Another idea was that Christ inaugurated a new familial affinity group, establishing an intimate connection with God. The most essential background for the language of Jesus as son of God, however, is the image of kingdom. In ancient Near Eastern mythology and legend, the king was always the son of the god or goddess. These various roots became interconnected during the christological deliberations of the fourth and fifth centuries, when the church affirmed that not only is Christ the son of God, but that also the Son of God is God.

A serious controversy in the contemporary church is the disagreement over the interpretation of primary metaphors. When is a metaphor so central to Christian speech that it moves from being a metaphor to being a normative label? A metaphor always implies both yes and no, while a label is unequivocal. Of the language of church as family, most Christians would concur that the speech is metaphor: the baptized community is both family and not family. But when we consider the language of God as father, considerable Christian disagreement arises over whether father language is metaphor—both true and not true—or accurate label. What does the church mean in calling God Father?

Sociologists like to reflect on the Nayar of South India, a matrifocal culture within which fathers play absolutely no role in the raising of the child. In the Greco-Roman world of the New Testament, however, the father was not only the biological source of human offspring and the economic head of the household. The title *father* was used in numerous first-century religious, social, legal, and governmental texts to describe any male in authority. Zeus/Jupiter was father. Army commanders were called father by their troops. In 2 B.C.E., the Senate of Rome conferred the title of Pater Patriae on Emperor Augustus. Thus, even though biblical scholars are quite accurate in demonstrating that first-century pious Jews did not regularly, perhaps ever, call God father in corporate prayer, the Greco-Roman culture called father every possible male authority figure, whether human, semidivine, or divine. In the first century the language of God as father was by no means distinctive. It can be argued that Christian adoption of father language was a logical result of the Hellenization of Judaism. Furthermore, New Testament scholars do not agree what precisely *abba* meant: a nearly unique invention of Jesus, the prayer of the trusting child, or the cry of the dying martyr. These historic inquiries may precede, but surely do not supersede, the pastoral issues involved.

The church continues to probe what the faith means by this imagery. Some Christians judge Father to be the divinely sanctioned name of God, sacred and immutable. Others honor the title as one divine metaphor among many, seeking to relativize its power by using alternative images. Still others avoid it altogether as a distasteful residue from archaic patriarchy. Some Christians claim that the imagery of God as father is religious authorization for the patriarchal family. Others describe divine fatherhood in a manner that criticizes stereotypical patriarchy in church and home. In the piety of many Christians, the imagery of father is momentous, either for good or for ill.

In the controversy raised by calling God father, we see an example of the astounding power of metaphor to shape minds and communities. It is ill-informed to dismiss a word as being only a metaphor. The imagery of God as father or the church as family can deliver totally opposite results: it enlivens some persons, embracing them with a joyous welcome, and it alienates others who reject both its patriarchal attitude and any community that enshrines this speech.

We must be aware of the problems of using the image of family in the liturgy. The contemporary fantasy of the happy family is far more shallow than a metaphor, which always brings with it ambiguity. Many persons spend years trying to free themselves from the psychological burdens of a destructive family system. Because U.S. census figures indicate that 25 percent of households are persons living alone, we cannot assume a family context at all. Family language in the church can serve to legitimate separation from the outsider, as if one's small affinity group is all that matters. Furthermore, an increasing number of Christians judge that the divine imagery of God as the father and Christ as the son reflects only the patriarchal society from which it arose and is best abandoned.

Yet life remains in the image; some of its possibilities are seldom explored. Some biblical commentators suggest that the first-century context of the New Testament speech implies that the language of brotherhood has less to do with affection and more to do with economic sharing. Thus the family imagery carries a justice dimension that is seldom highlighted. One sees a pattern among elderly people, that with their spouses dead and children grown away, their siblings are once again their closest connections. Thinking this way, the language of brotherhood and sisterhood implies commitment beyond choice, the givenness of members of one family as the longest-lasting bond.

The Christian family might be seen as more like the classic biological family than the contemporary affinity group. By our birth in baptism, we find ourselves connected and committed to others. We are not granted a choice to prefer only a few. Each Sunday we share the Spirit of peace with everyone sitting nearby, not solely with those who are our friends and relatives, for all are the family of God in Christ. The gift is reciprocal: I am family to them; they are family to me. In a society filled with lonely individuals longing for connection, the family in God can be gospel indeed.

Fire

ashes, burning bush, fire, tongues

Related chapters: LIGHT, SACRIFICE

In many world religions, fire is an image of divine presence, for both blessing and punishment. The lectionary emphasizes blessing. The paramount Christian use of fire occurs at the Easter Vigil, and this fire of the resurrection illumines all references to fire throughout the church year.

PSALM 105:37,   God led out the chosen people with silver and gold;
39   in all their tribes there was not one that stumbled.
      God spread out a cloud for a covering
        and a fire to give light in the night season.

THE EXSULTET   We sing the glories of this pillar of fire,
      the brightness of which is not diminished,
      even when its light is divided and borrowed. . . .
      May he who is the morning star find it burning—
      that morning star which never sets,
      that morning star which, rising again from the grave,
      faithfully sheds light on all the human race.

BIANCO   Come down, O Love divine;
DA SIENA   seek thou this soul of mine
      and visit it with thine own ardor glowing;
      O Comforter, draw near;
      within my heart appear
      and kindle it, thy holy flame bestowing.

      Oh, let it freely burn,
      till worldly passions turn
      to dust and ashes in its heat consuming.
      And let thy glorious light
      shine ever on my sight,
      and clothe me round, the while my path illuming.

The Word of God seems to honor the depiction of fire above all others. You will find it depicts not only flaming wheels, but also burning animals and even men who are somehow aglow. It places masses of lighted embers surrounding these heavenly beings and rivers roaring with endless fire. It speaks of fiery thrones and, invoking the etymology of the word "seraphim," it describes them as on fire and attributes to them the characteristics and the activity of fire. In general, whether the reference be to high or low within the hierarchy, the Word of God always honors the presentation of fire.

PSEUDO-
DIONYSIUS,
The Celestial
Hierarchy

As the flame of a fire has three qualities, so there is one God in three Persons. How? A flame is made up of brilliant light and red power and fiery heat. It has brilliant light that it may shine, and red power that it may endure, and fiery heat that it may burn. Therefore, by the brilliant light understand the Father, who with paternal love opens his brightness to his faithful; and by the red power, which is in the flame that it may be strong, understand the Son, who took on a body born from a virgin, in which his divine powers were shown; and by the fiery heat understand the Holy Spirit, who burns ardently in the minds the faithful.

HILDEGARD
OF BINGEN,
Scivias

FIRE FUNCTIONS AS a multivalent metaphor. We hear that despite the devastation wrought by a major fire in a beloved national forest, a fire that ruined the vacation plans of deeply disappointed tourists, some species of trees require periodic fire for their seeds to be released from the cones. Fire is both destructive and beneficial, and many of the world's religions use this ambiguity for symbolic purposes.

Even though people still gather around a fireplace on a winter night, and even though many worshipers love candlelight services, it is not easy to invoke for a technologically complacent assembly a sense of the power of flames. Our culture has distanced many people from the reality of fire. Fireplaces are desirable amusements, rather than lifelines. We turn up the thermostat, rather than build and tend an effective fire. Appliqued depictions of flames on banners cannot sufficiently convey the mystery of fire.

The ancients identified fire as one of the four elements that make up the universe, thus acknowledging the importance of fire for life on this planet. The ability to control fire, to kindle it at will and to use it for human purpose, is seen by some historians as a primary indicator of human society. When domesticated, fire allows the human community to alter nature for its own purposes. Darkness can become light, cold become warmth, food be cooked. Fire draws people around itself to form a circle of community. A home had a hearth. Fire was harnessed for rituals of purification and for the processes of manufacturing and metallurgy. The telescoped chronology in Genesis 4 claims that in the seventh generation of human beings, Tubal-cain operated a forge for producing both bronze and iron.

According to the ancient Greek myth, Zeus did not want humans to domesticate fire: only the deities were allowed such power and luxury. When Prometheus stole fire from heaven and gave it to humans, Zeus punished Prometheus by chaining him to the rocks and ordering the eagles to peck at his liver until the end of time. But, says the myth, with perpetual gratitude to the suffering Prometheus, humans do have fire, and civilization is on its way. The biblical stories assume that humans had domesticated fire from Eden on. The fires tended by human communities both alter nature and require work: thus it was that the Torah forbade kindling a fire on the sabbath.

Always fire destroys. Some living thing must die and be burned—a tree, a plant, an animal—in order that light, warmth, cooked food, and ritual purification are possible. Fire is mesmerizing to watch: a center of transformation that appears to have no center, a painful force that provides much relief for the community. Hindu burial practices demonstrate a religious use of fire as the vehicle of transformation and the transition from death to life. With such rituals the community testifies that there is no life without death, no rebirth without fire. According to the ancient legend of the phoenix, the millennium-old sole creature of its species must burn itself up in order for the new phoenix to emerge from the ashes.

The commonplace religious phenomenon of burnt sacrifice exemplifies the paradox of fire. The community destroys its own life—its produce, its flocks, its children—hoping to receive more and better life from the deity. The sacrifice might be understood quite literally, as if the deity is hungry and, like humans, prefers cooked to raw food. The sacrifice might be understood more symbolically: the deity wants proof that the suppliant is not selfish and is willing to give up goods. The fire might be understood as a sign of the religious enterprise, in which, like ore, the world must be purified of what is dross and prepared for its new use.

In the Bible, Cain and Abel offer burnt sacrifices to God. Leviticus 2–7 indicates how ritually detailed burnt sacrifices became later in Israelite history. In the biblical narratives of the conquest of Canaan, the Israelites' destruction of the resident population is legitimated because God ordered the burning of the cities. It is as if the goods are offered to God in thanks for the victory. The conquerors do not benefit by keeping the loot—except for example, in a detail reminiscent of the Trojan War, the 400 virgin girls who are saved alive as booty for the warriors (Judges 21:21). Subsequent use of incense in the temple substitutes a benign burning for the previous violent taking of life. Burning incense is a safe symbol of the people's offerings to God. The pleasant odor replaces the stench of burnt flesh, and the rising smoke illustrates the prayers rising up to God (Revelation 8:4).

Yet often it appears that fire destroys beyond any use, without any meaning. In the poetic essay *Holy the Firm*, the Christian author Annie Dillard questions the goodness of God before the enormity of human suffering by contemplating the young girl whose face gets seriously burned in a plane crash. When skin is burnt away, pain-killing drugs do not circulate within the body. We acknowledge the agony of burn victims, and so move from fascination with fire back again to primal terror.

Perhaps because of its mysterious power, fire was closely identified with the divine. Scholars suggest that at one time humans worshiped fire as itself divine, and that perhaps references in ancient religious texts to a perpetual fire in sanctuaries (for example Leviticus 6:13) indicate a second stage, in which the earlier worship of fire as divine evolved into reverence for fire as a sign of the divine. In Hinduism and in Zoroastrianism a primary deity is manifested as fire. In Egypt, the primary deity Re, the sun, is the origin of fire. Even in Buddhism, a religion that replaces divine imagery with talk of individual enlightenment, this human goal is described as if it were fire.

Also in the Bible, fire serves as a sign of God. In Israelite spirituality, God is not, like Zeus, hoarding the benefits of fire. Rather, the presence of God is seen as a fire in the burning bush (Pr17A°), and it promises freedom. The fire on top of Mount Sinai does not destroy the people. Rather, out from it comes the gift of the Torah. God gives light to the traveling Israelites by means of a pillar of fire. The theophanies experienced by Elijah (Pr4c°), Ezekiel, Daniel (Pr29B†), and Revelation 4 are marked by fire. The Bible personifies the might of God in the beings called angels, some of whom are called seraphs, burning fire-beings. In such passages the biblical writers describe the mysterious power of God as if it were like fire, without which humans cannot survive, but which is always escaping our control.

Fire serves also as a sign of evil. Persian dualism, influential in the thought patterns of the late Hebrew Scriptures, provided the imagery behind biblical legend of the fall of Lucifer (Luke 10:18). The name Lucifer means the bearer of light: the fire that once served God came to serve only itself. Praise turned itself toward destruction, and the fire that was divine became malformed into lightning, a force of evil. Residents of Jerusalem used the imagery of Gehenna, the perpetually burning garbage dump outside the city walls, as a picture of what life would be outside the embrace of the community of faith.

For the most part in the Bible—the book of Job is a marked exception—evil is not inexplicable, random, or the unfortunate result of natural forces. Since God is honored as the ultimate power, even what is perceived as evil must have come from the divine hand. Events such as earthquakes are interpreted as signs of divine displeasure. An angel with a flaming sword prohibits humans from approaching the tree of life. Fire destroys the wicked inhabitants of Sodom and Gomorrah. Fire consumes the Israelites who are complaining against the LORD. The well-known New Testament parable of the sheep and the goats describes eternal punishment as perpetual fire (LastA). Fires will destroy Gog and Magog at the end of time. Hell is described as a lake of fire and sulfur.

Usually in the Bible divine judgment afflicts the enemy, or at least the other guy. The prophetic writings are filled with warnings that God's fiery anger will consume even the chosen people who are unfaithful, and the apocalyptic literature, especially Ezekiel, foretells that at the end of time God's fire will burn up everything that is evil. Because most often divine wrath is targeted at the people outside the gathered religious community, assemblies of the chosen people have sometimes heard these messages as warnings to remain among the insiders, for whom God's fire is a divine blessing, not a devastating punishment. Because God's people enjoy divine favor, fire serves their purposes.

The lectionary takes this tendency another step. The Bible is literature expressing the worldview of the Jewish and early Christian insider, and, further, the lectionary is a selection from that literature meant especially to support and shape the contemporary baptized community. Contemporary theologians are far less sure than ancient people were about the fire of divine wrath, and many who grant its possibility give it minimal attention in proclamation. Because the goal of the lectionary is to proclaim the resurrection in all its fullness, condemnations of the outsider and predictions of divine punishment play a small role throughout the liturgical year.

This pattern is evident in the lectionary's use of Isaiah 66. The lectionary reading (Pr9c[†]) appoints verses 10-14, in which God's city is likened to a comforting nurse and mother. The selection stops before verses 15-16, which foretell the fire of divine fury. Again, the reading from 1 Corinthians 3 (Ep7A) includes verses 10-11,16-23: the omitted verses 12-15 threaten the fire of the day of the Lord. It is as if the lectionary heeds the story in Luke when James and John ask Jesus to rain down fire from heaven on the unbelievers, and Jesus rebukes, not the unbelievers, but the disciples (Pr8c). Currently most Christian churches minimize talk of hell. That the God we know in Christ is a deity overflowing with mercy suggests that the liturgy give little attention to God's punishing fires and no time at all to the perennial human desire for retaliation.

The lectionary includes several stories from ancient religious narrative in which God is seen as fire. We read of the throne of God (LastB) and of the mysterious flames that consume Abraham's sacrifice (Le2c). God's fires will burn away the chaff, threatens John the Baptist (Ad2A, Ad3c). But thanks to the purification wrought by the divine fire, as promised in the book of Malachi (Pr28c), God will keep the faithful ones safe from the fire (VigilABC). The fire on Sinai did not harm the Israelites (Pr19c[†]). The fire in the burning bush promises freedom (Pr17A°), and when the despairing Elijah hears the voice of God, God is in the sound of silence, not what we might expect, in the fire (Pr14A[†], Pr7c°). In a reading from James, the human tongue is likened to destructive fire, while God is described as a spring of water and a thriving fig tree (Pr19B). We, not God, are the fiery destroyers.

One reading in the lectionary superbly conveys the ambivalence of the imagery of divine fire. A passage from Hebrews (Pr16c) states that Christians have come not to the blazing fire that threatens their destruction, but rather to a joyous, perfect heavenly city. Yet the reading concludes with the sentence, "For indeed our God is a consuming fire." God is like fire, but for transformation, rather than destruction.

Several times in the church year, fire is the dominant metaphor throughout the liturgy. On Pentecost we read the story from Acts 2 in which "tongues as of fire" alight on each believer. According to Jewish liturgical practice, Pentecost was the celebration of the giving of the law on Sinai, when God appeared to the people in flames of fire on the mountaintop. Luke narrates the formation of the church by telling of another gift from God. This time fire appears not upon a mountain but upon each believer: the Spirit of God is present now in the people of the community. Fire on our foreheads is a way to say that the law is now written in everyone's hearts.

Fire is implied in the ritual of Ash Wednesday. More and more congregations on a lengthening list of denominations are adopting the imposition of ashes to mark believers at the beginning of Lent. The popularity of this ritual suggests that people are willing, indeed, glad to sign their bodies with a symbol of purification, death, and the hope for rebirth. We are willing, at least once in the year, to admit to the truth of our need for purification. That the ashes come from last year's palms circles the year around and places onto the believer the death-become-life that is the paschal mystery.

The consummate use of fire in the lectionary occurs at the Easter Vigil. As with the imposition of ashes, increasing numbers of Christians are reviving the ancient Easter Vigil as the church's most complete ritual expression of resurrection faith. The current practice of the assembly gathering outdoors to light the fire developed from the northern European pagan practice of inaugurating springtime by kindling a fire on a mountaintop. According to tradition, St. Patrick broke the law by taking to himself the right to kindle this sacred fire and by dedicating it to the resurrected Christ, rather than to the pagan springtime deities. This springtime fire is called by the liturgy "the light of Christ," kindled anew each year by the assembly in the night of Easter, shown high to us all on the paschal candle, and shared around the community with individual candles. In the Exsultet, the poem composed in perhaps the fourth century that praises the resurrection, the fire of the candle is likened to the radiance of God, to the pillar of fire that led the people the promised land, and to "the morning star which never sets," who is Christ. For the Christian, classic religious imagery of the divine is applied to Christ, and at no time more fully than at the Easter Vigil. Although ancient peoples worshiped fire itself, we worship Christ, imaged as the fire in our midst.

Many hymns, especially those suggested for Pentecost, baptism, and celebrations of the ministries of the church, incorporate the imagery of the Holy Spirit as of fire. We see the customary paradox of the image of fire in Bianco da Siena's "Come down, O Love divine." The hymn was written during one of the outbreaks of the Black Plague and was sung by flagellants, the penitents who processed to churches and shrines beating themselves, reciting prayers, and begging divine mercy, for they assumed that the plague was punishment for their sins. Only God's purifying fire could save them from God's avenging fire. However, the burning fire that is God is praised as *comforter*.

As the lectionary and the festivals of the year hold before us flames of fire, it is hoped that we are able to see in those fires an evocation of the gospel itself. All references to fire should recall for Christians both the fire kindled at the Easter Vigil and the fires on the community at Pentecost. The flames symbolize the resurrection of death to life and the transformation of the community by the Spirit of the resurrection. This gospel of Easter and Pentecost continues to flame throughout the year. Christians remind one another in their weekly assembly that the presence of God before us is good news; divine purification is good news; and the proclamation that God's Spirit is dancing on everyone's forehead is good news. Along with the ancients, we gather around the mystery of fire as if it were God. But different from many of the ancients, we recognize in that fire the mercy of God. Even the ash on our foreheads at the beginning of Lent is good news, a reminder that if we hope to have flames of fire on our forehead, some ash will be there as well.

Fish

boat, fish, fishermen,
Jonah, Leviathan, net

Related chapters: CREATION, RESURRECTION OF THE BODY

The biblical use of fish is not only a narrative detail about people's livelihood and menu. Religion in the ancient world used the fish as an image of divine life, which helps account for the connections between the image of fish and Christ's resurrection.

PSALM 104:25-
28

O LORD, how manifold are your works!
    In wisdom you have made them all;
    the earth is full of your creatures.
Yonder is the great and wide sea
with its living things too many to number,
    creatures both small and great.
There move the ships,
and there is that Leviathan,
    which you have made for the sport of it.

BENEDICITE,
OMNIA OPERA

All you powers of the Lord, bless the Lord;
    You whales and all who move in the waters, bless the Lord;
    praise and magnify God forever!

CESÁREO
GABARAIN

You have come down to the lakeshore
seeking neither the wise nor the wealthy,
but only asking for me to follow.

Sweet Lord, you have looked into my eyes,
kindly smiling, you've called out my name.
On the sand I have abandoned my small boat;
now with you, I will seek other seas.

You know full well what I have, Lord:
neither treasure nor weapons for conquest,
just these my fish nets and will for working.

You who have fished other waters;
you, the longing of souls that are yearning:
O loving Friend, you have come to call me.

Thanks to our sacrament of water, by washing away the sins of our early blindness, we are set free and admitted into eternal life. We, little fishes, after the example of our *ichthus* Jesus Christ, are born in water, nor have we safety in any other way than by permanently abiding in water; so that most monstrous creature, who had no right to teach even sound doctrine, knew full well how to kill the little fishes, by taking them away from the water.

TERTULLIAN, *Treatise on Baptism*

The saints will be within their Creator just as the fish in the sea; they will drink all they want, without becoming tired and without lessening the amount of water. The saints will be just like this, for they will drink and eat the great sweetness of God. This sweetness cannot be decreased any more or less than can the water of the sea.

MARGUERITE D'OINGT, *The Mirror*

CONSIDERABLE EVIDENCE INDICATES that in the ancient world many cultures used the fish as a religious symbol. For some coastal societies, cosmogonic myths recognized the water as the source of all life and represented fish as closely connected to the divine. Other peoples were fascinated by the vast numbers of fish eggs, and consequently used fish as a symbol of fecundity. Archaeologists have found instances of fish functioning as symbols of both male and female genitals. From India to Mexico are examples of fish deities or divine mermen and merwomen. Some scholars maintain that the Philistine deity Dagon was depicted as a merman and was understood to be the son of the sea goddess Atargatis. Some historians suggest that in Asia Minor during the Roman Empire, widespread religious cults included the sacrificing of fish. The apocryphal story of Tobit indicates a reverence for the powers of the fish. Guided by the angel Raphael's advice, Tobias is able to banish his fiancee's demons by burning the heart and the liver of a fish and to heal his father of blindness by applying on his eyes the fish's gall.

On the other hand, as the legendary sea monster demonstrates, the fish was also demonized. Assyrian art often depicted the sea monster, a primordial fish that personified chaos and threatened destruction of the people. According to the Babylonian creation story Enuma elish, Marduk, the male warrior, conquers and destroys Tiamat, the female sea monster, and constructs the earth out of her body. This myth identifies the sea with nature and female procreativity. The Tiamat monster is remembered in the Old Testament under the names Rahab and Leviathan. In Psalm 74, the people recall God's mighty power in creation, which included "crushing the heads of Leviathan." According to Psalm 104, God did not need to conquer Leviathan, because God created the monster, for sport. The image of a fish monster continued in medieval church art, where it was common to include a bare-breasted mermaid in depictions of creation, the Garden of Eden, or the flood, as a personification of the chaos of the sea. Some medieval churches included a merman underneath the waters of the Jordan in depictions of Jesus' baptism. So it seems that for millennia, an evil fish has swum about in human imagination.

It is not surprising that fish were used to signify both good and evil, both the creative matrix and the chaos monster. That good and evil are perilously close is something that we like to deny in our daily lives, but that archetypal symbols disclose. The great fish both swallowed up but then granted rebirth to the prophet Jonah, and when Jesus cited this story (Matthew 12:40), he used the belly of the fish as a symbol both of his coming death and of the resurrection. Rabbinic legends display this same pattern when claiming that the main course that will be served at the messianic banquet at the end of time will be the Leviathan, the chaos monster finally conquered, cooked up, and served as food for the people. This ancient identification of the fish turned from evil to good lies behind the contemporary practice of Jewish families serving gefilte fish at the annual seder meal.

In the New Testament, the image of fish is used in two ways. At least four of the twelve disciples—Peter, Andrew, James and John—are described as fishermen who left their nets to follow Jesus (Ep3A, Ep3B, Ep5C). Were this only historic memory rather than symbolization, we would wonder how these unemployed men (and their families?) survived. These narratives mean to underscore the religious conviction that the call of Christ radically alters one's purpose in life. The narratives have given rise to commonplace evangelistic vocabulary that, in preaching the gospel, we are fishing for people.

In several gospel narratives, fish engender a less literal, more symbolic resonance. The miraculous draught of fishes is told twice in the gospels, once in Luke at the call of Peter (Ep5C), and once in John after the resurrection, when Peter is once again called to ministry (Ea3C). These gospel traditions tie together the stories of the miracle of the fish and the call. Perhaps the evangelists retained the Jewish connection between fish and the messianic age. In Jeremiah's description of the return of the exiles (Jeremiah 16:16), God promises that also the fishermen will come back home, and in Ezekiel's dream of the new Jerusalem (Ezekiel 47:9-10), the water flowing from the temple will be filled with fish of a great many kinds, and people will fish from it with nets. Several times the gospels report that Jesus preached to the crowds on shore from a boat (Pr10A, Ep5C).

Over the centuries preachers have tried to interpret the Johannine detail of 153 fish caught in the net. According to the fourth-century biblical scholar Jerome, an ancient zoology text claimed that 153 varieties of fish existed on earth. Contemporary scholars cannot find the reference that Jerome cites: perhaps Jerome fudged a bit here, making up a quote to stress a religious meaning. Augustine's interpretation of the 153 fish is undeniably imaginative. He begins by citing seven as the number of life, completion, and immortality. Seven times seven is 49; plus one, as though to return again to the beginning, gives us fifty, for Pentecost. He then multiplies fifty by three, for the Trinity, and gets 150. Finally he adds three, for the Trinity, and arrives at 153. Although Augustine demonstrates a method of biblical interpretation quite alien to us, his hermeneutical principle is clear: the fish have symbolic meaning.

In other New Testament narratives fish are connected with the messianic age. The gospel accounts of the multiplication of loaves (Pr13A, Pr12B) include fish as the food Christ serves on the mountain. In two resurrection appearances (Ea3B, Ea3C) Jesus eats fish with the disciples. In John's account, Jesus even cooks the fish. The tie between a fish meal and the life of Christ might be traced to Old Testament allusions to fish at the end-time, Roman cults of sacred fish meals, or historic memories connecting Jesus with fish suppers.

The early church often used the image of the fish. Fish appear in catacomb art, suggesting a connection between the fish and the resurrected Christ. One particularly striking room in the Roman catacomb of San Sebastiano depicts in a series of pictures the entire story of Jonah and the fish. Several depictions of the eucharist show a fish on the paten. In one, Christ the Fish is shown on the anchor of the cross, with smaller fish, representing Christians, swimming nearby. Legend has it that a Syrian Christian realized that the Greek word for fish, *ichthus*, was also an acrostic for "Jesus Christ, God's Son, Savior," and so provided an extremely popular symbol for Christians, seen on ancient sarcophaguses and automobile bumper stickers alike. The ichthus remains an important liturgical symbol. Many churches include the image of the fish in stained glass, on wall paintings, and on vestments and paraments.

The art on many ancient baptismal fonts depicted fish, and baptismal catechesis of early centuries utilized the imagery of fish. Often cited is Tertullian's reference to Christians as little fishes and Christ our ichthus. Mystics wrote metaphors incorporating the image of the fish. Ecclesiastical iconography appropriated the symbol of the fisher for Peter. The pagan myth of the Fisher King became Christianized into the grail legend. In the Christian version, the wounded Fisher King, who heals the land, has become merged with Christ. Given the positive biblical references to the eating of fish, it is odd that medieval practice gave the Christian fish dinner a wholly penitential character. In parts of pagan Europe, fish was eaten on Fridays to celebrate the fecundity of the sea goddess, and some Jews ate fish on Fridays in anticipation of both the sabbath and the eschaton. Perhaps it was the socioeconomic reality—meat was expensive—that accounted for the medieval association of fish with penance.

For many contemporary worshipers, many if not all symbolic references

are unknown. Nowadays fishing is either an increasingly precarious livelihood, due to reduced stocks and the government's ecological regulations; or
fishing is a pleasurable pastime, in which the necessity of securing food has
turned into a relaxing activity devoid of any goal except itself. It is apparent,
then, that if the image of fish is to have much religious meaning for today's
church, considerable interpretive creativity is required. We are baptized by
God's water, and we survive in God, as fish in the sea. The archetypal danger, in ancient times called the sea monster and now described as a shark,
need no longer terrorize us. Like Jonah, we can be sustained by God's life
through what we assumed was death. One image of the Trinity is of three
fish fanning out from a shared single head. The good news is the fish can
evoke for us God's creation, Christ the ichthus, and the Spirit of the meal of
the resurrection. Where there is the image of fish, there is God.

Food

banquet, barley loaves, Bethlehem,
bread, fast, feast, manna, milk and honey,
salt, wine, wineskins

Related chapters: FISH, HARVEST

The most common biblical image is food. God gives all living
creatures their food; God feeds the church at the eucharist; Christ
is called Bread; feeding the hungry is a fundamental description of
the Christian life. The Bible describes God's beneficence as feast,
God's displeasure as famine, and our penitence as fasting. The
church is called to actualize the image of bread in both its liturgy
and its daily life.

PSALM 119:103   How sweet are your words to my taste!
           They are sweeter than honey to my mouth.

EUCHARISTIC   We implore you mercifully to accept our praise and thanks-
PRAYER   giving, and, with your Word and Holy Spirit, to bless us,
your servants, and these your own gifts of bread and wine;
that we and all who share in the body and blood of your
Son may be filled with heavenly peace and joy.

17TH CENTURY   O Bread of life from heaven,
LATIN HYMN   O Food to pilgrims given,
O Manna from above:
Feed with the blessed sweetness
of your divine completeness
the souls that want and need your love.

Come then, and let us hasten to the mystical Supper. This day Christ receives us as his guests. This day Christ waits upon us; Christ the lover of all humankind gives us refreshment. The fattened calf is slaughtered. The Lamb of God who takes away the sin of the world is slain. The divine gifts are set before us. The mystical table is prepared. The life-giving chalice is mingled. God the Word incarnate entertains us. Wisdom, who has built herself a house, distributes his body as her bread, and gives his blood as her wine to us to drink. O fearful mystery! O ineffable work of the divine Wisdom! Life bestows itself on mortals as food and drink. You have tasted the fruits of disobedience. Taste now the food of obedience.

Eat of me, who am life, he exhorts us. Eat of life which never comes to an end. Eat my bread: for I am the life-giving grain of the wheat. Suck the fatness of my divine food, and grow fat.

CYRIL OF ALEXANDRIA, HOMILY 10

You, eternal Father, are the table that offers us as food the Lamb, your only-begotten Son. He is the most exquisite of foods for us, both in his teaching, which nourishes us in your will, and in the sacrament that we receive in holy communion, which feeds and strengthens us. And the Holy Spirit is indeed a waiter for us, who serves us charity for our neighbors.

CATHERINE OF SIENA, PRAYER 12

No single religious image is more common, obvious, and yet multivalent than the image of food. On a literal level, food is what humans require for life. Thus religious communities since the earliest records of religion have appealed to the deities for food. Sometimes the nature of these appeals was regional, because the inhabitants of each geographical locale require a unique combination of soil and seed, weather and herd, for there to be enough food for the community. The move to monotheism afforded one deity power over all food availability, no matter where the people lived. Food shared between persons signifies an acknowledgment of shared life: thus come about religious rules regulating what and with whom we are to eat.

On a symbolic level, good food became an image for everything that we need from God. The phrase *mother's milk*, originally referring to the infant's drink from its mother, later became a metaphor for all the sustenance and care of a parent, and eventually came to signify any desired necessity. In the same way, the image of food evokes not only nutrition, but all the good that only God can give. Similarly, bad food functions in myth and legend as a symbol of evil: the poisoned apple for Snow White and the candy treats for Hansel and Gretel are two of many examples in folklore in which food promises death rather than life.

Because the image of food is so ordinary, the task for those who use the lectionary need not be, in this case, to trace obscure details about the original meaning and usage of the image, but rather to comprehend the immensity of the image. Let us consider one example. In Genesis 1, an essential part of the creation is God's designation of plants as food: God gives both animals and humans the breath of life and every green plant for food. In Genesis 2, the LORD God gives the man the fruit of all the trees of the garden, presumably also the tree of life, excepting only the tree of knowledge of good and evil. In Genesis 3, illicit food symbolizes the archetypal temptation, and when the man and the woman are expelled from the garden so that they will not be able to eat from the tree of life, the man is required to till the ground for their food. In Genesis 4, the sacrifices presented by both Cain and Abel are foodstuffs, the products of the farmer and the herder. It is startling that it is Cain, the son obeying the expectation to till the soil, who offers an unacceptable sacrifice. Thus in each of these primordial tales, food is a central image. One could page through the entire Bible extending this exercise, traveling through scripture as if it were a colossal grocery store.

Judaism was always and remains to this day an essentially down-to-earth religion. What God gives is life here and now. Jesus is speaking in a familiarly Jewish way when he urges his followers to trust in God for their food (Pr3A). Just as God feeds the birds, so God will feed the people. One of the most significant among the Jewish ancestral memories is that even during their nomadic decades in the Sinai, when the people could not till the ground for food, God provided the miraculous food of manna (Pr20A°, Pr13B†). Exodus treats the word *manna* as if it were a pun. Literally meaning "What is it?" *manna* comes to denote "bread given by God." It is as if food from God is the believers' answer to the fundamental human inquiry, "What is this?"

Ancient Judaism interpreted the scarcity of bread as divine punishment. The reign of King Ahab and Queen Jezebel brought on famine, and only the hospitable widow of Zarephath, who was willing to share her last piece of bread, was granted by God a continuous supply of food (Pr27B†, Pr5c°). The saga of Joseph is an example of divine providence in the face of famine. Because Joseph was faithful, he, his hungry family, and all of Egypt were able to eat (Pr15A°, Ep7c). Because eating is a partaking of the goodness of God, fasting indicates that the supplicant sought divine forgiveness. The idea is that the people who are fasting are practicing death: they are signifying their ultimate dependence on God by minimizing their natural dependence on food. So the community is asked to sanctify a fast as part of its plea for divine forgiveness (AshWABC).

Just as famine was a sign of divine testing, the joys of a feast were gifts from God. The promised land is repeatedly described as flowing with milk and honey (Pr17A°, Pr26B†), that is, a land in which good foods, both staples and treats, are plentiful. One reading appointed as a proclamation of the resurrection (VigilABC) is the poem from Isaiah 55, in which God promises a feast of rich food and wines, free to all who come. An alternate reading for Easter Day (B) is the poem from Isaiah 25, in which God promises that on the mountaintop a "feast of rich food, a feast of well-aged wines" will be spread on that great and final day of salvation.

Throughout the Hebrew Scriptures, food is used as a metaphor for the word of God. In the poem about Wisdom in the book of Proverbs (VigilABC), she is serving up a meal of bread and wine to all who along with her rely on the promises of life from God. The tales of the wise and faithful Daniel begin with a narrative version of this same idea, that we are to be nourished by God's word. Daniel and his three friends refused to eat the food served up in the court of the pagan king. After eating only vegetables and water, "they appeared better and fatter than all the young men who had been eating the royal rations" (Daniel 1:15). As the psalm has it, God's word is our honey.

Especially significant in Judaism is the sharing of food within the human community. Because food was recognized as the gift of life from God, with whom one ate became important: sharing food implied sharing God's life. Anthropologists use the term *commensality* to refer to the phenomenon in a culture of sometimes elaborate rules about what one can eat with whom. Recall that the Egyptians would not eat with the Israelites (Genesis 43:32). During the American civil rights protests, the laws about different races not eating together at lunch counters illustrated that people can be passionately concerned about who is welcomed at their table. This ancient fear of contamination by strangers at table probably accounts for the current hesitancy among some Christians to share a eucharistic cup with persons with AIDS. The use of individual drinking glasses at communion suggests not so much reasoned and rigorous hygienic practice as archetypal patterns of commensality that stand up poorly in light of Christ's eating habits.

An important story in the Hebrew Scriptures about commensality is the meal at Mamre. At Mamre, Abraham thinks that he is graciously hosting a meal for three strangers, only to discover that as they talk, God is conversing with him and promising that Sarah will bear her longed-for child (Pr6A°, Pr11c[†]). Thus food offered a stranger becomes a meal of promise shared with God. Eastern Orthodox Christians, especially, have revered this narrative as a way to depict the church's life with the Trinity. Painted by Andrei Rublev, the most famed icon of this meal at Mamre presents three mysterious figures sitting at a table on which is a single large chalice at the bottom of which is a tiny lamb. As we gaze at the icon, we are drawn into it, joining the circle of the Three, sharing the cup of life with God.

The primary food narrative in the Old Testament is the passover story. What developed into the annual passover celebration was a conflation of two quite different ritual practices: the springtime sacrifice of the first of the flock as a gift to the deities, priming the divine pump for the fertility of the herds; and a springtime feast within the community, sharing food from God. As with most Jewish festivals, the historical memory of the people provided a third overlay. Not only does God give the herd new lambs and the community its meal; God also gives freedom to the oppressed. For Israelites and their contemporary descendants the Jews, the seder is an elaborate family meal, at which the menu carries symbolic meaning. The lectionary appoints the description of the passover meal for the outset of the Triduum (MThABC), not only because the synoptic gospels say that Jesus' meal with the disciples before his arrest was a passover celebration. More significant than that, the Christian rites of Holy Week, like the Jewish passover, are the annual celebration recalling divine salvation. Christians hold before themselves their slain Lamb, his blood on their door, its meal of shared life, and the promise of freedom for the oppressed. Jews and Christians alike learn from this annual ritual that all meals are memories of God's salvation, yet another course of the banquet God alone can serve.

The more we see the role that food played in biblical Judaism, the more we understand what the New Testament is saying about Jesus Christ. Jesus was born in Bethlehem, a word that means "house of bread." He preached that his followers are to be food for others, salt in the world (Ep5A), that without which humans cannot survive. The sermon on the mount records Jesus as preaching that we are to give food to any who ask (Ep5A). In each of the gospels, Jesus enacts the miracle of manna yet again by miraculously providing food to the thousands in the desert (Pr13A, Pr12B, Pr13B). Many medieval churches displayed in parallel depictions the manna falling from heaven onto the Israelites and the bread Jesus shared with the multitudes. Oftentimes the artists drew the bread in the two pictures identically, resembling the wafers served at eucharist.

As the lectionary makes clear in year B, it is not only that Christ provides the bread. Rather, according to John's striking symbolic language, Christ is the bread (Pr14B, Pr15B, Pr16B). Not only does the church eat bread from God; we also eat bread that we recognize as being God's very self. Eating this bread we come to realize that all our life, like all our bread, comes from God, and that with God our life is full, bread or not. Christ is the incarnation of God's gift of bread.

Many preachers complain that in the summertime of year B the lectionary dedicates five full weeks to the Johannine discourse on Christ the bread. Yet the variation of details, especially for those churches that use the complementary Old Testament readings, offer a rich fare for these tables. Proper 12 cites the story of Elisha's multiplication of barley loaves, undoubtedly the reference behind John's stipulation that the loaves were barley, the bread of the poor. Proper 13, citing the exodus story of manna and quails, focuses on Christ as the new manna. Proper 14, citing the story about Elijah's miraculous meal before his forty-day journey to the mount of God, uses the imagery of the cycle of life and death and the journey between earth and heaven as language to describe the Christian life. Proper 15 cites Wisdom's banquet of bread and wine as it describes Christian eucharist. This week would be an appropriate occasion to describe the figure of Wisdom, who is making her comeback in newly composed hymns and prayers. Proper 16, citing the narrative of the covenant at Shechem, concludes the Johannine discourse with

Peter's creed: "Lord, to whom can we go? You have the words of eternal life," and we are back once again to the bread, the milk and honey, who is Christ.

The New Testament also utilizes the image of the feast. The beloved parable of the prodigal son concludes with a grand feast that the father provides for the wicked runaway (Le5C). Several of Jesus' parables of the kingdom are situated at a wedding feast (Pr23A, Pr17C). Such feasts are characterized by excess of food and drink in the sharing, but in Judaism find their deep religious resonance by recalling the promise of the messianic banquet. So it is that many of the post-resurrection appearances in Luke and John include eating (Ea3A, Ea3B, Ea3C). That Christ served up a breakfast of fish to the disciples recalls the Jewish legend that at the messianic banquet, the main course would be fish—the sea monster Leviathan cooked up and eaten. Just like the Jews of old, so Christians also encounter the saving God while at table.

The narratives concerning Jesus' eating habits are seen by many biblical exegetes as pivotal events leading up to his trial and execution. It appears from the New Testament that Jesus broke all the rules of commensality. By the turn of the common era, probably in an attempt to keep themselves wholly Jewish and uncontaminated by Hellenistic society, strictly observant Jewish men would not eat with those variously described as sinners: tax collectors, herdsmen, peddlers, tanners, Gentiles, Samaritans, the physically deformed, the ignorant and illiterate masses, and, to a certain extent, women. The stories of Jesus record his transgressing these boundaries time after time, eating with undesirable people as if they were equals. Such disregard for the conventions of commensality was religiously shocking, especially when, for orthodox Jews, sharing food with others implied sharing God with them. As well, Jesus broke sabbath rules about food preparation and hygienic rules about hand-washing. Perhaps the gospel reading in which this aspect of Jesus' ministry is most evident is at the beginning of Mark (Pr3B). Jesus is dining with tax collectors and sinners, refusing to participate in religiously appropriate fasts, likening himself to the groom at a wedding, and warning that his new wine will not be able to be contained by old wineskins. Those of his listeners who knew their Hebrew Scriptures would have found these claims at least startling, and perhaps also sacrilegious.

So it is at a meal that the church has assembled weekly since the first century. Admittedly, sharing with one another and God the bread and wine of Christ did not always resemble a meal, and a tiny wafer with little or no wine is a far cry from the meals that Jesus shared. We ought not forget that Jesus was accused of being a glutton and drunkard. Much of the Christian liturgical reform of the twentieth century was rooted in a rediscovery that eucharist is giving thanks over food, and many liturgical changes were aimed at making the bread and wine resonate more fully and clearly with all the biblical stories of God's gift of food. The persistence of medieval practices that obscure the origin of eucharist as food shared with Christ shows how resistant religious people are, of whatever century or religion, to altering their eating habits. Let us hope that in the course of this new century the weekly meal of Christians will become more of what it ought to be: a realistic image of God's gift of food, a profound symbol of the messianic banquet, the first serving from which the leftovers are brought to those who were absent, and the inspiration of substantial contributions for the hungry of the world. Perhaps it is time for congregations to separate donations for the maintenance of the church itself from contributions for the hungry, the better to proclaim to the world that God is food for all.

Christian eucharist makes clear that we eat the food of Christ with one another. The food is shared around the table. Thus a liturgical design in which communicants encircle the table is perhaps the most appropriate, and liturgical practice in which standing participants look at one another around the table, seeing those with whom they share God's food, is a worthy reform. The food comes not solely to me, but to us: the *you* in biblical passages that echoes in liturgical texts is a plural *you*. The messianic promise that all the hungry of the world will be fed makes the church reach out to feed others and to send food to all those who are absent, members and strangers alike. In that we share food with one another and with the hungry world, we experience the Trinity: not only God as creator of food and Christ as the food we share, but also the Spirit, alive in the community and eager to embrace yet more people in the divine circle of life.

That this weekly meal is called *eucharist*, "thanksgiving," should lead Christians to more regular thanksgiving at every table. The second-century martyr Justin, in describing the Christian movement to pagans, wrote, "We always give thanks"; that is, the weekly eucharist was not the only, but rather the most elaborate, of the phenomenon of Christians giving thanks. The regular thanksgiving of Christians over food flows into a habit of thanksgiving, the practice of seeing God as the food we need, and of being grateful.

In recent decades some Christians have sponsored passover seders. The reasons behind this practice are understandable. Many Christians attending a Jewish seder are delighted by the complexity of its symbolic referents, as well as with the religious conviviality of the ritual, and many are fascinated to learn what the meal may have meant to first-century Jews. Yet the notion of Christians hosting a seder is to be resisted. The seder is the holiest ritual event in the lives of devout practicing Jews: it is not an object lesson for curious Christians. Scholars have demonstrated that the contemporary seder is a medieval development that can tell us litle about Jesus' meal practice. Whatever constituted the seder during the first century developed in two parallel though distinct directions: one was to the medieval and contemporary Jewish seder, and the other was to the church's Easter Vigil.

For Christians, the annual Vigil meal, held the night of Easter, is, just like for the Jews, the celebration of God's salvation and the sharing of its joy with the community. For Christians, the primary example of salvation is the resurrection of Christ, rather than the exodus, and the community is the baptized assembly, rather than the family. The task for Christians in this century is, perhaps inspired by study of the Jewish seder, to reenliven our own annual ritual of God's salvation by celebrating the Easter Vigil with the symbolic complexity that it deserves. That a full seder takes hours to complete intrigues many people: however, so does an abundantly celebrated Easter Vigil. Excellent videos are available for those Christians who wish to learn about the seder practice of contemporary Jews.

Many contemporary issues relate to the image of food. Perhaps because nobody wishes to insult Christians who are overweight, little attention is given in the church to the disparity between America's excess of food, with its increase of obesity and consumption of junk food, and the millions of the world's peoples who are hungry or starving. The rise of vegetarianism in the developed world is a welcome symbol of the concern among some of the wealthy of the world to eat lower on the food chain. It is interesting that the idyllic poem of Genesis 1 indicates that God intended humans to be vegetarians. God is our food, and in the Christian tradition we recognize the holiness of food, not by overeating, but rather by sharing that food of God with the hungry.

Some Christians are reviving Lenten fasts, with one or another religious emphasis. In some cases the ritual serves as a penitential practice, a diminishment of the self before God. In other rituals, the point is our identification with the hungry, similar to the hunger meals served at summer camps and religious retreats, in which the participants are randomly selected either to be seated at table with candles and served an elaborate four-course dinner, or to be crowded onto the floor in a corner of the room and handed a bowl of oatmeal. Any use of religious fasting, however, should include an awareness of the phenomenon in our culture of crazy eating, either too much food or too little food, obesity or anorexia, and be sure that the ritual practice makes supremely clear its Christian intent.

The good news is that God gives food. The food that comes from God is as essential to our life as is milk for the infant, and the celebration of food in a shared feast is a fundamental way that humans create and nurture community. As the book of Ruth describes, in a time of famine a few destitute women were able to glean the leftover barley harvest, and from this food came the joy of a wedding and a newborn child Obed, who became the grandfather of King David. The eucharistic liturgy is based upon the claims that food from God brings life to the community and that the life of our community is food from God. It is easy to say that God gives food. The saints remind us of the further step, that God is the food we need.

Garden

Eden, garden, Gethsemane,
Mary Magdalene, wilderness

Related chapters: HARVEST, MARRIAGE, TREE

Ancient desert societies used the image of the garden to depict
paradise or the monarch's abode. For many Christians, the garden
was the antithesis of the wilderness and so symbolized spiritual
fulfillment. In the lectionary, the garden is paradoxical: the garden
of Eden and the garden in John's passion are sites of both life and
death.

PSALM 92:12-13   Those who are planted in the house of the LORD
       shall flourish in the courts of our God;
they shall still bear fruit in old age;
       they shall be green and succulent.

OFFERTORY   The earth is filled with the fruit of your work.
VERSE,   You cause the grass to grow for the cattle,
PROPER 14   and plants for us to cultivate,
that we may bring forth food from the earth
       and wine to gladden our hearts,
oil to make our faces shine
       and bread to strengthen our hearts.

JAROSLAV J.   God, you made this world a garden,
VAJDA   every harvest bearing seed.
Loving God, today as ever
you anticipate our need;
you are ready with your answer
long before we plead.

Take us through that other garden,
tragic, dark Gethsemane,
where our Savior faced our future,
set to win our amnesty:
Seed of woman, Seed of promise
from a barren tree.

Now a universal garden,
seeded with your living Word,
grows with peace and love and beauty,
songs of freedom there are heard;
by your mercy, by your Spirit,
thankful hearts are stirred.

One day between Easter and Ascension I went into the garden before Prime, and, sitting down beside the pond, I began to consider what a pleasant place it was. I was charmed by the clear water and flowing streams, and the fresh green of the surrounding trees, the birds flying so freely about, especially the doves. I asked myself what more was needed to complete my happiness in a place that seemed to me so perfect, and I reflected that it was the presence of a friend, intimate, affectionate, wise, and companionable, to share my solitude. And then you, my God, source of ineffable delights, did but inspire the beginning of this meditation to lead it back to yourself.

GERTRUDE
OF HELFTA,
*The Herald of
Divine Love*

We are a garden walled around,
chosen and made peculiar ground,
a little spot inclosed by grace
out of the world's wide wilderness.

ISAAC WATTS

Let my Beloved come, and taste
his pleasant fruits at his own feast.
"I come, my Spouse, I come," he cries,
with love and pleasure in his eyes.

Our Lord into his garden comes,
well pleased to smell our poor perfumes,
and calls us to a feast divine,
sweeter than honey, milk or wine.

A GARDEN IS A SMALL PLOT of cultivated nature. We distinguish a garden from a forest, which is not cultivated; and from a field, which is large and planted with a single crop; and from a nursery, which grows plants for sale. A garden is usually near a dwelling, and it requires considerable care. In the garden grow flowers for human enjoyment or vegetables for family use. A garden is nature domesticated, designed to provide people with pleasure and to meet their needs.

Judaism, Christianity, and Islam arose in a desert climate. By contrast, any garden that produced flowers, fruit trees, and vegetables implied a ready supply of water. Such abundant water contrasted starkly with the daily drudge of usually the women hauling back from the well just enough water to meet the family's needs. The garden described in Genesis 2, which like other mythological paradises is located at the center of the world, is set at the source of four rivers. These rivers are said to have watered the entire earth, lying right-angled as a sign of the ordering of nature for human needs.

The ancient world offers many examples of the garden as the symbol of abundant life. In some stories, the deities reside in a garden; in others, the original human paradise was a garden, with convenient food and plentiful water. In the Qur'an, heaven is described as a magnificent garden. The hanging gardens of Babylon symbolized the superiority of its culture over neighboring peoples. Some monarchs owned a spectacular garden, its walled luxuriance a demonstration of the wealth of the crown and a constant reminder of the distance between the life of privilege and the peasants' daily grind. Usually the garden included a fountain in its center, further symbolizing the ease of life the monarch enjoyed. Egyptian tomb paintings often showed houses with gardens, perhaps a reference to life after death.

The Bible does not talk much about gardens, perhaps because neither the nomadic life nor the harvests typical of an agricultural economy make much of what we call gardens. However, in the Old Testament, kings enjoyed private gardens. King Ahab steals land from Naboth to use for the palace vegetable garden; several wicked kings, Manasseh and Amon, are buried in their palace gardens; the weeklong banquet at which King Ahasuerus entertains his male friends takes place in the palace garden. It fits with the biblical theme of justice for the poor that none of these palace gardens is a site of God's gracious activity. In Isaiah, gardens are cited as the location of idolatrous sacrifices. The books of Joel and Amos, in describing the plagues of locusts that God sends in judgment to an unfaithful people, state that the gardens have been destroyed. According to several passages in Ezekiel, the splendid gardens of the enemy kings of Tyre and Egypt resemble God's paradise.

Several Old Testament poetic passages use the image of the garden as a metaphor for the good life. Some exilic poetry promises that the Jews' life in exile, like their harsh years in the wilderness, will become again like the abundant life in God's watered garden. The biblical book that most exploits the image of the garden is the Song of Songs. The woman and her lover, the king, meet in a paradise-like garden. The lovers' ecstasy, like the garden itself, is richly described with imagery of flowers such as rose of Sharon and lily, and trees such as apple, fig, palm, and pomegranate. Not only is the king's garden a private walled enclosure, the walled garden serves also as a metaphor for the female womb (4:12) and the fecundity of sexual love. Some interpreters suggest that the Song of Songs presented a critique of the Genesis tradition, by situating ecstacy, rather than evil, in the garden.

It was through a tradition of interpretation of the Song of Songs that garden imagery became important in medieval Western Christianity. Because the Song of Songs is an explicit sexual poem that does not even mention God, it was as an allegory that the church fathers found its religious meaning. The lovers were Christ and the church, or God and the human soul. Bernard of Clairvaux wrote 86 lengthy sermons on the Song of Songs, indicating the extraordinary interest that medieval monastics had for the poem. Many cloistered monasteries laid out their community's buildings around a garden with a fountain in the center. The garden was enclosed by a pillared walkway, with each pillar carved to represent a tree. Thus the monastery pictured itself as returning to the garden of paradise. The community was removed from worldly sins and, influenced by the teaching of Jerome, the monks imagined themselves as living an asexual existence like Adam in Eden before the fall.

Because of the story in John 20 of Christ's appearance to Mary Magdalene, much medieval church art used garden imagery to depict the resurrection. For example, the sequence of biblical pictures called the Biblia Pauperum, much reproduced in the thirteenth, fourteenth, and fifteenth centuries in books and on church walls, depicts the resurrection in two sets of scenes. First, in a picture illustrating Matthew 26, the women are looking in the tomb and find it empty. This story is shown parallel to Song of Songs 3:1, "I sought him whom my soul loves, but found him not." In the second set of scenes illustrating John 20, Christ appears to Mary Magdalene, and this narrative was made parallel to Song of Songs 3:4, "I found him whom my soul loves." Christ is encountered in the burial garden; Christ, the first of the new creation, appears as a gardener.

A comment here about Mary Magdalene: When in the sixth century Pope Gregory taught that the penitent of Luke 7 was a prostitute who was also Mary Magdalene of John 20, the way was prepared for centuries of homilies and artistic representations of the prostitute Mary Magdalene who in faith replaced sexual love with adoration of the risen Christ. Careful biblical reading demonstrates that Gregory's simplification was wrong. Fascination with sexuality being what it is, mistaken depictions of Mary Magdalene abounded, and still are popular in religious imagery; not only in high art, for example, Fra Angelico's painting in the Dominican friary in Florence, but also in popular art, such as Hollywood movies. In the song "I come to the garden alone," the person walking in the garden, waiting for the lover's talk in her ear, is Mary Magdalene. We do best, when we proclaim John 20:1-18 (VigilABC or EaABC), and when we commemorate Mary Magdalene on July 22, to avoid altogether the medieval notion that she was a prostitute, and rely rather on the biblical testimony that in the garden she was the first witness to the resurrection and, as the early church said, the apostle to the apostles.

In the lectionary, garden is neither wholly bad, the unjust domain of the wicked king, nor wholly good, the ecstatic paradise of the lovers' tryst. The two main references in the lectionary to a garden occur in Genesis 2–3 (Le1A, Pr5B[†]) and in the Johannine passion and resurrection (GFrABC, EaABC). Each deserves careful attention.

Similar to many ancient Near Eastern myths, Genesis describes God's original paradise for humans as a garden. Like other gardens of God, Eden is the source of the world's four rivers and offers plentiful fruit for the animals and humans living there. However, the description of Eden includes reference to the tree of knowledge of good and evil and to a place where there is good gold, and the reader senses that trouble is coming. In the biblical tradition, even the original paradise is two-sided: in the middle of the garden is a mysterious tree, with fruit that occasions the complexity of human consciousness and a serpent who talks us into death.

So it is that the Bible knows no mythical perfection. If humans are there, so is ambivalence. The canonical Old Testament, although occasionally referring to the garden of God, never once refers to the story of Adam and Eve. Jews usually claim Abraham, not Adam, as their progenitor. The New Testament does not refer to a primordial garden. In Romans, Paul contrasts Adam with Christ, and in 1 Timothy a Christian author condemns women as inheritors of Eve's guilt. It is clear that a mythical paradise is not a domi-nant idea in the Jewish and Christian scriptures.

The lectionary appoints the Johannine account of Christ's death and res-urrection to be read each year. In contrast to the synoptic gospels, the Gospel of John refers to the olive grove of Gethsemane as a garden (John 18:1), and to Christ's burial site as a garden (19:41). Only John uses garden language to describe the site of Christ's betrayal and burial, which like the wicked kings' gardens, symbolizes injustice. Christ is buried in a garden with excessive monarchical extravagance: John 19:39 mentions a hundred pounds of myrrh and aloes. Yet this burial garden, surprisingly, becomes the place of the resurrection, the new life of Christ springing up for the community. If Eden seemed a paradise in which we find death lurking, John's garden is a place of betrayal and death, from which is born life for all the world.

The biblical image that stands opposite the garden is the wilderness. A formative Israelite memory was the forty years of wilderness wanderings. The Sinai desert meant scarce food and water. That Jesus' ministry began with forty days in the wilderness (Le1a, Le1b, Le1c) means to recapitulate the history of Israel. Jesus' temptation in the wilderness was not a monthlong religious retreat. Rather, like Israel, Jesus lived a precarious existence, wan-dering in the wilderness far from any mythic garden of God.

The church found the wilderness imagery useful. Although medieval monasticism chose the image of the garden for its communal life, earlier monks and nuns understood their stark existence to be a return to the wilder-ness. Antony became a hermit in the desert, hoping to escape the evils of the world. Life in the wilderness meant complete reliance on God, and so daily life exemplified religious faith. For some spiritualities, Lent became the time of year that, like Israel and Jesus in the wilderness, we turn away from all that fosters death and instead await the coming life from God in the garden of Easter. Giving up something was a sign of choosing life in the wilderness.

Our technological urban culture is finding the image of the wilderness enormously popular. Trekking into the wilderness takes many forms in our society, from daylong family hikes in the woods, to death-defying attempts to survive alone as far as possible from human civilization. When the wilderness finds its way into Christian imagination, it is important to remember that in the Bible the wilderness is neither a pleasant vacation spot nor a hazardous solo adventure. The wilderness is the place where, whether alone or with the entire community, one stands with God in the struggle to resist evil.

In the nineteenth century, urban development made it less possible for Christians to use their churchyards as the place of Christian burial. Instead, churches began constructing garden-like cemeteries on the outskirts of town. A twentieth-century version of the burial garden took the form of columbarium gardens on church property. With artistic plantings and memorial sculptures, garden cemeteries mean to suggest the paradise of heaven that the dead were now enjoying and to soften our horror in thinking of death. Many people judge that American culture carried the sanitizing of death too far, however, and many churches are reexamining current burial practices to evaluate how we ritualize and recall death. For the believing Christian, death need not be covered over with a garden. In Christ the community can face death with realism; we can say "die," rather than "pass away." Yet in Christ even death can be pictured as a garden, a place redeemed by God's merciful life.

The task for Christian interpretation of the garden image is to keep it from becoming flat and one-dimensional. Especially in an urban culture, people's minimal experience with gardens can lead to a sentimentalizing of the symbol. In the garden as Christians encounter it, the tree of knowledge of good and evil stands alongside the tree of life. We meet Christ where he was buried. Here is gospel: We discover that the cemetery is a garden, the wilderness is a garden. The proclamation is that in the place of death, God gives life for all the people to enjoy.

Harvest

firstfruits, harvest, passover, vineyard

Related chapters: Day of the Lord, Garden

Biblical writers, living in an agricultural economy, often used the image of the harvest. Passover, Pentecost, and Booths were religious festivals overlaid onto the agricultural calendar of harvest times. Because soil was poor and rainfall scarce, God was credited with a bountiful harvest, and the image of harvest evoked all of God's gifts.

PSALM 65:10,
12, 14

You prepare the grain,
    for so you provide for the earth.
You crown the year with your goodness,
    and your paths overflow with plenty.
May the meadows cover themselves with flocks,
and the valleys cloak themselves with grain;
    let them shout for joy and sing.

OFFERTORY
VERSE

Let the vineyards be fruitful, Lord,
and fill to the brim our cup of blessing.
Gather a harvest from the seeds that were sown,
that we may be fed with the bread of life.

HENRY ALFORD

Come, you thankful people, come,
raise the song of harvest home.
All is safely gathered in
ere the winter storms begin.
God, our maker, does provide
for our wants to be supplied.
Come to God's own temple, come,
raise the song of harvest home.

Even so, Lord, quickly come
to your final harvest home.
Gather all your people in,
free from sorrow, free from sin,
there, forever purified,
in your garner to abide.
Come, with all your angels, come,
raise the glorious harvest home!

Just as the bread broken was first scattered on the hills, then was gathered and became one, so let your church be gathered from the ends of the earth into your kingdom.

THE DIDACHE

One day, quite an influential man in the community urged me to speak from Micah 4:13: "Arise and thresh, O daughter of Zion." I took his desire to the Lord, and was permitted to speak from the passage after this manner: In 710 B.C. corn was threshed among the Oriental by means of oxen or horses, which were driven round an area filled with loose sheaves. By their continued tramping the corn was separated from the straw. (Corn is not threshed in this manner by us, but by means of flails, so that I feel I am doing no injury to the sentiment of the text by changing a few of the terms into those which are the most familiar to us now.) The passage has a direct reference to all God's people who were and are commanded to arise and thresh. They are commanded to go to God, who alone is able to qualify them for their labors by making their horns iron and their hoofs brass. The gospel flail should be lifted up in a kind and loving spirit. To the glory of God I wish to say that the unconverted man who gave me the text gave his heart to God, together with many others, before we left Detroit.

JULIA A. J. FOOTE, *A Brand Plucked from the Fire*

In our society, the time of harvest is experienced entirely differently by different people. Urban residents, shopping in fully stocked grocery stores year-round, can be oblivious of the cyclical pattern of seedtime and harvest. What with refrigeration and international commerce, grocery stores give the impression that food of all varieties is perpetually available. Meanwhile, rural farmers, although they too may grocery-shop, are economically dependent on harvest, and so they are continuously attuned to the vagaries of growth and production. It is likely that the medieval practice of the Lenten fast was a spiritualizing of the fact that in late winter, Europeans were running out of food. Today, in developed countries, we know about such scarcity of food mostly by watching television news, where we witness the reality that drought and disaster still destroy harvests, and countless people with them.

Israel's ancient memories were of a nomadic past and a herding economy. The Bible's first story of the antagonism between the herder and the farmer, Abel and Cain, suggests that even God prefers the herder. Yet archaeologists demonstrated that grains (barley and wheat) and legumes (lentils and peas) were cultivated in Palestine since about 7000 B.C.E. From 3000 B.C.E., farming also included fruits, olives, figs, dates, and pomegranates. The herder may have been the mainstay in the past, but the Israelite people were kept alive by agriculture and were dependent on a successful harvest. Thus harvesttime was of central importance to the community. Later, urbanized Israelite society added pressure on the rural farmer to produce enough food for everyone, a fact that was likely one of the major grievances of the Palestinian peasant in New Testament times. Neither in the past nor the present is it accurate to romanticize the precarious lifestyle of the small farmer.

A famous harvest story in the Bible is one of no harvest, the famine that forces Joseph's clan to move to Egypt. In the ancient Near East, hierarchical governing systems were able to amass and store food in cities. Yet it is not Egypt's wealth and organizational capabilities that are seen as saving Israel. Rather, credit is given to God who inspired Joseph with wisdom and to Joseph who forgave his brothers. Thus even without harvest, God is praised for providing food for the people.

Because of the scarcity of rain and the rocky soil of the land, a successful harvest was by no means assured. According to Israelite worldview, God owned the land, and God gave the harvest. Although the farmers worked all year round for food, their dependence rested solely on God. Amos speaks of God sending rain on one field, but not on another. Yet the trust that God would provide, and would provide plenty, was one of the foundations of the ritual of sabbath. Because the community trusted that, thanks to God's beneficence, food would be sufficient even without any labor one day each week, the people could rest on sabbath. Furthermore, there would be harvest in excess, so that one year in seven would be jubilee, and the fields would lie fallow. Of course, it is unlikely that anything like a sabbatical year was actually ever practiced. Yet the hope that the farmer and the field can rest one year in seven indicates both Israel's religious faith in God and the back-breaking labor constantly endured by the farmer.

A tenth-century Canaanite inscription called the Gezer calendar indicates that seven months of the year were absorbed with harvesting: one month of barley harvest, beginning at the spring equinox and concluded in mid-April; one month of wheat harvest, from mid-April to mid-May; two months of grape harvest, from mid-May to mid-July; one month of fruit harvest, from mid-July to mid-August; and two months of olive harvest, from mid-August to mid-October. Harvesting consumed more than half the year for agricultural laborers, and it was this harvest calendar upon which the Israelite religious calendar was superimposed, such that the observance of religious feasts was also a celebration of the phenomenon of the harvest.

For example, Passover begins on the first full moon after the spring equinox. Thus Passover fell at the outset of the barley harvest and signifies, both in the commemoration of the exodus and with the actual harvest of the staple crop, God's gift of life for the entire community. Pentecost, the Feast of Weeks, fell fifty days later, at the end of the wheat harvest and the beginning of the grape harvest. This timing gave a context to the accusation (Acts 2:13) on Pentecost that the disciples were filled with new wine. At the close of the seven-month harvesting, in mid-October, fell the Feast of Booths, Sukkoth. When the last harvest had been gathered in, the people remembered the time when as nomads they relied, not on their harvest, but rather on the generosity of God.

Whether or not the later urban dwellers made these connections, the original fixing of presumably historical remembrances of the passover or the wilderness wanderings reinterpreted the agricultural calendar that was already in place. Judges 9:27 records that the Canaanites partied at harvesttime. Settling on their territory, the Israelites took those natural and cultural times of festival and used them to recall their historic connections with the saving God. In interpreting the readings in the lectionary, we need to know that as the people moved further from their agricultural roots, harvest became increasingly used as a metaphor for God's historic and continual saving of the people.

An example of this pattern is seen in the book of Ruth. The story's primary image of human need is the hunger of the poor. Famine forced Naomi out of Judah, and it was the barley harvest during which Ruth's marriage to Boaz was contracted. We know that the Passover celebration marked the beginning of the barley harvest. The story of Ruth superimposes all its images of new life—plentiful harvest, marriage, childbirth, milk in Naomi's breasts, and a future for Naomi's line—onto the festival of Passover, which already celebrated God's gift of life for the people. Jewish practice reads the book of Ruth at Pentecost, the wheat harvest, thus layering the story of fruitful women, barley, and Passover onto the celebration of the harvest of wheat at Pentecost.

The language of harvest continues through the scriptures. The psalms praise God for good harvests. On the other hand, the prophets such as Elijah interpret drought, and the consequent failure of harvests, as a sign that God is punishing the people for their infidelity. Later prophets, such as Amos, rail against the people for unjust distribution of the food of the harvest.

Many New Testament narratives are situated in the cities, but Jesus' parables and preaching use harvest as an image of the faithful life and of the fulfillment of God's design. At times of harvest, the ancient Israelites were to bring to the priests the firstfruits, both as sustenance for the clergy caste and as a symbol of gratitude. This idea of firstfruits functions metaphorically a number of times in the New Testament. Just as the ancient farmer brought the first and best to God, so also Christians were to give back their firstfruits to God. In 1 Corinthians (Eac) Paul uses the firstfruits language to describe the resurrection of Christ. The harvest imagery helps Paul to picture Christ's resurrection as the end of this age of planting and the beginning of God's new age of reaping life. God is the giver of harvest, and Christ himself the harvest God gives.

In the lectionary, most of the references to harvest are, like Paul's description of Christ's resurrection as the firstfruit of creation, metaphoric. In Advent, John the Baptist refers to the coming messiah as the one who will complete the harvest, by discarding the chaff and storing the grain (Ad2A, Ad3C). Each liturgical year after the Easter season is over, the lectionary speaks of the kingdom of God in harvest imagery. In some pericopes, the harvest is ready and workers are needed (Pr6A, Pr9C). In the parables of the kingdom, God's reign is likened to a seed that will mysteriously grow until the harvest (Pr11A, Pr6B). A reading from Third Isaiah (Pr3c†) complements the early preaching of Jesus: just as God brings about the growth of the seed to harvest, so the tree that grows in God will bring forth good fruit. This passage from Isaiah 55 is also appointed for the Easter Vigil, as one of the many Old Testament pericopes that the church uses to refer metaphorically to the resurrection.

Many citations from the New Testament in the lectionary use harvest imagery to describe the effects of the faithful Christian life. The parable of the sower (Pr10A) speaks of the size of the harvest the church can expect in the lives of the faithful. It is interesting, in light of Matthew's talk of a harvest of hundredfold, sixtyfold, and thirtyfold, that crop yields in ancient times in the fertile crescent ranged from twenty to seventyfold. For comparison, times of medieval European famine brought yields of only threefold, while contemporary agribusiness produces yields of 200 to 300. Yet as we have come to expect in the biblical worldview, although the apostles are planting and watering the crop of the church, it is God who gives growth to the harvest (Ep6A).

It is striking that the Old Testament often employs the imagery of the vineyard as God's people. Even though grain is the necessary staple for existence, grapes provide the added joy of communal life. That Israel is not God's field of grain, but rather God's vineyard, suggests the extraordinary goodness of the people's life with their God. Yet the vineyard sometimes yields only wild grapes (Pr22A†), and this imagery recurs in the New Testament as well. Perhaps the church will harvest only rank growth (Pr17B), although we who live united in the Spirit ought to be reaping eternal life (Pr9C) and bearing good fruit (Pr10C).

Another use of harvest imagery in the lectionary has to do with the endtime. Several New Testament writers speak confidently of the imminent end of this world, and especially Matthew uses harvest imagery to describe the coming of the end. The weeds growing in the wheat fields will not be destroyed until harvest time (Pr11A). The workers in the vineyard will get their reward only at the end of the day (Pr20A). These two parables suggest opposite outcomes for the end of time, the first that only the good wheat will be harvested, and the second that even the last worker will be fully paid. In Lutheran parlance, Matthew 13 is more law, and Matthew 20 more gospel.

Harvest language has remained in church use. We recall phrases such as *the harvest of souls* as a way to talk about active evangelization. African American Holiness churches have called *the threshing floor* the open area between the seating and the altar. When persons come forward to accept the faith and receive church membership, they stand on the threshing floor, ready to have their chaff beaten out. Knowing this language is important for understanding the imagery in James Baldwin's novel *Go Tell It on the Mountain*. The language of harvest and threshing can be useful both in speaking about the endtime and in focusing on the daily fruitfulness of those who grow together in the Spirit of Christ.

In ancient times, some of the native tribes of the American Southwest lived in pit dwellings, round enclosures below the surface of the ground. Some centuries later, in historic times, these same tribes moved into aboveground houses, but they continued to use the pit-dwellings, now called *kivas*, as religious structures. The men descended into the kivas to conduct their rituals, as the ordinary situation of the past became a religious experience in the present. We can describe this social change as a move from a literal use of a structure to a metaphoric use of it: dwelling became sacred space.

A similar situation exists for the biblical language of harvest. In ancient times, language about harvest generally referred to the literal harvests of a subsistence-level agricultural community. In later times, for example during the life of Jesus, language about harvest was more likely to refer metaphorically to a religious concept or a holy event. For today's churchgoer, the language of harvest may be of either sort: literally naming their precarious livelihood, or metaphorically speaking of good deeds or life's end. Both the literal and the metaphoric understandings may be in the same Sunday assembly. The language of harvest encountered in the lectionary can be interpreted broadly enough to include both the farmer struggling against weather and prices and the shopper eating cantaloupe in January.

In the United States, the societal autumn harvest festival, Thanksgiving, occurs very late in the agricultural year. For many Americans, Thanksgiving is the annual event most closely resembling a classic religious festival, since it includes family reunions, a substantial meal served with more formality than is usual, ritually important foods, traditional behavior patterns, and table prayer. Some Christian churches continue the practice, seen for example in medieval ember days, of meeting for liturgy at the harvest festival. Many communities now use this paraliturgical event as the best time of the year for ecumenical prayer services. When church members assemble for the ancient religious practice of thanking God for their plentiful harvest, two explicitly Christian activities can occur: prayer for all the world's hungry, and a collection for the poor.

Harvest is a commonplace liturgical metaphor that can draw us, not only to our own full dinner table, but in two other directions as well. One is to the triune God, the Bread who is God, the firstfruit who is the resurrected

Christ, the fields of mown grain that is the Spirit in the community. The second direction is toward all those who suffer from lack of the harvest we tend to take for granted. We do well to add a second couplet to the traditional table prayer:

Come, Lord Jesus, be our guest,

and let these gifts to us be blest.

Blest be God, who is our Bread.

May all the world be clothed and fed.

The harvest is one of the lectionary's most communal images, suggesting large fields, cooperative labor and community feasting, and for this reason is particularly important for a society that tends too often to focus on the individual. Harvest is communal, the image extensive, as is our shared life in the church.

Heaven
Earth
Hell

hades, heaven-earth-hell,
heavens opening, Sheol

Related chapters: Resurrection of the Body, Wind

The cosmic map assumed by most biblical writers pictures a three-
tiered world: heaven, the home of divine beings; earth, the home
of humankind; and hades, the place of the dead. This ancient
imagery figures in the description of Christ's death, resurrection,
and ascension. An alternate cosmic map present in the New Testament imagines heaven as the place of eternal reward and hell of
eternal punishment. Although humans are fascinated with the
afterlife, the Bible offers no uniform teaching about it, nor does
the lectionary give it much attention.

PSALM 115:16-
17

The heaven of heavens is the LORD's,
    but the LORD entrusted the earth to its peoples.
The dead do not praise the LORD,
    nor all those who go down into silence.

APOSTLES'
CREED

I believe in Jesus Christ, God's only Son, our Lord,
    who . . . was crucified, died, and was buried;
he descended to the dead.
On the third day he rose again;
he ascended into heaven,
he is seated at the right hand of the Father.

VENANTIUS
HONORIUS
FORTUNATUS

"Welcome, happy morning!" age to age shall say;
"Hell today is vanquished, heaven is won today!"

Source of all things living, you came down to die,
plumbed the depths of hell to raise us up on high.

Free the souls long prisoned, bound with Satan's chain;
all that once had fallen raise to life again.

As the earth gladly accepts the rain from Heaven,
just so, Adam who was held captive in Hades,
awaited the Savior of the world, the Giver of life.

ROMANOS,
Resurrection III
KONTAKION

"Wherever you may turn, you see on all sides
tombs which are emptied, and you, Hades,
   shameless one, naked.
Christ has lifted me to the heavens;
you, he has put to flight;
he took my body that he might make it new;
he will make it immortal and cause it to share his throne.
My pledge of surety is now on high,
but you are trampled on below by those who cry,
'Where, O Death, is your victory, or where your strength?
God has destroyed your strength
   through the resurrection.'"

At the moment of death, the soul goes to its appointed
place with no other guide for it but the nature of its sins;
and—in the case of mortal sin—hell is its proper place.
Were the sinful soul not there where the justice of God
wills it, the soul would be in a still greater hell. Then it
would be out of that divine order which is a part of God's
mercy.

CATHERINE OF
GENOA,
*Purgation and
Purgatory*

THE CHRISTIAN IMAGERY of heaven and hades/hell has undergone several millennia of development, and still no Christian consensus exists today about the meaning of this language. To understand the lectionary's use of this imagery, it is helpful to distinguish between its two strands, which appear sometimes separately and sometimes intertwined. First we will consider the more ancient meaning of this imagery, heaven-earth-hades as the cosmic map. Secondly we will deal with the use of this language as a description of a good and an evil afterlife, still popular in Western imagination.

In a nearly universal human phenomenon, cultures propose a cosmic map by which they picture the universe and describe the human place within it. The cosmic map assumed by most biblical texts was not unique to the Israelite people, but was shared with many neighboring cultures. This map proposed that the universe consisted of three layers. Following the stereotypical human orientation that up is good and down is bad, the highest layer, described as the dome of the sky or the area above the sky, was the abode of superior beings of one kind or another. Hebrew called this either heaven or the heavens. The sun, stars, wind, and rain that issued from the heavens were signs indicating the power of this divine realm. Job 38:7 refers to the stars as sons of God, that is, as supernatural beings residing in the heavens, near where God dwells above all.

The middle layer was the earth, home for humans. This layer was usually thought of as a disk, with mountains at its perimeter. Often such cosmic maps understood that the capital city is the navel of the world (Ezekiel 5:5) or the site of a primordial theophany.

The lowest layer was the underworld, sometimes the realm of the god of the dead, usually the place where the dead went. The Hebrew Bible called this level Sheol. In the story of Korah's revolt against Moses, the men, their families, and their household goods die by falling down into Sheol. Job's poem indicates that Sheol is characterized by silence; its inhabitants cannot serve or praise God, because they are dead.

In the versions of this cosmology held in ancient Egypt and Sumer, the original material of the universe was water. The earth is now suspended in water. The water above the sky provides the rain, and water below the earth figures in references to the river that must be crossed on one's way to the underworld. The narrative of Noah's ark describes the windows of the heavens opening so that the rain can pour down. Perhaps the phenomenon of the human womb suggested that life is surrounded by water.

Such a three-level universe was a common cosmology. In the Norse version, the three levels are held in place by Yggdrasil, the cosmic tree of life. However, not all prescientific societies imagined the world in this way. Ancient Chinese cosmology proposed a quite contemporary view of the stars and planets as suspended in infinite space, and a medieval Western view, reflecting the writings of Aristotle and Ptolemy, proposed concentric circles in which the earth is the center. For centuries, however, scientists in Christian societies have found it necessary to argue their data against a literalist belief in the biblical cosmologies. Galileo, for example, pleaded unsuccessfully that Psalm 104:5—"You set the earth on its foundations, so that it shall never be shaken"—was poetic metaphor, not scientific description. The intensity of the fundamentalist movement in the twentieth century is in part due to the anthropocentric simplicity of biblical cosmologies in contrast with the mind-boggling evidence cited by contemporary scientific cosmologies. Yet even when scientifically accurate descriptions of the universe are accepted, the language of God-up and death-down echoes in our speech and the three-tiered universe remains in our imagination.

Some readings in the lectionary presume this three-level cosmology. The specifics of the dream of Jacob's ladder (Pr11A°), the ascension of Elijah (TranB, Pr8c°), the vision of Stephen at his lynching (Ea5A), and the discussion of being caught up to the third heaven (Pr9B) all assume a universe in which God resides up in or above the sky. The narrative of the death of Elijah is about going up to be with God, not about his getting an eternal reward. To get to God, one goes up. When God speaks, the voice descends from the upper world to humankind in the middle layer. The same cosmology stands behind the narrative of Jesus' baptism (BapA, BapB, Bapc). Matthew says "the heavens were opened to him"; Mark, "he saw the heavens torn apart"; Luke, "the heaven was opened." In John, it is the Baptizer who sees the Spirit descending from heaven like a dove. All these narratives suggest that God resides up above and that communication between humankind and God is conducted between two layers of reality, the earth and the heavens.

The ascension narratives bring this imagery into prominence in Christian speech. The theological assertions of faith are that Christ went to God and so resumed the place of the divine, and that believers will at their end go to God. Luke relates this truth by the narrative of the ascension in which the three-tiered universe figures. In Luke 24:51 and Acts 1:9, Luke indicates that Jesus must go up to be with God. In the heavens is God's throne, where from God's right hand Christ will reign as a kind of prime minister.

Countless Christian churches depict this ascension scene on wall paintings. Without careful interpretation, the narrative could suggest that Christ has gone away from the church. The church fathers taught just the opposite: that as Christ went to God, his body became available to all the church. In the fifth century, Pope Leo preached that Christ ascended into the eucharist. Martin Luther taught that Christ ascended, not to some distant place, such as the right hand of God, but into the cosmos. Thus even centuries before contemporary cosmology, theologians recognized Luke's language as being metaphoric.

Ascension Day presents a challenge to contemporary Christians. Because the festival must not indicate some acceptance of an archaic cosmology, we must be able to interpret the cosmic map for its contemporary meaning. The language of Christ ascending to God is a metaphoric way to describe the apostolic belief that Jesus did not end his life and destiny in the grave, but rather rose (note again the metaphor of up) to be with God. The good news is that Christians are not pretending to accept an ancient cosmology, but are affirming their faith that in Christ we too will conquer death. Current liturgical practice discourages an older Ascension Day ritual of snuffing out the paschal candle after the reading of the gospel. Such a rite suggests a divine absence that minimizes the life of the Spirit of Christ in the assembled church. Contemporary practice stresses the unity of the fifty days of Easter culminating in Pentecost, rather than a focus on the Lucan distinction between the fortieth and the fiftieth day.

Not only on Ascension Day is the three-level universe in liturgical speech. The Apostles' Creed includes all three levels of the cosmic map. Christ died, descended to hades, rose again, and ascended into heaven. The most recent English translation of the creed, presented to all English-speaking Christians by a worldwide ecumenical translation committee, offers the phrase *he descended to the dead*, judging that the contemporary word *hell* mistranslates what the authors of the creed meant. In the fourth-century worldview, going to hades meant really dying. Jesus did not, as some gnostics suggested, wait out the weekend in suspended animation. According to Christian theological reflection, the death of Christ is salvific. Thus his genuine death became important to proclaim. Christ has done it all and been all places: he lived and he died; he has been above the earth, on the earth, and below the earth.

Many religions' narrative myths tell of a hero who descends to the realm of the dead, to rescue a dead relative or to do a favor for a deity. Hercules, for example, must complete a mission in hades as the most difficult of his labors.

Especially the Orthodox churches found the idea of Christ's descent to hades a useful image. Called the harrowing of hell—to harrow meaning to pillage or plunder—Christ's descent to the place of the dead came to be spoken of quite literally. While in hades with all the world's dead, Christ preached the gospel to them (1 Peter 3:10). Christ was said to have brought up from hades to heaven—that is, he transferred from the realm of the dead to life with God—all righteous Jews and godly pagans. Eastern Christianity reveres an icon of this harrowing of hell: Christ is standing upon the broken doors of hades, and he is pulling Adam and Eve up from hades into paradise. This story solves the perennial question about what happens to pious persons who did not know Christ. For the literal mind, Jesus' adventures in hades kept him occupied on Holy Saturday. For the mind that sees the language as metaphor, the harrowing of hell is language that affirms Christ's saving power over all humankind, those who lived before him as well as we who follow after. Christ's conquest of all space is parallel to his conquest of all time.

Although the cosmic map of heaven-earth-hades remains here and there in the liturgy, it is a later development of this imagery that figures significantly in contemporary imagination. So let us now consider the religious worldview in which hades has become hell.

Some ancient religious and philosophical systems posited the idea that part of each human person was immortal. One's individual destiny extended throughout time, after death, and for all of eternity. With an eternity for reward or punishment, the human desire for justice could be satisfied, for although we seldom see goodness rewarded and evil punished here on earth, the gods would settle accounts after death. Ancient Egyptian myth suggested that after death the heart was weighed against a feather to determine its relative goodness and thus its eternal fate. During Israel's political subjugation in intertestamental times, the faithful people did not experience the fulfillment of God's promises to them, and many came to believe that the righteous would be rewarded in some later realm. God's blessings came not now, but later. For some Jews, the future realm would be a newly created earth with resurrected bodies. Other Jews came to accept the idea of individual reward or punishment after death.

The apocryphal and pseudepigraphic literature written during the several centuries before Christ contains descriptions of the places of eternal reward and punishment awaiting the good and the evil. Some first-century Jews used the term gehenna to designate the place of everlasting punishment. The name originated as a symbol of utter desecration, because it was in the Valley of Hinnom that King Ahaz offered his child as a burnt sacrifice to Molech, and the location later became the site of a perpetually burning garbage dump. The noun indicating burning refuse came to designate the fate of those who were to be punished by God.

This development exemplifies the layering of religious imagery. The idea of eternal punishment, the disgraceful memory of child sacrifice, the disgusting refuse rotting outside the town, the horror of fire: All these elements superimposed on to each other figured in the development of Christian image of hell. Although in some early Greek mythological tales the underworld is divided into two areas, one pleasant for reward and one wretched for punishment, the later idea is that only the evil go down to hades, which has come to be imagined as a fiery hell. The good go up to be with God.

The language of heaven and hell occurs several times in the lectionary, most memorably in Jesus' parable of the rich man and Lazarus (Pr21c). Usually, the settings of parables are not taken literally. We do not, for example, teach that God's abode is really a vineyard. Yet the parable in Luke 15, with its vivid image of Abraham and the poor man up and the rich man far distant "in agony in these flames," corresponds so precisely to stereotypical religious imagination about the afterlife that its imagery has regularly been literalized. The lectionary also quotes Jesus as speaking of eternal punishment (Ep6A, Pr21B). Although the church stopped short of literalizing the demands—that believers are never to call someone fool, that believers should be cutting off their hands—it literalized the punishment described for sin.

Historians, sociologists, and psychologists might together confer on why the imagery of brutal and everlasting torture became such a commonplace religious thought for centuries of the Western church. In Dante's *Divine Comedy*, by far the most fascinating part details the nine circles of hell. Countless sermons dwelt on the horrors of a literal hell. Numerous church wall paintings and stone carvings showed grotesque monsters, deformed naked persons, and even clergy in full liturgical regalia boiling in vats of fire, with human entrails here and there. In the famous sermon "Sinners in the Hands of an Angry God," Jonathan Edwards said, "God holds you over the pit of hell, much as one holds a spider or some loathsome insect over the fire, abhors you and is dreadfully provoked. You are ten thousand times more abominable in his eyes than the most hateful and venomous serpent is in ours." One wonders what this reveling in hell was all about.

Although the thirteenth and fourteenth centuries were obsessed with hell, later centuries turned Christian attention to heaven. Especially nineteenth-century preachers described heaven as a kind of family reunion or perpetual summer vacation. Such a notion would have sounded quite off the mark to medieval celibate theologians, for whom heaven meant the presence of God, not dead friends and relatives. Language about the hope of living forever with deceased loved ones remains a staple of beloved hymns and of some funeral rhetoric.

A controversial question among contemporary Christians is whether the promise of eternal life is to be understood as in any way congruent with historic language of heaven and hell. Most contemporary religious Jews do not believe that eternal reward or punishment for individuals will be disbursed. But many Christians are raised to fear hell for themselves, to judge which other folk deserve to go there, or to understand religious observance as an insurance policy against eternal punishment. However, a growing number of Christians around the world reject teachings about hell, finding unacceptable the idea that a loving God could condemn anyone to eternal torture.

Several quite different voices raise concerns over talk of a personal heaven. Some Christians set aside a literal belief in heaven, assessing that heaven evolved from an archaic cosmology, expresses an immature hope for reward, and reflects more than anything else the human desire for immortality. If nearly everyone gets to heaven, the human does not really, finally, die. Some Christians concerned with ecology suggest that by focusing on life in heaven far away, the church lessens interest in God's created earth here and now. Liberation theologians teach that the medieval conception of heaven allowed Christians to avoid their task of bringing the reign of God to people's lives now. Christians with strong scientific interest wonder to what degree talk of heaven and hell moves the faith into a fantasy world, replacing realistic assessment of the earth with archaic imagery.

Even in ages past, some Christians sought to minimize our perennial fascination with immortality. John Chrysostom is quoted as saying, "What care I where heaven is, when in the liturgy I am in heaven?" A similar idea was expressed by Cyril of Jerusalem, who said of the phrase "Our Father in heaven" that God was to be found in the community of the faithful who were praying. The lectionary suggests that the idea of eternal punishment and reward, expressed in vivid though archaic imagery, is only a minor part of Christian reflection. Hell does not figure at all in the Apostles' and Nicene Creeds, and heaven is expressed in the ambiguous phrases "the life everlasting" and "the life of the world to come." (The creeds do refer to a parallel though distinctly different idea, "the resurrection of the body" or "of the dead.") The mythic story in Revelation 12, describing a war in heaven among the angels that brought about the fall of Satan, who then fell down out of heaven and, as the source of evil, resides in hell, is appointed for the day of St. Michael and All Angels, rather than a Sunday celebration.

The lectionary reflects the fact that Christian theology focuses on the resurrection of Christ and on that resurrected life within the living community.

Yet heaven must mean far more than life in the church. It is not clear to what extent the fulfillment of God's promises presumes a realm beyond this one that heaven language attempts to convey. Surely the church's use of the languages of cosmic map or eternal destiny ought never suggest that Christians are ignorant of scientific knowledge, or that religious belief is fantasy, or that Christians enjoy condemning others to punishment, or that Christians trivialize the sorrow that death brings to survivors. Many popular films and books present the picture of a blissful personal immortality that is devoid of the presence of God or the issue of justice. Rather, the good news of the biblical language of heaven is that God, who is beyond all we know, fills the universe and lives forever. Our faith is neither that God presides over an archaic world nor that we have become immortal beings, but that we humans find our life in worshiping the God who is God and in bringing God's justice into this world.

Israel

chosen people, congregation,
Ephraim, Israel, Jacob, Judah,
land, nation, people of God,
promised land, remnant

Related chapters: CITY, COVENANT, OUTSIDER

The Bible contains many collective nouns that designate the
people of Israel or their homeland, terms like *Israel, Judah, the chosen people,* and *the promised land.* In the lectionary, these terms usually function as metaphors for the community of the baptized.

PSALM 148:11-
13A, 14

Kings of the earth and all peoples,
    rulers and all judges of the world;
young men and women,
    old and young together:
Let them praise the name of the LORD.
The LORD has raised up strength for the chosen people
and praise for all loyal servants,
    the children of Israel, a people who are near to the LORD.
    Hallelujah!

PRAYER AT
EASTER VIGIL

O God, whose wonderful deeds of old shine forth even to our own day: By the power of your mighty arm you once delivered your chosen people from slavery under Pharaoh, a sign for us of the salvation of all nations by the water of baptism. Grant that all the people of earth may be numbered among the offspring of Abraham and may rejoice in the inheritance of Israel; through your Son, Jesus Christ our Lord.

JOHN MASON
NEALE, AFTER
12TH CENTURY
LATIN HYMN

Oh, come, oh, come, Emmanuel,
and ransom captive Israel,
that mourns in lonely exile here
until the Son of God appear.
    Rejoice! Rejoice! Emmanuel
    shall come to you, O Israel.

Oh, come, oh, come, great Lord of might,
who to your tribes on Sinai's height
in ancient times once gave the law
in cloud, and majesty, and awe.

Oh, come, strong Branch of Jesse, free
your own from Satan's tyranny;
from depths of hell your people save
and give them victory o'er the grave.

"Jacob" is everyone who conquers; by the power of Love, he conquered God, in order to be conquered himself. After having conquered, so that he was conquered and received the blessing, he will further help those who are also conquered but not yet wholly conquered, and still walk upright on their two feet and do not limp, as do those who have become Jacob. Whoever wishes to wrestle with God must set himself to conquer in order to be conquered; and he must start to limp on the side on which there is anything else for him besides God alone.

HADEWIJCH, *The Jacob Letter*

It is in chanting the Psalms that we too are leaving Egypt. It was in Christ that Israel crossed the desert, and it is in Christ that we, the tribes of Israel, are going up to Jerusalem. Just as the whole people of God is still crossing the desert to the Promised Land, still passing through the Jordan, still building Jerusalem and raising God's temple on Sion, so each individual soul must normally know something of the same journey, the same hunger and thirst, the same battles and prayers, light and darkness, the same sacrifices and the same struggle to build Jerusalem within itself.

THOMAS MERTON, *Bread in the Wilderness*

FOR MOST OF THE YEAR the lectionary appoints weekly readings from the Hebrew Scriptures, which means that Christians hear many references to Israel, to other ancient names, such as Ephraim, Jacob, and Judah, and to collective nouns, such as the chosen people, the congregation, the nation, the people of God, and the remnant. The term *Israel* might well cause confusion because of its contemporary usage, while other of the terms might be too obscure to have any meaning for worshipers. Each of these terms is a label in historic Judaism, but in the lectionary, they most often function as metaphors for the baptized community. Let us begin by considering the proper names, which originate as names of significant male characters and become designations for the descendants of that person.

The name Israel was said to have originated as God's renaming of the patriarch Jacob, after he wrestled with the angel. Although the text (Genesis 32:28) says that the name means "the one who strives," its etymology seems actually to be "Isra-el," that is, El, God, prevails. Subsequently, although the names *Jacob* and *Israel* were used interchangeably both for the man and for his descendants, the term *Israel* became the dominant label for the entire people of whom he was the patriarchal ancestor. Thus in different biblical passages, *Israel* might refer to Jacob, Jacob's family, the twelve tribes, the united kingdom under David, the northern kingdom, the southern kingdom of Judah, the remnant in exile, the ethnic group that saw itself as the continuing people of God, the Christian church, or the Jews who did not accept Jesus as messiah.

Although soon enough Christians included Gentiles in their community of faith, the church of the New Testament originated with people of the line of Israel, and the church continued to worship the historic god of Israel. According to the oldest passages of the Hebrew Bible, the tribe of Israel had its own deity. Naturally, a desert people would have different needs, and thus a different deity, than a coastal people. The people in a geographic area were to worship the deity of that locale, and in return the deity fed and protected the tribe. A detail in the story of Elisha healing Naaman, the Syrian, illustrates this concept. Naaman was so impressed with the power of Elisha's god that he packed up two mule-loads of earth to take home with him, as if the soil would bring the power of its deity back with Naaman to Syria. Another example is the exodus story itself: the god of Israel, YHWH, saved the people of Israel. YHWH's commitment was to the chosen people of Israel, not to the Egyptians, whom YHWH defeats and destroys. This ancient history of local tribal deities helps explain the tone of exclusivity that undergirds some biblical references to Israel.

The exclusive tribal deity evolved into the one God of the whole earth. In the exile, when the people of Israel were no longer in Israel, the prophets spoke of only one god over all the earth. This monotheism comforted people who were now distant from the promised land, the location protected by their tribal deity. Such monotheism was essential for the development of Christianity, because the church could assert that the God of Israel was the God also of persons not descended from the man Israel. There is only one God, and so all people can become members of the one people blessed by the one God.

The first Christians were a sect within Judaism, and early Christians saw themselves as continuing the faith associated with Israel and his descendants. Occasionally, the New Testament books use the term *Israel* pejoratively to refer to those Jews who did not accept Jesus as messiah. Because the lectionary intends that biblical readings address the assembled believers, not persons who are absent, most of these passages are not appointed in the lectionary. For the most part, the term *Israel* when heard liturgically is a metaphor for the church. An ancient tribe that named itself by its patriarch worshiped a deity who is now our God. Their god is our god, YHWH's promises our hopes, and their name metaphorically our name. Jesus is quoted as having intended his ministry only for Israel, yet several decades into the Christian movement, Christian writers were applying the name Israel to non-Jews who are baptized. By calling itself the new Israel, the church claims to stand in the tradition of the faith of Abraham, Isaac, and Jacob and to appropriate for all the baptized the promises made to Israel's descendants.

Linguistic philosophers teach that no isolated word possesses meaning: the meaning of a word can be determined only within its context in a sentence. This assertion is surely true of the word *Israel*. Because the church's practice of referring to itself as Israel continues in the language of the liturgy, the challenge for interpretation of the image is considerable. The issue is further complicated, since 1948, by the existence of a country called Israel, largely but by no means wholly populated by ethnic Jews, of whom only a minority are religious Jews. Thus in the intercessions, Christian assemblies may well pray for Israel, meaning the State of Israel. Or they may pray for religious Jews, for example at the autumn Jewish new year and at the springtime Pesach. Of course, no single Jewish meaning defines the word *Israel*. The word may refer to a secular nation or a religiously observant community descendant from ancient Israel, and among religious Jews, Israel may be heard as a literal piece of land or as a metaphoric reference to the promises of God.

A second issue with Christian use of the term *Israel* is the church's history of anti-Semitism. Replacement theology not only borrowed the language of Israel for the church, but stole the language of promise from the Jews. Much of the church taught that God had rejected the first Israel, replacing it with the second and true Israel, the church. It is understandable that early Christians sought to distinguish their faith community from that of the Jews. It is far less understandable that the church settled into a tradition of anti-Semitism. An increasing number of Christian communities now reject this attitude and proclaim that God continues care for both the children of Israel and the family of the baptized. One need not displace the other.

Perhaps the most stark usage of the image of Israel in any Christian liturgical text is the complex, poetic, penitential litany called the Reproaches. Developed in the tenth century and appointed for use on Good Friday, this litany presents God as chastising the church for its unfaithfulness. The refrain, citing Micah 6:3, quotes God's lament that in spite of God's care for the people, they are still guilty of sin. Typical of Christian liturgical language, the Reproaches use the image of Israel as metaphor for the church and the imagery of the exodus as metaphor for salvation. The idea is that on Good Friday, the church confesses its sins before God who says, "I led you forth from the land of Egypt, but you have prepared a cross for your Savior." Even though God brought the church into the freedom of salvation, we continue to crucify Christ with our actions.

Because of the history of anti-Semitism in the West, the Reproaches came to be interpreted as an anti-Semitic exercise in which the church condemned the Jews for killing Christ. Believers moved from confessing their own sins to condemning the outsider. Perhaps liturgical catechesis was also to blame, by forgetting that usually in the liturgy Israel refers to the church. This unfortunate history led many churches to abandon use of the Reproaches. For those who wish to revive this metaphoric confession, an excellent rendition is available in several recent Protestant service books. The contemporary text makes the metaphoric nature of the language evident:

I offered you my body and blood,
    but you scatter and deny and abandon me,
and most explicitly,
    I grafted you into the tree of my chosen Israel,
    but you turned on them with persecution and mass murder.

I made you joint heirs with them of my covenants,
but you made them scapegoats for your own guilt,
and you have prepared a cross for your Savior. [1]

Christian assemblies who wish to continue the tradition of praying the Reproaches on Good Friday do well to use this text.

Only metaphorically do we call ourselves what we are not, in this case Israel. Because the church is not literally Israel, the current interest in Christians holding seders is to be discouraged. It is historically inaccurate to claim that the contemporary Jewish seder is anything close to the passover ritual that Jesus used. The first-century passover ritual developed in two different ways: among Jews, after the destruction of the temple, into the medieval and contemporary seder, and among Christians, into the Easter vigil. The seder is one of the two holiest religious rituals of the Jewish people and ought not be hosted by Christians. We would find it odd, to say the least, were synagogues to celebrate the eucharist, and although some Jews may not be concerned over Christian seders, others Jews find the practice utterly offensive.

Christians wishing to learn more about contemporary Judaism can study the text of the haggadah, view one of the excellent educational videos produced by Jewish groups, or get themselves invited to a genuine Jewish seder. Attempts to Christianize a seder are particularly problematic. Christians already celebrate paschal salvation with the Easter Vigil. At the Vigil the imagery of the church as Israel is paramount. The resurrection of Christ is our release from slavery, and baptism is our escape across the Red Sea. Easter is the occasion of our victory dance. Christians read the exodus story at the Vigil not to remember the history of another people, but to claim the images of that story as their own.

One more contemporary issue must be cited here. Some communities of Christians have seen only themselves as the elect. In appropriating the language *Israel* to themselves, they adopted also the ancient notion that they alone had access to God: they alone are the chosen people. Recall that the storyteller of Exodus 14 does not weep for the dead Egyptians, since the ancient people of Israel cared explicitly for their own tribal destiny. However, the contemporary Jewish ritual of the seder asks those at table to lessen the wine in their goblets by ten drops, one for each of the plagues of Egypt, in sorrow for the suffering of others. Similarly, over the centuries many Christian communities have come to care also for the outsider. Many biblical selections in the lectionary urge just this, that God's promises are meant for all the world and divine mercy is surprisingly more inclusive than we ever imagine.

We need to be mindful of these complexities when looking at the lectionary's use of the image Israel. When Christians read that God intends to gather Israel (Ep2A), we mean not only the Jewish people, but also our-selves, perhaps the entire world. When we hear "Save the remnant of Israel," we mean ourselves (Ch2ABC). When we recall Jeremiah's confes-sion of Israel's sin, we are confessing our sin (Pr25c†). When we hear that God is a father to Israel, we mean that God is also our father (Pr25B†). The ten commandments are meant to address not only all the congregation of the people of Israel (Ep7A). Although for example the command to keep the sabbath is meant for ancient Israelites and for contemporary religious Jews, we must discover in what way the commandments are addressed also to Christians. If the reading is not addressed to us, we should be reading something more appropriate in the eucharistic assembly. The lectionary does not appoint for Sunday reading, for example, the menstrual taboos, because the church judges those passages to be unrelated to the baptized community.

The lectionary presents us with many synonyms for Israel, other terms that function in the same metaphoric way. We are not only Israel, we are also Jacob (Israel's birth name), Judah (one of the sons of Jacob), and Ephraim (one of the sons of Joseph) (Pr25B†, Bapc, Pr25c†). We are of Abraham and Sarah (Pr16A†). The penitential ritual originally proclaimed in Zion (AshWABC) became for Christians the season of Lent. The priest Ezra is reading the Torah also to us (Ep3c). That these images are presented in the lectionary requires high levels of adult catechesis in our churches. We can-not expect hearers to make any metaphoric sense of these readings if they do not recognize these names and cannot recall their stories.

Sometimes the readings use terms such as *the nation* and *the land*. In Ezekiel's memorable vision of the valley of the dry bones (VigilABC, Le5A), *the whole house of Israel*, God's *people*, and *the land of Israel* are all meant to include Christians, who experience at Easter the resurrection of their own dry bones. Christians read the promise made to Abram (Le2A) because we see that God is metaphorically making us into what the ancient text called *a great nation*, that is, a single people protected by a benevolent God. One pop-ular image in hymnody is *the promised land*, more obscurely *our portion*, that is, the land that our God has destined us to occupy. Most Christians and Jews recognize *land* to be, not a literal piece of property on this globe, but rather God's protection of our life, God's gift of wholeness. For Christians, such a land is at the least the community of the church.

The New Testament generalizes this imagery into the idea *the people of God*, and many contemporary Christians find this language helpful. Christians are now God's own people (Ch2ABC, Pr10B, Ea5c). Care must be taken to keep this language from becoming sentimentalized, as sometimes *the family of God* language does, or serving as license for exclusionary attitudes. The reading from Isaiah 25 reminds us that the feast on the mountain that YHWH will serve up is meant for all peoples.

In other passages, the idea of the people of God pervades, without the explicit word *people*. For example, Paul speaks God's blessings to the Corinthian congregation in totally corporate language. We must think *you all* when the English says, "the God of love and peace will be with you" (TrinA). As a people in community, Christians receive the peace of the risen Christ. John's version of *the people* is the image *one* (Ea7c), and during Eastertide descriptions from Luke's book of Acts characterize this people: they are continually at prayer (Ea7A); they meet for meals and share a common life, equalize money and possessions, and care for the needy (Ea4A); they are of one heart and soul (Ea2B); they elect leaders (Ea7B); they preach Christ around the world (Ea6c). Undoubtedly, Luke's depiction of the primitive Christian community—many peoples having become one people in Christ under the authority of several men, living in astonishing harmony with one another—is highly idealized. We do well to read these descriptions of the church not as history, but as images of the promised life we share in the Spirit.

The Jewish artist Marc Chagall was asked to supply the art for the baptistery in the church in Assy, France. His depiction of the Israelites crossing the Red Sea hangs on the wall by the font and is a superb example of Christians using Israel as metaphor in their own religious expression. The words *Israel, Judah*, and *the promised land* convey many different meanings, and so we must work hard to catechize our communities into the Christian meanings of these images. Quite simply, all these terms are metaphors that try to say *the people of God*. All these images proclaim a countercultural message: In a society that glorifies the isolated individual and marginalizes God, these images affirm that our life is life together and that our life together surrounds and is surrounded by God. Our identity is communal; we know ourselves as a people; and it is in our wrestling with God that we come to our strength and purpose.

Journey

goal, highway, journey, prize

Related chapters: ISRAEL, MOUNTAIN

The image of the journey, common in world religions, usually implies an arduous physical or psychological search for the ultimate spiritual goal. Although literal religious journeys are not required of Christians, the image is used as a metaphor for Christ's mission, the communal life of the baptized, and the commitment of the individual believer.

PSALM 139:2   You trace my journeys and my resting-places
and are acquainted with all my ways.

PRAYER BEFORE   Lord God our Father, you kept Abraham and Sarah in
TRAVEL   safety throughout the days of their pilgrimage, you led the
children of Israel through the midst of the sea, and by a star
you led the Wise Men to the infant Jesus. Protect and guide
us now in this time as we set out to travel, make our ways
safe and our homecomings joyful, and bring us at last to
our heavenly home, where you dwell in glory with your
Son and the Holy Spirit, one God forever.

WILLIAM   Guide me ever, great Redeemer,
WILLIAMS   pilgrim through this barren land.
I am weak, but you are mighty;
hold me with your powerful hand.
Bread of heaven,
feed me now and evermore.

Open now the crystal fountain
where the healing waters flow;
let the fire and cloudy pillar
lead me all my journey through.
Strong deliverer,
shield me with your mighty arm.

We took a route by which we would go down the length of the center of the valley where the children of Israel camped while Moses was ascending and descending the mountain of God. At the very head of the valley, we saw the place where Moses stood before the bush as God spoke to him. As we set out from the bush, the guides pointed out first the place where the camp of the children of Israel stood, and then the place where the calf was made. Next they showed an enormous rock, on which Moses, in anger, broke the tables he was carrying. Next we were shown the place where the seventy had received of the spirit of Moses, and then the place where the children of Israel had lusted for food. We were also shown where manna and quails had rained on them.

EGERIA,
Diary of a Pilgrimage

We ought to note carefully the words our Savior spoke, "How narrow is the gate and constricting the way that leads to life!" He says the gate is narrow to teach that entrance through this gate of Christ (the beginning of the journey) involves a divestment and narrowing of the will in relation to all sensible and temporal objects by loving God more than all of them. As this path on the high mount of perfection is narrow and steep, it demands travelers who are neither weighted down by the lower part of their nature nor burdened in the higher part.

JOHN OF THE CROSS,
The Ascent of Mount Carmel

THE WORD JOURNEY is rare in daily speech. We take trips, or go on hikes, or set out on vacation, or join an expedition, or move from one residence to another; but none of these is exactly a classic journey. A journey is a quest, an ordeal, an arduous search for a distant goal of enormous significance. In a journey, the way is uncertain, the road full of dangers. We who drive along the interstate highway in a comfortable car with food, shelter, and entertainment readily available may live in constant motion, and yet never experience a genuine journey.

History gives us a fuller appreciation for the meaning of journey. We think of those prehistoric movements of entire peoples to escape enemies or to locate a new food source. Medieval explorers were ignorant of both their route and their destination. American immigrants and refugees fled European religious intolerance, political injustice, and economic hardship. These journeys were not pleasurable jaunts, but were judged as less horrific than remaining in the present untenable situation. The journals of the pastor Henry M. Muhlenberg, who journeyed to colonial America to organize the Lutherans in Pennsylvania, describe how while on shipboard the crew and passengers ran out of drinking water, and how the rats, desperate to quench their own thirst, would lick the sweat off the faces of the sleeping people. Movies depicting the westward pioneers usually romanticize the journeys. Family members did not sit for the ride in the covered wagons, because the weight would have been too onerous for the oxen. The overland diaries of pioneer women record the numbers of graves lining the wagon route of each day's journey. The pioneers' journeying toward a new home encountered continuous uncertainties and life-threatening dangers nearly beyond our imagining.

When we contemplate a classic journey, we see why many religious traditions invoke the image of the journey to describe the spiritual quest. To discover and to embrace ultimate reality requires a continuous and often difficult movement away from what is trivial or evil and toward what is valuable and good. World religions attest that this journey is seldom a pleasurable jaunt or an invigorating hike. In some traditions, pilgrimage is urged or required. For pious Muslims, the hajj is both a literal journey to the holy places of the religion's founders and a symbol of one's perpetual journeying from secular to sacred realities. The physical journey exemplifies the spiritual journey incumbent on the faithful.

In the fourth century, European Christians began in earnest to explore the Holy Land. Queen Helena located what she thought were sites from the life of Jesus and discovered what she believed to be the true cross. Her journey inspired the tradition of pilgrimages to the places associated with Jesus and the apostles, and later with the saints and even legendary folk. We know of these journeys from serious accounts, such as Egeria's, as well as from popular descriptions of the practice, such as Chaucer's *Canterbury Tales*. Although in medieval times such pilgrimages were sometimes laid on public sinners as a penance, literal journeys to holy places were never a requirement for faithful Christian life.

Psychologists offer considerable discussion of the individual's interior journey. Carl G. Jung identified the journey as a primary universal archetype of transcendence. He described the visions of shamans as a journey into a deeper level of consciousness that results in healing for the people. The Jungian idea is that individuals, assisted by a wide variety of techniques, are encouraged to journey deeper into the meaning of life. The popularity of blank books designed for journaling is one example of the contemporary expectation that thoughtful persons approach life as if it were a journey into the meaning of the self.

Throughout the church's life texts of Christian spirituality use the imagery of journey to describe the psychological aspects of faithful life. The mystics invoked the image to illustrate the arduous nature of the continuous search for God. Two of the most influential spiritual writings of the Christian world describe religious journeys: the epic poem *The Divine Comedy*, by the fourteenth-century Christian Dante, who must journey through hell and purgatory on his way to glimpse heaven, and the allegory *Pilgrim's Progress*, by the seventeenth-century Puritan John Bunyan, whose Pilgrim abandons family and friends for the solitary journey to the Celestial City. The immense popularity of these two imaginative works can be interpreted as a sign of our attraction to the image of the journey.

Some biblical journeys are individual ones. Elijah, for example, travels alone to the mountain of God (1 Kings 17). Soon enough, however, the individual is turned toward the community: Elijah is sent right back to the capital city to get to work. Abraham does not journey alone; rather, Abraham, Sarah, and all their household journey forth from their ancestral home toward a new promised land. The Israelite people engage in forty years of nomadic journeying in the desert, traveling from slavery to their promised land. After the exile, the Jews journey back once again to Palestine.

Jesus' life retraces these mythic journeys. His parents journey to the city of David for his birth. Jesus journeys away from a murderous king. He journeys to and from Egypt. He spends, not forty years, but forty days, in a solitary journey in the desert. He journeys to and from the holy city of Jerusalem. The resurrection accounts suggest a final journey for Jesus: according to Mark, Jesus returns back to Galilee; in the books of Luke and Acts, he ascends into the skies; according to John, he is back again eight days later with the assembly.

The church's liturgical year recalls these journeys. In Advent, we journey with the crowds to hear John the Baptist, and we journey with Mary toward Bethlehem. In Lent, we journey into the desert with Jesus; in Holy Week we journey to the cross and the empty tomb; and in the fifty days of Easter we journey around the world, embodying the Spirit of the risen Christ. The point is not that we are reenacting the travels of ancient Israel or following Jesus around. Rather, each year the entire people of God journey again the road toward what holds highest value: their communal celebration and embrace of God's gift of life. Like the Israelite people, we journey away from slavery and into God's promised land. Along with the author of John we journey out of darkness into the light of God.

The lectionary accompanies us on our annual journey. We read the journey of Abraham and Sarah (Le2A, Pr5A°), repeated references to Israel's wanderings in the desert, the annual accounts of the crowds journeying to John the desert (Ad2A, Ad2B, Ad3B, Ad3C), and the annual account of Jesus' stay in the desert (Le1A, Le1B, Le1C). Prophetic poems promise God's protection on our journey: "They shall mount up with wings like eagles, they shall run and not be weary, they shall walk and not faint" (Ep5B). After Pentecost each year (Pr6A, Pr9B, Pr9C) come the accounts of Jesus sending out the twelve, or the seventy, in their missionary journeys, and we go out with them.

Biblical readings use journey as a metaphor. In John (Ea5A), in a variant of the journey image, Christ is the way, the truth, and the life. The passage from Mark 8 (Pr19B) describes the Christian as following Christ and carrying the cross. Paul likens the Christian life to the journey of the Israelites in the desert (Le3C). In a variant of the journey, the epistles compare the Christian life to a race (Ep6B, Le5C), for we "press on toward the goal for the prize." Hebrews 11 culminates with the imagery of a race and calls Jesus the pioneer in this race (Pr15C).

Another variant of the journey is the language of the highway. The Israelites juxtaposed their memories of nomadic wanderings in the desert with their observations of Babylonian, and later Roman, straight roadways.

These highways, usually constructed at great public expense in honor of the deity or the monarch, were the site of massive religious or civic processions. Isaiah 35 (Ad3A) is one of several Isaiah passages that promise that a holy highway will be laid in the desert by which all the nations will with ease be able to travel to the holy city. This highway is recalled in Advent (Ad2A, Ad2B, Ad2C) in the preaching of John the Baptist. The Christian idea is that baptism into the body of Christ is the highway along which we travel together toward our renewed life.

The Pima Papago, a Southwestern American Indian tribe, traditionally described human life as a maze through which the individual must journey, searching for its center. In the contemporary popularity of walking a labyrinth, it is as private psychological exploration that our culture utilizes the image of journey. Although in some ways similar to other ventures, the Christian liturgical journey is different from that of the Pima Papago, different from what self-help manuals describe. The very fact that we attend to the lectionary exemplifies the journey as experienced by Christians. We encounter the Bible, not hiking alone up a dangerous mountain, but standing together in the Sunday assembly. We receive the word, not in isolation, but with the help of centuries of Christian hymnwriters, preachers, poets, mystics, theologians.

The Christian journey is marked by distinctive emphases: we journey as a community; Christ is the journey by which we travel; the neighbor in need is the midpoint of the maze. The Christian life is not a solitary journey toward personal illumination or transformative escape, a lonely search that might be successful but all too often fails to deliver what was desired. Here is the good news: We journey together, with all the baptized of past and present. We search for what we already have—the presence of God and the cry of the needy. Our goal is ensured, for we arrive in Christ no matter how far we have traveled. I am accompanied by all the faithful, surrounded by all the needy, upheld by the triune God.

Judge

advocate, law, judge, justification

Related chapters: Day of the Lord, Kingdom, The Poor, Wisdom

The medieval Western church often depicted God as an angry judge. During the twentieth century, the opposite image was popular: God automatically forgives everyone everything. The lectionary draws us into a deeper consideration of the judge image. As the psalms say, the creation itself rejoices when God's justice is manifested on earth.

PSALM 96:12-13   Then shall all the trees of the wood shout for joy
before the LORD who is coming,
 who is coming to judge the earth.
The LORD will judge the world with righteousness
 and the peoples with truth.

NICENE CREED   He will come again in glory to judge the living and the dead.

APOSTLES'
CREED   He will come to judge the living and the dead.

BERNARD OF
CLUNY   The clouds of judgment gather;
the time is growing late;
be sober and be watchful;
our judge is at the gate:
the judge who comes in mercy,
the judge who comes in might
to put an end to evil
and diadem the right.

And I saw a figure who is leaning against the pillars, who represents God's Justice. She arises after Wisdom and by the Holy Spirit works in all the justice of human beings. She seems to be as broad as five people standing side by side, for she takes in all five human senses and uses them to abide in the law of God, and she contains and keeps all the commandments God instituted for those who love her. She has a large head and clear eyes, with which she is looking acutely into the heavens; for Justice, in her supreme goodness, has shown people a bright vision in the incarnate Son of God. Those human deeds that weigh people down do not cling to her, but only those that lead them to justification and life. For God is just; and she, fighting against the devil, shows it in her exhortation to other virtues, which work for God.

HILDEGARD OF BINGEN, *Scivias*

God so orders this corporeal world in its external affairs that if you respect and follow the judgment of human reason, you are bound to say either that there is no God or that God is unjust. But the light of glory tells us differently, and it will show us hereafter that the God whose judgment here is one of incomprehensible righteousness is a God of most perfect and manifest righteousness. In the meantime, we can only believe this.

MARTIN LUTHER, *The Bondage of the Will*

THE BIBLE PRESENTS GOD as the creator who made not only humankind but also the laws by which humans are to live. The Pentateuch states that not only the ten commandments of the covenant, but also hundreds of other religious and social laws, come from God. That God is the judge of all the world is said to be a terror only to those who are evil. All faithful people are to be joyful at the coming of the judge, because justice will come to reign in an unjust world. The New Testament continues this pattern. In the sermon on the mount, Jesus delivers a more interiorized, thus more pervasive, law. The authors of the pastoral epistles, promulgating standards for the Christian community that include even clothing regulations for the women, probably believed that their understanding of law came from God, who both makes the law and judges our ability to keep the law.

The image of God as judge was oppressively dominant during medieval Europe. Perhaps the civic and ecclesiastical authorities stressed God's judgment in order to ensure social order and to bolster their own authority. Because they believed that God was judge, and that God had put them in charge, then it followed that their judgments enjoyed divine sanction and support. Yet, partly because of the church's threats of hell and purgatory, God as judge became a fearful image to many believers. Countless medieval churches depict Christ as the stern judge, either in a stone carving on the door's tympanum or in a painting on the front wall of the sanctuary. One entered the church building or stood throughout the liturgy under the unblinking gaze of the Judge. The elaborate system of penances that permeated European medieval society reflected this fear of divine judgment. Much Marian devotion developed in compensatory reaction to Christ as judge. Mary was depicted as protecting the faithful, as pleading to her Son and softening his heart from judgment to mercy. Popular folk religion suggested that if the divine judge were to close the gates of heaven against you, you would need only go to heaven's back door, where the merciful Mary would let you in. So it is no surprise that Reformation preachers, especially Martin Luther, stressed the forgiveness of God. Belief in Christ brought justification: to believers, God was a loving father, not an exacting judge. Although some Protestant traditions continued a strong emphasis on divine judgment, twentieth-century piety suggests that

Luther's emphasis triumphed. Not justice, but forgiveness is popularly understood as God's primary activity.

Several contemporary situations heighten our difficulty in understanding God as judge. As people become aware of other ethical systems than their own and realize the cultural patterns undergirding any set of laws, it seems naive to imagine God as the lawgiver. Critical biblical readers must reject the idea that God literally gave the law as recorded in the Bible. If God is understood as lawgiver, it follows that God is judge; if laws have arisen in other than divine ways, however, then God as judge also fades. To the extent that the human potential movement, which stresses the innate goodness of the individual, has replaced the classical Christian doctrine of sin, errors are understood as mistakes, even growth experiences, rather than as instances of the wretched systemic condition that alienates the culpable human from the divine judge.

The twentieth-century psychological movement contributed to the decline of the church's use of the image of judge. Guilt is often interpreted, not as the objective condition of one who has broken a just law, but as the subjective state of one whose sense of right and wrong may have been malformed by home, society, or religion. Because we can no longer imagine in a naive way that God handed down to us our moral code, we do not agree which activities are evil or whether our guilt is appropriate. A recent study of sermons based on the parable of the prodigal son demonstrated that the dominant theme was that we should all avoid mimicking the angry older brother by judging others. God, like the loving father, does not judge, but forgives.

What you think of God as judge depends a good deal on which side of the world's uneven justice you experience. Liberation theology, articulating the lot of the world's poor and oppressed peoples, sounds again the song of the psalms. Those who suffer poverty and degradation eagerly await the coming of divine justice, singing with joy when they see God as judge arriving. Here is an alternate image of Mary: not Mary the Queen who sneaks you into heaven when the Judge isn't looking, but Mary the lowly peasant whose Magnificat rejoices at the coming of justice for all the downtrodden of the earth. Liberation theologians proclaim that God's judgment is aimed against social injustice, against the rich's misuse of the poor and the rulers' trampling of the masses, rather than at each individual's mistakes and instances of selfish behavior.

Some church traditions continue to stress God as judge, and some avoid such language. Some think of God's judgment as more concerned with personal, perhaps especially sexual, morality, and others speak of social justice for the poor. We all are called to balance our use of the language of judge: God is judge, and God is not judge; God is just, while in many instances God appears quite unjust, or at least beyond our human sense of justice; Christ is judge, yet the Spirit is advocate. Believers are to refrain from judging one another; yet we are called to name injustice when we see it. The lectionary's variety of uses of the judge image can help us into a deeper, wider understanding of divine communal justice.

The three-year lectionary includes several different uses of the biblical idea of God as judge. As the one with the power to make earth, God also has the authority to hold creatures accountable to the law. In a Hosea reading (Pr21A[†]), God speaks with the voice of the stern judge, contending against the people and their complaint that God is unjust. In this reading, God claims the right of judge, yet concludes by urging the people to turn and live. God judges justly (Ea4A), God judges righteously (Pr20B[†]).

The lectionary option that reads semicontinuously through the Hebrew Scriptures in the summer and fall includes readings in which the faithful express anger and alienation from God as judge. A speech from the despairing Job (Pr23B°) proclaims that God appears unjust, and in a caustic condemnation of humankind, Jeremiah assures the people that the judge will not relent (Pr19C°).

But in the lectionary God is nearly always the forgiving judge. Luke uses the parable of the unjust judge (Pr24C) to describe a forgiving God who grants justice to the elect. In a passage from Isaiah that recurs in the lectionary (PasA, PasB, Pr19B, Pasc), other people are adversarial and declare us guilty, but God vindicates us. According to Isaiah 55 (VigilABC, Le3C), God is judge, but one who abundantly pardons: God's justice is beyond human justice. The lectionary does not include the narrative of the destruction of Sodom and Gomorrah. Rather, it includes the story of Abraham's pleading for the city and God's willingness to forgive the entire city for the sake of the few faithful (Pr12C[†]). If we did not know the story of the burning of the cities, the lectionary would lead us to believe that God heeds the pleas of the believers for mercy for all. In another example of the lectionary's stress on mercy, the vineyard's owner is persuaded to keep the fig tree alive one more year (Le3C). In another, the terrified Isaiah hears the angel remove his guilt and sin (Ep5C). The Christian belief that God's dealings are characterized by mercy repeats the teaching in the Talmud, which uses the numbers of Exodus 20:5-6 to say that God has 500 times more mercy than justice.

Any fear of God in biblical narratives, for example, the people's terror at Sinai, is far less than the delight in God's law that the psalmist celebrates. Living in disregard of the law will turn us into chaff blown away; living within the law forms in us the endurance and fruitfulness of a mighty tree. Psalm 119 praises the law as God's self-disclosure. The idea is that if we live according to the law, we live in communion with God and one another, since the covenant's commandments (Pr22A°, Le3B) are a prescription for just life within the community.

In describing salvation as justification, Paul elaborated the image of God as judge. Paul's training as a rabbinic lawyer is evident in his repeated use of legal-sounding terminology: law, judgment, condemnation, righteousness, trespass, reconciled, appeal, sin. For Paul, Christ replaces Torah. Christ's death and resurrection reversed the judgment of the divine court. We are justified, says Paul, not only declared innocent by the judge, but genuinely freed from guilt for sin, thanks to Christ. Although the book of James claims that Abraham was justified by his works, the book of Hebrews and the words of Paul claim the opposite: it was faith that justified Abraham (Le2A). The lectionary includes significant sections of Romans, 2 Corinthians, and Galatians that rely on this imagery (Le1A, Le2A, Le3A, Pr4A, Pr5A, Pr6A, Pr10A, Le4C, Pr6C).

Considerable obstacles block our reception of this classic Christian emphasis on justification, much of which occurs in the second reading of the day. The Pauline passages are not easy listening, and the legal language of his argument can sound alien to people unfamiliar with this imagery. Some assemblies reduce the lectionary's readings from three to two: how often is the second reading dropped? Many preachers attend to only one reading each week: how often is this reading the epistle? Yet for those who try to weave together the three readings, the second reading usually concerns itself with the assembly of believers, and it offers a path down which to walk, a way to apply the images found in the narratives, the poems, and the prophetic speeches to the congregation there assembled. The interplay of the three readings can help keep the justification language alive and well among us.

The gospels present two different uses of the judge image in relation to Christ. It is Christ as judge, rather than God as judge, usually depicted on church walls and windows. Jesus is the one "ordained by God as judge of the living and the dead" (BapA, EaA). We must appear before the judgment seat of Christ (Pr6B). Judgment will occur when the Lord comes again (Pr3A), on a day fixed by God (Ea6A). One popular image of what is often called "the second coming" is the parable of the Last Judgment in which Christ, referred to in the parable as Son-of-man, king, lord, and "as a shepherd," is judge of all (LastA).

Yet according to the Gospel of John, the Son came into the world, not to condemn the world, but to save. In the lectionary, this opposite function—

not to judge, but to speak on our behalf—is credited by John to the Advocate (Pentв, Ea6c). Although Christ is no longer among us, the Spirit of Christ is alive and well in the community, and this spirit is one of advocacy and of forgiveness. The members of the community are to intercede for one another. We are to be one another's defense counsel. That like Abraham, we plead for one another before the divine standard of justice, is an idea often neglected.

The lectionary's use of the language of judging is the plural. Many speakers of English forget that the *you* of so much of the New Testament and the liturgy is a plural pronoun. Its being plural is obvious in many languages, but in English, the singular and plural *you* are not distinguishable. (What was originally the English singular pronoun, *thou*, has become obsolete, and *you*, originally plural, is used for both singular and plural.) Furthermore, with American culture so individually focused, many people hear the biblical and liturgical *you* as referring to *me*, rather than to *us*. The Johannine idea that the Spirit in the community will be our Advocate assumes a communal reality. It is to *you-all* that Christ promises the Paraclete.

The lectionary also includes passages about the human practice of judging. The Hebrew Scriptures speak a good deal about the role of the tribal leader, the priest, and the king as judge. The social leaders that the Old Testament terms *the judges* were rulers and military saviors rather than juridical figures. Yet God expects all the faithful to live in justice and to judge rightly in their dealings with others. Inspired by God's justice, we are to judge our neighbor with justice (Pr25A[†]) and "to establish justice in the gate" (Pr23B[†]), ensuring a just society for the poor. However, the lectionary's selections also urge us to avoid judging one another, leaving judgments to God (Pr19A).

Just as the typical child comes to realize that life is not fair, so all the world's major religious traditions inquire into why there is so little justice in human society and whether divine powers are willing to intervene to ensure justice. Seen in its biblical light, the image of the divine judge is good news. We can trust that at least God exemplifies justice, and we hope that in God justice will finally be achieved and celebrated by the whole creation.

Furthermore, the image of the judge calls the church to be faithful to the implications of the gospel. Not only are we thankful that Christ vindicates us from divine judgment: we are to enflesh the Spirit of God in this world, making society more and more a place marked by justice for all. Each week our weekly intercessions pray for the United Nations, for governmental leaders, for legislators, for judges, for law enforcement officers, for the poor, for refugees, for oppressed minorities, for victims of war and abuse, for an increase of justice in the world. These prayers serve not only to beg that God come as judge, but also to convert ourselves into the spirit of divine advocacy. Remade into the image of Christ, we are to speak the word of God's justice in the world.

The task is difficult. Granting the complexity of moral issues and social problems, we do not always know what is just. Within the church will be continuous discussion about the best route to a just world. The church must be alert against self-congratulation. Even the idealized language of communal love that we read in John's gospel can develop into the criticism of the outsider that we find in the Johannine epistles. Here is the paradox: God as judge is good news for the whole world. Martin Luther argued that this claim makes sense only if we are ready to redefine justice. Here is the challenge: to welcome God the judge with singing, and to proclaim justice as good news for the whole world.

Kingdom

anointing, Christ, crown, David,
king, kingdom, messiah, right hand,
seal, Son of God, throne

Related chapters: BATTLE, CITY, DAY OF THE LORD, ISRAEL

The image of the kingdom of God pervades the scriptures and is central to the texts of Christian liturgy. The language of Christ as king is important to the lectionary. Believers of the twenty-first century, however, encounter many problems when interpreting this complex imagery.

PSALM 145:1,   I will exalt you, O God my Sovereign,
10, 13   and bless your name forever and ever.
All your works praise you, O LORD,
    and your faithful servants bless you.
Your kingdom is an everlasting kingdom;
    your dominion endures throughout all ages.

THE LORD'S   Your kingdom come.
PRAYER

ISAAC WATTS   Jesus shall reign where'er the sun
does its successive journeys run;
his kingdom stretch from shore to shore,
till moons shall wax and wane no more.

People and realms of every tongue
dwell on his love with sweetest song;
and infant voices shall proclaim
their early blessings on his name.

Blessings abound where'er he reigns:
the prisoners leap to lose their chains,
the weary find eternal rest,
and all who suffer want are blest.

The Kingdom of God is greater than all report, better than all praise of it, more manifold than every conceivable glory. The Kingdom of God is so full of light, peace, charity, wisdom, glory, honesty, sweetness, lovingkindness and every unspeakable and unutterable good, that it can neither be described nor envisioned by the mind. The citizens of heaven are the just and the angels, whose king is Almighty God. In the Kingdom of God, nothing is desired that may not be found. In the Kingdom of God is nothing that does not delight and satisfy. In the eternal Kingdom there shall be life without death, truth without falsehood, and happiness without a shadow of unrest or change.

PATRICK,
SERMON FOR
ADVENT

Jesus' messianic proclamation centers on his interpretation of the tradition of a coming Reign of God. He does not evoke the hope for the Davidic Messiah. Jesus seems to express a radicalized view of the concept of a coming Reign of God as a time of the vindication of the poor and the oppressed. Jesus' vision of the Kingdom is neither nationalistic nor other-worldly. The coming Reign of God is expected to happen on earth, as the Lord's Prayer makes evident (God's Kingdom come, God's will be done on earth). It is a time when structures of domination and subjugation have been overcome, when the basic human needs are met (daily bread), when all dwell in harmony with God and each other (not led into temptation but delivered from evil).

ROSEMARY
RADFORD
RUETHER,
Sexism and
God-Talk

$\approx$

THE LANGUAGE OF THE KINGDOM is the most recurrent and most formative image in the Bible. In the Old Testament, this kingdom is implied in many aspects of the Israelite belief, for example the evolution of the tribes into the nation-state, God's anointing of a king, the mythic status of David, the dream of national sovereignty, and the liturgical affirmation that YHWH is Sovereign. Jesus' fundamental message was the proclamation of this kingdom, called the kingdom of God by Mark and Luke and the kingdom of heaven(s) by Matthew. That believers named Jesus Messiah indicates the paramount importance of kingdom imagery. Furthermore, the kingdom myth is the source of the Father-Son language used in trinitarian speech. Thus to call Christ the Son of God requires first us to see Jesus as the messiah, the anointed of God's kingdom.

According to the myths of the Babylonians, Canaanites, and Egyptians, those peoples that wielded influence on the people of Israel, the primordial chaos at the beginning of time was conquered when the deities appointed one of their own as a champion to slay the prehistoric monster and to establish a safe place for the people to reside. Characteristically, the primary deity was male, the champion was male, the monster was female, chaos was the sea, and home was the capital city for what became the succession of divinely appointed kings. Although the mythic stories focused on the exploits of the champion-made-king, the legend itself was the creation myth of the people. Before the champion saved them, there was no earth for humankind. Thanks to the victorious divine king, they were now a settled people, civilized, residing in a city, enjoying the protection that hierarchical order ensured. The myth celebrated not only the ruler, but also the people, the community, the kingdom.

The first twelve books of the Bible trace Israel's adaptation of this myth. According to these records, first they were no people. After the exodus, they became a confederation of tribes over whom only God reigned. Still later, national sovereignty located in a capital city looked more attractive than either the traditional matrifocal or later patriarchal nomadic tribal culture. Although both Moses and Samuel (Pr5B°) are quoted as warning the people that oftentimes kingship does not provide what the myth promises, Israel evolved into a kingdom with a similar kingdom myth as its neighbors.

Subsequent historical memories bore witness to the truth of these warnings. Recall, for example, King David's violation of Bathsheba and Uriah (Pr12B°, Pr6c†), King Ahab's thieving (Pr5c°), and King Herod's treachery (Pr10B). Despite the flaws of kings, the people were formed by YHWH into a kingdom. They were to serve YHWH; YHWH set up King David to protect against Israel's enemies; David ruled from the capital city Jerusalem, which came to be described as the center of the world. The idea was that the king, anointed by God, ruled in God's stead over the kingdom that God established.

Here is where father-son language enters Jewish and Christian religious vocabulary. According to the prevalent cultural myth, the champion who became the first king was divine, and his descendants were named son of the deities. In some of the oldest versions of the myth, the deity was female, but later the male deity adopted the subsequent kings as son and heir. The king, now honored as the son of God, reigned over the kingdom with divine sanction and semidivine authority. Although the language of the king being son of the gods fell out of use in later millennia, the notion of the divine right of kings persisted in Europe until the French Revolution. Discussion about the meaning of the titles *Father* and *Son* for the Trinity must recognize that the language of Jesus as the son of God originated, not in a familial metaphor, but in the kingdom myth of the ancient Near East. We need to understand which were original and which were acquired meanings of an image.

This complex of ideas is articulated especially in what are called the royal psalms. In Psalm 2 (TransA) God adopts the king and names him son and begotten of God. In Psalm 110 (AscABC) God places the victorious king at the right hand of heaven's throne to serve as assistant ruler. It is God who rules. The king is God's right-hand man. The so-called enthronement psalms celebrate the reign of God through the king and describe the joy, not only of the people, but also of nature itself. These psalms are appointed in the lectionary to praise the birth of Jesus: Psalm 96 is appointed for Christmas Eve, Psalm 97 for Christmas Dawn, and Psalm 98 for Christmas Day.

The importance of these psalms for early Christian reflection on the identity and purpose of Jesus cannot be overestimated. The royal myth that the adopted king reigns from God's right hand as the son of God became the normative language used to describe Christ. These psalms are cited as the words of God spoken at the baptism of Jesus. In Acts 2 (Ea2A) the Davidic legacy is cited, and in the accounts of Jesus' trial and crucifixion, the imagery of divine kingship echoes the royal psalms that early believers would have known by heart.

Some of the first readings during Advent refer to the Davidic myth of the divinely appointed king who will reign over the kingdom that God restored to safety and prosperity. Reminiscent of Egyptian art in which a great tree stood behind or in place of the pharaoh, some ancient Near Eastern poetry described the king as the kingdom's tree of life. It is a branch of this Davidic tree that Jeremiah anticipated (Ad1c, Pr11b†). Like David of old, the coming king will originate in Bethlehem (Ad4c, Pr11b°). To parallel the gospel reading of the annunciation, the lectionary appoints God's promise to David that his kingdom will be secure forever (Ad4b). The readings for Christmas from Isaiah repeat the imagery. The child will inherit the throne of David (ChEabc), through which the reign of God will bring life and health to the people (ChDyabc).

In the passion narratives, the Davidic myth of kingship is both presented and broken. This king is not a king. In the synoptic gospels, Jesus uses the apocalyptic imagery of the Son-of-man being seated at the right hand of God, and he does not deny the title King of the Jews (Pasa, Pasb, Pasc), the charge nailed to the cross. His crown, later glorified in ecclesiastical art, was an instrument of torture. In John, the symbols of divine kingship, for example the purple robe, are poignantly paradoxical, and in conversation with Pilate Jesus states that the language of the kingdom does not mean what anyone would imagine it to mean (GFrabc). At Epiphany, the magi who seek the Davidic king give homage to only a poor newborn (Epabc), and at his temptation Jesus refuses to take the throne (Le1a, Le1c).

Even though Jesus is no king, he acquired from his followers the status of divinely authorized king. The title Christ, that is, the Anointed One, the Messiah, was the Jewish encapsulation of the Davidic myth. One would arrive whom God would designate as head of the kingdom. Who do people say that I am? asks Jesus, and Peter, as leader in the community, answers, "You are the Messiah, the Son of the living God" (Pr16a). Because our Bible translations are Christian, our English versions of this verse capitalize the nouns *Messiah* and *Son*, although the Greek makes no typographical distinction. We must continue to probe the meaning of the title *Christ*. Constant thoughtless use might suggest that Christ is part of Jesus' given name, rather than a complex and paradoxical title.

Some users of the three-year lectionary title the last Sunday of the year Christ the King. This Sunday is characteristically a time when the paradox of the imagery gets obscured by triumphal processions and enthusiastic hymns. Yet the gospel readings from John 19 (Lastb) and from Luke 23 (Lastc) make clear that king language is metaphor for one who is not a king. Naming this Sunday Reign of Christ is somewhat better, but perhaps simply saying the Last Sunday of the Year is best. In other Christian festivals as well, the paradox of the language is apparent. At Christmas and Epiphany, the king is a helpless newborn; at Jesus' baptism the beloved son is an itinerant preacher; his purple robe garbs him before execution; and Christ's ascension to the right hand of God describes his absence from the community. The Zechariah text lauding the arrival of the king is set beside Jesus' revelation to infants and description of his yoke (Pr9A†), and according to Revelation, at the center of the throne is the lamb.

The fundamental New Testament language is not of a king but of a kingdom. The goal of a Davidic king is the safety and prosperity of the kingdom. In Ephesians and Colossians, the praise of the resurrected Christ as king is part of a prayer for the church (LastA, Lastc), and in Revelation, the kingdom becomes priests serving God (LastB, Ea2c). The narrative of Samuel anointing David (Le4A) is read parallel with the story of Jesus' anointing the eyes of the blind man, for the point is that we are now anointed by God to reign with the divine spirit. The focus is not only on a king who effects all that is good, but also on us who bear the royal seal of baptism. A similar emphasis is held by most religious Jews, who understand the biblical messiah language as metaphoric speech that refers to the community: it is the community of faith, inspired by God, who will make the world ready for God.

The synoptic gospels indicate that Jesus consistently preached the coming of the kingdom. Perhaps this preaching was mostly characterized by enigmatic sayings, such as Jesus' single sentences recorded in Mark (Pr6B) or his claim that the kingdom belonged to children (Pr22B). Perhaps Jesus' preaching included long imaginative stories, as Matthew records (Pr11A, Pr19A, Pr20A, Pr21A, Pr23A, Pr27A). Many biblical scholars speculate that especially the allegories (for example, Pr10A, Pr22A) reflect more of the Matthean community's attitudes toward Judaism than of Jesus' own preaching style.

The primary prayer of Christians, called the Lord's Prayer, the Our Father, or the prayer of Jesus, gathers up many classic Jewish themes into Jesus' proclamation of the kingdom. "Your kingdom come," we pray, as did Jews before us and to this day. Both the petition that God's kingdom come and that God's name be honored pray for a world in which God's reign is realized. What will characterize this divine dominion? All will enjoy daily bread and all will have their sins forgiven. Bread and forgiveness: each person will be able to survive, and everybody together will unite into a cooperative community.

What precisely the imagery of the kingdom refers to sits at the center of a debate ongoing throughout the history of the church. In the second century Justin Martyr reported that some Christians believed in a literal millennial kingdom soon to arrive, while others received the biblical speech about the kingdom as allegory of eternal life. Today a small group of believers interpret the kingdom of God as a future state on earth, necessitating either a transformation of individuals or a reformed political reality. For others, the kingdom refers to the church itself, either at present or in a future perfected state. For still others, the kingdom is a wholly spiritual reality, having to do with either a believer's emotional state during an intense religious experience or life after death. Most teachers of the faith combine several of these interpretations, so that for mainstream Christians the language of the kingdom always carries at least two meanings, one here already and one only fully realized in the future. Eschatology—the promise that the kingship of Christ and all that it will effect will arrive in the future—continues to be variously interpreted by Christian preachers.

During the twentieth century a group of biblical scholars constituted what was called the metaphor school. Norman Perrin, Robert W. Funk, John Dominic Crossan, and Sallie McFague are among those who described Jesus' proclamation of the kingdom as religious metaphor and Jesus as a master of metaphor. Because Jesus preached metaphor, we cannot be surprised at the diversity in interpretation, for metaphor is open-ended and capable of accumulating meaning. The community judges some interpretations creedal, some optional, some rejected. One can think of the history of biblical interpretation as the many layers of meaning that Jesus' enigmatic metaphors suggested to believers, and the various pieties and denominations as groups emphasizing different facets of the many biblical metaphors.

Speaking of Jesus as king or as the son of God is the odd speech of metaphoric paradox. Yet the language can easily become literalized. Ecclesiastical art depicting Jesus in royal robes or triumphalistic hymns reminiscent of a coronation need to be juxtaposed to Jesus' identification with the poor and to serious attention to the world's injustices. That many contemporary Christians do not live in a kingdom and perhaps do not even respect that classic form of civil society makes the task of interpretation a considerable challenge. Most Christians who do have a queen or a king understand the monarch as nothing but a figurehead. The Bible invoked the imagery of king with high intent, not with nostalgic charm. Our proclamation of Christ as king ought not imply either historic sexism, in which a man must be in charge, or infantilism, a faith that reduces us to children who need to follow orders.

It is unfortunate that most of the church's consideration of this imagery has focused on king, rather than on kingship or kingdom. About kingship: the idea of Christ's kingship was historically important to Christians. It provided crucial psychological freedom from the oppression of governmental structures. Often it became the source of strength for the Christian community's resistance to unjust rule. Christ's reign, his mercy and justice, was the dominion within which the Christian community found its life. About kingdom: the idea of the community of believers realizing itself as God's kingdom was, similarly, a comfort in times of oppression and an inspiration for unified action within and outside the circle of faith. Especially in the sacramental life, the images of Christ's kingship and the church's kingdom are important. The baptized are sealed with holy oil as a sign that believers are anointed by the Spirit of God, as was Jesus, to reign in the kingdom of God. The phrase from Luke 17:21, often cited as "the kingdom of God is within you," is more correctly translated "the kingdom of God is among you"; that is, the kingdom is realized in your (plural) midst, rather than in your (singular) heart.

Some women theologians propose the spelling *kin-dom* to stress the communal aspect of the imagery and to reduce the patriarchal origin of the term. We might alternate the words *kingdom*, *kingship*, *kin-dom*, *reign*, *dominion*, *realm*, and *rule* in order to show the various facets of the biblical image. The hope is that the image can be one, not of oppression or reminiscent of archaism, but of mercy and the communal life of justice. The good news is that the kingdom can be a metaphor for God's very self. Together we live in God as in a kingdom, united by the Spirit and calling the whole world into divine peace.

Light

blindness, darkness, day, light,
morning star, night, sight, star, sun

Related chapters: CREATION, EMANATION OF THE DIVINE, FIRE

In Christian literature, light is a metaphor for God's very self and
for all that is related to God: creation, the word, Christ, salvation,
and the baptized life. Christian liturgy incorporates this central
biblical image with its use of light imagery at its primary celebrations, for example Easter, Christmas, Epiphany, and baptism.

PSALM 18:29   You, O LORD, are my lamp;
              my God, you make my darkness bright.

THE EXSULTET   May the light of Christ, rising in glory,
               dispel the darkness of our hearts and minds.
               Exult, O earth, enlightened with such radiance;
               and, made brilliant by the splendor of the eternal King,
               know that the ancient darkness
               has been banished from all the world.
               . . . Wherefore, dearly beloved,
               who stand in the clarity of this bright and holy light,
               join with me, I ask you,
               in praising the lovingkindness of almighty God.
               . . . May he who is the morning star find it burning—
               that morning star which never sets,
               that morning star which, rising again from the grave,
               faithfully sheds light on all the human race.

AMBROSE   O Splendor of the Father's Light
OF MILAN   that makes our daylight lucid, bright;
              O Light of light and sun of day,
              now shine on us your brightest ray.

              True Sun, break out on earth and shine
              in radiance with your light divine;
              by dazzling of your Spirit's might,
              oh, give our jaded senses light.

              The Father sends his Son, our Lord,
              to be his bright and shining Word;
              come, Lord, ride out your gleaming course
              and be our dawn, our light's true source.

You must note that hardly any of the light coming from the King's royal chamber reaches these first dwelling places. Even though they are not dark and black, as when the soul is in sin, they nevertheless are in some way darkened so that the soul cannot see the light. The darkness is not caused by a flaw in the room—for I don't know how to explain myself—but by so many bad things like snakes and vipers and poisonous creatures that enter with the soul and don't allow it to be aware of the light. It's as if a person were to enter a place where the sun is shining but be hardly able to open his eyes because of the mud in them.

Teresa of Avila, *The Interior Castle*

Now morning being come, Christian looked back, not out of desire to return, but to see, by the light of the day, what hazards he had gone through in the dark. So he saw more perfectly the ditch that was on the one hand and the cowage that was on the other, also how narrow the way was which lay betwixt them both. Also now he saw the dragons of the pit, but all afar off, for after break of day they came not nigh. Yet they were discovered to him, according to that which is written, He discovereth deep things out of darkness, and bringeth out of light the shadow of death. About this time the sun was rising, and this was another mercy to Christian. Then said he, His candle shineth on my head, and by his light I go through darkness.

John Bunyan, *The Pilgrim's Progress*

ONE OF THE MOST COMMONPLACE ARCHETYPES in human history is light. On this planet the life cycles of plants and animals depend upon light. Because our existence is constituted by and around light, scientists demarcate the universe by its solar systems. Many peoples speak of also intellectual maturation and spiritual growth as light. What the Buddha achieves is enlightenment. The ancient Aaronic blessing says that God's face shines; artistic convention depicts holiness as if it were a visible circle of light; and contemporary cartoons draw a light bulb to indicate a character's good idea. From the profound to the trivial, light indicates all that is good.

Ancient religious myths acknowledged this dependency on light by noting in their cosmogonies the primordial separation of light from darkness. According to the Zoroastrian dualism of ancient Iran, this separation set up an eternal conflict between the power of light and the forces of darkness. Humans must continuously struggle against darkness for the light. In some other worldviews, for example indicated by the yin-yang symbol, the opposites fit harmoniously together, each containing a small circle of its opposite.

In many cultures, the sun itself was divine. Especially in cultures such as Egypt and Mexico with hierarchical political organizations, sun worship prevailed, as if the monarch on the top of the social triangle was legitimated by the power of the sun in the sky. Among the Aztecs, persons at the base of the socioeconomic triangle were sacrificed to the sun, which required human blood as payment for its shedding of light. Some biblical scholars speculate whether the presence of the sanctuary lamp, described in Leviticus 24:2, suggests an earlier light worship of the Israelite ancestors.

Like many other world myths, the story in Genesis 1 (VigilABC, TrinA, BapB) gives light primary place, but the biblical storytellers make clear that people ought not worship the sun as the origin of light. The sun was not created until the fourth day: light came not from the sun, but from God, and light ought to inspire humankind to worship God. In Islam also, the lamp that hangs in the niche of each mosque points out the direction toward Mecca: a light shows the way to God. When Christian artists painted the annunciation with a light beaming down onto the virgin Mary, theologians explained that the mystery and might of the extraordinary pregnancy came from God.

Many intensely metaphorical biblical passages, such as Genesis 1, the Psalms, the poems in Isaiah, John, the Johannine epistles, and Revelation, are filled with light images. Light can be a metaphor for God's self, as when God's face shines. Light can be a symbol of God's creative powers, as in the creation stories in Genesis 1 and Job 38. Especially in the psalms, light functions as a metaphor for the word of God, from which comes knowledge of human salvation and by which the faithful can see how and where to walk. The prophets speak of salvation as if it were light coming to the nations. The incarnation of God in Jesus is described as the light of the world, and God's people are described as people of the light: people who, rejecting the paths of darkness, travel together in the light toward the light who is God.

Light is contrasted with its opposite, darkness. In most biblical poetry and narrative, darkness is what is apart from God. Matthew's parables use the term *outer darkness* to suggest the final alienation from all that comes from God. God led the people of Israel with a pillar of fire, without which the people would have been lost in night. In John's gospel, blindness is a symbol for spiritual ignorance: the narrative of the man born blind (Le3A) is meant not only to affirm that Jesus had miraculous powers, but to proclaim that all the readers of the gospel were born in and reside within darkness, unless and until they come to be illumined by Christ. When on Good Friday Christ, the light of the world, was extinguished, all the gospels tell of extraordinary darkness covering the land. John's gospel says of the moment when Judas left the last supper, "and it was night" (John 13:30).

However, as Isaiah 45:7 says, God makes also the night. As poets, the mystics of the Christian tradition searched for unique ways to describe God, and so although it is commonplace to describe God as light, the mystics, who see differently from the rest of us, said that God is darkness. In asserting that God is night, they are saying not only that our God is far more than the natural light we know, but also that the word *light* is wholly inadequate to describe the total otherness of God. Even stereotypical religious imagery fails in describing God.

It would be good if at least several hymns in common use included the mysterious language that God is both night and day, darkness and light. Without our recognizing that God is also night, we fall prey to a dualism in which easy separation is made between all that is good and all that is evil—a separation that should never satisfy baptized sinners. Light is not actually God: light is only a metaphor for the things of God, and if we never call God also darkness, we come to literalize the light of God. One example of this problem is seen in hymns in which darkness is equated with evil. Such expression might border on racist notions that all things closer to white are better than things closer to black. So although light is only one image of God, and an inadequate one at that, the three-year lectionary grants to texts and rituals of light preeminent place. We will consider here the Easter Vigil, baptism, the twelve days of Christmas, and daily prayer.

During the first century, the Jewish celebration of passover included a late-night waiting for the Lord. The seder meal was both a remembrance of the exodus and an anticipation of the coming of the messiah. It was as if the ritual of remembrance served to remind also God of the people's need, as if retelling the exodus would encourage God to send the messiah. In the decades after the death of Jesus, it is likely that Jews who were his followers kept up the night ritual, for they anticipated that the messiah would return soon to save them. Naturally, at any nighttime religious ritual in which people implore God to send salvation, whether the seder or the weekly sabbath, lamps or candles take on ritual significance. The Jewish woman begins the sabbath by lighting the sabbath candles, as if she, like God, is beginning creation anew in the creation of light.

Two Christian rituals developed from the use of the paschal light. Southern European churches came to craft enormous paschal candles, mounted in paschal candlestands that reach 10, 12, even 20 feet high. The light of the paschal candle was a symbol of the risen Christ, shining from the tomb of death into the world's darkness. Many churches are restoring the use of a paschal candle, which annually is marked with the date of the year as well as with the Alpha and Omega, names of the eternal God. The candle leads the Easter procession and remains lit through Pentecost Sunday. The medieval practice of extinguishing the paschal candle after the gospel reading on Ascension is now discouraged by most liturgical reformers, as suggesting in too literal a way that Jesus is now gone from the church. This light of Christ, "the morning star," is lighted again at each baptism throughout the year and stands next to the coffin at a Christian funeral.

Another ritual was developing in northern Europe. Especially in the latitudes in which winter is marked by extended darkness, a springtime pagan ritual, overseen by a designated priestly authority, included lighting of the springtime fire to signify the return of light to the land. The people may not have distinguished whether the priest celebrated the sun's return or effected the sun's return. The legend of St. Patrick tells that, against the law, he himself lighted the springtime fire and, preaching his new religion, proclaimed Christ as the light. Churches today are reclaiming this ritual by assembling in the night of the Easter Vigil, both to mark the return of spring by lighting a fire—the date of Easter is set in relation to the Northern Hemisphere's spring equinox—and to proclaim the resurrection: The light of Christ: Thanks be to God!

The Easter Vigil is not only the proclamation of the Easter gospel of the empty tomb. For the Vigil, the lectionary appoints four, or seven, or twelve, of the Old Testament stories about God's creative salvation. The first reading is God's creation of the universe, which opens with the creation of light. The Vigil presents God's light in a paradoxical way, for it is dark night; one large candle stands in the center of the candlelit room. Only in forthright honesty about darkness can our rejoicing about light have its deepest meaning. As the narratives of the resurrection say—"the first day of the week was dawning," "very early on the first day of the week, when the sun had risen," "at early dawn," "while it was still dark"—Christ rose at the close of night. Although some communities schedule the Vigil early enough in the evening for children's participation, it is best if the night sky is already dark, so that the outdoor ritual of light makes symbolic sense.

Twentieth-century liturgical reforms attempted to reconnect Easter with baptism. Instructed by the ancient church, many communities are moving toward the Easter Vigil as the most appropriate time for the parish baptisms. Baptism is not predominantly a family ritual about a new baby, but a Christian celebration of the resurrection in the life of another person. Early Christian writings about baptism commonly refer to Christian initiation as illumination. Narratives about conversion, for example the man born blind in John 9 (Le4A) or Paul's conversion in Acts 9 (Ea3A), employ the image of light as a symbol of enlightenment of the new believer. Contemporary baptismal rituals include the presentation of the baptismal candle, which is to be lighted from the paschal candle, for the newly baptized believers are now among those who are themselves a new creation and who carry in themselves the light of the resurrection. Christians are encouraged to light their baptismal candle at home each year on their baptismal anniversary. Newly composed baptismal hymns include the image of light. The Sunday of the Baptism of the Lord is another appropriate time for parish baptisms, and its readings incorporate light imagery: Isaiah sees God coming as a light to the nation, opening blind eyes (BapA), and the Genesis creation of light is told once again (BapB).

The birth of Christ was not observed in any way for the first three centuries of Christianity. About the time of the legalization of the Christian religion, in the mid-fourth century, the cultural celebration of the winter solstice was seen as the natural time to observe the birth of the light of Christ. Winter solstice was observed in some places at the close of our December, in other places one week into January: thus came about the geographical variations in the focus on Christmas Day and Epiphany. In the extreme north, the cultural calendar had come to be several weeks off the natural solstice. Thus the mid-December festival of St. Lucia's Day also became an annual celebration of the light of Christ.

The readings for Christmas Day make clear the ancient connection with solstice. "All the ends of the earth shall see the salvation of our God," says Isaiah 52. The reading from Hebrews 1 recalls the creation story of Genesis 1 and calls Christ the "reflection of God's glory." The poem of John 1 is the fourth gospel's way of proclaiming the incarnation. The world has been created anew. The light that comes from God is other than, greater than, the natural light of the universe: it is the person of Christ. We do not know whether the author of John knew the birth narratives that Matthew and Luke tell. But, in typical Johannine fashion, the author chose a more metaphoric way than the synoptics did in proclaiming Christ. Luke talks of the light of the angels in the sky; Matthew describes a brilliant star; Mark 4:22, in referring to the secret messiah, speaks of what will come to light. But for John, secondary imagery of light is unnecessary: Christ himself is the light of the world.

Many parishes omit a liturgy on Christmas Day, and thus present the Christmas story only from Luke 2. This exclusion is problematic for a number of reasons. Not all faithful Christians, particularly older persons who live alone, can or wish to attend an evening service; many Christmas Eve services are marked by family hype that does not readily include persons outside a happy family circle; some Christians are not engaged with family or friends on Christmas Day. But, social realities aside, attention to the images in the lectionary would lead parishes to maintain a Christmas Day liturgy that proclaims the light of John 1. According to John 1, the incarnation is bigger than the story of the manger. Christ is not only a newborn, but is the light of God shining from before creation. On Passion Sunday, the narrative of Palm Sunday serves as a processional reading for a liturgy at which the entire Passion is the gospel. Some parishes are copying this model at their single Christmas liturgy: Luke 2 is read in an opening procession, perhaps to a crèche, and the gospel is proclaimed from John 1. We go from the manger to the light.

The commercialization of Christmas several weeks before December 25 has reached unprecedented proportions. Department stores now advertise after-Christmas sales the second week of December. Strings of lights are used, not on December 25 to herald the birth of Christ, but from the third week of November on to highlight one store over another. It is not surprising that societies set far from the equator celebrate the winter solstice in a big way. Our giving of gifts, lighting of candles, hanging of evergreens, and feasting are natural ways to decry the night. While the sun hides, candles are lit; although trees are bare, green branches are brought indoors; although no food is growing in the fields, tables overflow with mounds of food.

Yet just as Christians do not celebrate Easter during Lent (isn't it silly to think of singing Alleluia on Good Friday?), so the churches need to resist the abandonment of Advent. Advent is the church's observance of the darkness. As the reading from Isaiah 2 says, we are only beginning our walk toward the light of the Lord (Ad1A). Advent acknowledges the silence of God, the night of human society, the shadows in the human heart. Advent pleads for the coming of the light, well aware that even on Christmas Day much remains in dark sorrow: the week after Christmas is a time of many suicides.

So although for stores Christmas is over sometime on December 25, the lectionary suggests that the light is now beginning to shine. If the sanctuary is decorated with evergreens or trees during Advent, only the candles of the Advent wreath are lit. Multiple lights appear only at Christmas. Christmas concerts and parish partying occur during the twelve days of Christmas, rather than during Advent. In ritual, the community practices its faith: the rituals of Advent allow us to practice our trust in God at times of darkness. Without such intentional focus on the darkness, Christians will be ill-equipped to deal with suffering, to endure the death of loved ones, to face disaster, to stand alongside those whose lives are permeated with darkness.

The image of light continues through the twelve days of Christmas to the festival of the Epiphany. Some churches observe this day on the nearest Sunday, while others keep January 6 in harmony with those nationalities for whom Epiphany is the primary gift-giving celebration. The opening poem from Isaiah 60 (EpABC) is a masterpiece of light imagery. Christ the light has come, and we all are to arise and shine, see the dawn, lift up our eyes, and be radiant. In the Ephesians reading, the apostle testifies that thanks to the coming of Christ, we can all see the mystery of God's plan for salvation. According to the narrative of the magi, those who are wise follow a light to Christ. The magi were not three kings, but an undetermined number of religious seekers of knowledge and truth: the masculine plural noun *magi* could have included also the female sibyls of the ancient religious world.

The light who is Christ is not exhausted over the twelve days of Christmas. As the Nicene Creed says, Christ is forever light from light. The lectionary continues this light throughout the Epiphany season. The Isaiah poems add their light imagery to the Epiphany season (Ep2A, Ep3A). The church's exploration of the light continues until the Transfiguration, when the disciples see in a vision of spectacular dazzling brightness the divinity of their master Jesus.

On the mountaintop Jesus is like the glory and fire on Sinai (TransA); like a lamp in a dark place and the morning star in the sky, heralding the day (TransA); like the chariots of fire that brought Elijah up to God (TransB). He is the image of the God shining in our newly created hearts (TransB). Like Moses, having seen God, we shine (TransC), for we are being transformed into the image of divine light (TransC).

The lectionary does not leave the light of God in Christ. As baptized believers, we now carry the Spirit of that light in our lives. Perhaps influenced by the Zoroastrian dualism in which life is a perpetual struggle between the kingdom of darkness and the kingdom of life, the authors of the Dead Sea Scrolls found useful the imagery of becoming children of light. A number of epistle passages in the lectionary similarly rely on the image of light. We are now children of light and must keep awake, resisting the darkness (Le4A, Pr28A). We have been recreated by the light (Pr4B). The three years conclude with our thanks that we have been rescued from the power of darkness and brought into God's light (LastC).

As with the year's turn from winter to summer, the earth's turn from night to day is a time to see in God the brightest light of our life. Many Christians, newly attuned to ecology, find in these natural cycles significant rituals for their faith. God gives not only some kind of supernatural light, but also the necessary natural light of day and of summer. We keep the cycle and praise God, grateful for both the new creation of the Christian community and the old creation of the marvelously functioning universe.

Each day for the last fifteen centuries, Christians who pray morning and evening prayer mark the natural daily turn of darkness to light as a sign of Christ. The canticle for morning prayer, the song of Zechariah, speaks of the dawn from on high breaking upon us, shining on those who dwell in darkness and the shadow of death. For the believer, just as the natural dawn breaks into night's darkness, so Christ brings light to the community. In evening prayer, the lighting of the candle recalls the Easter Vigil. Although night is coming, we can rest in peace, for "Jesus Christ is the light of the world, the light no darkness can overcome." The Greek hymn to Christ the light, *Phos hilaron*, sung by Christians at evening prayer since at least the fourth century, is readily available in various translations and paraphrases.

Church architecture is one place to see the importance of the image of light for worshiping communities. Romanesque buildings offered bigger windows than were previously possible: the largest Romanesque churches of Europe are flooded with natural light. Five hundred years later, Reformed churches recognized in the light shining through clear windows a symbol of the light of God on the faithful, without interference. For Quaker Christians, light is the predominant image of the community: sitting in natural light, they see in one another inner light that comes from God's presence within. The opposite approach has been taken by the Taizé community. Their worship space is kept in considerable darkness, with the hundreds of votive lights shining as Christ in a dark world.

Electricity creates an obstacle for contemporary Christians. Many people have little experience with genuine darkness. Because artificial light is so readily available, we rarely experience fear of the night, and candles' effect on us is significantly less than for people in the past. Yet candlelight services are still enormously popular, the small flickering light still an archetypal symbol of the light we too easily take for granted. We are far from those ancient peoples who, as winter approached, feared that the sun was dying and that the light of the world would be extinguished. Yet the light of utopia is still harder to imagine than the darkness of disasters, and currently dystopian novels and films play on this ancient fear by depicting a society gone dark by anarchy or war, a civilization turned to night through the brightness of nuclear bombs. So perhaps, electricity notwithstanding, the image of light still has its place of power.

Many biblical poems and narratives weave the imagery of blindness into the image of light. We need to be particularly attentive to how blind persons receive this imagery. Some blind Christians are offended that their disability is appropriated as a symbol of spiritual ignorance and depravity. Others willingly offer their condition as an image of the disability we all share. As is the case with all the images in the lectionary, not all Christians will respond emotionally in the same way to an image. We have a dual task: to be sure we are not being gratuitously offensive, while at the same time offering such a plethora of images that all worshiping Christians will find, somewhere in the Sunday's liturgy, an image important and particularly appropriate for them. Although one image may not be my favorite, it may be yours: I will use each image, if not for myself, then for you.

Marriage

bride, bridegroom, Cana, lover,
marriage, marriage supper

Related chapters: COVENANT, ISRAEL

The Bible uses the image of marriage to describe God's commitment to the people, and the joy of finally meeting God is called a
wedding feast. The New Testament also reverses the image, urging that human marriage mirror God's everlasting faithfulness to
us. However, the biblical image of marriage assumes male dominance and thus needs careful application in the contemporary
world.

PSALM 45:15-16   In embroidered apparel she is brought to the king,
    after her the bridesmaids follow in procession.
With joy and gladness they are brought,
    and enter into the palace of the king.

PRAYER
AT MARRIAGE   Faithful Lord, source of love, pour down your grace upon _name_ and _name_, that they may fulfill the vows they have made this day and reflect your steadfast love in their life-long faithfulness to each other.

JOHANN FRANCK   Hasten as a bride to meet him,
eagerly and gladly greet him.
There he stands already knocking:
quickly, now, your gate unlocking,
open wide the fast-closed portal,
saying to the Lord immortal:
"Come, and leave your loved one never;
dwell within my heart forever."

The Bridegroom is not only loving; he is love. God requires that he should be feared as the Lord, honored as a father, and loved as a bridegroom. Which of these is highest or most lofty? Surely it is love. When God loves, he desires nothing but to be loved, since he loves us for no other reason than to be loved, for he knows that those who love him are blessed in their very love. The bridegroom asks nothing else but love, and the bride has nothing else to give.

BERNARD OF CLAIRVAUX, SERMON 83 ON SONG OF SONGS

Our Redeemer became our Bridegroom. The bride became exhilarated at the sight of his noble countenance. Under this immense force she loses herself. The less she becomes, the more flows into her. The more loving God is to her, the higher she soars. The more his desire grows, the more extravagant their wedding celebration becomes. The narrower the bed of love becomes, the more intense are the embraces. The sweeter the kisses on the mouth become, the more lovingly they gaze at one another. The greater the distress in which they part, the more he bestows upon her. The more God's praise is spread abroad, the greater her desire becomes.

MECHTHILD OF MAGDEBURG, *The Flowing Light of the Godhead*

⁓

ANCIENT RELIGIOUS MYTH is filled with stories of marriage, or at least of sexual mating. Mother Earth lies down, and Father Sky mounts on top of her, and from their intercourse comes creation. The Egyptian Geb and Nut, the Canaanite Yarih and Nikkal, and the Greek Zeus and Hera are examples of marriage among the deities. From these divine marriages comes life for the world. By extension, patriarchal monarchies regarded the king's marriage, often extravagantly celebrated, as promising fecundity for the entire people. Psalm 45 recounts just such a royal wedding, in which the virility of the king—"Strap your sword upon your thigh, O mighty warrior"—is ensured by his marriage to the princess, who will provide the king with sons.

The Bible contains its own metaphoric version of the myth of divine marriage. Although both the Hebrew and the Greek texts refer to God with predominantly male terminology, the Bible refrains from mentioning any divine genitals or describing divine sexual intercourse. Some contemporary scholarship speculates that, at least in popular piety, YHWH was indeed understood in explicitly masculine terms and merely replaced Baal as the consort of the fertility goddess Asherah. But in the biblical texts themselves, this religious tradition of recognizing divine marriage shows up only as metaphor. The exilic prophets used marriage imagery to describe God's commitment to the Israelite people without implying any literal sexual activity.

Even without explicit sexual references, the scriptures' use of the language of divine marriage can be problematic for contemporary people. The image relies on the archaic assumptions that the male is the dominant marriage partner and that the female is the passive and grateful recipient of the male's procreative attention. In this worldview, the husband supports the wife while the wife honors her husband: in the metaphor, *husband* is God and *wife* the believers. The scriptures suggest another vision of marriage: Hosea says that YHWH's love is more affectionate than domineering. God is not to be termed *baal*, that is, "lord," but is characterized by "steadfast love." In either case, the divine-human relationship described in the Bible's marriage language is quite other than our contemporary expectation of marriage as a state of equality and mutual interdependence. At least in first world countries, marriages between persons of vastly different rank or age tend to be viewed with disapproval. We must be sure to separate the biblical proclamation of the divine marriage between God and the people from our current expectation of equal participants in marriage, for God is not at all our equal. Perhaps biblical citations of God as our husband can be balanced with language in which God is married to us. The verbal form eliminates the suggestion that males, like God, are dominant, while still retaining the idea of the bonds of committed love.

Metaphoric use of the image of divine marriage continued in the church. The New Testament employs the image of marriage to describe the relationship of Christ and the church. Ephesians 5 turns the metaphor around, using the example of Christ and the church to describe human marriage. The Exsultet, the poem that originated in the fourth century and is sung at the Easter Vigil, lauds the time of the resurrection as the night in which "heaven and earth are joined, things human and things divine." In the medieval Easter liturgy, rubrics ordered the candlebearer to spill some wax into the baptismal pool, in an obvious suggestion of sexual intercourse. Medieval mystics, struggling to realize their connection with God in a time when the liturgy obscured, rather than celebrated, this affectionate bond, explored the marriage imagery to the fullest in their extraliturgical poetry. Not only the church, but the individual soul became married to God. Catherine of Siena and other women testified to what is called a mystical marriage, through which in an overpowering emotional experience they apprehended Christ's loving embrace of their unworthy self. Protestant hymnody retained this language in hymns describing the end-time or the eucharist. The sexual innuendos in Johann Franck's "Soul, adorn yourself with gladness" are surprisingly explicit.

Marriage remains a powerfully positive metaphor for life. Despite our contemporary divorce rate, couples continue to hope that their marriage will ensure present joy and future stability. A growing number of homosexual couples are asking the society and the church whether they, too, may participate in a marriage ritual, to appropriate for themselves this undergirding and overarching image of life: life rendered happier, deeper, wider, safer, by being shared with the beloved. Yet contemporary use of biblical descriptions of marriage poses the dilemma that most past societies understood marriage in ways very different from our current culture.

Biblical discussion of human marriage is both prescriptive and descriptive, and both treatments are complicated. The several millennia covered by the biblical record encompassed an evolving understanding of marriage. The most ancient legal prescriptions are wholly androcentric, delineating which women are a man's appropriate marriage partners: this status is dependent largely upon which man currently has charge of the woman in question. In several extreme examples, David acquired his first wife Michal in payment for delivering to her father King Saul the foreskins of a hundred Philistines, and the prophet Nathan, threatening David with divine punishment, says that God will take his wives away and give them to his neighbor. Both divorce and multiple wives were a man's right. The marriage code associated with the reforms of Nehemiah required a man to divorce any non-Israelite wife. Yet in the first century, within Roman urban society, some Jews asserted that faithful monogamy is God's design, and Jesus is remembered for urging that men relinquish their right of divorce.

Each of these marriage patterns is described as if it reflects God's intentions. Even the androcentric maxims concerning marriage included in the book of Proverbs, some of which border on misogyny, are included in the word of God. But despite historical changes in marriage patterns, the biblical texts indicate that a man marries, and a woman is married. He *takes* her. Even the sexually celebratory poem the Song of Songs cannot do much to update the Bible's archaic view of marriage, since the poem does not refer to its mutually aggressive lovers as a married couple. Paul in 1 Corinthians 7 is exceptional: in reflecting on when divorce might be acceptable, he admits that he is using his own judgment in this matter, and he speaks of the sexuality of the couple as mutually responsible and interdependent.

The more ancient biblical narratives indicate that the dominant marriage pattern was endogamous polygamy, with the man or the man's family securing wives from the extended family. Some narratives indicate that, in a pattern familiar to readers of ancient war stories, wives might be battle booty. As urban culture brought about a change in what had been optimum living arrangements under nomadic or rural life, polygamy seems to have been retained only by the community's high status males, for example, the kings. It is not clear when the ideal of monogamy became popularized. In both Genesis accounts of creation, neither of which are as old as some of the Israelite narratives, monogamy is presented as God's idea for human society. Yet the creation stories offer differing views as to the purpose of marriage: Genesis 1 stresses marriage as a method of procreation, and Genesis 2 as the remedy for loneliness.

By the rise of the common era, urban life had made monogamy the preferred marriage arrangement, and the church's ethics reflected this social change. Granting that one sign of the decline of the Roman Empire was the extreme sexual excesses practiced by at least the upper class, the call in the New Testament for sexual fidelity resembles that of other religious movements highly critical of promiscuity. It is surprising, granted the Jewish stress on marriage, that so many of the New Testament characters were apparently unmarried and that abandoning one's marital responsibilities was considered religiously praiseworthy, rather than morally reprehensible. Perhaps this sentiment reflected believers' expectation of the nearness of the eschaton.

We see that the Bible contains contradictory messages about what marriage is and what God thinks about it: society is polygamous, society is monogamous, marriage indicates a man's status, marriage bonds Jacob with his beloved Rachel, Dinah's marriage to a foreigner is forbidden, Boaz's marriage to a foreigner is blessed, marriage is God's preference for humankind, marriage is rejected by the committed Christian. In light of this complex picture, contemporary Christians do well to advance opinions about marriage with some humility. Study of nature suggests that in creation countless sexual arrangements are determined largely by how and how long the young are reared. In this light, it follows that people, moving into urban work patterns from a subsistence rural economy, replaced polygamy with monogamy. Were these people religious, they might see this change as divinely sanctioned. Whether in our time of available contraception and extended adolescence, patterns of faithful sexual relations come to be reconfigured, is a source of deep disagreement among Christians. The Bible provides no easy answers to our contemporary questions concerning premarital sex, cohabitation, homosexual unions, and divorce. Perhaps the biblical images of divine marriage as a sign of everlasting love, rather than its descriptions of various cultural patterns, can serve as the primary source of the church's continued exploration into what commitment between two Christians creates and requires.

Although our society is consumed with sexual issues, the lectionary hardly addresses these topics at all. The so-called divorce texts occur twice in the lectionary (Ep6A, Pr22B). In one option the reading is tied to the creation story in Genesis 2, which provides the passage that Jesus cites in rejecting divorce. The poem of Genesis 1, which says that both females and males, created simultaneously and equally in the image of God, is appointed to be read at the Easter Vigil, as if such a description of perfection in marriage is itself a sign of Christ's resurrection and of the world being created anew. In the pericope about the woman with the seven husbands (Pr27C), the issue is not marriage, but life after the resurrection. The marriage sections of the household codes (Galatians 5 and Colossians 3) were omitted from the Revised Common Lectionary. The decision that first-century expectations for the upright family are not necessarily applicable today extends the prior lectionary decisions that omitted the slavery sections of these same household codes from the Sunday proclamation.

It is as a metaphor for God's devotion to the people that language about marriage occurs most often in the lectionary. The Old Testament's most striking examples of this imagery are included: Jeremiah's passage about our marriage to God (Le5B) and Hosea's call to fidelity (Pr3B). Memories of the ministry of John the Baptist repeat the imagery of the messiah as the bridegroom. The parable of the ten bridesmaids (Pr27A), the parable of the wedding feast (Pr17C), and the imagery of the end-time as the marriage banquet (Ea5C) all continue the ancient metaphor that life with God is as joyous, fruitful, and permanent as a mythical marriage. In the Johannine miracle of the water turned to wine at Cana (Ep2C), the primary point of the story is not that Jesus attended weddings. Rather, John uses the marriage narrative to proclaim the gospel that the Spirit of Christ is making all things new, bringing joy and fulfillment to the entire world.

In marriage, two opposites come together to make a mysterious unity. Marriage thus provides the church with a treasured image of life with God and life within the community of believers. Yet as with many powerful images, the biblical picture of marriage can do both good and harm. It can bring to arid liturgical practice the joyous wine of the wedding feast; it can enliven a dead spirituality with the imagery of marital ecstasy; it can recall the church to its commitment as a partner with God. That God marries the people suggests a primary proclamation of both Judaism and Christianity: God loves humankind. But biblical imagery of marriage can also reinforce archaic views of male dominance or stigmatize Christians who live the single life. Perhaps it is true that the stronger the metaphoric image, the more care we must take in employing it.

Mother

eagle, hen, Mary, mother,
nursing, Rachel weeping

Related chapters: CREATION, FAMILY

The biblical image of mother is mainly a natural image of birthing
and breastfeeding. The church has used the mother image to
describe baptism and life in the church, as though God is father
and the church is mother. Some contemporary Christians, hoping
to balance the Bible's androcentric imagery, now refer to God as
mother.

PSALM 131:3-4

I still my soul and make it quiet,
like a child upon its mother's breast;
  my soul is quieted within me.
O Israel, wait upon the LORD,
  from this time forth forevermore.

EUCHARISTIC
PRAYER

Holy God, Creator of all and Source of life,
at the birth of time
your word brought light into the world. . . .
By your Spirit bless us and this bread and cup,
that, held and nourished by you,
we may live as your children.

JEAN JANZEN,
AFTER JULIAN OF
NORWICH

Mothering God, you gave me birth
in the bright morning of this world.
Creator, source of every breath,
you are my rain, my wind, my sun.

Mothering Christ, you took my form,
offering me your food of light,
grain of new life, and grape of love,
your very body for my peace.

Mothering Spirit, nurturing one,
in arms of patience hold me close,
so that in faith I root and grow
until I flower, until I know.

Now the saving warmth of the eternal font invites you. Now your Mother adopts you to make you her child. Lo, the sweet wail of the newborn is heard! Lo, the most illustrious brood of the begotten proceeds from the one womb! Run, then, forward to the Mother who experiences no pains of labor although she cannot count the number of those to whom she gives birth. Happily you are going to drink the new milk together. This regeneration, this resurrection, this eternal life, our Mother has given to all. Fly to the fountain, to the sweet womb of your virgin mother.

ZENO OF VERONA, *Seven Invitations to the Baptismal Font*

The metaphor of God as mother is built not upon stereotypes of maternal tenderness, softness, pity, and sentimentality, but upon the female experience of gestation, birth, and lactation. This experience in most animals, including human beings, engenders not attributes of weakness and passivity but qualities contributing to the active defense of the young so that they may not only exist but be nourished and grow. In the picture of God as mother, God is angry because what comes from her being and belongs to her lacks the food and other necessities to grow and flourish. The mother-God as creator is necessarily judge, at the very basic level of condemning as the primary (though not the only) sin the inequitable distribution of basic necessities for the continuation of life in its many forms.

SALLIE MCFAGUE, *Models of God*

THE MEANING OF MOTHER IMAGERY in the ancient world was determined by one of two archaic biological misunderstandings about human procreation. For the first: The earliest human records studied by anthropologists suggest that the male role in procreation was not yet understood. Consequently, the mother was revered as the sole source of life. Ancient practices in which the menstruating woman, too mysterious and powerful for regular social contact, was isolated outside the community point to this awe of the procreative woman. In some cultures this sense of the female coincided with both worship of a mother goddess as the primary deity and a matrifocal social structure in which mothers raised their children with minimal involvement of the child's father. The line in the second creation story, in which the man leaves his parents and goes to his wife (Genesis 2:24), recalls just such a matrifocal society in which the power of the mother was recognized by social structures of female dominance. This contrasts with the culture represented in the story of Rebekah leaving her family to live with Isaac's household. Anthropologists continue spirited debates about ancient mother goddess veneration and disagree to what extent the hundreds of female images unearthed by archaeologists—figurines characterized by huge breasts, bellies, and hips—indicate mother goddess worship, ancient pornography, or iodine-deficiency among Neanderthals.

Now the second biological misunderstanding: Perhaps connected with the rise of pastoral herding, when humans could watch the results of the mating of animals, many communities came to judge the male as the supremely powerful procreative sex. Later called "the flower-pot theory," this biology saw the woman as merely an incubator for the tiny fetus that was inserted into her by the male. Some historians connect this new biology with the evolution of cultural patriarchy. Mother goddesses were demoted, to become consorts or mothers of the dominant father gods. Polygamy became the norm: if one woman was not a good flower pot, another woman would do.

This pattern is evident in the biblical story of Hannah, whose husband still loves her, although his second wife, Peninnah, functions as his childbearer. According to this biology and culture, the child born to the woman is the property, not of the mother, but of the father, from whom the child came. Such a worldview underlies many biblical stories: for example, that David's and Bathsheba's firstborn son dies is God's punishment for David's sins of theft and murder. In the story of the extraordinary birth of John the Baptist, the father Zechariah receives the angel's promise, names the child, and understands its mission.

Mother imagery coming to us from either of these two historical world-views will be to some degree off kilter for contemporary people. Because we know that neither the mother nor the father is the mysterious and powerful sole source of life, we do well to grant to neither parent a status that disregards the other. Religion, which ought to correspond to, rather than contradict, what we know of the world, should give mother imagery its due honor, without dismissing or demoting the father image. Such a balance is not easy to achieve.

In current usage, the term *mothering* refers not only to conceiving and birthing an infant, but also to nurturing the child. Such mothering may last two years or two decades. As far back as human records attest, wealthy mothers did little of the nurturing of their own offspring, but hired or forced other women or men into the mothering responsibilities. Thus the inquiry into what mothers did must always clarify whether the mothers were rich or poor. In some cultures, mothering was handled in communal rather than individual ways, with groups of adults tending many children together. In other cultures, children functioned as adults from about the age of seven, while in ours, persons in their mid-twenties can still be dependent upon mothers who willingly continue mothering tasks through a third decade.

In thinking about mothering, we need to be aware of the nineteenth-century phenomenon called the Cult of True Womanhood. The changes brought about by the industrial revolution meant that fewer family units were economic partnerships involving shared work by wife and husband. The family farm, in which both adults divided up the chores, gave way to the factory, which provided cash for a lengthy day of work away from the home. In reaction, the Cult of True Womanhood prescribed the mothering role for all true women, whose sole social responsibility was to bear and rear children in a home financed by an attending husband.

In late medieval Europe, when middle class women, copying the upper classes, began to board their infants with nurses rather than breastfeed the babies themselves, the clergy reacted by commissioning church art that depicted Mary with an exposed breast, feeding the baby Jesus. In accord with the Cult of True Womanhood, nineteenth-century clergy preached extravagant praises of the mother and her extraordinary power over children and husband. The invention in 1906 of Mother's Day culminated a patriarchal century of sentimentalizing the mother's role in society. Yet scholars of folklore remind us of the countless legends of the bad mother and wicked stepmother, tales that indicate that mothers can not only give life, but also suffocate it. Churches that observe Mother's Day in any way need to reflect seriously about the pros and cons of this cultural celebration and about how such a focus on some women in the community can become a Christian experience.

For the most part, the biblical image of the mother is a symbol of birthing and nurturing. This contrasts with the biblical father image, which symbolizes the social role of the parent. The Bible contains many stories of women coming to pregnancy and childbirth. The many biblical stories narrating which woman is head wife and how the wife becomes a mother may indicate an ancient matrifocal society in which mothers had far more significant power than in later Israelite times.

By the time the stories were written down, either the man or God is credited with the pregnancy. After Eve bears Cain, the first human child, she says, "I have produced a man with the help of the LORD" (Genesis 4:1). Sarah, Rachel, Samson's mother, Hannah, Elizabeth, Mary: in all these central stories of faith, divine intervention was required. Natural mothering is not enough: the life that God promises is more than the life of nature. Neither Judaism nor Christianity is a nature religion; biblical religion nurtures faith in the God who blesses outside and beyond nature. Thus life comes ultimately from God. Yet childbirth remains a primary image of divine blessing. Ancient Israelite people saw offspring as their most pressing need, and in story after story, God meets this human need with the birth of a baby. Although God meets the people's social needs by granting them kings, the Old Testament court narratives suggest that kings were a far less successful route to fulfillment than was the mother's birthing of a baby.

Mother goddess worship was a central feature in the religions of Egypt, Canaan, and the Greco-Roman world, and it is probably in reaction against these prevailing religions that the Bible only rarely likens God to a mother. Historians of religion see this technique repeated throughout history. The significant imagery in a preceding religion is radically reinterpreted by a succeeding religion as part of the process of destroying the power of the first religion. However, the three-year lectionary includes several of these few passages. God will love the chosen people as much as, even more than, a nursing mother (Pr3A[†]), and will comfort the city as would a mother her child (Pr9C[†]). Also male leaders are likened to mothers: Moses complains that God is expecting him to act like a nursing mother to the people (Pr21B[†]), and Paul likens himself to "a nursing mother tenderly caring for her own children" (Pr25A). The beneficent city wherein God resides is also like a nursing mother (Pr9c†). The lectionary also includes images of animals mothering. God is likened to a mother eagle, who catches any faltering fledglings on her outstretched wings (Pr5A†), and Christ likens himself to a mother hen, protecting her chicks (Le2c).

The christological festivals of the Annunciation and the Visitation employ the image of childbirth as the metaphor for God's salvation. The commemoration of the Nativity of John the Baptist, which originally coincided with the summer solstice, superimposes the imagery of childbirth of the forerunner onto the natural phenomenon of the decreasing sunlight in the Northern Hemisphere. As John the Baptist says of Jesus, "He must increase, and I must decrease" (John 3:30). The lectionary option to read semicontinuously through the Hebrew Scriptures includes the birth narratives involving Sarah (Pr6A°), Moses' mother (Pr16A°), Naomi (Pr27B°), and Hannah (Pr28B°).

The primary use of the mother image in the lectionary occurs at Christmas (ChEABC). Some Christians laud the incarnation as parallel to the resurrection as a sign of God's action in the world. That the mighty God comes to the world by means of the nearly total vulnerability of a poor, disenfranchised, unmarried woman is one image of the surprise of divine mercy. The task in our culture, in which religious Christmas carols are piped throughout malls to help increase sales, is to keep the story of Jesus' childbirth from sentimentality. Genuine childbirth is never cute; nor was it likely, despite imaginative medieval preachers, that Mary's childbirth was painless, bloodless, lovely. Our use of the imagery of childbirth as a sign of divine mercy can be stronger for our honest appreciation of what actual childbirth is like. Many crèche sets include not only the mother, but also the ox and the donkey of Isaiah 1:3, who recognize the child as their master.

The lectionary includes stories about Mary (Ad4A, Ad4B, Ad4c, Ep2c, GFrABC, and during the Christmas season). Although Mary plays a minimal role in the Revised Common Lectionary, she has played an enormous role in Christian imagination. Even though Paul seems to have known nothing about her and Mark suggests that Jesus' family were concerned for his sanity, Luke depicts Mary as the ideal female disciple, eager to receive the word of God. Here the ancient world's archaic biology, which considered a mother the passive recipient of the father's seed, assists the Lucan message: Mary, the true mother, like the true Christian, receives and nurtures the gift of divine life.

Past centuries witnessed an increasing and sometimes excessive fascination with Mary. A second-century legend tells of the midwife at the stable discovering that Mary's hymen was still intact. The fifth-century's theological reflection moved to name Mary not only mother of Jesus, but, since Christ is God, also the mother of God. That Christians built churches honoring Mary on sites of mother goddess temples helped elevate Mary from Luke's lowly woman to the thirteenth-century's Queen of Heaven. During the nineteenth century Mary came to be called *our* Mother, and in some popular piety Mary is far more devotionally important than the triune God. Currently, although some Roman Catholics are moderating their historic emphasis on the role of Mother Mary, some Protestants are rediscovering her, glad to find a mother figure in the Bible for our praise. Perhaps a healthy and balanced use of Mary as mother figure is possible in our future: a Mary who in personifying the image of mother can be all, but not more, than a mother might be, functioning as a significant metaphor for the creative energy that the Spirit of God engenders in all who believe. An example of this maturing Mary is the sculpture by Elizabeth Frink entitled *The Walking Madonna*: a larger-than-life bronze old woman, bones showing through her meager dress, striding across the lawn toward God's future.

Mothers mourn: this sorrow the lectionary forces us to remember. We read of the slaughter of the innocents, and of Rachel weeping for her dead children (Ch1A). That Herod's murder of the babies of Bethlehem is recalled during the twelve days of Christmas exemplifies the lectionary's attempt to speak God's truth to a world of suffering.

Some Christian teachers are nervous about the church's adoption of the mother metaphor at a time marked by a resurgence of neopagan earth religion. Perhaps some of the contemporary adaptation of ancient earth religion is a fad, but unquestionably, some persons raised as Christians are participating in a variety of nature religions, most of which use mother imagery for the earth itself, for the life force identified with nature, or for the creative female self. Most of these religious expressions recognize no transcendent deity; rather, the ultimate reality is the life of the universe, called Mother Earth or the Great Goddess. The ancient idea of the earth as mother left its mark on Christian hymnody: "Dear mother earth," we sing in a customary translation of St. Francis's Canticle of the Sun. Christians need to distinguish their use of imagery from other cultural uses of these same images. But Christians need not reject mother imagery simply because other religions find it significant.

Concerning the earth as mother: The ecological movement requires Christians to attend with increasing concern to the matrix of life on this planet and to revere God's earth as a mother. Here Mother Earth imagery may be helpful. Yet contemporary Americans need to reflect on use of *she* for the earth, since referring to the earth as mother sometimes implies problematic ideas, such as imagining one gender or another for God, accepting an archaic biology, or endorsing a receptive passivity in females.

Concerning the church as mother: Especially the medieval church used this imagery. Commonplace were depictions on the walls of churches in which a great woman, Mary or Mother Church, is opening her cloak to protect a crowd of naked people. Currently, renewed baptismal practice can encourage churches once again to enjoy the image of church as mother, who births her children, washes the newborns, pours oil on them, and clothes them in white garments, embracing them as new members of the family. In baptism we are born from above (Le2A, TrinB), and by believing in Jesus we are born of God (Ea6B). Our baptisms are coming again to resemble, not someone sprinkling a cactus, but the community bathing a newborn. This is Mother Church at work.

Concerning God as mother: Hymns are a good vehicle for introducing underused imagery. A new body of hymns, found in recent hymn collections, includes imagery of God as mother. The church can use the image of God as mother, no less than God as fortress or light, without jeopardizing the orthodoxy of trinitarian faith. Were we free to compare God to a great variety of animate and inanimate realities while refusing to liken God to a mother, one would have to inquire whether an unconscious misogyny is operative.

Concerning Christ as mother: Julian of Norwich is the most renowned among many medieval mystics who called Christ their mother. Medieval biology believed that the milk in a lactating woman was her menstrual blood reconstituted: thus the poets could claim that the blood of the eucharist was milk from the side of Mother Christ. Some contemporary people might find this image charming, while others may find it only bizarre. Sometimes in the church's history the image of Christ as a solicitous mother was offered as an antidote to the presentation of God as a nasty father, who is intent on disciplining wicked offspring. Here we see that the image of Christ as mother may be either intriguing or problematic.

Concerning each other as mother: In the church, we are mothers to one another. I am to be mother to you, you are to care for me. The way the church enacts the mothering love of God is by mothering one another, bearing one another, nurturing one another, honoring each other. Such a metaphoric use of mother is more appropriate in the church than a focus on the women who are literally mothers. Women who are mothers might be pleased with their role or in despair over their situation: they can be gladly fulfilling their tasks or quite dismissive of these responsibilities. In the baptized community, however, the Spirit of God makes us all mothers to one another, and we can always use encouragement for this aspect of our life together.

Mountain

mountain, Sinai, transfiguration, Zion

Related chapters: CITY

Similar to many ancient religions, biblical religion reveres mountains, not for their natural beauty, but as the earthly place closest to the divine and thus a likely spot for a theophany. As a site where we meet God, mountains figure in significant events in Jesus' life: his preaching, transfiguration, and ascension.

PSALM 68:15-16

O mighty mountain, O hill of Bashan!
　　O rugged mountain, O hill of Bashan!
Why do you look with envy, O rugged mountain,
at the hill on which God chose to rest?
　　Truly, the LORD will dwell there forever.

PRAYER
OF THE DAY,
TRANSFIGURATION

Almighty God, on the mountain you showed your glory in
the transfiguration of your Son. Give us the vision. . . .

SUSAN PALO
CHERWIEN

In the desert, on God's mountain,
Moses saw the bush aflame,
wondered at the fiery foliage,
heard the crackling call his name.
May we notice bushes burning;
may we wonder at the flame.

Later in the wild of Sinai,
from another mountain height,
bringing promise to his people,
Moses shone with God's own light.
May we, not consumed, yet burning,
guide all to the mountain height.

Christ brought the apostles up to the mountain that he might show them, before his resurrection, the glory of his divinity. This was so that after he had risen from the dead, they might know that he had not received this glory as the reward of his labor, as one who had had it not, but that he had had it from all eternity, together with the Father and the Holy Spirit. It was therefore this glory of his divinity, which was hidden and veiled to humanity, that he revealed to the apostles on the mountain. And there appeared to them Moses and Elijah talking with him. The prophets were filled with joy, and the apostles likewise, in their ascent of the mountain. The prophets rejoiced because they had seen Christ's humanity, which they had not known. And the apostles rejoiced because they had seen the glory of his divinity, which they had not known.

EPHRAEM,
SERMON FOR
TRANSFIGURATION

Afterwards the angel bore me up to a towering mountain, and placed me on the mountainside. And as I looked up to the summit, a light so great and brilliant appeared there that I could scarcely bear to look at it. "This is the mountain," the angel said, "that you began to climb three years ago, and this is how far you have come. You will climb the rest of the way, and when you reach the top, you will not regret all your toil."

ELISABETH
OF SCHOENAU,
Visions

MUCH HUMAN LANGUAGE speaks as if things that are higher up are honored more than things that are lower down. Linguists refer to this up/down imagery as orientational metaphors. Some examples of up being better than down are: "my spirits rose," versus "I'm feeling down"; "I'm at the peak of health," versus "the cat dropped dead"; "it's a lofty career," versus "I'm at the bottom of the class"; "I have high standards," versus "it was a low-down thing to do." Perhaps this pattern of speech developed because the human eyes, mouth, and brain are high up on the human body. Perhaps the practice of burial in the ground contributed to the linguistic pattern that down is bad. For whatever the varied reasons, up is good, and things that are higher up transcend the common lowliness of things that are lower down.

A prime example of this human tendency is the imagery of mountains. Throughout recorded human history, mountains have functioned as archetypal symbols of transcendence. Many of the world's mythologies include stories of a cosmic mountain. The cosmic mountain has been variously described as the peak of the created world, the navel of the earth, the abode of the deities, a prized place of worship, a destination of pilgrimage, an honored location of theophanies, the site of ascensions, or the burial place of godlike persons. Either the deities live on the distant volcano or mountain range, or humans can approach as close as possible to the divine by ascending the mountain, or the community connects with the deities by constructing a mountain-like temple from which to worship. Examples of mountain-like temples are the Mesopotamian ziggurat, the Buddhist stupa, and, in the Western Hemisphere, the pyramids in Mexico.

The Bible contains many examples of the imagery of the holy mountain. In Genesis 22, Mount Moriah, called "the mount of the LORD," the location of which is disputed, is the place on which Abraham is spared the sacrifice of Isaac. Israelite history recalls a sacred mountain from the nomadic period: Moses first experiences a theophany in the form of the burning bush while on Mount Horeb, which is called "the mountain of God" (Exodus 3:1). God appears to Moses on top of this same mountain, in Exodus 19 called Mount Sinai. On this same Mount Horeb God causes water to gush out from the rock. Later Elijah walks forty days and forty nights to reach this same "Horeb the mount of God."

Israel's life in Canaan recalls other sacred mountains. The contest between Elijah and the prophets of Baal, during which the deity is expected to rain fire down from heaven, takes place on Mount Carmel, since it is from a mountaintop that the people can expect contact with their deity. Later, the mountain is more closely situated near Jerusalem. The book of Zechariah states that the day of the LORD will begin on the Mount of Olives, and perhaps in accord with this text, the gospels indicate Jesus' visit to the Mount of Olives on the eve of his death. Both the Old and New Testaments talk in mythic language of Jerusalem itself as Mount Zion, the eschatological center of the world, the place where finally in the end-time God will dwell among humankind (for example, Revelation 21:10), serving up a feast for all.

The centuries of Judaism and Christianity continued the age-old fascination with mountains and mountain imagery. Jerusalem, although actually a plateau surrounded by hills and valleys, is repeatedly described as a mountain, the *axis mundi* of God's earth and the locus of religious life. Jerusalem and the hills of Rome served as pilgrimage sites for many Jews and Christians. That many churches have been built on the tops of mountains suggests not only that the builders wanted their edifice visible for miles, but also that similar to the pyramids of ancient times, churches are set up high, close to God. The iconographic practice of depicting the skull of Adam at the base of Christ's cross comes from the medieval legend that Golgotha, "the place of the skull" (Mark 15:22), was the mountain at the center of the earth, and this despite the gospels not indicating that Calvary was a hill. At this spot, claimed popular piety, both Adam and Christ died, thus marking the place of both human death and God's reversal of death on the cross.

Many contemporary secular people respond to mountains with emotions similar to those of ancient religious folk. We look at a magnificent mountain and feel both greater and smaller than we are, emotions common to religious experience. The current practices of hiking, mountain climbing, and skiing bring urban dwellers close to mountains. A parallel to ancient sacred pilgrimages is the phenomenon of wealthy adventurers attempting to climb Everest. It is as if the height of human activity is imagined as scaling the highest possible mountain. To go up is to go to the best place. Hikers carry oxygen to counteract the light-headedness brought on by the altitude; Buddhist pilgrims ascending Mount Fuji interpret the light-headedness as the experience of spiritual transcendence.

The lectionary uses mountain imagery in mainly two ways. The first use is christological. On the mountain we encounter God in Christ, and the most significant use of the image occurs each year on Transfiguration Sunday. Before the church begins its Lenten symbolic climb to Golgotha, there is first, on the Sunday before Ash Wednesday, the theophany on top of a glorious mountain. In year A, the mountain in Matthew's account is likened to Mount Sinai, on top of which "the appearance of the glory of the LORD was like a devouring fire." Moses ascends this mysterious mountain and converses with God for forty days and forty nights. In years B and C, the second reading's discussion of Moses' veil recalls the story, narrated in year C, that when Moses descended from Sinai, his face glowed so blindingly from the vision of God that he had to wear a veil when speaking to the people. According to the story of the transfiguration of Christ, the disciples, along with Moses of Sinai fame and Elijah of Horeb fame, experience the splendor of God on a mountaintop. The surprise is not that God appears on a mountain—that is commonplace religion—but that by looking at Jesus we can see God. The ascension is said to have occurred from a mountain, identified as a mountain in Galilee (TrinA) or the Mount of Olives (Ea6A).

For the sermon on the mount (Ep4A and following) Jesus, presented as the new Moses, speaks to the people the word of God. The church proclaims that Jesus himself is the word of God speaking from the mountaintop; in Jesus the church encounters the God of the mountain. The reading from Hebrews (Pr16c) articulates this same christology. The mountain that incited the terror of divine judgment—"if even an animal touches the mountain, it shall be stoned to death"—is replaced now with Mount Zion, described as the assembly around Jesus, who is the mediator of the new covenant.

The second important use of mountain imagery in the lectionary is eschatological. Perhaps the best example is on the first Sunday of the three-year lectionary. In Isaiah 2 (Ad1A) the "mountain of the LORD" will itself rise up as the place from which God's word goes out to all people and to which all the world will be drawn. In Isaiah 25 (Pr23A[†]) this mountain is the site of the great feast at the end of time. A splendid option for Easter Day is a reading from Isaiah 65 (Eac). Here the newly created world, in which there is no weeping, no premature death, no hunger, is the holy mountain on which "the wolf and the lamb shall feed together." The famed Quaker artist Edward Hicks depicted this holy mountain repeatedly in his dozens of paintings of The Peaceable Kingdom, in which the animals, wild and tame, are grouped together with children on a hill in the foreground of the scene— with William Penn and the Lenape conferring peacefully beneath a tree.

Always, however, in Christian imagery, we look for the *but*. The *but* in Christianity is that, there is finally no sacred mountain to which the faithful must travel. No mythic or historic spot is especially holy. To the Samaritan woman who inquires whether Mount Gerizim or Jerusalem is a holier place,

Jesus replies, "The hour is coming when you will worship the Father neither on this mountain nor in Jerusalem" (Le3A). In the church, God is revealed every Sunday as the lector reads from the reading desk. The word read in the community is God's word, the reading desk the only holy mountain we need. Perhaps our lectors would read more magnificently if they knew they were reading from the mountain. The feast that Isaiah proclaims will be spread out on the mountain for all peoples, this feast of rich food and well-aged wines, is already the eucharist. The church does not require or even urge the faithful to make pilgrimages up some mountain. The good news is that the only pilgrimage we make is to church each week.

Some current spiritualities are popularizing mountain retreats as individual exercises in personal self-awareness. In contrast, the Bible's stories of ascending the mountain to encounter God always have a communal cast. After encountering God at the mountain in the burning bush, Moses must connect with his brother and go back to attend to the people. At Sinai, Moses receives instructions to deliver to the whole people. Elijah, pouting on the mountain, is reminded that he is not alone, and he is sent back to 7,000 others in the midst of a conflicted political situation. Jesus on the mountain preaches to the crowds, and even at the transfiguration, a community of the disciples together witnesses the encounter with God. In Christianity, ascending the sacred mountain is not a task for the lone hiker. Through the Spirit of God we are united into one on the mountain. We assemble to receive the vision of God, and this vision transforms us from solitary pilgrims into a community of faith in this world.

Name of God

Father-Son-Holy Spirit, I AM,
Immanuel, Jesus, Lord, LORD,
the name of God, YHWH

Related chapters: EMANATION OF THE DIVINE

Many religions past and present name their deity, and knowing the deity's name gives the worshiper access to the divine. The biblical record concerning the name of God and the name of Jesus is complex. Granting the contemporary Christian discussion about the traditional triune name, this image is one of the most controversial in the lectionary.

PSALM 68:5   Sing to God, sing praises to God's name;
exalt the one who rides upon the heavens;
     the name of our God is the LORD; rejoice before the LORD!

RITE OF BAPTISM   I baptize you in the name of the Father, and of the Son, and
of the Holy Spirit. Amen.

THOMAS   The God of Abraham praise,
OLIVERS   who reigns enthroned above;
Ancient of everlasting days,
and God of love.
Jehovah, great I AM!
By earth and heaven confessed;
I bow and bless the sacred name
forever blest.

Before the great Three-One
they all exulting stand
and tell the wonders God has done
through all their land.
The listening spheres attend
and swell the growing fame
and sing the songs which never end,
the wondrous name.

Enjoyment consists in clinging to something lovingly for its own sake. The things therefore that are to be enjoyed are the Father and the Son and the Holy Spirit, in fact the Trinity, one supreme thing, and one which is shared in common by all who enjoy it. It is not easy, after all, to find any name that will really fit such transcendent majesty. In fact it is better just to say that this Trinity is the one God "from whom are all things, through whom all things, in whom all things" (Rom. 11:36). In the Father is unity, in the Son equality, in the Holy Spirit the harmony of unity and equality; and these three are all one because of the Father, are all equal because of the Son, are all linked together because of the Holy Spirit. Have I said anything, solemnly uttered anything that is worthy of God? On the contrary, all I feel I have done is to wish to say something; but if I have said anything, it is not what I wish to say. How do I know this? I know it because God is inexpressible.

AUGUSTINE,
Teaching
Christianity

O high eternal Trinity!
O our redeemer and resurrection!
O fire ever burning,
O light-giving light:
you are the One Who Is,
and I am the one who is not.

CATHERINE
OF SIENA,
PRAYER 20

297

The line from Shakespeare, "A name? What's in a name? A rose by any other name would smell as sweet" expresses a decidedly modern view of naming. According to this line, a name is a random set of letters arbitrarily assigned to designate something; no intrinsic connection links the group of letters and their referent. We are accustomed to this notion of naming in our culture. Acronyms such as GOP become standard designations, trade names such as Kleenex function as common nouns, and names on e-mail addresses can be chosen by whim.

This common contemporary view contrasts starkly with the more ancient understanding that a name was a constituent feature of a thing. When God promises to bless Abram, it is Abram's name that will be great (Le2A, Pr5A°). When Abram, Sarai, and Saul undergo a fundamental life change, they change their name. According to Genesis 1, God has the power to name the things of the earth, which indicates God's authority over them. The androcentric story in Genesis 2 extends this authority to the man, who names everything God did not yet name, including woman. The man knew the essence of things and was granted authority to order them; therefore, he could name them. We see this high view of naming when adults legally change the name their parents gave them at birth, or when an oppressed group rejects a designation laid upon it and selects its own nomenclature. The phrase "Stop in the name of the law!" also indicates the symbolic importance of the name and its inherent power.

In religion also, to know the name of someone or something gave the knower access to it. How might the residents of Athens gain what they needed? They invoked the goddess Athena. Her name was not incidental; rather, her name was a key to her identity and significance. Knowing the name of the deity is one step along the way toward magical incantations, in which recitation of the divine name might influence the deity to grant benefits to the intercessor or to alter the universe. Some mantras are the deity's name, repeatedly endlessly. Also in the Bible the name of God is a central image. That God has a name, that knowing the divine name is a privilege granted to some, that invoking the divine name brings benefits, and that for Christians Jesus shares the divine name are a few of the ideas that permeate the Old and New Testaments.

The resolutely monotheistic Islam acknowledges only one God: there is no other. Without any confusion between several deities, God does not need any designating name: the word *Allah* is simply the Arabic noun for god. The ninety-nine attributes of Allah are not names, but mostly adjectives, descriptions of the God whose name is nothing other than God. The liturgy of Coptic Christians is also full of reference to Allah, that is, to God. However, the contrast between Islam and Judaism is striking. Biblical religion arose within cultures—Mesopotamian, Egyptian, Canaanite, Babylonian, Greco-Roman—that boasted dozens of deities. Each tribe needed to be clear about its divine names, in order to access the power and protection of its deity. For example, in the story of the contest between Elijah and the adherents of Baal (Pr4c°), both sides are calling upon the name of their god, who is expected to respond to the invocations with the power of fire from heaven. The Hebrew Scriptures record various designations for God. Jacob's deathbed blessing of Joseph names God the Mighty One of Jacob, the Shepherd, the Rock of Israel, the God of your father, and the Almighty. A passage in Isaiah (Pr11a†) names God the Sovereign of Israel, the Redeemer, the First and the Last. In a story of nearly as much importance for Judaism as that of the burning bush, Jacob, after the night of wrestling, asks for the name of the mysterious being (Pr13a°, Pr24c†). Here God refuses to divulge the divine name, and instead grants to Jacob a new name, Israel, a theophoric name that incorporates *El*.

Various names for God appear in the Hebrew Scriptures. *El*, translated God, was the high god of the Canaanite pantheon. Since the word is the generic noun *god*, it often occurred in apposition to a word specifying which god. *El Elyon*, God most high, is associated with the story of Melchizedek and recurs throughout the Old Testament. *El Olam*, everlasting God, uses royal imagery, because the term is the same as would be used in greeting a monarch: "O King, live forever!" *El Shaddai*, traditionally translated Almighty God, meant something about peaks, perhaps God of the mountains, perhaps Goddess of the breasts, and was also a divine name with a pre-Israelite history. The original meaning of God *Sabaoth*, "of hosts," is also obscure. At different times in biblical history the primary referent of Sabaoth was to divine power, to the divine beings in heaven, to the armies that a tribal deity could authorize, to the planets and stars in the sky, or to the nine ranks of angels. The contemporary translation of "Holy, holy, holy," the Sanctus hymn, renders this term "power and might." The Hebrew Bible often uses the word *Elohim*, the plural for *El*. Scholars debate why this plural noun, which used a singular verb, became normal usage. Perhaps the term indicates an early leaning toward monotheism, in which a multiplicity of deities is replaced with only one god. Perhaps the name suggests the plurality of majesty within God.

According to Israelite tradition, God revealed the divine name to the chosen people. Moses asks to know God's name, the knowledge of which will confer on him the authority he needs for the task before him (Pr17ᴬ°). God reveals to Moses the divine name, and although ancient piety did not record nor do contemporary scholars agree upon the precise translation or meaning of yhwh, the exodus story says that the name, and its inherent access to power, came from God.

Some scholars claim that yhwh was a divine name in use in the eastern Sinai prior to 1300 b.c.e. and speculate that it was around the time of Moses that the Israelite people adopted the worship of this deity. At the crossing of the Jordan after the wilderness wanderings, Joshua refers to other deities that their ancestors had worshiped. The words in the first commandment usually translated "before me" actually mean something like "in front of my face," a spatial phrase implying that Egyptian and Canaanite deities have no place in the cultic shrine of Israel, which is dedicated to yhwh alone. In the song of Deborah, one of the oldest poetic pieces in the Bible, the "god of Israel" is named yhwh (Judges 5:3), and in the biblical books such as Deuteronomy in which Israelite tribal identity, religious consolidation, and cultic centralization are paramount, the name yhwh is repeatedly used. In the wisdom literature, after the tribal religion evolved into monotheism, the word *God* tended to replace the older designation yhwh.

Ancient Israelite piety kept its distance from God, in order not to transgress too closely to ultimate power, claiming that it could not look at God and survive. Consequently the tradition refrained from referring to God's very self, instead offering substitutes of some part of God for the whole. We see a remnant of this practice when subjects address a monarch, not as *you*, but as *your majesty*. The Bible uses several such substitutions: God's mighty hand and outstretched arm, the word of God, God's backside, heaven. Throughout the Hebrew tradition, the most common substitution is the phrase *the name of God*. Not only does one's name stand for one's being, it is as if the part of God that is on earth is God's name. First the ark is seen as the place of the name of God (Pr10ᴮ°); later, the temple is seen to be the place where God's name dwells and from where God can be correctly invoked (Pr4cᵗ, Pr16ᴮ°); still later, Jerusalem itself is where God's name dwells. The Aaronic blessing is understood as placing God's name onto the people themselves.

To come in the name of yhwh is to arrive as a divine emissary or with divine protection. David approaches Goliath "in the name of the Lord of hosts, the God of the armies of Israel" (Pr7ʙ°). Psalm 118, a thanksgiving for victory, introduces the line extremely important in Christian usage: "Blessed is the one who comes in the name of the Lᴏʀᴅ." All four gospels record that as Jesus entered Jerusalem before his death, the people called out Psalm 118, acknowledging Jesus as the one who comes into the holy place of God's name, the one who bears the name, or authority, perhaps even the identity, of God (Pᴀsᴀʙᴄ). For centuries, Christians praying their great eucharistic prayer have sung both the Sanctus hymn, which praises God in the words of Isaiah's temple vision, and the Benedictus qui venit, which praises Jesus, who arrived in Jerusalem "in the name of the Lᴏʀᴅ."

At the beginning of Israelite use of the name ʏʜwʜ, God's name was pronounced: otherwise the oral tradition could not have developed. Reverence for the divine name led to its being proscribed in worship. Many contemporary Jews maintain this proscription by replacing the divine name with the noun *Hashem*, meaning "the Name," and the suggestion for Christians to render ʏʜwʜ as Yahweh has been criticized for its disregard for Jewish sensibilities. Over time, however, the Israelites substituted the male noun designating authority, *Lord*, for the divine name. Although most worship books do not make this typographical distinction, some Bible translations render ʏʜwʜ as "Lᴏʀᴅ" and *Adonai* as "Lord." In the Septuagint, both were translated as "Kyrios." Greek-speaking early Christians who were fluent in Hebrew would have realized that Kyrios was not a literal rendering of the divine name. However, calling God Kyrios meant that for believers, the Roman emperor was not the lord. Furthermore, since Lord was also the cultural title of respect afforded Jesus, the same designation could refer both to God and to Christ. This pattern established the standard used within the Christian church ever since.

Considerable discussion is taking place in the church today about rendering ʏʜwʜ as Lord, since the translation replaces the mysterious I ᴀᴍ with a male honorific. Some contemporary psalm translations, in rendering the nearly hundred times that the psalter refers to God's name, translate ʏʜwʜ as "God," hoping to minimize male terminology. Yet the church's christology searches for a single name to designate both God and Jesus, and English-speaking Christians have not yet agreed on a replacement for *Lord*.

The name of Jesus is a major theme in readings in the lectionary. The name Jesus refers back to Joshua, the successor to Moses. That Jesus comes to share the divine name is most evident in John's gospel, in which the divine name ɪ ᴀᴍ (Pr24ᴀ) is taken on by Jesus himself (GFʀᴀʙᴄ, Pr12ʙ). The high priestly prayer suggests that God gave the divine name to Jesus, who now extends its power over the church (Ea7ᴀ). The divine name is a culmination of many other designations that John's gospel gives to Jesus. In John 1 alone, we read Word (ChDyABC); Lamb of God, Son of God, Rabbi, Messiah (Ep2A); son of Joseph, King of Israel, and Son-of-man (Ep2B). Another divine designation is Gabriel's name for the coming Jesus, Emmanuel (Ad4A), found in Isaiah 7:14 as well as in Psalm 46: "the LORD of hosts is with us." Throughout the entire New Testament, it is the usage of *Lord* for Jesus that grants to Jesus the power of the divine name. An impressive first-century hymn recorded in Philippians (PasABC) makes this connection explicit: God gave to Jesus "the name that is above every name," before which we bow. In Hebrews 1 (ChDyABC), the unique name God grants to Jesus is *Son*.

Many readings, especially the selections from Acts during the Easter season (Ea3B, Ea4B, Ea2C, Ea7C), indicate that the Christian life proceeds from and in the name of Jesus. In Mark, Jesus cites the authority of his name as having empowered even a stranger to exorcise a demon (Pr21B). After the ascension, Jesus' followers can effect those same miracles in his name, and Luke's gospel anticipates that disciples will be persecuted because of Jesus' name (Pr28c).

Both Old and New Testaments share a pattern. In prior cultures or neighboring peoples a divine name, or, in Jesus' case, a standard personal name was used. The emerging religion rejects most previous holy names as false. But some of the previous designations are taken over by the emerging religious tradition, which reinterprets the divine name in the light of its own experience of grace and claims that salvation comes through these names. Invoking other divine names is at the least a useless activity, at the most idolatry.

The contemporary church asks whether there is a name of God. Some theologians, intent on preserving Christian tradition, argue that just as YHWH is the Jewish name of God, *Father, Son, and Holy Spirit* is the Christian name of God (TrinA). New Testament quotations ground the name Father in Jesus' own usage (the Gospel of John; also Pr11A, Ch1B, PasB, TrinB, Pasc). These theologians teach that the threefold name, the divine name granted to the church, must be used in all orthodox Christian prayer. Substitutions would dilute the uniqueness of baptismal faith and tend toward heresy.

The opposite suggestion by other Christians is that this first-century terminology of Father-Son-Holy Spirit developed within the Greco-Roman world in which Father was the standard title for Jupiter and Son of God was a stereotypical way to refer to a male monarch. For these Christians, the formulation in Matthew 28 represents neither the complete Christian truth nor the only way to articulate the mystery of God, but rather one example of the hellenization of the Jewish tradition that became Christianity. According to this position, although Father-Son-Holy Spirit retains a privileged place in Christian prayer, the mystery of God's being is finally unnamable, and any attempt to close off doctrinal debate by enforcing an androcentric solution is unwelcome. Currently Christians around the world are discussing whether some other idiom is acceptable for the ritual language at baptism. The New Testament indicates that the earliest baptisms were done in the name of Jesus (Bapc). Could the idiom used at the baptism ritual and in blessings be open to variation? The theological discussion continues.

January 1, the eighth day after Christmas, is the remembrance of Jesus' circumcision ritual, as well as being the first day of each secular calendar. On this day Christians celebrate the divine name with readings that recall the terms *Lord*, *Abba*, and *Jesus*. We stand before the uncertainty of the new year in the name of our God, united in God's Spirit with all others who come in the name of the LORD, proclaiming God's justice along with the prophets who, like Jeremiah, spoke in God's name.

In a society in which the word *Christian* often functions as a synonym for *nice*, it is important for the church to grow deeper into the meaning of our name. Because many Christians receive the name of Christ in their infancy, some churches are working toward a more effective ritual of confirmation than is currently practiced. At such time, and perhaps at other designated central points in a person's life, adults publicly state their intention to continue their life under the name of God, and the whole community reflects together on what such a dedication to the name of God might imply.

The fifth-century hymn written by St. Patrick, "I bind unto myself today," is a gift from the past to contemporary believers. The hymn shows its pagan origins, for the singers bind themselves also to the powers of nature. But along with Patrick Christians bind themselves to the name of the Trinity and to the powers of that name of God. The church continues to sing this premodern, almost magical formulation of protection, and meditates on the significance of living under two names: one's own given and chosen name, and the name of the triune God. The book of Revelation says that in the end-time, God's name, no longer unknown or secret, will be written on everyone's forehead (Ea6c). The good news is that, by the power of the Spirit, the church can be the place where Christians reside in the name of God, practicing the peace and the justice of the end-time.

Outsider

alien, Babylon, Egypt, foreigner,
leper, outsider, prostitute, Samaritan,
tax collector, uncircumcised

Related chapters: BATTLE, CROSS, ISRAEL, THE POOR

Like many ancient religious texts, the Bible contains condemnation of the outsider. Yet the New Testament presents Jesus as an outsider. The lectionary appoints especially those biblical passages in which God and the community welcome, rather than ostracize, the outsider.

PSALM 87:3, 4   I count Egypt and Babylon among those who know me;
            behold Philistia, Tyre, and Ethiopia:
         in Zion were they born.
      Of the city it shall be said, "Everyone was born in Zion,
            and the Most High shall sustain it."

BIDDING   Let us pray for those who do not believe in Christ, that the
PRAYER,   light of the Holy Spirit may show them the way of salva-
GOOD FRIDAY   tion. . . . Let us pray for those who do not believe in God,
           that they may find the one who is the author and goal of
           our existence.

KOH YUKI   In a lowly manger born,
         humble life begun in scorn;
         under Joseph's watchful eye,
         Jesus grew as you and I;
         knew the sufferings of the weak,
         knew the patience of the meek,
         hungered as but poor folk can;
         this is he. Behold the man!

         Visiting the lone and lost,
         steadying the tempest-tossed,
         giving of himself in love,
         calling minds to things above:
         sinners gladly hear his call;
         publicans before him fall,
         for in him new life began;
         this is he. Behold the man!

One day three Britons by birth approached Kildare and asked for Brigit. Two of the Britons were blind and one was leprous. They met Brigit at the door of the church and asked her to cure them. She invited them in to eat and said she would pray for them. They told her that it was because they were Britons and not Irish that she refused to cure them. She was moved by their reproach and took holy water to bless them. Immediately, the blind men could see and the leper was cleansed.

TALES OF
St. Brigit

As Christ came not only to serve people with leprosy, healing and cleansing them in body, but he also wished to die for them, sanctifying and cleansing them in their soul, so St. Francis, longing to be entirely conformed to Christ, used to serve victims of leprosy with very great affection, giving them food, washing their sore limbs, cleaning and washing their clothes, and, moreover, frequently and fervently giving them kisses. And so it happened many times that God by his power simultaneously healed the soul of one whose body the Saint healed, as we read of Christ.

*The Little
Flowers of
St. Francis*

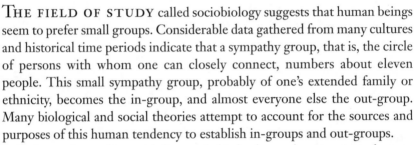

THE FIELD OF STUDY called sociobiology suggests that human beings seem to prefer small groups. Considerable data gathered from many cultures and historical time periods indicate that a sympathy group, that is, the circle of persons with whom one can closely connect, numbers about eleven people. This small sympathy group, probably of one's extended family or ethnicity, becomes the in-group, and almost everyone else the out-group. Many biological and social theories attempt to account for the sources and purposes of this human tendency to establish in-groups and out-groups.

In its moderate form, this human habit leads to ethnocentrism, the tendencies to assume one's own culture is the best and to interact with other cultures according to one's own biases. When these biases are negative, we use the word *prejudice*; when the biases evoke excessive fear and hostility, we talk about *xenophobia*. Our word *barbarian* is instructive in this regard. Originally the Latin word designated one who was not of the tribe and thus who was strange; yet the word came to mean one who is a dangerous threat to the in-group. Yet even nature deplores an extreme preference for the in-group: genetic studies demonstrate that the practice of exogamy—marriage outside the group—is important for the birthing of healthy human beings.

It is easy to see how during ancient Bible times religion helped to support ethnocentrism. If the sympathy group provides the means of security, granting that the small group of persons care enough about each other to protect one another from outside harm, and if religion understands that one task of the deities is the protection of the people, then it is likely that the religion will support, if not intensify, ethnocentrism. The gods and goddesses wanted their favorite ethnic group to survive and thrive. Even though in contemporary Jewish practice everyone celebrating the passover seder lessens the wine in their glasses ten drops in sorrow for the suffering of the Egyptians, the story in Exodus does not suggest that God grieved over the slaughter of the Egyptian army. YHWH is fighting against the deities of Egypt. YHWH is the deity of the people of Abraham, Isaac, and Jacob, not the God of Pharaoh's people. Two millennia of Christian history record many similar events, in which the in-group of Christians assumes that God directs them to harass, isolate, and even exterminate the out-group.

Scholars of religion use the word *henotheism* to describe the religious practice in which each ethnic group or geographical area follows its own deities that must be honored by that tribe and in that place. Moving to another area raises the question of whether to switch to the deities of the new place. The Israelites' migration to Canaan involved a test of whether their ancient tribal deity YHWH would be efficacious in the new place, or whether in this area worshiping the local deities Baal and Asherah might be a smarter idea. After Naaman the Syrian traveled to Elisha the Israelite to be healed of leprosy, he took back home with him two mule-loads of soil: Naaman's hope was to commandeer the power of the deity of that place by bringing home some of the earth over which that deity presided.

The Bible contains many examples of what we would call xenophobia, in some cases even genocide. Many times God's people hear God telling them to separate from the outsider. Moses and the Egyptians, Joshua and the Canaanites, Samson and the Philistines, Nehemiah and those Jews who during the Babylonian exile contracted mixed marriages: these stories assume that God's people are to identify themselves as different from the outsider and to refuse contact with, if not slaughter, the outsider. Many biblical texts use the proper nouns *Egypt*, *Canaan*, *Philistine*, and *Babylon* to designate the evil alien. How to treat the out-group is the subtext of the story in Genesis 34 of Dinah's rape. That the rapist is named Shechem, which is not a man's name, but the name of a Canaanite city, indicates the in-group and out-group aspect of the story. Although Shechem wishes to marry Dinah, Dinah's brothers carry out their deception and revenge because he is an outsider.

Yet nearly all of the Bible's rejection of the outsider is omitted from the three-year lectionary. In the lectionary, the Bible's stories of in-groups and out-groups are presented so as to include, rather than to reject, the outsider. For example, Genesis narrates in detail Lot's foolish choice of settling on land too near the pagan cities of Sodom and Gomorrah, the immoral behaviors of the urban dwellers, and God's destruction of the cities. Of this entire story the lectionary includes only the story of Abraham pleading with God that the city be saved (Pr12c†). The New Testament records the attitude of Peter, who early on believed that God's mercy in Christ was meant only for Jews and did not mean to include the outsider Gentiles. Yet in the lectionary, we hear of Peter's dream that nothing is now unclean: there is for Christians no outsider (Ea5c).

A striking tale of including the outsider is appointed in the Revised Common Lectionary: the story from Luke 8 of Jesus healing the demoniac. The demoniac lives in the Transjordan, outside Jewish areas, and runs about naked among the tombs. His demons find their new home in a herd of swine (Pr7c). All these traditional categories of the outsider—one who is not Jewish, has a demon, associates with the dead, wears no clothing, resides near pigs—do not keep Jesus away.

An example of how the lectionary treats the outsider is in its use of the Bible's leper stories. Ancient Israelite behavioral codes required the community to isolate to a place outside the camp people with various skin diseases and bodily discharges. Scholars are not sure exactly what physical maladies Leviticus 13–14 refers to, but the rules are strict. The so-called lepers, viewed as threats to society because of their supposedly highly contagious disease, are relegated, along with the latrines, to outside the camp. If they presented themselves to the priest as cured, the examination occurred outside the camp. When a house was judged to have leprosy, the stones removed from the walls were thrown outside the city. The tale of Aaron and Miriam challenging Moses' authority, in which only Miriam is punished (Numbers 12), indicates that, stricken with leprosy, she must be isolated outside the camp until she is healed. According to these ancient stories, God instructs the people to designate the person with leprosy a social outcast.

Which stories of leprosy were chosen for the lectionary? That lepers will be healed is listed as one of the signs of the arrival of the messiah. We read the early synoptic story of Jesus healing the person with leprosy (Ep6b). Jesus not only heals the leper, but also touches the person. We read the story of Jesus healing the ten persons with leprosy, one of whom, by being a Samaritan, is doubly an outsider (Pr23c). The lectionary includes the story of the healing of Naaman (Ep6b, Pr23c†, Pr9c°), but the reading as stipulated in the lectionary concludes before the grim ending of 2 Kings 5, in which Elisha's thieving servant Gehazi is punished by contracting leprosy.

Similarly, many biblical passages identify the foreigner as a potentially dangerous person whom it is wise to avoid. The Israelite was not to eat the passover with a foreigner; the Israelite was allowed to charge only a foreigner interest on a loan; the visionary Ezekiel stipulates that foreigners will not be granted entry into the sanctuary. Especially the foreign woman was viewed as a threat. The wisdom literature warns a young man to avoid them, and the court narratives blame Solomon's foreign wives and Ahab's Canaanite wife Jezebel for leading their men astray. Foreigners are outsiders who threaten tribal identity, national security, and religious purity.

In the lectionary, however, the foreigner comes off far better. Ruth was a foreigner who becomes the great-grandmother of King David (Pr26b°, Pr27b°). Jonah is shown to be wrong in his prejudice against the Ninevites (Vigilabc, Pr20a†, Ep3b). Solomon's great prayer at the dedication of the temple anticipates the time when also foreigners will come to worship there

(Pr16b°, Pr4c†). Gospel readings include the stories of the Gentile woman's faith (Pr15a) and the Gentile centurion's plea (Pr4c). The lectionary's selections from Hebrews include the reminder that it is the Christians who are themselves foreigners here on earth (Pr14c).

The same pattern exists with the Samaritan. Originally, Samaria was the capital city of the northern kingdom of Israel. Later, the term referred to the northern kingdom. Still later, southern dwellers of Judah began to use the term *Samaritans* as an ethnic designation of the northerners. By the time of the New Testament, *Samaritan* was a derogatory term. When in John 8:48, the people of Judah, enraged at Jesus' teaching, call him a Samaritan demoniac, they are being as offensive as possible. Although first-century Jews treated women as unclean during their menstrual period, some Judeans believed that Samaritan women menstruated since birth: thus Samaria's women were far more unclean than Judea's women. The lectionary does include the instruction of Jesus to his followers, to preach the gospel to Jews, but not to enter Samaritan villages (Pr6a).

However, in the classic Lenten baptismal readings, Jesus receives water from the Samaritan woman at the well and converts her, and she immediately becomes a preacher of the good news (Le3a). We hear the stories of the Good Samaritan (Pr10c) and of the thankful Samaritan healed of leprosy (Pr23c). All people with leprosy were ostracized from society, and the group of lepers that Jesus healed included both Jews and Samaritans, people who would normally not associate with one another. Some exegetes think that the comment in John 10 about "other sheep that do not belong to this fold" (Ea4b) is a reference to Samaritans. The lectionary's selections make clear that Christians welcome the outsider as did Christ.

Tax collectors were employees of the military dictatorship and thus were despised by the population as collaborators. As well, because their salary was acquired by their unregulated overcharging of taxes and fees, tax collectors were assumed to be cheats. Several readings cite tax collectors as a class of moral reprobates (Pr5a, Pr9a, Pr18a). Yet Jesus cited tax collectors as moral folk who love their neighbors (Ep7a). The New Testament records that Matthew was a tax collector, and in the parable of the two sons, Jesus said that the tax collectors will enter the kingdom before the upstanding priests and elders (Pr21a). In the parable of the Pharisee and the tax collector and in the story of Zacchaeus, it is the tax collector whom God blesses (Pr25c). A further example of the outsider in biblical parlance is the prostitute, a woman outside even the community's moral proscriptions since she was outside family structures and unattached to any man. Yet Jesus claims that prostitutes will enter into the reign of God before the religious leaders (Pr21a).

According to the linguistic world of the Bible, the term *the uncircumcised* referred not only to Gentile males, but to Gentile people male and female. When Exodus 12 stipulates that the uncircumcised cannot eat the passover, we assume that *the uncircumcised* referred also to non-Jewish women. In Romans Paul refers to the Gentiles as the uncircumcised, and Jeremiah and Acts use the term as a metaphor for those who hearts are not ready to receive God. One could designate an entire population of males and females by referring to male anatomy. *The uncircumcised* is one instance of many male terms sometimes meant to include women and sometimes not. The biblical reader may not be sure when *kings* included queens, if *brothers* includes sisters, if *apostles* were only male. Contemporary translations meant for public reading might well clarify these whenever possible, for example, by rendering *the uncircumcised* as "those who do not circumcise their males." Yet distinct from the many negative references in the epistles to the uncircumcised, the lectionary includes the passage proclaiming that in Christ there is no longer "circumcised and uncircumcised" (Pr13c).

For the pious Jew, perhaps the most extreme class of outsider was the crucified. To be hanged naked on a tree until one was dead was a particularly repugnant method of execution that took place outside the city walls. Christian theology teaches that Christ was the ultimate outsider, and by his splayed arms invites and welcomes all the outsiders. The lectionary's use of lepers, foreigners, Samaritans, tax collectors, and the uncircumcised indicates that just as Christ was on the outside of what was thought holy, so the word of God proclaims that all outsiders are to be seen in a new light. Depending on one's life situation and experience, different types of people get viewed as the outsider. Perhaps it is those who are poor, or unwashed, or incarcerated, or alien, or unemployed, or terminally ill, or sexually different; it may, on the other hand, be those who are incredibly rich or socially successful. Americans are raised to so avoid death that those who are dying come to be shunned as the outsider. Yet because of the cross, Christians see Christ in the face of each outsider. Twentieth-century Christians Dorothy Day and Gustav Gutierrez are among those who call us, not only to smile at the outsider, but to live with the outsider, for it is among the outsiders where Christ is.

The group of images designating the outsider illustrates well how the lectionary works as metaphor. Take for example the leper: thankfully, people with various serious skin ailments are no longer misdiagnosed as lepers and ostracized outside our communities. Thus a gospel reading about leprosy functions for us not as a literal directive from God, but as an image for us to contemplate: Who are our lepers? Whom do we fear? Whom do we ostracize? And if we judge ourselves as an outsider, we are the thief on the cross, welcomed inside the church by the presence of the body of Christ.

Practical implications for the liturgy flow from a consideration of the outsider. Some church naves provide space, and not in the back row, for wheelchairs. The church is recognizing the incongruity of baptizing children but then dealing with them as outsiders, excommunicating them to the nursery. Music from cultures other than our own is being included in the liturgy. Theologians are rethinking the relationship between Christianity and other world religions. Yet the church has a long way to go. For example, worship books include few hymns that attend to the outsider, and nearly no hymns recognize when we ourselves are the outsider. Conversely, some churches mean to eliminate any sense of the outsider by expecting little of the worshiper or the member, as if everyone is instantly an insider. Yet the Sunday liturgy is a ritual: ritual is symbolic communal behavior, a practice that holds the group together in its beliefs by its participatory action. Those who design Christian liturgy are perhaps best helped not by pretending that nobody is outside the assembly, but by urging each member of the assembly to welcome the outsider in the next pew. Rituals cannot provide the welcome that Christians themselves are to embody.

The hope is that attending to the outsider on Sunday morning will be practice for our lifelong turn toward the outsider. Francis of Assisi is a model of such a commitment. His radical acceptance of the gospel impelled him to embrace the leper. Francis left his comfortable home for life with the outsider. He welcomed the foreigner, he visited the sultan during the crusades. The lectionary offers the leper, the foreigner, the Samaritan, the tax collector, and the uncircumcised as images of the outsider whom we are called to embrace. There, outside, we will find Christ. And it will be good news, that there is no longer anyone we need to hate.

The Poor

the poor, the rich, shepherds, widow

Related chapters: OUTSIDER, SERVANT

Although many societies neglect and ostracize people who are poor, the readings proclaim the biblical teaching that God values the poor and blesses them. Christians have evidenced wide variations in how they think about and deal with the world's poor. Metaphorically we all are the poor.

PSALM 12:5   "Because the needy are oppressed,
and the poor cry out in misery,
     I will rise up," says the LORD,
     "and give them the help they long for."

CANTICLE   You have shown strength with your arm,
OF MARY   and scattered the proud in their conceit,
casting down the mighty from their thrones
     and lifting up the lowly.
You have filled the hungry with good things,
     and sent the rich away empty.

HARRY E.   Cure your children's warring madness;
FOSDICK   bend our pride to your control;
shame our wanton, selfish gladness,
rich in things and poor in soul.
Grant us wisdom, grant us courage,
lest we miss your kingdom's goal.

Francis's companions asked him, "Are you thinking of getting married?" Francis answered in a clear voice: "You are right. I was thinking of wooing the noblest, richest, and most beautiful bride ever seen." His friends laughed at him, saying he was a fool and did not know what he was saying; in reality he had spoken by divine revelation. The bride was none other than that form of true religion which he embraced, and which, above any other, is noble, rich, and beautiful in its poverty. He was already a benefactor of the poor, but from this time onward he resolved never to refuse alms to anyone who begged in God's name, but rather to give more willingly and abundantly than ever before.

LEGEND OF
St. Francis
and Lady
Poverty

We who live in this country cannot be as poor as those who go out to other countries. We are the rich country of the world, like Dives at the feast. We must try hard, we must study to be poor like Lazarus at the gate, who was taken into Abraham's bosom. The Gospel doesn't tell us anything about Lazarus' virtues. He just sat there and let the dogs lick his sores. He would be classed by any social worker of today as a mental case. But again, poverty, and in this case destitution, like hospitality, is so esteemed by God, it is something to be sought after, worked for, the pearl of great price.

Dorothy Day,
"The Pearl of
Great Price"

USUALLY ONE'S OWN ECONOMIC SITUATION helps determine one's opinion about the poor. Are you yourself poor? Almost nobody reading this volume is genuinely poor. Were your ancestors poor, or were they wealthy benefactors? Does your family and cultural tradition believe that hard work brings money? Are your associates successful in achieving the economic gains due their labor, or is society stacked against you and yours? Whom exactly do we mean by *the poor*?

Not only contemporary Christians, but also the Bible evidence various attitudes about the poor. Biblical legal texts speak of the obligation of those with money; those who lend money are not to charge the poor any interest, and farmers must ensure that after the harvest some gleanings will remain for the poor. The wisdom literature usually suggests that poverty is one's own fault; yet Job heartily disputes this claim. The prophets see poverty as the result of an oppressive ruling class that must change its ways; the psalms pray that at least God will "hear the cry of the poor." The book of Ruth illustrates God's blessings upon the poor. One of the seven Hebrew nouns that can be translated "the poor," *anawim*, goes even further in connecting religious piety and humility before God with the poor of the land.

The books nearer to the ministry of Jesus, either in time or in tone, recall his life among the poor of the land. Yet reading the book of Acts we see that the Jesus movement evolved into a church that wanted to survive, and even thrive. Because such an organization needed money, Luke presented wealthy believers with considerable respect and praised their benefaction to the poor. Especially the author of James judged that care for the poor is a preeminent sign of Christian life.

Over the centuries, the Christian church has evidenced the same multivocality as the Bible itself. Faithful believers of every economic situation lived as if their approach to the poor was the one approved by God. On the one hand, some Christians assume that poverty is good, or at least that the poor are blessed by God. The genuinely poor, who usually are without platform to voice their opinions, are seen as a model of trust in God as they seem to accept their lot as God's will. Some Christians chose to become poor. Francis of Assisi judged money, and the evolving capitalist economy of Europe, to be worldly evils that must be wholly rejected. Medieval European history tells many saints' legends of those born into wealth and status who gave it up to live in sometimes extreme privation in monastic life. Much of this romanticizing of poverty resulted from a biblical understanding that Jesus himself was poor, and so to take Jesus as one's model, one must also be poor. Undoubtedly, the ways that money corrupted persons and thwarted social order were apparent to many believers, who saw as their only recourse the total abandonment of money.

The close of the Middle Ages marked the establishment of capitalism in the West. Particularly among economically successful Protestants the opinion grew that money is God's reward for work well done, and such money can serve the society in many ways, including by feeding the poor. The late nineteenth century saw the emergence of what has been termed the gospel of wealth, a conviction held by some Christians that God's good news was money. Meanwhile, throughout the centuries many wealthy Christians believed that generous contributions to the poor was one way they expressed to God their gratitude for a life of privilege.

So the church lives in ambivalence about money. This ambivalence, openly discussed by many contemporary Roman Catholic vowed religious, addresses one of the classic three monastic vows, which is to a life of poverty. Yet as participants in our society, these sisters and brothers recognize poverty as a great social evil that the church must combat. How can one be vowed to an evil? What is meant by *poverty*? One of the most influential Christian movements of the twentieth century was liberation theology, led by theologians within the community of the poor. The movement enabled the poor themselves to speak out, resulting in eloquent expressions of God's preferential option for the poor. The mainstream church tends to listen with compassion and charity, without joining the life of poverty.

Advocates of the distinctive positions, from the gospel of wealth to liberation theology, may be dissatisfied with the lectionary's presentation of the poor. Usually the biblical texts are open to a wide range of interpretations. For example, the propers for All Saints Day include in year A the Matthean beatitudes (also Ep4A) and in year C the Lucan blessings and woes (also Ep6C). Liberation theologians can see in Jesus' praise of the poor (Matthew: "the poor in spirit"), the meek, the hungry, and the persecuted a primary illustration of the biblical message of God's preferential option for the poor. Especially in the Lucan version, the rich are explicitly condemned for having already received their consolation.

Other interpreters see in these passages an alternate value system that only metaphorically speaks about money. It is not that the poor will now or eventually be fed, but that they will have the kingdom of heaven, itself a metaphorical reality. The same interpretive ambivalence is evident in Paul's discussion of charity for the poor (Pr8B). Jesus is cited as a model for Christian charity: he became poor, so that through his poverty you might become rich. Probably Paul meant to refer, as does the hymn quoted in Philippians 2, to Christ's relinquishing the divine throne in order to live a human life. This passage seems to point to Jesus' life of literal poverty. Yet at its conclusion Paul's sentence becomes metaphorical: through Christ's poverty we become rich, not literally, of course, but spiritually. In this passage Paul advocates what we might associate with a mainstream Christian middle class value and ethic: that the rich are to share out of their abundance to meet others' need.

The lectionary includes prophetic condemnation of the rich. This biblical strain says that people are poor, not because of God's fault, or fate's, but because of the greed and dishonesty of the rich. Amos says that if the rich were not breaking or stretching the law, there would be no poor (Pr20c°, Pr21c°). According to Luke's memorable parable of the rich man and poor Lazarus, the rich man bears full responsibility for not having fed, clothed, and nursed the beggar on his doorstep, and his disregard for the poor lands him in a place of torment (Pr21c). The parable of the last judgment conveys a similar message (LastA). Although the parable does not mention the words *poor* or *poverty*, it is because people did not feed the hungry, clothe the naked, nurse the sick, and visit the prisoner that they are sent into eternal punishment.

Several other readings can be seen as stressing God's blessings on the poor. In the Lucan narrative of the beginning of Jesus' preaching ministry (Ep3c), Jesus took to himself the words from Isaiah 61: the long-awaited anointed one is sent "to bring good news to the poor." In the Lucan birth narratives, the angels brought the good news of the birth of the messiah first to shepherds. A first-century audience would recognize shepherds as representatives of the poor. Our sentimentalizing of shepherds ignores the fact that in the urban culture of that time, shepherding was considered an undesirable trade; shepherds could not maintain a kosher lifestyle and did not respect property boundaries. The reading from James says explicitly that God has chosen the poor (Pr18B). Consequently, believers are to honor the poor, by for example giving a poorly dressed person a prominent seat in the assembly. Without such honoring of the poor, wrote the author of James, our faith is meaningless.

A recurring way that the Bible images the poor is as the widow. The social ideal was that everyone would marry, that a couple would bear sons, and that old people would be supported by their sons. Of course this ideal was not always realized. Thus an old woman, who was too old to work, who had outlived her employable husband, and who had no sons to care for her, became a stereotypical image of the poor. Widows are pictures of those who are genuinely destitute and socially powerless, and throughout the scriptures the people of God are urged to care for the widow, the community caring for those who fall through the social net.

Several well-known gospel stories use the widow to exemplify Jesus' concern for the poor. After condemning the immoral practices of the rich, Jesus praised the poor widow who contributed two small copper coins to the temple's treasury (Pr27B). In this episode Jesus suggested that it is not the amount of money that God notices, but only the faith and intention of the believer. In the miracle of the raising of the widow's son from death (Pr5c), Jesus saved the widow from the absolute destitution that would be hers were her only son dead. We see this use of the widow most fully in the book of Ruth (Pr26B°, Pr27B°). The short story presents the reader with three widows struggling through a famine. By Naomi's knowledge of Israelite law and by Ruth's chutzpah in urging Boaz's hand—beware of sentimentalizing the extraordinary and inappropriate behavior of Ruth—God was able to give the poor widows everything they needed: home, husband, a son, even milk in the grandmother's breasts.

It is not only widows, but other ostracized women as well who become symbols of the poor. The song of Mary is perhaps the Bible's most explicit statement of God's countercultural love for the poor (Ad4c). God has rejected the proud, the powerful, and the rich, while blessing the lowly and the hungry. This song, probably one that Luke's community received from intertestamental times, is put into the mouth of a young, poor, powerless, and pregnant woman, an archetypal image of *the poor*. The song parallels the song of Hannah, in which God is praised for caring for the feeble, the hungry, the barren, the poor, the needy, even those already in Sheol. Appropriately, this song is put in the mouth of a barren woman, a person ostracized for not being able to bear the son that her husband and society expect of her.

The biblical emphasis on God's care for the poor was realized in the liturgy of the early church by a weekly collection for the poor. The idea was, as Justin Martyr explained in the second century, that Christians present offerings to God by presenting food and goods to the needy. The contemporary church continues this practice. Congregations might distinguish money collected for internal church expenses, such as salaries and parish maintenance, from what is collected for the poor. That congregations find it easier to raise money for capital campaigns than for poor relief demonstrates how countercultural it remains to care for those in need.

In the weekly intercessions, congregations pray for the poor. The scriptures are full of promises that God hears the cry of the poor. Although it is not always easy to see or believe this assurance, the church continues to trust that God will attend to the needs of the poor. The Spirit of God, who anointed Jesus to preach good news to the poor, is now resident in the church, and believers are anointed in their baptism by that Spirit to bring the good news to the poor. The least that Christians who are not poor can do, anointed by that Spirit, is hold the needs of the poor before God every single week.

Yet the biblical passages hold more than the literal meaning of our care for those who are in economic need. The biblical language of *the poor* can also be metaphorical: the poor are all of us. Some biblical interpreters believe that in the psalms, the *anawim* is primarily a metaphor for all pious persons who look to God for life. Even if we have enough or too much money, we are all poor in one way or another: poor in our sharing, poor in our understanding of others, poor in our dedication to the things of God, poor in facing down death. Yet the lectionary readings bring us the good news, that no matter in what way we are poor, we come to participate in the riches of God through our baptism. In the community formed around the triune God, all of us, poor in some way, share a life that God alone can give.

Prophet

Moses, prophet, rabbi, scroll,
voice in the wilderness, word

Related chapters: Day of the Lord, Emanation of the Divine, Spirit

Although popularly the prophet is seen as predicting the future, the biblical prophet is far more, even other, than that. The prophet speaks the word of God, which always recalls divine justice and promises divine mercy. For Christians, the paramount prophet is Christ, the word of God, and the liturgy is a prophetic proclamation of the word.

PSALM 40:1, 3, 11

I waited patiently upon you, O LORD:
    you stooped to me and heard my cry.
You put a new song in my mouth,
    a song of praise to our God;
    many shall see, and stand in awe,
    and put their trust in the LORD.
Your righteousness have I not hidden in my heart;
I have spoken of your faithfulness and your deliverance;
    I have not concealed your love and faithfulness
    from the great congregation.

CANTICLE OF ZECHARIAH

Blessed are you, Lord, the God of Israel,
    you have come to your people and set them free.
Through your holy prophets, you promised of old
to save us from our enemies,
    from the hands of all who hate us,
to show mercy to our forebears,
    and to remember your holy covenant.
And you, child, shall be called the prophet of the Most High,
    for you will go before the Lord to prepare the way,
to give God's people knowledge of salvation
    by the forgiveness of their sins.

SARAH E. TAYLOR

O God of light, your Word, a lamp unfailing,
shall pierce the darkness of our earthbound way
and show your grace, your plan for us unveiling,
and guide our footsteps to the perfect day.

From days of old, through blind and willful ages,
though we rebelled, you gently sought again,
and spoke through saints, apostles, prophets, sages,
who wrote with eager or reluctant pen.

Undimmed by time, those words are still revealing
to sinful hearts your justice and your grace;
and questing spirits, longing for your healing,
see your compassion in the Savior's face.

I told them I was like Jonah; for it had been then nearly eight years since the Lord had called me to preach his gospel to the fallen sons and daughters of Adam's race, but that I had lingered like him, and delayed to do at the bidding of the Lord, and warn those who are as deeply guilty as were the people of Nineveh. My sermon applied wholly to myself, and added an exhortation. God made manifest his power among the people. Some wept, while others shouted for joy. Here by the instrumentality of a poor colored woman, the Lord poured forth his spirit among the people. The Lord gave his handmaiden power to speak for his great name, for he arrested the hearts of the people, and caused a shaking amongst the multitude, for God was in the midst.

The Religious Experience and Journal of Jarena Lee

Who is it that is supposed to articulate the longings and aspirations of the people more than the preacher? Somehow the preacher must be an Amos, and say, "Let justice roll down like waters and righteousness like a mighty stream." Somehow, the preacher must say with Jesus, "The spirit of the Lord is upon me, because he hath anointed me to deal with the problems of the poor. . . ."

Well, I don't know what will happen now. We've got some difficult days ahead. But it doesn't matter with me now. Because I've been to the mountaintop. And I've seen the promised land. Mine eyes have seen the glory of the coming of the Lord.

MARTIN LUTHER KING JR., "I See the Promised Land"

A PROPHET IS ONE who speaks for the deity. The prophet sees into and beyond current events and conveys a message to the people from the deity. The people must determine whether the prophet is true or false, to be honored as divinely inspired or to be ignored. Ancient Near Eastern texts indicate that in many nation-states various kinds of prophets used varieties of techniques, and it is not at all clear, when the Hebrew Scriptures speak about a prophet, exactly what kind of person the author was envisioning. We do not know what the prophet's religious and cultural responsibilities were, even whether the venerable designation of prophet was awarded to such a spokesperson during life or only after death. More conservative biblical scholars feel capable of describing the personalities of the major prophets, while more critical scholarship suggests that all we have is the texts, pastiches compiled over decades and even centuries. It is helpful to think through a list of different types of prophets, some of which are explicitly referred to in the Bible, others of which may or may not have been active through Israelite history:

1. Some prophets were diviners who would identify the meaning of present actions by reading the state of the liver of a sacrificed animal, the location of the stars, or the casting of lots.
2. Some were miracle workers, who by the power of the deity were able to change the situation, heal the sick, or produce extraordinary conditions. Elisha was remembered as a miracle worker. Some of these prophets made use of incantatory rituals, capitalizing on the inexplicable power of words to connect the divine and the human.
3. Some prophets spoke, sang, or declaimed while in some kind of induced ecstasy. The story of the prophets of Baal and Asherah indicates self-mutilation as one form of inducing ecstasy. While in ecstasy, the prophet's extraordinary words would bring wisdom to the people. Such prophets were literally beside themselves.
4. The ancient world made considerable use of oracles. A suppliant would come to the deity's shrine searching for answers, and the oracle would speak the answer from the gods. Sometimes a second person, one who interpreted the message of the oracle, was involved, especially when the oracle, such as the sibyls, spoke in riddles or gibberish.

5. Visionaries or seers, with or without trance states, were able to see and understand more than the ordinary person. In classical literature, some of these seers were described as driven mad by the horrors they foresaw and by the people's refusal to believe.
6. Some prophets interpreted dreams as metaphoric vehicles of divine will.
7. Some prophets were revered sages who embodied the wisdom tradition in their person.
8. Some prophets were employed as court appointees, serving the monarch's desires. Understandably, some court prophets spoke to the ruler in such a way as to keep their posts.
9. Some prophets were social critics who analyzed the community's distress as brought on by the people themselves, their immorality, their lack of communal care. In the biblical record, some prophets courageously speak social justice directly to the king.

It is clear that the designation prophet is a wide one. The prophet's emphasis might have been on current need or on future events. The suppliant may have been a nation, a religious community, a monarch, or an individual petitioner. The prophet may have been a socially prominent person or an outcast, a miracle worker or an author. The prophet's words may have been insane babbling or the metaphoric masterpieces of Second Isaiah. The lectionary presents narratives and words of the prophets that are judged either useful to us today or instructive as images of Christ, for many of these prophetic types came to be woven together in the gospels' depiction of Jesus.

In the scriptures and the subsequent Jewish and Christian theological traditions, prophets were highly revered, at least after their death. The overall theme of all prophetic messages was positive. Although many prophets decried something in the current situation, the prophet usually promised that God will forgive, God will renew, God will speak mercy, healing, victory. Something better will come in the future. Indeed, one of the distinguishing characteristics of the world's three monotheistic religions is their positive outlook: God will improve things, one way or another, sooner or later.

The Jewish tradition designated Moses as the greatest prophet, from whose authority came the Torah. Moses was responsible for conveying to the people the words and wisdom of God. He spoke for God to the people, and he was the intermediary for the people to address themselves to God. In Jewish tradition, the focus of the prophet is the reestablishment of the relationship between God and the people. Repeatedly, God calls the people to keep the covenant, worship only YHWH, and honor one another in the community. According to the prophet, life in the community could be vastly improved, and God's words through the prophet told the people how: by renewing their religious and social responsibilities.

When Christians have read the Hebrew Scriptures, their interest has tended to be on the prophet's promises for God's mercy in the future. This focus is not surprising, since the Christian religion centers on Christ. The church proclaims that preeminently in the words of Christ we see the truth of our condition; that in the life, death, and resurrection of Christ we hear God's word for our salvation; and that through Christ will come finally the redemption of all. The emphasis for the church on the words of the prophet is not so much on covenant as on eschatology: God will bring about a future that is better than the present. In approaching the Hebrew Scriptures, Christians tend to be more interested in the prophets, and contemporary Jews in Torah.

The readings in the lectionary maintain the ancient idea that God speaks, which is of course metaphoric language, since the literal meaning of *speak* implies use of a mouth from which audible words come. However, even without a literal belief that deities talk, a common religious conviction is that the deity has a will that can be communicated to followers. In the Judeo-Christian tradition, that divine will is for justice and mercy—the Talmud says that God has 500 times more mercy than justice—and that through the prophets we can come to know God's will. The prophets speak God's word, that is, proclaim God's will, and that word is subsequently written down and read aloud by rabbis. The Christian tradition developed this idea further by incorporating the Greek philosophical idea of *logos*, the word. For Christians the ultimate way that God speaks is through the embodied Word who is Christ, the ultimate prophet.

Although Christians do not usually call Jesus a prophet—Islam does refer to Jesus as one of the three greatest prophets—Jesus likens himself to the great prophets Elijah and Elisha (Ep4c). Luke records that at the outset of his ministry, Jesus opened the scroll of Isaiah and suggested that he was himself the embodiment of the anointed prophet (Ep3c). Jesus suggested to the imprisoned John the Baptist that he was the one the prophets hoped for (Ad3A). The gospel writers make clear their conviction that Jesus is the one the prophets of old sought. On Christmas Eve the lectionary appoints Isaiah 9, with its promise for the ultimate Davidic king. Jesus was said to have interpreted "Moses and all the prophets" as referring to himself (Ea3A). Early Christian preachers, for example Philip, interpreted the prophet Isaiah as referring to Christ (Ea5B), and on Pentecost the church saw the fulfillment of the promise in Joel (PentABC).

The lectionary includes narratives of the most famous of the Israelite prophets: the seventy elders who received the spirit of Moses, and Eldad and

Medad who did not (PentA, Pr21B[†]), Samuel (Ep2B), Elijah (Pr8c[†]), Elisha (Ep6B, Pr9c°), Jeremiah (Ep4c), and Jonah (VigilABC). Although critical scholarship views the books of First Samuel, Jeremiah, and Jonah as belonging to quite different genres, first-century Jewish reading of these writings grouped them all together as similarly being mouthpieces of God, and New Testament writers would have felt free to borrow and adapt phrases and themes from all these prophets in their portrayal of Jesus.

The lectionary includes many speeches and poems attributed to these and other prophets. In one series within the Revised Common Lectionary, the prophets are read more or less chronologically over the summer and fall, while in the other series, and for both during the nonfestival half of the year, prophetic readings are set next to those gospel pericopes that they illumine. Isaiah and Jeremiah, judged the most pertinent prophets for Christian use, recur repeatedly over the three years. Some lectionary selections describe the task of the prophet, the marks of a true prophet, and the hope for future prophetic vision (for example, Pr7A[†], Pr8A[†], Pr17A[†], Pr15c[†]). For Christians, these passages illumine the person who is the very Word of God.

Another New Testament use of the prophet is its presentation of John the Baptist. Called by some Christians the last Old Testament prophet, John the Baptist typified one kind of Hebrew prophet: a loner and social critic who threatened divine punishment if the people did not reform their lives and turn back to God (Ad2c, Ad3c, Bapc). The expression "a voice in the wilderness" is apt. A slight misreading of Isaiah 40:3, the phrase recalled the Israelite wilderness wanderings, the people's desire for land and home, and the prophet's task to call out the way. As we would expect in a Christian narrative, John both figuratively and literally (Ad2A, Ad2B, Ad3B, BapB) points to Jesus as the one who will embody the eschatological age. The Revised Common Lectionary includes the gospel narrative of the death of John the Baptist (Pr10B). One way to interpret this grim reading is as a parallel to the death of Jesus.

According to the New Testament, the prophetic powers of the Spirit of God continue. Paul asserted that in the body of the church are prophets who are inspired by God (Ep3c). When Paul described his own work as an apostle and writer, he employed the imagery of the prophet (EpABC, Ad4A, Ad4B, EaB, Pr5c, Pr23c, Pr24c). Called and set apart by God, Paul reminded his readers of the prophets of old who similarly spoke out the grace of God. First to the prophets, so now to Paul, God revealed divine mysteries, mysteries Paul now proclaims. Several New Testament writers claimed also for future leaders in the church the continuing power of speaking the word of God (Pr14A, Pr24A). This message is strong in the Johannine epistles (Ea2B).

Protestants in particular have found the imagery of the prophet useful for their insistence that God continues to speak through the preaching in worship. Many current evangelists testify to a personal experience that recalls the call narratives of the Old Testament, and even the secular world accords the designation prophet to prominent religious social critics such as Martin Luther King Jr. and Desmond Tutu. The task of discernment is always on the faithful; even though the call of God to prophetic preaching may come to the individual, it must be validated by the community. So the churches have designed various methods of examination and rituals of authorization for those who are to preach the word of God. In some churches, the process entails years of study, a period of internship, and a historic ritual of certification. On the other hand, in the Amish communities, each year on a certain Sunday the men file into the service and pick up their hymnal, in one of which is a marked piece of paper: the man who picks up that hymnal is the preacher for the next year. The idea here is that God is choosing the preacher, since God knows who can best proclaim the word. Although some Christian assemblies are somewhat casual about who preaches the word, the churches need to recall that the preacher continues the revered role of the prophet by proclaiming the perhaps unpopular mercy and justice of God.

The biblical talk about hearing the word raises for contemporary interpreters the issue of the deaf. The lectionary includes pericopes in which Jesus heals those who were deaf. Perhaps these miracle stories stand in direct continuity with a history of prophetic writings: the goodness of God's mercy is exemplified metaphorically when the deaf come to hear. Just as with the biblical narratives of persons who were blind or lame, use of these stories calls for sensitivity. Usually the passages call for metaphoric interpretation, suggesting that all of God's people are more or less unwilling to be open to the word of God. Yet contemporary deaf communities include those who prefer their deafness to others' hearing. A related issue arises from the contemporary practice of printing out the readings in weekly service folders so that the assembly reads along with the proclamation, rather than hearing it. Parishes are better off training lectors who can proclaim the readings well, rather than resorting to readers so poor that the texts must be printed out. It is, finally, ill advised to assume that the many members of the Sunday assembly are literate.

We need to beware of oversimplifying the prophetic messages. The prophets pointed to specific examples of social injustice and proclaimed, sometimes metaphorically, the mercy of God. The applications of these examples and metaphors can be numerous. A passage in Matthew is helpful in this regard. Several times in the gospels Jesus is quoted as likening himself to Jonah. Recall that to first-century listeners, Jonah was viewed not as a memorable character in a short story, but as revered prophet of God. So how is Jesus like Jonah? Matthew 12:40 says that the similarity lies in the three days that both were entombed, and verse 41 says that the similarity lies in their preaching of God's judgment. Here is the twofold image of the prophet as one who proclaims both God's mercy and God's justice. And both are good news: that God seeks justice is good news for us all, and that finally we will all receive mercy is the best news of all.

Resurrection of the Body

empty tomb, Jonah, Lazarus,
resurrection of the body

Related chapters: CREATION, DAY OF THE LORD,
HEAVEN-EARTH-HELL

The language of the resurrection of the body originally referred to
the restoration of God's people Israel. Used by early Christians to
describe God's vindication of the executed Jesus, the imagery of
resurrection became wedded to Greek ideas of immortality and
developed into a primary image of the faith. In the New Testament
and the church are various understandings of what the imagery
means.

PSALM 16:9-11   My heart, therefore, is glad, and my spirit rejoices;
     my body also shall rest in hope.
For you will not abandon me to the grave,
     nor let your holy one see the pit.
You will show me the path of life;
     in your presence there is fullness of joy,
     and in your right hand are pleasures forevermore.

PROPER PREFACE,   It is indeed right and salutary that we should at all times
SUNDAYS AFTER   and in all places offer thanks and praise to you, O Lord,
PENTECOST   holy Father, through Christ our Lord; who on this day
overcame death and the grave, and by his glorious resurrection opened to us the way of everlasting life.

JOHN OF   Come, you faithful, raise the strain
DAMASCUS   of triumphant gladness!
God has brought his Israel
into joy from sadness,
loosed from Pharaoh's bitter yoke
Jacob's sons and daughters,
led them with unmoistened foot
through the Red Sea waters.

'Tis the spring of souls today:
Christ has burst his prison,
and from three days' sleep in death
as a sun has risen.

For today among the twelve
Christ appeared, bestowing
his deep peace, which evermore
passes human knowing.
Neither could the gates of death
nor the tomb's dark portal,
nor the watchers, nor the seal,
hold him as a mortal.

In the beginning, we see, it was not an ear rising from a grain, but a grain coming from an ear, and, after that, the ear grows round the grain: the order indicated in this similitude clearly shows that all the blessed state which arises for us by means of the resurrection is only a return to our pristine state of grace. We too were once in a fashion a full ear; but the burning heat of sin withered us up, and then on our dissolution by death the earth received us, but in the spring of the resurrection, the earth will reproduce this naked grain of our body in the form of an ear, tall, well-proportioned, and erect, reaching to the heights of heaven, and, for blade and beard, resplendent in incorruption, with all the other godlike marks.

TEACHINGS OF MACRINA, On the Soul and the Resurrection

If you would be wise, ask him who is wisdom. When it is too dark for you to see, seek Christ, for he is the light. Are you sick? Have recourse to him who is both doctor and health. Have no fear whatever of death, for Christ is the life of those who believe. Would you know by whom the world was made and all things are sustained? Believe in him, for he is the arm and right hand. Are you afraid of this or that? Remember that on all occasions he will stand by your side like an angel. If you are afraid that your body is failing and have a dread of death, remember that he is the resurrection, and can raise up what has fallen.

NICETA, The Names and Titles of Our Saviour

THE RESURRECTION OF THE BODY is one of the most central images that express the Christian faith. The birth, life, and death of Christ find their meaning in his resurrection; the celebration that most fully articulates baptismal faith is Easter; and the weekly meeting and meal of believers recurs on each Sunday, the day of the resurrection. Christians maintain a diversity of interpretation as to the meaning of resurrection of the body. This ambiguity begins already in the Bible. The earliest biblical use of resurrection imagery means something quite other than what Christians generally mean by it, and the New Testament writers record in quite different ways the experience of persons encountering the resurrected Christ.

Continuous repetition of a figure of speech tends to turn metaphor into definition. Because the church seldom calls God Rock, the language is recognized as metaphor, but because the church calls God Father regularly, some people imagine God to be literally a father in the sky. Probably because language of resurrection is so central to Christian faith, and because people want to escape the finality of death, the imagery has consistently been literalized. People wonder whether finding Jesus' bones would invalidate Christianity, and conferences address the question of what a video camera set up at the tomb on the first Easter Day would have recorded. Although some Christians take comfort in a wholly literal meaning of the language of Christ's and their own resurrection, other Christians judge the language to be supreme metaphor, a figure of speech that suggests an eschatological reality itself beyond words.

One of the primary goals of religion is the search for a response to death. By prayers and rituals of healing, religion attends to the approach of death in the individual. By appealing to the deity for rain and sun, religion hopes to fend off or delay the death that threatens the land itself. By acts of charity and the maintenance of justice, religion hopes to counter death within the society. By doctrines of life after death or of the reincarnation of the soul, religion suggests that the deity, not death, is the ultimate reality and that religion can conquer the death of the individual.

In the worldview of the ancient Hebrew people, humans are mortal, and death is the end of the life that comes from God. The story of the garden of Eden says that God expelled the man and the woman out into the world so that they would not be able to eat from the tree of life and live forever: to be human is to die; only the gods live forever. Humans are bodies into which God breathed life. At death, the breath returns to God, and the body returns to dust. There is silence in the grave. With no breath and no body, there is no human life.

During the exile, resulting both from increased influence of other religions and from the dread that God seemed not to be saving the people in this life, Jewish texts began to include metaphoric references to a second life beyond this one. God promised that sometime in the future the people of Israel would be raised up to productive life. The stunning imagery of Ezekiel's vision of the dry bones in Ezekiel 37 is the most well-known of these texts (VigilABC, Le5A). The whole house of Israel will rise again from the death of their captivity. Here death is itself an image, the dry bones a metaphor for the exiled nation-state. God says, "I will put my spirit within you," and as typical in the Bible, the *you* is plural. Life is in the community, so the second life will also be of the community. In Ezekiel, then, the imagery of the resurrection of the body is about the restoration of the nation-state. Some scholars see in Hosea a similar metaphor for the restoration of the people. Here the myth of Baal's death and resurrection was applied to the people of Israel as a whole.

During the following centuries, when Jewish hopes for a restored community were still not realized, the movement of apocalypticism grew. The biblical book of Daniel and many apocryphal and pseudepigraphal texts affirm that eventually, after this human time is over, a second time will begin. Only in that future time will martyrs be honored, the oppressed freed, the prophets vindicated, the whole house of Israel thrive once again. For some authors, the idea was that only the righteous would rise again to a restored life, while others imagined also punishment for the wicked. More and more the nation-state was spoken of in terms of its inhabitants. Life will come not only to Israel, but to its individuals, especially to those who, like the martyrs, were exemplary believers who suffered for their faith and whose death cried out for vindication.

Some exceptions to this general historical pattern of thought include healings so extraordinary that God actually returned the breath of life to a dead body. Elijah revived the widow's son (Pr5c) and Elisha the Shunammite woman's son (2 Kings 4). Jesus raised the daughter of Jairus (Pr5A), the son of the widow of Nain (Pr5c), and Lazarus (Le5A). Peter revived Tabitha (Ea4c), and Paul Eutychus (Acts 20:9-12). The Lazarus story is the most interesting, because John's gospel is more likely than the synoptics to use narratives symbolically. We note, for example, that both the Lazarus

337

story and the empty tomb narratives involve a weeping Mary, a time period of three days, a stone, and the burial bandages. In all these biblical examples of bodies restored to life, however, the second life of the individual was no different from the original life. Breath was restored to the body, but these people would die again. These stories are about resuscitations, something quite different from what Christianity came to mean by resurrection of the body.

Matthew records that at the earthquake on Good Friday "many bodies of the saints who had fallen asleep were raised," and that on Easter morning, these other persons along with Jesus "came out of the tombs and appeared to many" (Pas A). Philipp Melanchthon, in exegeting this text, wrote, "Among those saints raised were doubtless the first parents. Eve spoke lovingly with Mary. There were Rachel, Sarah, and the other holy mothers, and those fathers themselves: Adam, Seth, Noah, and others." It is not clear how literally Melanchthon meant these words or what he thought subsequently happened to these raised persons.

Other significant exceptions to the rule of death were Enoch, Moses, and Elijah. These three extraordinary believers are described as going to a life with God that continued after their death. Enoch became a primary figure in Jewish apocalyptic. In the New Testament's transfiguration stories, Moses and Elijah appeared, talking with Jesus (Matthew, Mark) and in glory (Luke). The synoptics describe Moses and Elijah as being glorified supernatural presences. Yet even the possibility of joining Moses and Elijah in an otherworldly continued existence with God after death is something different from resurrection of the body. Moses and Elijah went to God directly after their earthly life: resurrection of the body is something promised in the future. The much-loved citation from the speeches of Job, with its controverted translation (Pr27c), expresses only the faith that after death those who are faithful will see God. Perhaps what Job meant is that no matter what happens, even death, God would finally vindicate him.

These varied stories articulate the faith that God conquers death. The religious idea is that if humans do not fear death, they will be able to live in a more peaceful and generous manner than if they do. The ultimate reality is not my death, but God. So the people tell their stories of faith: the breath of life comes from God, and God cannot die; the people as a whole will be restored; if not now, then at the end of time the righteous will live again; some individuals who died have their life restored to them; and at least extraordinary individuals enjoy existence with God after their death. For Christians, the most central way to say that God conquers death is not with phrases such as breath of life, restoration of the people, resuscitation of the corpse, or, like Elijah, ascending in a whirlwind into heaven, but rather, resurrection of the body.

New Testament word studies provide detailed analyses of the New Testament descriptions of the resurrection of the body. Here is only a brief summary of the data. Paul wrote that Christ was raised according to the scriptures, by which he probably meant passages such as Psalms 16:9-11 and 118:13-24. Paul's discussions of the resurrection of Christ, especially in Romans 6 and 1 Corinthians 15 (VigilABC, Pr7A, EaB, Ep5C, Ep6C), use the verb *appear* and equate Christ's appearances after Easter Day with that to Paul years later. Christ's resurrection is only the firstfruits of God's vindication of the just. In Paul's most sustained discussion of a final resurrection of the body, he introduces the oxymoron spiritual bodies (NRSV, translating *soma*) as distinct from physical bodies (*sarx*). The new body will be as different from the old body as heaven is different from dust. Human bodies are described in the Bible as made from dust; the resurrected body will therefore be in every way different, having put on immortality. Here Paul incorporates Greek philosophical imagery into his Jewish religious background.

During the decades in which the gospels were written, the narratives concerning Easter Day grew from a story of the empty tomb into detailed memories of encounters with the raised body of Jesus. In Mark, nobody sees Jesus; in Matthew his disciples see him; in Luke, Jesus eats with his followers; in John, Thomas touches Jesus' wounded side. The further from the event, the more precisely literal are the narrative details. That twice Christians added a conclusion to the stark ending of the book of Mark indicates a subsequent desire to provide more comforting and persuasive narrative details to the mystery of the fate of Christ. Many scholars consider the book of Hebrews an early Christian essay. Its author speaks of Christ's ascension to God being like incense: Christ arose to God in the sacrificial act of his death. No language of resurrection of the body or empty tomb appears in the book of Hebrews.

Because resurrection of the body is language of image, rather than of fact, Christians interpret it with a wide range of meaning. At least, the language gives the church a picture of the power of God over death. The relationship between God and God's people is finally indestructible. To biblical Jews, human life without the body was unimaginable. Thus for God to give us new life, new bodies were required. Medieval belief in a literal resurrection of the body was seen in the church's prohibition of cremation, the idea being that by cremation a person was hoping to avoid the promised resurrection. Contemporary physics keeps us from any such naive thinking. The many ways that God gives life out of death are all, more than less, miraculous.

339

A literal interpretation of this language was encouraged by religious art. The church's early iconographical tradition popularized the imagery of Christ raising Eve and Adam from hades to heaven, their bodies intact. Many medieval churches, from small country churches to the Sistine Chapel, adorned their interiors with graphic depictions of the last judgment, always pictured as the resurrection of the body; that is, to draw humans after death, the artist drew wholly recognizable human bodies. It is difficult to draw this language without rendering it naively literally.

The church uses the language of resurrection not only in relation to a last judgment. Especially Romans 6 and Colossians 2 speak of baptism as burial with Christ and describe coming up out of the waters of baptism as being raised with Christ. So it is that some churches constructed baptismal pools to resemble tombs, and the rite of Christian baptism and many baptismal hymns incorporate the imagery of baptism as resurrection. In its baptismal use, being raised from the dead is a metaphor to indicate the ultimate significance of baptism and the total transformation that it effects in the lives of believers. One answer to the question of what the resurrection is: we have already been raised, in our baptism.

A similar metaphoric use of the imagery of resurrection of the body is found in explication of the eucharist and the church. The Easter narratives of the empty tomb say, "He is not here. He is risen." If the body of Christ is no longer in the tomb, where is it? The church gives several answers. Luke suggests it was on earth for forty days, a standard biblical number to designate a long period of religious time, after which the body rose once again, this time into heaven. Thus Luke portrays Christ's resurrection as a two-step process: in the first, Jesus is returned to earth, in the second to God. Another answer to this question of the location of Jesus' body is suggested in the narratives of the last supper: believers recognize that the bread they share is the body of Christ. No longer dead and rotting in a tomb, the body of Christ is now omnipresent at the assemblies of Christians, giving life. Thus an answer to the inquiry about Christ's resurrected body is that it is the bread of the weekly meal.

A third answer to this question is suggested by Pauline ecclesiology: the assembly itself is the body of Christ. The Spirit of God, that is, the divine breath of life, is now in the church, and all that Christ did for the world is now the task of the church. Christ is not in the tomb: Christ is, rather, in the assembly, which is eating the bread and sharing the life of God with all the world. To search for the body of Christ, Christians do not excavate first-century tombs: they go to church on Sunday. Thus the church's sacramental language applies the ultimate imagery of resurrection of the body not to some single unique event at the end of time, but rather to the meaning of baptism, to the weekly eucharist, and to the reality of the assembly of the faithful. The promise that in the future God will give a second life to the faithful people is realized each time that the baptized community shares its meal. By sharing the body of Christ, the community becomes more fully the body of Christ.

It is because of the resurrection that Christians meet on Sunday. Although some Christian cultures have kept Sunday as a sabbath, and although many contemporary people would do well to introduce a measure of sabbath into their frenetic lives, it is not a weekly day of rest upon which Christian assembly is based. Rather, it is the meal, the assembly a week later, as John's gospel tells us, at which we recognize Christ alive in our midst. This Sunday meeting constitutes the Christian ritual. As the proper preface for Sunday suggests, on this day Christ rose from the dead. Not twenty centuries ago, but today Christ arose, and in this assembly at its meal we experience the power and presence of that body of Christ. As with the Jews of the first century, there is no contemporary Christian consensus as to whether at the end of time a literal resurrection of the dead will take place (Pr27c). But the community of Christians does agree that our Sunday together, reading the scriptures and sharing bread at the table, shows to us, as it did to the disciples at Emmaus (Ea3A), the risen Christ.

Attention to the readings appointed for the Easter Vigil broadens our interpretation of the resurrection. Paul wrote in 1 Corinthians that Christ was raised according to the scriptures. The scriptures Paul refers to, of course, are the Hebrew Scriptures, and it is to immerse ourselves into these Old Testament stories that the Vigil appoints four, or seven, or nine, or twelve readings. The selection of the readings means not to provide a summary of Old Testament history, but rather to present significant examples of how God raises people from death. The two central readings, creation (Genesis 1:1—2:4a) and the exodus (Exodus 14:10-31, 15:20-21), are both resurrection stories. As with baptism, both stories depict God bringing new life out of the chaos and destruction of the waters. We join with Miriam to sing the song of victory (15:20-21), just as on Easter Day we join with Mary (Greek for "Miriam") to encounter the risen Christ.

Likewise, the flood story describes God as bringing a new creation out of the destruction of the old one. The story of the sacrifice of Isaac is more graphic, and to some people more troubling, than the other narratives, perhaps because the terror of death is more personalized than in the flood or the exodus stories. One single, likeable boy, rather than nearly all the human and animal populations, or the enemy army, is slated for death. As a metaphor for Israel itself, Isaac is saved from death and given a new life from God.

The other vigil readings continue the pattern of presenting ways to proclaim the resurrection. The resurrection is like a feast shared and a seed sprouting (Isaiah 55), Lady Wisdom inviting us to share a meal of bread and wine (Proverbs 8 and 9), the gift of a new heart and spirit (Ezekiel 36), the valley of bones raised to new life together (Ezekiel 37), the victory and marriage celebration in the renewed city (Zephaniah 3), the saving of Jonah (Jonah 3), the land flowing with milk and honey (Deuteronomy 31), and survival within the fiery furnace (Daniel 3). All these readings follow an interpretive model laid out by Jesus in speaking about Jonah (Matthew 12:40). The language of the Hebrew Scriptures (for example, Jonah saved from hades in the belly of the fish and restored to a second life after three days) functions for Christians as a picture of what God promises to Christ and to all believers in the resurrection.

It is hoped that the restoration of the Easter Vigil throughout the church will deepen and broaden the oftentimes literal interpretation of the resurrection of the body. The narratives of the empty tomb will be heard as primary among many accounts of God's saving power. Furthermore, believers who worship at both the Vigil and on Easter Day encounter two different accounts of the empty tomb each year, the synoptics at the vigil and John in the morning, and so we are faced with the fact that even the stories of Easter Day are mysterious and diverse.

At funerals, the language of resurrection of the body is often replaced with language of immortality, if not in the rite, then in preaching and conversation. Immortality is a commonplace human idea that at the time of death is decidedly comforting. Socrates is said to have welcomed death, which would free his immortal soul from his troublesome body. But this idea is not a Christian one. Both Judaism and Christianity see the body as God's good creation, and for Christians the language of the resurrection of the body praises the God who gives life to the matter of the earth. Although a literal re-creation of human-like individual bodies may await us at the end of time, the Christian faith is not focused on such a personalized future expectation. According to eschatological thought, the future is already appearing in the present. We are already now to experience in baptism, in eucharist, and in shared life and mission some of what the faith means by the resurrection of the body.

Sacrifice

altar, blood, high priest,
lamb, Lamb of God, offering,
passover, priest, sacrifice

Related chapters: SERVANT, TEMPLE

The Bible both commands and criticizes sacrifice. The church uses the image of sacrifice metaphorically to describe both Jesus' execution and the church's worship. Throughout the history of the church, the use of the language of sacrifice has often generated controversy.

PSALM 51:17-20

Had you desired it, I would have offered sacrifice,
  but you take no delight in burnt-offerings.
The sacrifice of God is a troubled spirit;
  a broken and contrite heart, O God,
  you will not despise.
Be favorable and gracious to Zion,
  and rebuild the walls of Jerusalem.
Then you will be pleased with the appointed sacrifices,
with burnt-offerings and oblations;
  then shall they offer young bullocks upon your altar.

PRAYER AFTER
COMMUNION

Almighty God, you gave your Son both as a sacrifice for sin
and a model of the godly life. Enable us to receive him
always with thanksgiving, and to conform our lives to his;
through the same Jesus Christ our Lord.

CHARLES
WESLEY

Victim Divine, your grace we claim,
as here your precious death we show;
once offered up, a spotless lamb,
in your great temple here below,
you did for humankind atone;
and now you stand before the throne.

You stand within the holiest place,
as once for guilty sinners slain;
your blood for sinners intercedes,
redemption for the world to gain.
Your blood shall still our ransom be,
the payment made to set us free.

Sacrifices do not sanctify a person, for God stands in no need of sacrifice; but it is the conscience of the offerer that sanctifies when it is pure, and thus moves God to accept the offering as from a friend. Inasmuch, then, as the church offers with single-mindedness, its gift is justly reckoned a pure sacrifice with God. For it behooves us to make an oblation to God, and in all things to be found grateful to God our maker, in a pure mind, and in faith without hypocrisy, offering the firstfruits of his own created things. The church offers this pure oblation to the Creator, offering to him, with giving of thanks, the things taken from his creation.

IRENAEUS, "A Sincere Sacrifice"

In speaking with persons interested in helping the poor who suffer most, and who asked me what I supposed would tend to hasten a really better and wide-spreading state of comfort for them, I have sometimes burst out that I thought it needed the life-blood of persons working for this end. By "life-blood" we mean the life we live in days and energy given, actually, with heartfelt willingness, to this object of our existence—the being compassionate. It is "life-blood" because it is the most terrible and complete sacrifice, if thoroughly made, that we can choose, and the instinct to staunch our life-blood often strives to assert itself. Nothing less than this sacrifice will save the poor from continued degradation.

ROSE HAWTHORNE LATHROP, "Sacrifices for the Poor"

No image in the Christian tradition is more convoluted than sacrifice. The ambiguity begins in the Bible. Comprehensive biblical encyclopedias explain that no consensus among biblical scholars indicates what sacrifices were offered to God when, where, how, and to what end, throughout the centuries of biblical history. Narrative descriptions of sacrifices do not accord with prescriptions concerning sacrifices as encoded in the law. The layering and interweaving of biblical traditions make it impossible to construct a grid that would trace the development of Israelite sacrifices from the springtime rites of the nomadic tribes to the meticulous rituals of the second temple. To add to the complexity, numerous theories in the study of religion offer mutually contradictory proposals as to what practitioners actually thought they were doing in their sacrificial offerings. This biblical complexity need not paralyze users of the three-year lectionary, because specificity about ancient sacrifices is not judged important for Christian proclamation.

Yet the language of sacrifice is found through the New Testament and in both preaching and polemic throughout the centuries of the church. Because Christians did not maintain the practice of slaughtering an animal in ritual before God, the word *sacrifice* in Christian usage is always metaphoric. Admittedly, those Christians using the metaphor of sacrifice were not always conscious of the poetic nature of their speech. The history of the word *sacrifice* exemplifies the fact that when an image is used repeatedly, it comes to be accepted as literal fact, rather than received as multivalent metaphor. The challenge in interpreting sacrifice imagery today is complex. Any metaphoric image calls for multivalent interpretation; the Christian language of sacrifice recalls biblical usage that itself is multivalent; and many contemporary people find the imagery of sacrifice alien, if not repulsive.

To examine the lectionary's use of sacrifice imagery, we begin with the Triduum. The primitive church struggled to make sense of Jesus' death, and the Old Testament complex of sacrifice references was found to be most useful. On Maundy Thursday the lectionary appoints the directions for the passover sacrifice; on Good Friday the lectionary appoints both the prophetic poem from Isaiah 53 and a passage from the book of Hebrews, the

New Testament book that most develops sacrifice imagery; and the Easter
Vigil includes the narrative of the sacrifice of Isaac. Each of these readings
presents a somewhat different nuance to the language of sacrifice in reference to Christ.

On Maundy Thursday is the reading from Exodus in which God established the passover sacrifice (MThABC, Pr18A°). Scholars assume that a
springtime ritual in which nomads killed a lamb in order to insure the life of
the flock far antedated the passover. Perhaps for the nomads the lamb's blood
was a gift of life to the deities, in exchange for which the flock and the community would enjoy a fertile year. Exodus 12 recontextualized and reinterpreted the characteristic nomadic ritual. Rather than herders performing
sympathetic magic to ensure fertility, God ordered the sacrifice. The lamb's
blood smeared on the door protected the family from a plague of death that
God sent to punish the oppressor. The processes of nature and the cycle of
the year were overlaid by a story involving the deity, the tribe, and their history of oppression. This pattern is characteristic of the historical focus in
Judaism.

In placing this reading at the outset of the Three Days, Christians add
another layer. Since the first century the church has used the imagery of a
lamb's blood effecting safety as a primary way to see how Jesus' blood, so
unjustly shed, might be understood. We are saved, not like the nomads from
hungry wolves, nor like the Hebrew slaves from the angel of death, but from
sin, despair, and eternal death. The sacrifice of the passover lamb presented
the church with an image that helped make sense of the execution of Jesus.
Like the ancient lamb chosen from the flock, Christ was slain to ensure the
people's safety, and like the passover lamb eaten in a communal feast, Christ
provided the food for a joyous ritual meal.

The church moves to Good Friday and the complex poem from Isaiah 53
(also Pr24B[†]). The Servant Songs of Second Isaiah express the hope that
some servant of God will suffer in the stead of the whole exiled people. The
suffering of the one will release the people from their suffering. Woven into
the poem of Isaiah 52:13—53:12 are several references to sacrifice. The servant will go silently like a lamb to the slaughter, and vulnerable like sheep
before herders. The poem then refers to the suffering of the servant as an
offering for sin, thus recalling one kind of Israelite sacrifice in which, after an
animal was slaughtered, the priest sprinkled the blood of the dead animal on
the veil of the temple. The Isaiah passage suggests that the death of the
meek lamb is the vehicle by which God sees the sorrow and suffering of the
faithful. The picture of sorrow is quite different from the evocation of the
passover, at which nothing is made of the suffering of the lamb. The seder is

a meal of joy and expectation. Yet Christian tradition blended Exodus with Isaiah, the meanings intermingling with one another.

Sacrifice as a fundamental way to interpret the execution of Jesus is seen throughout the book of Hebrews, from which the second reading for Good Friday is taken. Hebrews does not contain a coherent description or understanding of Israelite sacrifice. The author joins the image of the tabernacle with that of the temple and focuses on the ritual of the Day of Atonement. Called Yom Kippur by contemporary Jews, this day is the most solemn of the Jewish calendar. On Yom Kippur the people stand before the reality of death and the guilt occasioned by sin. By fasting from food, sex, and bodily washing, and by a day of prayer, Jews practice dying and appeal to God for continued life. The Good Friday reading from Hebrews 10 (also Ad4c) or Hebrews 4 (also Pr23b) likens Christ to the high priest, who in biblical times offered the most important yearly sacrifice on this day.

According to the author of Hebrews, Christ was high priest anointed by God (Pr24b), yet still was one with his brothers and sisters (Ch1a); Christ as high priest was himself sinless (Pr25b); and he offered on the altar the blood not of animals but of himself (Pr26b). Thus the sacrifice of Christ need not be an annual event, but became the single archetypal propitiatory sacrifice for all time. Here what is sacrificed is not a lamb for a feast, nor an animal for its blood, but rather Jesus himself as both the high priest dressed in elaborate robes and the victim slaughtered on the cross. With this metaphoric language, early believers sought a justification for the tragic end of their hopes in Jesus as messiah. Increasingly, the way to refer to Jesus' execution was as an atoning sacrifice. By calling Christ both the victim and the high priest, the inappropriateness of the victim language was acknowledged.

The Triduum also gives us the reading of what has long been ironically called the sacrifice of Isaac (also Pr8a°). Although Isaac escaped sacrifice, the Jewish tradition gave so much attention to the obedience of Abraham that midrash spoke as if Isaac had been sacrificed and raised to life. The Christian tradition often juxtaposed Isaac and Jesus. Many medieval churches depicted parallel pictures of Isaac carrying wood, often in the shape of a cross, and Jesus carrying his cross. The church used the story to suggest that just as God provided a ram so as to save Isaac from death, so God provided Jesus to save believers from death. Christ is not lamb, but ram.

As a reading at the Vigil, the Isaac story stresses not the death of Christ but the resurrection, the transformation from death to life. What we thought would lead to death—human sacrifice—instead bears life. So at the Vigil, the sacrifice of the ram is a metaphor for our escape from the fear of death, our return back to our home alive and well. The gruesome aspect of this ancient story has bothered many Christians, both sophisticated theologians—we think of Soren Kierkegaard's meditations in *Fear and Trembling*—and faithful worshipers. Yet also other narratives appointed for the Easter Vigil present divine demands in ways unpopular today. In the flood story, God destroys nearly all human and animal life on earth, and at the Red Sea God brings about the death of the Egyptian army. These biblical stories are not pleasant fairytales, but the church found them useful images of the death and life we encounter in Christ. Feminist theologians suggest that the sacrifice of Isaac is metaphorically powerful because it is all too true: countless Christian women have been expected to sacrifice their selves for the men in their lives and have believed that God desired their sacrifice.

If the church speaks as if Jesus' death was literally a sacrifice, as if God killed Jesus just as the ancient nomads killed a lamb, the imagery remains alien, archaic, an icon understandable only to some of those catechized into it. If the church speaks as if its own meager worship is a sacrifice, it evaluates the ritual far more seriously than the prophets or Jesus suggest we do.

In a society in which self-fulfillment and personal happiness are among the highest goals, however, the language of sacrifice offers the baptized assembly a countercultural set of values. Sacrifice imagery suggests that Christians might have to give their own blood so that the oppressed can go free. In spite of death, the community can rejoice at its communal meals; even God was willing to give up divine life so that mortals could live. Together in community we are able to admit our guilt and to face our death, because we acknowledge that individual status and individual existence are not the most important things in the world. Sacrifice is not the end, but the beginning. What the world assumes will destroy life is, surprisingly, the way new life is born. Julian of Norwich likened Christ's shed blood to the blood poured out of a mother's womb in childbirth. There is no birth without blood, no life without death, no shared spirit without sacrifice.

The lectionary includes the story in Luke 2 of what the author calls "their purification" (Ch1B). This fascinating narrative conflates two Hebrew rituals: the mother's purification from the blood of childbirth and the firstborn son's redemption from God. The first, the mother's purification, indicates ancient notions of the awesome power and social taboo of menstrual blood. That in the blood was the life of the person, and yet that women could pour out this blood with no ill effects, meant that many ancient societies established elaborate rituals surrounding menstruation and childbirth. Contemporary anthropologists describe how during the exile Jews heightened the redemptive power of the male blood shed in circumcision and intensified the taboo against the female blood of menses. It is as if male blood is good, and

349

female blood bad. Perhaps this ancient prejudice is still alive in contemporary resistance to female imagery connected with Christ. Because classical theologians taught that Christ assumed, not manhood, but human nature, the church might explore ways that also women's blood could serve as a metaphor for divine life.

The second ritual that Jesus' family undergoes, as conflated in Luke 2, is the redemption of the firstborn. It appears that the sacrifice of the firstborn son was a commonplace ritual in ancient Canaan. Cemetery excavations unearth many infant skeletons in jars. Jewish tradition substituted a redemption ritual, in which the child was presented to God, but an alternative sacrifice was offered to replace the human child. The rejection of infant sacrifice may stand behind the narrative of the sacrifice of Isaac, and this idea of redemption became a useful image for Christian explanation of how Jesus became humankind's substitute. The twelfth-century substitutionary theory of atonement developed by the theologian Anselm used this imagery to propose that God's justice required punishment for sin, and that Jesus substituted for us, taking our suffering onto himself. This theory survives in classic hymnody, although many mainstream Christian churches find it unhelpful in proclamation.

Some lectionary readings speak of the sacrifice of Christ in ways that combine the various meanings of the passover lamb, the atoning sacrifice, and the high priest. The Eastertide reading from 1 Peter (Ea3a) refers to the precious blood of Christ the lamb, which has ransomed our life; 1 John 4 (Ea5b) uses the language of the atoning sacrifice; and Revelation 5 (Ea3c) praises Christ as the Lamb that was slaughtered. The author of Ephesians can refer to Christ as a fragrant offering and sacrifice to God (Pr14b). The word *fragrant* evokes perhaps the most ancient idea of sacrifice: that the deity liked the smell of the meat cooking and consequently thought kindly of the one presenting the sacrifice. Later biblical writers suggested that it was the smell of incense burning, rather than of meat cooking, that God appreciated. One sees here an early move away from literal toward symbolic meaning.

Some lectionary readings repeat the strong prophetic criticism of sacrifice. The prophet Micah (Ep4a) preaches that God wants justice, not burnt offerings. In Isaiah 42 (Ep7b) God criticizes the sacrificial offerings of Jacob and Israel, and Isaiah 1 (Pr26c†) quotes God as being sick of the very sacrifices that God was said to have inaugurated. In the reading from 1 Corinthians (Ep4b), Paul considers whether Christians can eat food that was offered as sacrifice to idols. He decides that since those deities do not even exist, the sacrifices mean nothing. So, Paul says, help yourself to the food, unless other

Christians are offended by the action. Here ritual sacrifice is not as important as is pastoral concern for the members of the community. Thus while some biblical writers understand ritual sacrifice as of little significance, others find it the best language with which to understand the death of Christ.

Christian tradition further complicated the imagery of sacrifice. Like the reading from Hebrews 3 (Pr17c), early Christians talked about the church's praise as its sacrifice. Later the presentation (that is, the offering) of bread and wine was described as the church's sacrifice. The medieval church overused sacrifice language: the clergy were priests, serving as intermediaries between the human and the divine, who offered the body and blood in atonement for the sins of the people. This literalizing of sacrifice language intensified clerical privilege in medieval society, and it led to the rejection of sacrifice language by some Reformers. Contemporary Christians, both Roman Catholic and Protestant, are currently reviving the early understanding of sacrifice as metaphor, able to be used if not literalized.

The feast of the Presentation, February 2, presents clearly the metaphoric nature of sacrifice language. The Presentation is the fortieth day of Christmas, the close of the Christmas season. The passage from Malachi anticipates a coming one who like the Levites of old will present offerings to God, and the Hebrews reading calls Jesus a merciful and faithful high priest. Yet the gospel presents us with a forty-day-old infant boy, being bought back from sacrifice by an offering of two young pigeons. Both the ancient ritual of a worthy sacrifice and the perennial human desire for a priest meet their fruition in the infant Jesus. In this high metaphor, the sacrifice is not a sacrifice, the high priest is not a high priest.

Martin Luther argued that even as metaphor, sacrifice language is dangerous, because God's grace erases the religious need for any kind of literal or figurative presentation to the deity. Yet the language of sacrifice continues to be evoked in church life today. Many Christians apply sacrifice terminology to the stuff of worship. We call the table an altar, although no animal is slaughtered on it, and the wine is called blood. The collection for the poor is called an offering. Many churches inspire their members to more sacrificial giving by stressing that the offering goes to God, and some presiders employ a ritual gesture reminiscent of the Hebrew heave-offering, lifting up high the collection plates, as if God were up in the sky receiving the offering. Some Christian denominations call their clergy priests. All this metaphoric terminology suggests that the church joins with the millions of religious folk of all ages offering bloody sacrifices to the deity, as if we are ancient Mayans, cutting out a beating heart and offering it to the sun, in hopes that the sun will drink the victim's blood and rise again tomorrow. Yet we do nothing of the kind. Christians borrow the language of sacrifice to describe the sharing of bread and wine in the assembly.

Theologians face the difficult task of addressing the language of atonement. What kind of God wants sacrifice, whether of infant boys, yearling lambs, or an innocent man whom the church has named "his Son"? Does our God demand or appreciate sacrifice? Is *sacrifice* the best word to articulate the meaning of the death of Christ? Originally the language of sacrifice helped the church make sense of Jesus' execution by suggesting that he willingly participated in his death, as would befit the model sacrifice. Some theologians find more useful the idea that Christ's sacrifice was not so much in his death as in his life. He lived for others, and although that life brought about death, the living sacrifice brought life to the world. Simply repeating traditional language about Christ sacrificing himself for our sins will not be sufficient for proclamation in a post-Christian society.

Traditionally Christians have been called to a life of sacrifice. The nineteenth-century deist Elizabeth Cady Stanton shocked Christians by urging that Jephthah's daughter ought not be praised for her obedient self-sacrifice, a proposal made in nineteenth-century sermons. Rather, Cady Stanton wrote, women already sacrificed too much, and should instead strive for self-fulfillment. Liberation theologians of the twentieth century also suggested that Christians who enjoyed status and authority found it easy to urge self-sacrifice on the lower classes and on women. Christian therapists suggest that in some situations self-sacrifice is a behavioral pattern that only enables the neuroses of others. The church needs to find ways that its classic language of self-sacrifice can address these contemporary understandings of the meaning of the self before God.

One avenue for interpretation builds on communal interpretation. Perhaps the Servant Songs meant to identify the suffering one as the whole people of Israel. In Christian parlance, the sacrificed Christ is now embodied in the baptized community. In the power of the Spirit, it is the community, rather than the individual, that stands ready to be sacrificed for the good of the world. Such interpretation avoids the danger that the call to sacrifice gets directed to others.

For here is good news: We are freed from relentlessly pursuing our society's myth of happiness in the self. We can give up cultural goals in order to offer ourselves to other values. Enabled by the Spirit of Christ, the members of the community can let go of self, which will naturally diminish and die, and instead hold on to God's gifts to us and to the ongoing life of the earth. The task is to find the ways that the biblical imagery of sacrifice can be useful in proclaiming and appropriating this good news.

Servant

footwashing, Good Samaritan,
servant, slave, Suffering Servant

Related chapters: KINGDOM, OUTSIDER, THE POOR

Biblical culture was a slave society, and the biblical image of servant or slave usually assumes a positive meaning of interdependence. Our different worldview makes difficult our appropriation of
the lectionary's use of these images, for example, that baptism
makes us servants and slaves of one another.

PSALM 116:14   O LORD, I am your servant;
        I am your servant and the child of your handmaid;
        you have freed me from my bonds.

INSTALLATION   Our Lord, who came among us as a servant, calls us to faith
OF A LAY   and a life of loving service to our neighbor. You stand
PROFESSIONAL   among us as one called to render a particular service, a gift
LEADER   from God to inspire us to love and good works.

TOM COLVIN   Jesu, Jesu,
        fill us with your love,
        show us how to serve
        the neighbors we have from you.

        Kneels at the feet of his friends,
        silently washes their feet,
        master who pours out himself for them.

        Neighbors are wealthy and poor,
        varied in color and race,
        neighbors are nearby and far away.

        These are the ones we will serve,
        these are the ones we will love;
        all these are neighbors to us and you.

A Christian is a perfectly free lord of all, subject to none.
A Christian is a perfectly dutiful servant of all, subject to all.

MARTIN LUTHER,
*The Freedom
of a Christian*

This seemingly impossible role of service is possible for us all because it is not just a command. It is a gift of God. Service is God's gift because it is God who serves us. Think of it. God is the one who chooses to serve, not just to be worshiped or adored. The humanity of God is seen in that God chooses to be related to human beings through service. In Jesus Christ we have the representation of a new humanity—the beginning of a new type of human being whose life is lived for others. Here we see what it means to be truly and newly human. This is the image of God—freedom to serve others. The whole story of the New Testament revolves around this one theme: *diakonia*, service.

LETTY RUSSELL,
"The Impossible
  Possibility"

THROUGHOUT THE ENTIRE time frame of the Bible, the Mediterranean world practiced a slave economy. Society was structured in a relatively rigid hierarchy. Persons were born into, and usually remained within, one economic level of society. Captives or criminals could find themselves demoted into slavery, or free workers could fall into it because of debt. The laws of the various governments treated the service class as more or less human, and so details of the slave systems in Israel, Babylon, Assyria, Greece, and Rome differ one from another. At least in Greco-Roman society, what was called the household was not a contemporary nuclear family, but an extended hierarchical economic unit, with the *pater familias* ruling as the head of both familial relatives and all the persons serving them. The master owned the slaves, just as he legally owned his wife and children. Even in the commandments, what belongs to your (male) neighbor included his wife, male or female slave, ox, and donkey. The social expectation was twofold: the master had moral and legal obligation to care for the slaves, and the slaves were required to serve the master.

When encountering biblical slave language, we ought not assume cruel excesses, as for example the American antebellum enslaving of African Americans on plantations. Although some of us may imagine brutal scenes of Israelite slavery in Egypt, biblical scholars doubt that any such system ever marked the history of those tribes that later united as Israelites. Although biblical slaves could be bought and sold, the economic success of the society depended on a ready work force, which violent treatment would undercut. The commandments in the Pentateuch forbid also slaves from working on the sabbath.

Naturally, the Israelites preferred freedom to slavery for themselves. Yet the Hebrew tribes perpetuated a slave culture. The Hebrew Scriptures repeatedly demand compassion for the slave, urging Israel to recall the time that it had been enslaved. Deuteronomy 5:14-15 interprets the sabbath not as a reenactment of God's day of rest at creation, but rather as a day of freedom reminding Israelites of their own bondage. In the New Testament, Paul was able to send Philemon back to his master, because Paul viewed the master-slave society as the standard economic pattern, rather than as immoral oppression. The slavery in the biblical world in many ways resembled the

European medieval feudal system; some persons were perpetually tied to their employers, legally held there, without many of the rights of the free citizenry. Yet this system lasted for centuries as a stable and workable economic institution. The philosophical revolution we call the Enlightenment called for the end of any social system that granted one person ownership of another.

Biblical translators disagree whether the Hebrew *'ebed* and the Greek *doulos* are better rendered by our words *slave* or *servant*. The connotations of neither noun perfectly match the biblical situation. When Paul calls himself a *doulos* of Christ (Romans 1:1), some current translations say servant, and others slave. The American practice that most residents can become citizens and the American myth that all citizens are free and equal indicate a worldview in which language of servanthood is heard nearly as negatively as language of slavery. A behavioral pattern in which family members wholly ignored the presence of servants in the room, as if they were not humans with feelings, is long gone. In many restaurants now, waiters introduce themselves, as if they are friends. A current Roman Catholic Bible translation, the New American Bible, uses neither *slave* nor *servant* in its rendering of the Song of Mary (Luke 1:48), but *handmaid*.

That the biblical economic system is not accurately represented by either our vocabulary or our emotional response is only the half of it. The psychological movement has trained us to think of the self as the center of consciousness and will. The current safety demonstrations given to air travelers, to secure one's own oxygen first before helping others, is symbolic of the contemporary Western worldview that a healthy and whole individual attends first and foremost to the self. Dependence on others is supposed to be replaced by the free agency of each individual, and adulthood is often equated with personal independence. The Amish acronym *JOY*—"Jesus first, Others second, Yourself last"—seems to many Americans nearly as alien as does biblical slavery. Yet the biblical language of *'ebed* and *doulos* is explicitly language of dependence: the master depends on the slave-servant, and the slave-servant depends on the master.

A striking example of the biblical worldview is found in the New Testament's household codes. Placed at the conclusion of epistles that convey a more uniquely Christian ethic, the household codes (Ephesians 5:21—6:9, Colossians 3:18—4:1) repeat the typical ethical system of the Greco-Roman world: everyone is to obey the persons higher up than they, and everyone is to treat with some respect those who are lower. The passages urging masters to treat their slaves well were cited by Christians in antebellum America to defend the institution of slavery. Early twentieth-century lectionaries omitted the master-slave portion but retained the husband-wife hierarchy. The Revised Common Lectionary omits the household codes as being more indicative of first-century slave society than instructive for ours.

Only when we understand this biblical worldview can we appropriate the epistles' metaphoric use of the servant-slave image. It seems that Paul would find popular talk of individual autonomy naive and contemporary individualism beyond his experience. In Romans, Paul writes as if persons must be enslaved to something (Pr8a). We were enslaved to sin, and thus to death, but now are enslaved to obedience, and thus to life. Paul does not consider the image of enslavement to God negative: thus our difficulty in appropriating this language. In 1 Corinthians, Paul speaks again of Christian willingness to become slaves (Ep5b). He describes ministers as your slaves for Jesus' sake (Pr4b). In the paradoxical passage in Galatians, our freedom in Christ frees us from the yoke of slavery so that we can become slaves to one another (Pr8c). The eloquent passage from Philippians (Pasabc, Pr21a) includes what was likely a first-century hymn or creed and describes Christ as having relinquished the prerogatives of divinity to become an obedient slave. In response, every knee should bend. Christ became like a slave, and we are also to become like slaves. The image occurs in Jesus' apocalyptic sayings, in which the coming Son-of-man who is the lord and master will surprise the inattentive slaves (Ad1b).

In calling Christ a servant, the church is appropriating a metaphor found in the Hebrew Scriptures. The poems in Second Isaiah that scholars call the Servant Songs describe the one, either a faithful individual or the faithful people as a whole, who remains dedicated to the will of God despite continuous suffering. Christian tradition saw in Jesus Christ the epitome of such a suffering servant, and the lectionary appoints sections of the Servant Songs several times (Bapa, Ep2a), most notably as the long first reading each year on Good Friday.

The Good Friday readings bear the difficult task of proposing an explanation for the death of Christ: How does the unjust execution of a man long ago carry ultimately significance for the community assembled here today? The gospel, read from John rather than from the synoptics, proclaims a conquering Christ, the I AM, the one who in dying gave up his spirit. The second reading presents temple imagery from the book of Hebrews as one way to understand Christ's death, and the first reading, the servant song from Isaiah 53, presents him as the preeminent servant of God, fulfilling the divine will even in his suffering. Poetic phrases such as "shall be lifted up, shall be very high" are paradoxical on Good Friday, on which the lifting up is both crucifixion and exaltation.

The readings for Holy Week present yet more servant imagery. On Passion Sunday the Philippians reading praises Christ, "taking the form of a slave." On Maundy Thursday, usually thought of as the day to recall Jesus' last meal with his disciples, the lectionary presents us the complementary narrative of the footwashing. If the last supper makes us think about Christ as the host of a meal, presiding and overseeing, John's narrative of that Thursday evening presents us with the opposite image: Christ as the slave of the household, on his knees doing the dirty work. John's gospel enacts Paul's discussion of slavery to Christ, as Christ instructs his disciples to love one another by being slaves to each other. Yet John 8 counters this message with another paradox: we are no longer slaves to sin; indeed, we are not slaves to anybody; we are free, "sons" in the household.

Some Protestant churches take Jesus' command literally and maintain the practice of quarterly footwashing rituals. Many mainstream churches are seeking to revive the medieval ritual of annual footwashing on Maundy Thursday. Some communities understand this ritual as a clerical obligation, a sign of the leaders' mission to serve. Other churches widen the ritual to include the entire baptized community, so that all participants, lay or clergy, first have their feet washed and then wash the feet of the next worshiper. Perhaps where assemblies are reluctant to institute this ritual, the people guess the truth: the ritual is an extremely powerful symbolic enactment of the biblical theme of service.

Feminist biblical scholarship asks us to keep separate the various narratives of footwashing, in order that we do not confuse their quite different intentions. Jesus washed his disciples' feet as a sign of service and love. Quite different is Luke's story of a sinner woman (not identified as a prostitute) who washed Jesus' feet with her tears (Pr6c). Jesus used this event to illustrate not service and love, but repentance and adoration. This narrative is distinct from the story in Mark, who records the actions of a woman, wealthy enough to pour away nearly a year's income, who anointed Jesus' head (PasB), probably to signify her faith in him as messiah, the anointed one. When these stories get conflated, the important symbolic differences between them are lost.

Many gospel readings throughout the three years repeat the message that we are to serve one another. One of the most famous parables is that of the Good Samaritan (Pr10c), who serves even the despised foreigner. Jesus is quoted as saying that persons will be slaves to something, God or wealth (Pr20c). When God's faithful people are praised for their service, their response is to be: "We are worthless slaves; we have done only what we ought to have done" (Pr22c). Meanwhile, Jesus reversed the social expectations about class and rank by naming the servant to be the greatest one (Pr26A, Pr20B, Pr24B). In his community, Jesus indicates, the leader must serve. The church has seen in Mary a personification of this paradoxical leader-servant (Ad4c).

Many of the parables lay before us the troubling reality of a slave culture. The king forgives his slave's massive debt but later tortures him, until his debt is paid, so presumably forever (Pr19A). In the allegory in Matthew 21, the owner of the vineyard owns also slaves (Pr22A); the king in Matthew 22 owns slaves (Pr23A); the master in Matthew 25 both rewards and punishes his slaves for their conduct (Pr28A). In Matthew we find not only the Christians' life of service, but God as in some ways like the slave-owner. These pictures of an exacting master who owns, controls, and with justification tortures slaves is a far cry from a popular image in, for example, much contemporary hymnody, in which God is a benign, gentle friend who accepts us as we are.

At least since the career of Stephen, the church has identified persons who exemplify a life of service by calling them deacons. The churches developed the diaconate in a considerable variety of ways. Even in Acts, Stephen began by managing food distribution and ended by preaching. In the various churches, the diaconate is a lifelong career of service to the poor, service to the clergy, a step toward priestly ordination, or a term of attending to the practical responsibilities of parish life. Jerome, the fourth-century biblical translator, when encountering in Romans 16:1 Phoebe the deacon, decided that the text contained a scribal error, since he assumed that only males could be deacons. It is instructive to check several centuries of English-language Bibles to trace how Phoebe is designated.

In their interesting variety, the churches agree on this point: that the baptized community is to emulate a life of service. Here is one of the most striking countercultural messages of the Christian faith. Contemporary popular psychology urges persons to attend first and foremost to the only area of human life over which they can have any real control: their individual selves. Analytical psychology suggests that whole and healthy adults may appear to be helping others, but that actually they are making themselves contented in their serving. Furthermore, a crass version of our economic theory of capitalism suggests that serving the self, for example by making a million dollars, is the best way to serve the entire society, since one's wealth will accrue good for others. These powerful creeds can become mantras recited in their many versions throughout our lives in Western countries. Some Americans believe that adherence to these creeds will bring individual happiness and that individual happiness is the primary goal of life. To the extent that egocentrism is proclaimed as both the route and the destination of life's journey, the biblical message of service is extraordinarily countercultural. Christ relinquished divinity to become a slave. The last will be first; get down on your knees and wash someone's feet.

Liberation theologians remind us of the many times and ways that church authorities have admonished other persons to emulate the call to servanthood. It seems human nature to order other people to be loyal servants. Rather, the baptized are called to accept as good news that the individual is not the center of all things. God is the center, and in the Spirit of Christ the community can attend to God by serving one another. We can lay down the weary task of being a god by being a servant, and the joy of the community will attest that this is good news indeed.

Shepherd

flock, gate, lamb, sheep, shepherd

Related chapters: KINGDOM, SACRIFICE

The church makes considerable use of the biblical images of the shepherd, the flock, and the lamb. Many Christians find the metaphor of divine shepherd personally significant. Careful attention to the lectionary's use of this set of images will keep the language from misinterpretation and sentimentality.

PSALM 78:70-72

God chose David to serve,
    and took him away from the sheepfolds.
God brought him from tending the sheep,
    to be shepherd over Jacob, the chosen people,
    and over Israel, the chosen inheritance.
So David shepherded them with a faithful and true heart
    and guided them with the skillfulness of his hands.

COMMENDATION,
BURIAL OF THE
DEAD

Into your hands, O merciful Savior, we commend your servant *name*. Acknowledge, we humbly beseech you, a sheep of your own fold, a lamb of your own flock, a sinner of your own redeeming. Receive *him/her* into the arms of your mercy, into the blessed rest of everlasting peace, and into the glorious company of the saints in light.

EDINBURGH
PSALTER

The Lord's my shepherd; I'll not want.
He makes me down to lie
in pastures green; he leadeth me
the quiet waters by.

My soul he doth restore again,
and me to walk doth make
within the paths of righteousness,
e'en for his own name's sake.

Yea, though I walk in death's dark vale,
yet will I fear no ill;
for thou are with me, and thy rod
and staff me comfort still.

My table thou hast furnished
in presence of my foes;
my head thou dost with oil anoint,
and my cup overflows.

Goodness and mercy all my life
shall surely follow me,
and in God's house forevermore
my dwelling-place shall be.

Understand, therefore, beloved, how the exodus is new and old, perishable because of the slaughter of the sheep, imperishable because of the life of the Lord. O strange and inexpressible mystery! The slaughter of the sheep was found to be Israel's salvation, and the death of the sheep became the people's life, and the blood won the angel's respect. Tell me, angel, what did you respect? The slaughter of the sheep or the life of the Lord? The death of the sheep or the model of the Lord? The blood of the sheep or the Spirit of the Lord?

MELITO,
On Pascha

My brother said to me, "Dear sister, you are greatly privileged; surely you might ask for a vision to discover whether you are to be condemned or freed." I promised that I would, and this was the vision I had: I saw an immense garden, and in it a gray-haired man sat in shepherd's garb; tall he was, and milking sheep. And standing around him were many thousands of people clad in white garments. He raised his head, looked at me, and said, "I am glad you have come, my child." He called me over to him and gave me, as it were, a mouthful of the milk he was drawing; and I took it into my cupped hands and consumed it. And all those who stood around said: "Amen!" At the sound of this word I came to, with the taste of something sweet still in my mouth. I told this to my brother, and we realized that we would have to suffer, and that from now on we would no longer have any hope in this life.

PERPETUA,
ON HER
MARTYRDOM

THE NOMADIC TRIBES that predated the people of Israel practiced a herding economy. The memory of this nomadic history is retained in the stories of the forty years in the wilderness and the biographies of revered ancestors. Abel, the righteous of the first two brothers, was a shepherd. Abraham, Isaac, Jacob, Rachel, Moses, and David were all shepherds. Sheep and other herded animals provided the nomadic tribe with its staple foods and the raw materials for clothing and shelter. The daily tasks and annual patterns of herding determined the lives of females and males alike.

Scholars of myth report that oftentimes a community's staple food, whether seafood or sheep, banana or buffalo, figures as an essential part of that people's stories of self-identity. At the most ancient level of biblical storytelling, sheep are highly respected, for without their life, communal survival would not be possible. Contemporary interpretation of the Bible's sheep stories needs to balance its characteristic talk about how stupid sheep are with the economic reality that sheep were the primary life source for the people, God's gift of sustenance for the people.

When the nomadic tribes of the ancient Near East evolved into monarchies, the old image of the shepherd was appropriated as a model for the good ruler. In ancient texts, Gilgamesh, Hammurabi, and Ramses II are among the many authority figures who are likened to shepherds. Even deities, for example the Sumerian god Enlil and goddess Ningal, were compared to shepherds. In *The Republic*, Plato delineated the various ways that a ruler ought to be like a shepherd. Some historians theorize that the royal scepter evolved from the shepherd's crook. Thus when the Bible praises David as shepherd-king, it is not merely recalling a biographical memory that David was a shepherd before he became the king (Pr6B°, Pr11B†). By referring to Christ (Ea4A, Ea4B, Pr11B, Ea4C) or the king as a shepherd and to the people as the flock (Ea4B), the Bible participates in the stereotypical Near Eastern figurative speech in which a good leader was compared to a shepherd who cared for the flock, making sure it had food and protecting it from harm. Both Jeremiah and Ezekiel likened the poor leadership of the community's elders to the ministration of bad shepherds (LastA, LastC).

Later, when Israel settled into an agricultural economy and became increasingly urbanized, herding was seen in a different light. By the time of the common era, rigorously observant Jews classed shepherds along with tax collectors and Gentiles as persons with whom a devout Jew could not eat. The urban elite viewed shepherds as unclean persons who did not respect property boundaries and whose occupation resulted in their perpetual ritual impurity. Leftover from the old-world pattern, shepherds were poorly paid and lower class. That at Christ's birth angels appeared to shepherds (ChEABC, ChDnABC) indicates Luke's evaluation of shepherds as the migrant farm workers of that society.

The image of the shepherd, if not the reality, gained the patina of nostalgia. The practice of likening a ruler to a shepherd continued, even intensified. The shepherd evoked the good old days, when old-fashioned values were intact, tribal identity unblemished, and the religious covenant maintained. Although the only herders who interact with Jesus are the shepherds who come to the stable and the swineherders who lose their pigs into the sea, eight New Testament books either refer to Jesus as a shepherd or liken the divine mission to that of a shepherd. Perhaps because shepherding decreased as a social reality, it could gain in mythic importance, until, in Revelation, in the center of the heavenly city, where no flocks of sheep are found, the ruler is both shepherd and lamb (Revelation 7:17).

Despite the immense popularity of the imagery of Christ as the Good Shepherd, the lectionary contains relatively few references to this language. Psalm 23 is appointed for all three years of Easter 4, and on that Sunday the Johannine use of the shepherd image in John 10 is divided out between the three years. In year A, Christ is the gate of the sheepfold, an image that recalls the fact that herders in that part of the world lay their own bodies down for a night's rest in the gap of the fence, the body of the shepherd thus serving as the gate. In year B, the good shepherd who owns the flock is contrasted with the paid help who cares only for the self, not for the sheep. In year C, characteristic of John's gospel, the voice, that is, the word, of the shepherd is emphasized. When several flocks of sheep mingle, for example at a water hole, the sheep readily separate out into their owner's flock when they hear the voice of their own shepherd. This fact about sheep, rather than their dirty stupidity, is a helpful metaphor for God's faithful people, hearing the word and following it.

Often in the lectionary the shepherding imagery is applied to the people. We are the flock. People are like a sheep without a shepherd (Pr6A, Pr11B). The Lucan parable of the lost sheep (Pr19C) gives no specific referent to the shepherd: heaven rejoices. Yet the context makes clear that sinners are the lost sheep. In the parable of the last judgment (LastA) the saved are the sheep, the lost are the goats. In an Easter gospel, the risen Christ instructs Peter to "feed my sheep" (E₄3c). All these New Testament references rely on the passage in Ezekiel 34 (Last₄) in which God promises to shepherd the scattered and abandoned flock.

Our culture is perhaps the most individualistic in human history, and technological advances allow for increasingly privatized lives. This individualism intensifies loneliness, persons feeling disconnected from others or imagining that they have no need of others. Shepherding stresses the communal nature of the sheep. Our singular noun *flock* is one made of many. The church proclaims the good news that I am not alone. We are the flock, and we share a common life. Psalm 23, a popular choice for funerals, suggests to some Christians the individual as the one sheep Jesus is holding. Yet during the early centuries of the church, the church fathers used Psalm 23 as an allegory for baptismal catechesis. The green pastures were the weeks of catechetical instruction; the still waters was baptism; the soul's restoration was the revival by the Spirit; the path of righteousness was the new life of faithfulness; the oil was the chrism of baptism; the table and the overflowing cup referred to the eucharist. In this classic interpretation of Psalm 23, the emphasis is on the communal life of the sheepfold, enlivened by the Spirit of God through baptism.

Especially the clergy has taken to itself the label of shepherd. The bishop's crosier evolved from a shepherd's crook. *Pastor* as a noun means shepherd and as a verb refers to the tasks of the ordained minister. We do well to monitor our use of the adjective *pastoral* and adverb *pastorally*, which come sometimes to mean little more than *nice*. Such usage radically minimizes the arduous responsibility required of the shepherd.

Art historians identify a second-century statue of a young shepherd as the earliest extant depiction of Christ. Modeled after portrayals of Orpheus, the statue is clearly not a realistic depiction of a middle-aged preacher and healer, but a metaphoric image of the ever-youthful divine shepherd. The catacombs and sarcophagi present images of Christ the shepherd. Especially in this funereal art, the shepherd evokes a bucolic peacefulness, a sense that believers need not fear death because they remain in the care of a good shepherd. The third-century house church at Dura Europas included a fresco of Christ the shepherd. Several of the fifth- and sixth-century mosaics in the churches in Ravenna, Italy, depict Christ as the shepherd surrounded by the sheep. Even Moses is depicted as a shepherd.

Less popular during medieval times, the shepherd image was revived during the Romantic movement of the nineteenth century. In its criticism of industrialization and urbanization, Romanticism exaggerated the glories of the rural past, and the church's presentation of Christ shared in this Arcadian influence. We think of hymns such as "The King of love my Shepherd is" and "Jesus, tender Shepherd," as well as the popular nineteenth-century painting by Bernhard Plockhorst of the Good Shepherd. That Plockhorst's shepherd wears a white shawl-like mantle and is walking barefoot down a pathway indicates how unrealistic the picture of the shepherd had become. Churches with such an image prominently displayed must extricate Christ from the excessive sentimentalism the picture might evoke. Had Jesus been a meek and mild babysitter, he would not have been executed.

Ancient herding tribes practiced a springtime ritual in which the firstborn lamb was given back to gods, sacrificed perhaps as a thank-you gift, perhaps in a gesture of sympathetic magic, to ensure the fertility of the flock during the year. In the exodus, the Israelites historicized this ritual, connecting the lamb with the passing away not of winter, but of the angel of death and the condition of slavery. In either case—the fertility of the flock or the escape from Egypt—the lamb symbolizes new life for the whole community. Were a family too small to consume one lamb, two families were to share the meal, for the lamb meant life for all the people.

The passion narrative in John's gospel stresses the passover lamb as the image of Christ by noting that Jesus was crucified as the passover lambs were being killed and that he was offered wine on hyssop, hyssop being the fern-like herb stipulated in Israelite ritual as the means of sprinkling the blood of animals. As usual in the fourth gospel, narrative details are symbolic refer-ences to religious meaning rather than realistic historical memories. Christ is not only the shepherd and we the sheep, but is himself the lamb ensuring new life. The connotations of Christ as shepherd are reversed when Christ is the lamb.

The lamb has several other referents. The cry of John the Baptist, "Behold the lamb of God who takes away the sin of the world," has an apoc-alyptic message. The lamb that figures in the book of Revelation recalls the Jewish image of a conquering lamb that would appear in God's final vindica-tion of the just. Another use of lamb imagery in the Old Testament comes from certain passages of Second Isaiah, the poems of the Suffering Servant. The image of the sufferer as a slaughtered sheep provided background for early Christian reflection on Christ. He too stood silent at his trial and already in Acts was described with the imagery of Isaiah 53 (Ea5B). Yet another image of the sheep in the Hebrew Scriptures became significant in later Christian theology. Just as God provided a ram for Abraham's burnt offering (VigilABC, Pr8A°), so in Christ God provided a sheep to be killed in our stead. This imagery provides one of the biblical backgrounds for the medieval substitutionary theory of atonement. These various biblical uses deepen and enrich contemporary references to the flock and its sheep.

In the tenth century the Eastern church forbade the depiction in churches of Christ as the lamb, because apparently outsiders were misunderstanding the eucharist to be animal sacrifice. Yet in the fifteenth century Andrei Rublev, in his memorable icon of the Holy Trinity as the three visitors to Abraham and Sarah, drew a tiny lamb in the base of the chalice. So it is that in each age the church makes contemporary judgments about which biblical images work effectively to convey the gospel and which, for one reason or another, do not. One century's decisions may not hold for the next century, for one obstacle is replaced by another.

The danger in twenty-first century use of the image of the shepherd is sentimentality. By sentimentality we mean the practice of showing a one-sided image, a flat depiction that, because of its lack of ambivalence, conjures up only warm fuzzies. If the shepherd wears a long white robe, we may think unconsciously of only our mother's nightgown. If our depictions focus on one cute lamb, we forget the reality of the flock. Any way that we are able to give more layers, more shading, more connotations, to the shepherd, the flock, and the lamb helps save this complex biblical image from misinterpretation, sentimentality, and ultimately obsolescence.

Spirit

advocate, breath, spirit, wind

Related chapters: EMANATION OF THE DIVINE, FIRE, PROPHET, WIND

One possible translation of the Hebrew nouns *ruah* and the Greek *pneuma* is the English word *spirit*. Those biblical passages traditionally translated as "spirit" were essential in the development of trinitarian theology and are read at festivals of the Holy Spirit.

PSALM 104:30-
31

You hide your face, and they are terrified;
you take away their breath,
and they die and return to their dust.
You send forth your Spirit, and they are created;
and so you renew the face of the earth.

BLESSING AT
BAPTISM

Pour your Holy Spirit upon _name_: the spirit of wisdom and understanding, the spirit of counsel and might, the spirit of knowledge and the fear of the Lord, the spirit of joy in your presence.

JEAN JANZEN,
AFTER
HILDEGARD
OF BINGEN

O Holy Spirit, root of life,
creator, cleanser of all things:
anoint our wounds, awaken us
with lustrous movement of your wings.

Eternal Vigor, Saving One,
you free us by your living Word,
becoming flesh to wear our pain,
and all creation is restored.

O holy Wisdom, soaring power,
encompass us with wings unfurled,
and carry us, encircling all
above, below, and through the world.

You have it in the Gospel that the angel at a certain time went down into a pond, and the water was moved. And the one who went down first into the pond was made whole. What did the angel announce in this type, but the descent of the Holy Spirit, which would take place in our time to consecrate the waters when invoked by the sacerdotal prayers? That angel was the herald of the Holy Spirit, because through spiritual grace medicine was to be applied to the infirmities of our soul and mind. The Spirit fills all things, and possesses all things, and operates all things and in all things, just as both God the Father and the Son operate.

AMBROSE
OF MILAN,
*The Holy
Spirit*

Once upon a time we captured God and we put God in a box and we put a beautiful velvet curtain around the box. We placed candles and flowers around the box and we said to the poor and the dispossessed, "Come! Come and see what we have! Come and see God!" And they knelt before the God in the box. One day, very long ago, the Spirit in the box turned the key from inside and she pushed it open. She looked around in the church and saw that there was nobody there! They had all gone. Not a soul was in the place. She said to herself, "I'm getting out!" The Spirit shot out of the box. She escaped and she has been sighted a few times since then. She was last seen with a bag lady in McDonald's.

EDWINA
GATELEY,
"Prophetic
Mission"

The LECTIONARY'S USE of the biblical image of *spirit* illustrates how a religious tradition uses its scriptures. Only as interpreted in a specific way is the Bible authoritative in a faith community. Various Christian communities assign the right of interpretation to different persons, the hierarchy or the preachers or inspired laity. However, for most Christians, the first and fundamental stage of biblical interpretation rests in the community's biblical translation, because contemporary word choice reflects the tradition's interpretation of the biblical text. The translation of the biblical text carries in it, perhaps unconsciously, the objectives of the translator. A Christian translation committee, themselves formed by weekly proclamation in the eucharistic assembly, will encounter in the ancient text something different from what the Jewish translator hears. Many denominations require their preachers to learn at least Greek, if not also Hebrew, so that their proclamation is not captive to those biblical translations that are currently recommended.

The translations of *ruah* and *pneuma* exemplify ecclesial use of the Bible. In Hebrew, the noun *ruah* can be translated spirit, breath, or wind. That is, in biblical Hebrew, spirit, breath, and wind are a single indistinguishable complex concept. In Genesis 1:2, the translators must decide whether to render *ruah* as "a wind from God" (NRSV), "the spirit of God" (REB), "a mighty wind"(NAB), "a divine wind" (NJB), "the Spirit of God" (NIV, CEV), "the power of God" (TEV), or "rushing-spirit of God" (Everett Fox), and whether to capitalize any of these nouns. Some scholars suggest that *ruah* was mainly an onomatopoeic sound. However, it was as "Spirit of God" that *ruah* became important in Christian theology. Genesis 1 became a text to proclaim the triune God, since God, the word of God, and the spirit of God all figure in the creation of the heavens and the earth. (Herein lies the theological problem in referring to only the first person of the Trinity as Creator.) In the three-year lectionary, Genesis 1 is appointed for Trinity Sunday (TrinA). However, perfectly acceptable biblical translations may not introduce the noun *spirit* in Genesis 1 at all.

Ezekiel 37 (VigilABC, Le5A, PentB) provides another example. In the story of the valley of dry bones, most, but not all, translations use the noun *breath* in verse 5, the four *winds* in verse 9, and *spirit* (usually not capitalized) in verse 14, all three words being variants of *ruah* in Hebrew. Similarly, the

Greek *pneuma* can be translated life, wind, breath, or spirit. In John 20:22 (Ea2ABC), *pneuma* is the root of both the verb translated *breathed* and the noun *Spirit*. In John 3:8 (Le2A, TrinB), the words *wind*, *blows*, and *Spirit* all translate forms of *pneuma*. Although biblical languages do not distinguish between wind, breath, life and spirit, many languages and the three-year lectionary do. Because of this history of linguistic differentiation, and because this volume deals with biblical images in the three-year lectionary, this volume separates the words *spirit* and *wind* into two chapters. Readers of this chapter on SPIRIT are urged to consult also the chapter on WIND.

The scriptures demonstrate a development of the image of spirit from an ancient principle of life to the Holy Spirit of the Christian Trinity. Perhaps the earliest idea was the power of the life as seen in the mysterious winds. The Bible contains the idea that in God's breath and with God's wind came divine life to the people. In the narrative in Genesis 2 of the creation of the first human, the breath of God infused life to the clay manikin, and in the exodus narrative, the wind from God saved the people from death. In the early history of Israel, this spirit from God rested especially on charismatic leaders and ecstatic prophets; later, the king was said to be anointed with this spirit; visionary passages predicted that some day the spirit, this life from God, would rest on the whole people. As the manifestation of this spirit moved away from nature and toward religion or nationalism, the Hebrew continues to understand spirit as the method of communication between God and humankind, the vehicle by which God conveys life to the people. *Ruah* (spirit) and *dabar* (word) are parallel terms, both explaining how the divine is conveyed to the world. That spirit connotes extraordinary power opens the way for a spirit to be also the power for evil. For example, in Ezekiel 36 God's spirit, a new spirit, will replace our old spirit characterized by uncleanness (VigilABC).

Because of the imprecision of the concept of spirit, various Bible stories embody this divine spirit differently. The spirit is manifest in God's breath, which activates humans during their lifetime. The spirit is seen in wind, for example at the Red Sea (VigilABC). The spirit descends from heaven, the place of the abode of God, like a dove descending from the sky, for example at Jesus' baptism (BapA, BapB, BapC). The spirit alights on the faithful like flame: "divided tongues, as of fire, appeared among them, and a tongue rested on each of them" (PentABC). The spirit anoints Jesus (Ep3C), the verb invoking the memory that the priests (Exodus 28:41), prophets (1 Kings 19:16), and kings (1 Samuel 16:13) were consecrated with a ritual of oil.

New Testament writers personified the spirit and stress its various aspects. For Paul, the Spirit is the power of the resurrected Christ alive and operative in the community of the baptized: the Spirit of God is nothing other than the Spirit of Christ. The moral life of Christians is described as fruits of the Spirit. For John, the Spirit is the divine power that will perpetuate Christ's presence in the community. John's gospel uses the title Paraclete—helper, advocate—to describe the Spirit's double-sided activity of supporting the faithful with divine comfort and appealing to God for the faithful (Ea6a, Pentc).

Luke's depiction of the Spirit greatly influenced Christian imagination. Although Paul cites the resurrection as the time of Christ's incorporation of the Spirit, and Mark suggests that the Spirit came on Jesus at his baptism, Luke dates the entry of the Spirit to Jesus' conception. Luke's annunciation narrative (Ad4b) utilizes a pattern found also in Greek religious myths, that a personified power of the deity, called in Luke 1:35 both the Holy Spirit and the power of the Most High, brings about conception in a virgin woman. The idea is that the life of the child comes not from the father, but from the deity. In using such imagery, we do well to avoid both the Greek myth of sexual intercourse between a god and a human and literalist descriptions about Mary. Rather, the biblical idea is that the salvation we meet in Christ comes from God's creative power. Luke's understanding of the personified divine spirit led to many biblical translations capitalizing both Holy and Spirit throughout Luke and Acts.

The New Testament's personification of the divine spirit provided Christian theologians with material that described a triune God. Although the church fathers from the fourth and fifth centuries taught that all three persons of the Trinity are equal and that none operates alone, in subsequent centuries different arenas of the church emphasized either the Son or the Spirit. Scholarly theological reflection focused on Christ, while charismatic expression on the edges of the church celebrated the Spirit. Some theologians call for this millennium to more fully incorporate the Spirit into the whole of Christian life.

The Spirit has always burst out of the churches' categories and definitions. In the second century Montanists claimed unique inspiration by the Spirit of God. The medieval mystic mothers, overcome by visions in their convent cells, testified that the Spirit of God was sending the messages. Small Protestant movements claim authorization from the Spirit for novel activity. In the nineteenth century some conservative Protestant churches allowed women to preach, long before mainstream denominations did; because these churches ascribed so much power to the Spirit, they took seriously the women's anointing by the Spirit. Some feminist Christians choose to call the Spirit *she* and thus proclaim a distinctly female image of God as operative in the church.

One lectionary reading in particular deals with unforeseen manifestations of the Spirit. The almost comic narrative of Eldad and Medad indicates that some of the faithful were able to prophesy even though they missed the formal ritual over which Moses presided (Pr21в†). Yet Moses expresses the hope that God's Spirit will be manifest in everyone. The lectionary presents the image of spirit in the Pentecost readings of Acts 2 and John 20 and the reading of the dry bones vision in Ezekiel 37 (VigilABC, PentB, Le5A). In several Pauline texts, the Spirit is paramount. Our life in the Spirit (Pr10A), the firstfruits of the Spirit (Pr11A), our being anointed and sealed with the Spirit (Ep7B), the community's diverse gifts by the one Spirit (Ep2c), and living by the Spirit (Pr8c) capture Paul's attention. The passage in Romans 8 (Pr11A, TrinB), in which Paul writes of Christians calling God *Abba, Father*, stresses our life as led by the Spirit of God. Because the baptized people now embody the Spirit that Christ once embodied, we stand before God in the same relationship that Christ enjoyed. The verses 15-16 suggest that Paul is not laying down a law about the church's address in prayer as much as explaining the ongoing power of the Spirit of God among the baptized. The same movement from Christ to the assembly of believers is seen in the baptismal blessing that prays for the seven gifts of the Spirit. The list of seven, that is, the number of completion, quotes Isaiah 11:2, in its context a description of the one who will come from the root of Jesse. First the Spirit comes onto Christ, and now onto the baptized people of God.

The church celebrates the Spirit especially on Pentecost, festivals of the martyrs, and ceremonies of the conferral of the Spirit, such as confirmations and ordinations. The color is red. Bland depictions of flames attached to paraments and vestments, however, do little service to the biblical description of the Spirit of God. We cannot let our pictorial representations of biblical images trivialize them. A better celebration of the fire of the Spirit occurs at the Easter Vigil when the community gathers in the dark night to light a substantial bonfire from which all the worshipers light their small but lively flames. For Christians, the flame of the Spirit of God is the Light of Christ.

In some of the biblical images of inspiration by the Spirit, the recipient is an individual. However, many passages in Old and New Testaments describe the Spirit as alighting on the whole community. Contemporary baptismal practices seek to stress the communal nature of the gift of the Spirit. Private baptisms that are not emergencies are discouraged. The growing popularity of baptismal festivals is reshaping our understanding of God's Spirit. In Romans 8, the *you* who experiences the Spirit is a plural pronoun. It is in the baptized community that we experience most fully the

Spirit of the Creator, which for Christians is the same as the Spirit of the resurrected Christ.

The church has paid too little attention to the created earth itself, and many Christians are seeking to rectify this situation. Some assemblies now regularly include in the Sunday intercessions a petition for the earth, the land and seas, the animals, and the plants. According to Genesis 1:2, God's spirit hovered over the whole creation, not merely over the humans. In Psalm 104, all the animals, even the Leviathan, look to God for food. One could trace the history of the church by following the ecclesiastical discussions concerning whether God's Spirit is operative among the Gentiles, women, people with dark skin, children, homosexuals, the faithful of other religions, now even the animal kingdom. Throughout our debates, as the Hebrew and Greek nouns remind us, God's Spirit blows where it will. The divine Spirit is a mysterious wind, which we realize without seeing, which we honor without understanding. The good news is that the Spirit of God is always higher, always lower, more powerful and more pervasive, than we have yet imagined it to be.

Temple

ark of the covenant, house of God, temple

Related chapters: City, Kingdom, Mountain, Sacrifice

The Bible refers to the actual temples of Solomon, Zerubbabel, and Herod and to the eschatological temple of Ezekiel's visions. The temple was usually understood as the sacred place for God's chosen people, but some prophets hoped for the temple as the gathering place for everyone. In the lectionary, the temple is also a metaphor for Christ, the church, and the believer.

PSALM 65:1, 4   You are to be praised, O God, in Zion;
to you shall vows be performed in Jerusalem.
Happy are they whom you choose
and draw to your courts to dwell there!
They will be satisfied by the beauty of your house,
by the holiness of your temple.

PRAYER AT THE
DEDICATION OF
A CHURCH
BUILDING

Blessed are you, O Lord our God, king of the universe. The heavens and the earth cannot contain you, yet you are willing to make your home in human hearts. We are the temple of your presence, and this building is the house of your church. Accept us and this place to which we come. . . . Now, O God, visit us with your mercy and blessing as we dedicate this house to your glory and honor and to the service of all people in the name of the Father, and of the Son, and of the Holy Spirit.

NIKOLAI F. S.
GRUNDTVIG

Built on a rock the church shall stand,
even when steeples are falling;
crumbled have spires in ev'ry land,
bells still are chiming and calling—
calling the young and old to rest,
calling the souls of those distressed,
longing for life everlasting.

Not in our temples made with hands
God, the Almighty, is dwelling;
high in the heav'ns his temple stands,
all earthly temples excelling.
Yet he who dwells in heav'ns above
deigns to abide with us in love,
making our bodies his temple.

The soul, the conscience of the faithful, is also the temple and house of God. Should this soul bring forth wicked thoughts, towards the injuring of our neighbor, these will settle there like robbers in a cave, slaying one by one those who pass by, thrusting the swords of their malice into those who are without fault. The faithful soul is now no longer a house of prayer, but a den of thieves; scorning the innocence and simplicity of holiness, it tries to injure its neighbor. But since we are instructed without ceasing against all such perversities of conduct by the words of the Redeemer throughout the sacred pages, even now Christ is doing what we are told he then did: "And he was teaching daily in the temple." For Truth teaches daily in the temple when it carefully instructs the mind of the faithful.

GREGORY
THE GREAT,
HOMILY 39

Isaiah has wandered into the temple just as we might wander into St. Paul's Cathedral, perhaps not expecting to get much out of the time spent there. Suddenly he finds himself undergoing a great spiritual experience. He sees, not an impressive religious building, but the glory of the Lord, filling the temple. That which is revealed to him is that which is always there and seldom noticed, although it is the first term of all religion and the only reason that religion exists. It is the all-penetrating, unchanging splendor of the light of God.

EVELYN
UNDERHILL,
*The Ways
of the Spirit*

⁓

ACCORDING TO THE CHARACTERISTIC WORLDVIEW of the nation-states in the ancient Near East, monarchs received their authority to reign from the deities. Sometimes the first king in the line was a deity, and his sons inherited his divine right to rule. From approximately 3000 B.C.E., it was usual for the palace compound to include a temple. The temple was not a communal place of worship, but rather the earthly house of the heavenly deity. The god or goddess resided in that structure when on earth, and this divine residence confirmed the authority of the monarch. The temple secured the dynasty and symbolized the identity of the kingdom under the deity. So also, when David evolved from a tribal chieftain to the king of a new nation-state, he sought to replace the tabernacle with a temple worthy of his god. The centralization of government in Jerusalem meant that a single temple, controlled by the king, was preferred over local shrines. Although David did not oversee its building, he chose its site, and according to the tradition of Chronicles, helped design the liturgy.

This first Israelite temple, built by the aggrandizing king Solomon (Pr16b°), closely resembled Egyptian, Canaanite, and Phoenician temples. The deity's abode was an eastward-facing elongated cube situated within more or less elaborate temple grounds. That Solomon employed Phoenicians to build his temple did not alone account for the similarity of his temple to others'. Most people, Solomon included, think in the categories of their own time and place. Solomon's version of the monarch's house of God was famous as being perhaps the biggest and grandest in the region, as large as was architecturally possible for the available building techniques. Like its neighbors, Israel used the temple for its royal treasury, with some of its precious items being ritual objects for worship.

Built in the tenth century before Christ, Solomon's temple was destroyed in the sixth century, and several decades later it was rebuilt under Zerubbabel (Pr27c°). Because in the sixth century Israel was not a sovereign nation, the temple no longer symbolized divine legitimation of the dynasty. Rather, the temple was a solely religious structure tying the people to their god. The temple was repaired yet again by Herod, who vastly enlarged the temple grounds and made its courtyards, walls, gates, an adjoining fortress and reservoir conspicuous signs of wealth. The Gospel of John says that Herod's temple took forty-six years to construct. It was destroyed by Rome in 70 C.E., never to be rebuilt. What remains now in Jerusalem is the Wailing Wall, and on the temple site, understood by Muslims to be the site of Abraham's offering of Isaac, the mosque called the Dome of the Rock. Some Ultra-Orthodox Jews hope for a rebuilt temple, while most observant Jews judge the temple a religious artifact of their past. Yet the visions of Ezekiel imagine a final spectacular temple, marking the end of all exile, exceeding all earthly temples, bringing the abode of God here to this earth.

Not only the purpose and design of the Israelite temple, but also its iconography closely resembled that of its neighbors. The building on its platforms replicated the mythological cosmic mountain. Stone carvings and lotus capitals recalled trees, so as to evoke the garden of the gods or the mythic tree of life, a characteristic feature in ancient Near Eastern legends. The temple yard contained a large water basin, which scholars conjecture symbolized the sea that the divine powers tamed at creation. The mythological creatures called cherubs, constructed of body parts of the lion, the bird, and the human, were common in ancient Near Eastern iconography as the deities' mode of transportation. As honorific figures flanking the divine throne, cherubs accompanied the ark of the covenant. The cherubs are a particularly surprising cultural sharing, because the commandments seemed to forbid such image making.

More in keeping with the Torah, the Jerusalem temple was said to have contained, not a statue of the deity, but instead the ark of the covenant. The repository for the tablets of the law, the ark concretized the words of the divine, without depicting the deity. The ark had a long and complicated history. Biblical scholars are unsure about its appearance or its various uses over time, and nobody knows its fate. The ark was referred to as the footstool of God, because God's throne was transcendent, and as God's mercy seat, because YHWH was characterized by mercy. In spite of the strong similarities between the Israelite temple and those of its neighbors, Jews believed that God's being could not reside in anything as meager as a building. The Hebrew Scriptures reiterate Solomon's point at the dedication of the first temple that it was not God, but rather God's name that was enthroned in the temple.

Not only was ancient Judaism a religious tradition thoroughly marked by its own historic time and place: so also is ours. Throughout its two millennia the church has adapted cultural phenomena for Christian purposes. The basilica, the Roman assembly hall, became the standard design for the church building of the fourth and fifth centuries. Later when some Protestants conceived of worship as education, their church buildings were modeled on community lecture halls. For a short period in the twentieth century, new American churches resembled fast-food restaurants. When the pottery of folk artists gained popularity, many churches replaced their chalices with ceramic, even though it was neither as sanitary as silver nor as easy to use. The nonrepresentational art of the twentieth century led many churches to design stained glass windows that were splays of color, rather than ones depicting biblical or symbolic imagery.

Not only can we not escape our time: the incarnation would suggest that we not even try. The gospel proclaims that God seeks to reside in each culture through its language, its images, its arts, its social patterns. But always there is a twist. The church seeks ways to use the languages, the design, and the architecture of its culture to speak God's words, to proclaim not worldly values but God's mercy, to house not the latest affluence, but God's beloved poor. Although much of our buildings, our speech, our symbols, will resemble that of the wider society, some striking difference, some sign of the alternate values of salvation will be evident.

The Jerusalem temple features in several lectionary readings. Although the site of the boy Jesus talking with the teachers (Ch1C) sounds more like a synagogue than the temple, Jesus tells his parents that he must be in his Father's house. The prophecy from Malachi (Ad2C) foresees the temple as the place where the messiah will appear. Consequently, at the temptation of Jesus, the devil suggests that Jesus appear suddenly in the temple; for to appear in the temple is to stand in God's stead in God's house.

In the call narrative of Isaiah (TrinB, Ep5C), the temple is not only metaphorically the house of God; in Isaiah's vision, the temple becomes the throne room of YHWH. The gilded cherubim become flying fiery seraphs, singing God's praises. The cloud that settled on Solomon's temple at its dedication is present again, and incense fills the air. Statues of angelic figures come alive and talk to the terrified and unwilling Isaiah. Here the temple is the primary holy place, the place of angelic song, the spot at which God talks to the chosen ones, the site of religious ecstasy.

This extraordinary vision, at which Isaiah is forgiven his sin and commissioned to be God's mouthpiece, is the setting for the "Holy, holy, holy" hymn that countless Christians sing weekly at the eucharist. Our musical settings and the very spirit of our song should transport us into Isaiah's mystic vision. Paradoxically, it is at our simple Christian altars that we sing this song. In Isaiah's vision, the Jerusalem temple became the heavenly courtroom with angelic attendants of the Holy Sovereign. Each week at the eucharistic prayer, Christian meeting rooms become the Jerusalem temple become the heavenly court, for the church understands this table as God's throne, the bread and wine as the body of God. In an adaptation of the Hebrew words, Christians sing that the entire earth is filled with the glory of God. So the church is called to care for the earth, as the place of God's creation and the manifestation of God's glory. The "Holy, holy, holy" deserves our reverence, even amazement, and if we decide not to sing it, we need to find a worthy replacement for this multivalent song.

Several readings in the lectionary speak of the temple as more than the sanctuary for Israelites. In Isaiah 56, YHWH promises that in the future everyone will be welcomed at the house of God (Pr15A[†]). Even foreigners were to be welcomed for prayer. When Jesus was criticized for breaking the sabbath laws, he reminded the people that David violated the tabernacle by eating its sacred bread when his band was hungry (Pr4B). Jesus relativizes the sanctity of the temple and challenges the ancient idea that a small group of people can house God for their own private protection.

Some persons in the early Christian community continued their practice of temple worship. But as the decades moved along, and surely after the destruction of the temple in 70 C.E., Christians taught that the temple had been replaced. Like the participants of Qumran, some early Christians stressed that what had been the temple was now the community of the faithful. To meet God, Christians assemble to meet one another. The baptized people now house the Spirit of God, and so they can be called God's temple (Ep7A). The community is now holy. It is as if we could sing "Holy, holy, holy" to one another at the sign of peace and make profound bows to one another at communion. The community is now built into a spiritual house, with Christ as its cornerstone (Ea5A). Also in Peter's speech in Acts 4 and in Ephesians (Pr11B), the church is said to be the dwelling place for God. Another use of the temple image is found in Paul's discussion of sexual ethics. Paul describes the believers' bodies as God's temple and therefore claims that the parts of our bodies are holy, just as were the vessels of the temple (Ep2B). God resides in the bodies of the community: Paul's discussion contains the plural *you* throughout.

For Christians the image of the temple refers primarily to Christ himself. In the Johannine narrative of the cleansing of the temple, Jesus says that the temple that he will destroy and raise up is the temple of his body (Le3B); that is, God resides in Jesus. Christ is the locus of the divine spirit, the presence and the proclamation of God's name. The same point is made by the Lucan story of Peter's catch of fish (Ep5C). Paired with the call of Isaiah, this narrative shows Peter begging for forgiveness, just as Isaiah did. Isaiah is before a vision of the almighty throne, while Peter is on the shore kneeling before Jesus.

The temple image is central to the book of Hebrews. The author of Hebrews presents an allegory, that is, a sustained set of metaphors with elaborate parallels between one complicated image (here, the temple ritual) and something else (here, Christian faith). Appointed for Lent (Le5B), Good Friday (ABC), and for six weeks in year B (Pr23B, Pr24B, Pr25B, Pr26B, Pr27B, Pr28B), Hebrews uses temple imagery to state that Christ's death replaced Jewish temple rituals. Hebrews 9 expects the hearer to know that only the high priest could enter the Holy Place for the ritual of sprinkling the blood (Pr26B). Hebrews 10 concludes this series of readings (Pr28B, GFrABC) by drawing allegorical parallels between the temple's design, for example its curtain, and the actions of Christ. The sanctuary of the temple is likened to the stance of our faith. We enter to stand in the house of God by means of the confession of our hope. Our faith in Christ replaces the temple.

The contemporary church often individualizes the temple metaphor, using it to picture the believer who houses God. Usually, however, the Bible sees the community as the temple. The body of Christ refers mainly to the assembly of the faithful. The assembled community is the place where God dwells. The medieval emphasis on the tabernacle, that is, the storage container of the consecrated bread, as a location of high holiness has given way to a more New Testament idea of Christ, the community, and the sharing of the bread as referents for the metaphor of temple. The Christian presider leads the prayers and the rituals of a community within which the Spirit of God already resides. Here is the good news: Christians need not spend huge amounts of money on lavish temples to please a distant God. Our temple is Christ, and in baptism our temple becomes one another, each housing God for each other. Usually at the dedication of new church buildings, Christians refer to their structure as a temple and pray once again Solomon's prayer. Yet our buildings are temples only metaphorically, houses of God only because they are in the first place assembly halls for God's people.

But (there is always a but) humans learned over the ages that holy places are important, if not for God, then for their own devotion. Mid-twentieth-century experiments to worship without consecrated spaces or to eliminate objects of reverence underestimated the human need for religion, for places that symbolize the altered consciousness that follows the encounter with God. Christians do not need temples in order to meet God, but having met God within a certain community, we honor the site with a structure that symbolizes God's grace and houses those in whom in Spirit dwells.

Treasure

gifts, gold-frankincense-myrrh,
pearl, rich fool, treasure, widow's coin

Related chapters: KINGDOM, THE POOR

Human communities value rare metals and gems, and from this
treasuring of scarce products of nature come both personal happiness and international conflict. In the lectionary, treasure is an
image of a countercultural valuing of the things of God.

PSALM 119:11, 127
I treasure your promise in my heart,
    that I may not sin against you.
Truly, I love your commandments
    more than gold and precious stones.

MODEL PRAYER OF THE CHURCH
Almighty God, giver of all things, with gladness we give thanks for all your goodness. We praise you for the gift of your Son our Savior, through whom you have made known your will and grace. Help us to treasure in our hearts all that our Lord has done for us, and enable us to show our thankfulness by lives that are wholly given to your service.

ELEANOR HULL, AFTER NINTH-CENTURY IRISH HYMN
Riches I heed not, nor vain, empty praise,
thou mine inheritance, now and always:
thou, and thou only, first in my heart,
great God of heaven, my treasure thou art.

As Sixtus was led away to be jailed and tortured, he gave all the treasures of the church into Laurence's care to be dispensed to the poor. Blessed Laurence then sought out Christians by day and by night, and ministered to all according to their needs. . . . The soldiers, hearing of money, took Laurence and presented him to the general Decius. Decius said to him, "Where is the church's money, which we know is hidden with you?" Laurence requested a delay of three days. During the three days Laurence brought together the poor, the lame, and the blind, and then presented them before Decius in the palace, saying, "See here the eternal treasure, which never diminishes but increases. It is divided among these people and is found in all of them, for their hands have carried the treasure off to heaven."

JACOB OF VORAGINE, *The Golden Legend*

How can I explain the riches and treasures and delights found when the soul is united to God in prayer? Since in some way we can enjoy heaven on earth, be brave in begging the Lord to give us his grace in that he show us the way and strengthen the soul that it may dig until it finds this hidden treasure. The truth is that the treasure lies within our very selves.

TERESA OF AVILA, *The Interior Castle*

TREASURE IS A BEAUTIFULLY EVOCATIVE WORD; perhaps we smile as we speak it. Its primary meaning is an accumulation or store of small valuable items, gold and silver jewelry, precious stones, coins. Treasure hunters dig in the ground or dive into the sea to find caches of lost treasure. In that the word suggests a massive wooden chest filled with golden chains and loose gems, the primary meaning is archaic for our culture; the treasury of a European medieval cathedral contains valuable items no longer in use. A memory of such treasure exists in our words *treasurer* and *treasury*.

Usually today the word *treasure* is metaphoric. Lovers call one another "my treasure." The noun becomes a verb: we treasure the family photographs. Treasure is something valued, whether or not it has high monetary worth. The word nearly always carries a positive connotation. We tend not to use it sarcastically or ironically. Our culture nurtures its own myths concerning treasure: lotteries, television game shows, and casinos attest to the enduring fantasy held by particularly Americans that a hidden treasure awaits us, and finding it at the end of the rainbow will ensure our happiness.

The human fascination with treasure is found at the beginning of the Bible. In the second story of creation, in the passage laying out the geographical boundaries of the garden of Eden, the land of Havilah is described as having gold, "and the gold of that land is good." This proleptic reference to a human culture marked by mining, metallurgy, jewelry, and coinage is a poignant parenthetical remark in the middle of the description of a primordial paradise that needed no gold. Old Testament narratives include many stories about treasure. Abraham's servant presents Rebekah with gold bracelets and a gold nose-ring as part of his negotiation for Isaac's marriage. Aaron melts down the people's jewelry to mold the golden calf. When the Israelites destroyed Canaanite settlements, they were allowed to keep as booty anything that could be purified in fire: thus their keeping of captured treasure was sanctioned, although a percentage was to be contributed to the high priest. The books of Kings and Chronicles describe the treasure that adorned both temple and palace and became booty for various invading enemies. Much of the wisdom literature suggests that God rewards the righteous with earthly treasure. Job ends up with twice his original wealth. Yet in Psalm 119 and Proverbs 2, the word *treasure* metaphorically describes the glories of God's word—an understanding of the value of the Torah that contrasts markedly with Paul's opinion of the law.

In one interesting reference to treasure, Exodus 39 includes a detailed description of the high priest's vestment with its decorations of gold filigree and twelve precious stones. The idea here is that the holy man is marked out as a treasured person, his status as a mediator between God and the people symbolized by the treasure he wears. The author of Revelation envisions a transformation. Instead of the high priest and a temple adorned with treasures, the city itself is made of gold, the twelve precious stones are set into its foundation, and each gate into the city is crafted from a single pearl. The New Jerusalem replaces the high priest. Treasure characterizes not a holy man, but the entire people of God. The great single pearls that are the gates to the holy city call to mind the parable of the man who finds one pearl of great value (Pr12A) for which he sells all he owns. The pearl, a mollusk's coating of an irritating grain of sand, is an image of the treasure that God is and provides.

The three-year lectionary includes several gospel narratives that illustrate the tendency to treasure the wrong things. The rich man cannot bring himself to sell all that he has (Pr23B) and another man builds bigger barns (Pr13C). Alternatively, two poor women are depicted as appropriately treasuring their small coins, one by searching for a single lost coin (Pr19C) and another by contributing her few coins to the temple treasury (Pr27B). In these particular stories, men are depicted as amassing treasure and women as having few resources. In the contemporary world, we must judge when these gender stereotypes remain useful and when not. In most places around the world, this gender disparity in livelihood continues. Yet one wants to avoid the assumption that women are poor and helpless while men are rich and selfish.

A beloved gospel story of persons presenting their treasure freely to God is the Epiphany story of the magi. Many Christian preachers have suggested that the gifts of gold, frankincense, and myrrh symbolize the destiny of the child. The gold marks Christ as king, the frankincense honors Christ as God, and the myrrh anticipates his death and burial. The magi are not identified in Matthew as three kings. That the number of the magi is imagined as three comes from the number of the gifts, and that they are called kings comes from later Christian speculation on Psalm 72 and Isaiah 60, with their descriptions of foreign kings offering the Israelite king their gifts. Gold and frankincense are direct citations from Isaiah. The word *magi* refers to a group of religious seekers of wisdom, which in the ancient world would have included both male and female, magus and sibyl. Because the masculine plural would have been used even if women were included, perhaps we ought to picture both wise men and wise women presenting their treasures to the Christ child.

On Ash Wednesday, the gospel reading invites the faithful to the three classic disciplines of Lent: almsgiving, prayer, and fasting. The conclusion of this call to repentance sums up the Christian life with the imagery of treasure. Our treasure is to be not on earth, but in heaven, says the gospel reading. We are called to find our treasure, as we give alms, in the poor; as we pray, in the needy; as we fast, with the hungry.

Several epistle readings use the image of treasure to describe our life together in God. The grace of God has enriched the whole church (AdIB). Yet we have this treasure only in clay jars (Pr4B). Our treasure is countercultural, not the same as the treasure valued in our society. God's mercy and grace are the treasures of the community (Le4B).

Most readers of this volume live in capitalist societies. The economic theory behind capitalism is that an individual's accumulation of personal treasure is a social good because it eventually enriches the entire community. Christians who wish to live faithful lives within capitalism continue to reflect how to juggle this idea of treasure with that in the New Testament. What does it mean to treasure God? If God is our treasure, how do we preserve and honor this treasure? Where is the God we treasure? The faith maintains that the Spirit of that treasure is alive in the persons around the eucharistic table, and the St. Laurence legend records that in the poor and the maimed are the treasures of the church. These ideas cannot easily sit alongside the goals of capitalism.

The word *treasure* derives from the same root as the word *thesaurus*. A thesaurus is a storehouse of words, a treasury of synonyms to enrich communication. The liturgical language of the church is one such treasure of words, and this volume a thesaurus of our lectionary's vocabulary. This volume took its title from the gospel about the householder who takes from the storehouse treasures both new and old (Pr12A). The gospel of Matthew, steeped in Jewish traditional speech, knew that the Israelite language is old treasure, still conveying to the hearers the mercy of God. Yet the evangelist also realized that Christians had to discover new treasure, new words that express the meaning of Christ and the life of the church.

The verse about treasure old and new can be a formula used in assembling the texts for each Sunday's worship. There will be treasures old, words and images from the ancient Hebrew past, the church's early preaching, Christian hymnwriters, and the words of theologians and testimonies of believers in every age and various cultures. There will also be treasures new, both when the old treasure is seen in new light, and when new imagery is added to the storehouse. The liturgy can be such a trove, gems piled here, gold coins stacked there. The faithful come away from worship newly enriched by the treasure that God is and shares.

Tree

fig tree, fruits of the Spirit,
Jesse tree, mustard bush, tree of life,
tree of knowledge of good and evil, vine

Related chapters: Cross, Garden, Wisdom

Many cultures and religions use the image of the tree to symbolize wholeness in the cosmos, in the realm, in the community, and
in the person. These usages occur also in Christian imagery, as
well as the paradoxical use of the tree to describe the cross.

PSALM 52:8   I am like a green olive tree in the house of God.

PROPER PREFACE,   It is indeed right and salutary that we should at all times
PASSION SUNDAY   and in all places offer thanks and praise to you, O Lord,
holy Father, through Christ our Lord; who on the tree of
the cross gave salvation to all, that, where death began,
there life might be restored, and that the evil one, who by
a tree once overcame, might by a tree be overcome.

DELORES   Faithful cross, O tree of beauty,
DUFNER   tree of Eden, tree divine!
Not a grove on earth can show us
leaf and flow'r and fruit so fine.
Bearer of our Savior's body,
tree of life, salvation's sign!

Cross of pain transformed to gladness,
ever green and sheltering tree,
symbol once of shame and bondage,
now the sign that we are free!
Cross of splendor, cross of glory,
cross of love's great victory!

Christians, chant your grateful praises
for the tree of triumph won,
proof of overflowing mercy
and redemption in the Son.
To the cross of Christ give glory
while the endless ages run!

Picture in your mind a tree whose roots are watered by an ever-flowing fountain that becomes a great and living river to water the garden of the entire church. From the trunk of this tree, imagine that there are growing twelve branches that are adorned with leaves, flowers and fruit. Imagine that the leaves are a most effective medicine to prevent and cure every kind of sickness. Let the flowers be beautiful with the radiance of every color and perfumed with the sweetness of every fragrance. Imagine that there are twelve fruits, offered to God's servants to be tasted so that when they eat it, they may always be satisfied, yet never weary of the taste.

BONAVENTURE,
The Tree of Life

High eternal Trinity! O Trinity, eternal Godhead! Love! We are trees of death and you are the tree of life. What a wonder, in your light, to see your creature as a pure tree, a tree you drew out of yourself, supreme purity, in pure innocence! You made this tree free, you gave it branches. But this tree became a tree of death so that it no longer produced any fruits. You engrafted your divinity into the dead tree of our humanity. O sweet tender engrafting! So through you who are life we will produce the fruit of life if we choose to engraft ourselves into you.

CATHERINE
OF SIENA,
PRAYER 17

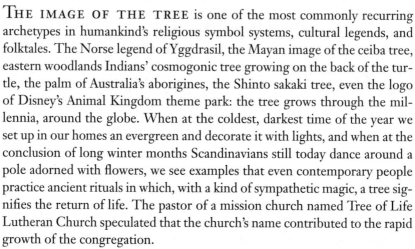

THE IMAGE OF THE TREE is one of the most commonly recurring archetypes in humankind's religious symbol systems, cultural legends, and folktales. The Norse legend of Yggdrasil, the Mayan image of the ceiba tree, eastern woodlands Indians' cosmogonic tree growing on the back of the turtle, the palm of Australia's aborigines, the Shinto sakaki tree, even the logo of Disney's Animal Kingdom theme park: the tree grows through the millennia, around the globe. When at the coldest, darkest time of the year we set up in our homes an evergreen and decorate it with lights, and when at the conclusion of long winter months Scandinavians still today dance around a pole adorned with flowers, we see examples that even contemporary people practice ancient rituals in which, with a kind of sympathetic magic, a tree signifies the return of life. The pastor of a mission church named Tree of Life Lutheran Church speculated that the church's name contributed to the rapid growth of the congregation.

In the ancient Near East and in several lectionary readings, the tree served as a pictorial representation of royal power and national identity. Egyptian court scenes on friezes or papyri depict a tree behind or in the place of the Pharaoh or a divine figure. Also in Ezekiel 17 (Pr6B) and 31, the tree is an image of the monarch or of statehood. Although the Davidic line appears dead and gone, God will replant one of its sprigs on the top of the mountain. The Isaian poems that anticipate the return of the Israelite kingdom (Ad2A, Ad1C) speak of the shoot from the stump of Jesse and the branch springing up for David.

Many churches are now reviving this symbol, for example by sponsoring Advent projects in which parishioners assemble banners that depict a Jesse tree. Such a tree is depicted in many medieval manuscript illustrations and stained glass windows, some of which show detailed biblical history. Usually the great tree grows up out of the loins of the reclining dead Jesse; on the ascending trunk and branches are images of kings and prophets from the thousand years between King David and Christ; and on the top of the tree is the Mary holding the infant Jesus. In the Lutheran church in Lohja, Finland, the entire interior of the church building is covered with a fifteenth-century wall painting intertwined with branches from a Jesse tree. A Jesse tree not only teaches Bible history: first came Jesse, then David, then Solomon, all the way to Mary and Jesus. A tree topped with the baby Jesus illustrates the crowning of the earth by God's incarnation in Christ.

A variation of the tree-as-king-and-nation occurs in the biblical image of Israel as a vine planted by God that is supposed to produce good grapes (Pr22a†, Ea5B, Ea6B, Pr15c°). For Christians, the vine is the church Christ planted, and the grapes both the eucharistic source of our communal nourishment and our fruitful lives. The tree depicts the faithful community. Biblical poetry likens the ungodly to useless weeds or short-lived grass, blown away by the wind, and the godly to a healthy, hearty tree, oaks of righteousness (Ep6c). These images are not so much Jungian pictures of the individual healthy psyche as they are images of the wholesome community of faith. Paul uses this image in his beloved fruits of the Spirit passage (Pr8c), in which the believers are like a fruitful tree. The lectionary also includes an example of the cosmic tree at the center of life. Although world myths provide dozens of examples of this religious image, especially in the Near East, in a climate where water is scarce and vegetation vulnerable, heaven came to be described as a bounteous garden at the center of which is an eternal tree of life. For the Muslim prayer rug, rather than draw a representational picture of the tree in paradise, the ancient desert people developed the paisley pattern as a stylized tree. The idea is that as the devout Muslims pray, they are practicing for life in paradise. The American Shakers believed that their utopian communes were already the beginning of the kingdom of God, so they depicted trees of life on their spirit-drawings. According to Genesis 2, the more mythic of the two Genesis creation stories, God created a perfect garden within which humans are to reside, and in its center was the tree of life. It is explicitly the power of the tree of life to grant immortality that caused God in Genesis 3 to expel Adam and Eve from Eden. Human life in paradise is over, and access to the tree of life is prohibited.

The lectionary includes only the happier part of the story (Ea6c). At the end of time, John's Revelation promises, all will eat from the tree of life in God's paradise. "And the leaves of the tree are for the healing of the nations," promises the visionary. Not only is one ancient nation-state to be revived, but all the nations of the earth will be made whole and will gather around God. This image of the healing tree is significant for the Gbaya Christians in Cameroon, who brought their traditional honoring of the *sore* tree for tribal rituals of healing and reconciliation into Christian iconography and liturgical speech.

The Genesis story includes a second symbolic tree. In the religious iconography of some Near Eastern peoples, the goddess of life resides in a tree or is depicted as a tree. The Canaanite Asherah was represented by a tree or a pole that was removed several times from the temple in Jerusalem. From these accounts we assume that veneration of the tree was practiced in some periods of Israelite history. Perhaps the attraction of the worship of Asherah inspired the Yahwist reformers to prohibit outdoor worship in groves of trees. Probably the identification of the tree with other religion accounted for how seldom the Old Testament likens God to a tree. One exception is the story of the burning bush. Those passages in the wisdom literature, for example Sirach 24, where the tree represents Sophia, the female divine Wisdom, are probably a continuation of the imagery of the goddess as tree.

In the narrative of Garden of Eden (Le1A), we encounter a rewriting of the story in which the tree goddess gives wisdom to woman. Following a classic pattern of the conquering peoples, in which symbolic stories of the conquered are inverted, also the Israelites reconceptualized the old tales, reversing their values. In their telling of the primordial event, the goddess was reenvisioned as a threatening animal, the woman a sinner, wisdom a knowledge of limits, and the tree of knowledge of good and evil a tree not of life but of death.

Any responsible contemporary meditation on the story in Genesis 3 needs to avoid interpretations that, although common in Christian history, are wholly inappropriate today. The interpretation that Eve was not only an example of humanity gone wrong, but also of womankind as the source of sin, permeates the writings of the church fathers, whose biological and sociological worldview accepted males as superior to females. In many situations our society still blames the woman for human tragedies. Contemporary Christians need not imagine as literal historic fact that the human race originated in two humans who were created immortal and sinless and later fell from that state. So what is the meaning of this myth? Although androcentric in its narrative, Genesis 3 provides a profound description of what constitutes human life. We are not children, naked, happy, eating from perpetually fruitful, even magical, trees. Rather, human life is characterized by neediness, ego, labor, sexuality and its pitfalls, deceit, and finally death. The gospel is that into this truth of human existence God speaks a word of promise. Behind the tree of knowledge of good and evil is a glimpse of the tree of life, waiting for us by the mercy of God.

The lectionary includes also examples of the tree of enlightenment. In world religions perhaps the most famous example of this image is of the Buddha, who attains enlightenment while sitting under the bodhi tree, a type of fig tree. Augustine reports that he was sitting under a fig tree at the time of his conversion experience. Jesus spotted Nathanael under a fig tree (Ep2B). Perhaps the similarity between the fig and testicles led to use of the fig as a symbol of vitality. Zaccheus climbs a tree to encounter salvation. The author of the ironic and humorous book of Jonah sits Jonah under a shady bush, which promptly withers away, rather than under a grand tree, as the site of his realization of the mercy of God.

For Christians, the most significant tree lies in paradox. Deuteronomy records that criminals who are particularly cursed by God and the community are to be executed by being hanged on a tree. Both Paul and Luke (Bap<small>A</small>, Ea2c) recall this image when they record primitive kerygmatic proclamation that Christ, who died on a cross, was hanged on a tree. Crucifixions, however, occurred on a pole permanently fixed into the ground, upon which a crossbar and the victim were hoisted. Therefore, early Christian preachers were not describing the execution. They were employing a shocking metaphor when they proclaimed the mystery of the death of Christ: that Christ, both victim and savior, both cursed by all and yet the source of all blessing, was killed on a cross, which was also a tree.

Some early exegetes grounded their use of the cross-tree imagery on a Christian addition to some Septuagint versions of Psalm 96:10, in which "from the tree" had been added to the phrase "The Lord reigns." This phrase is familiar to many Christians because the sixth-century hymnwriter Venantius Fortunatus included it in his famous hymn "Vexilla Regis": "Regnavit a ligno Deus"—"that God the nations' king should be / and reign in triumph from the tree." Composed for Radegund, the abbess of the convent in Poitiers, France, to celebrate the convent's receiving a fragment of the True Cross, the hymn is sung today by many Christians during Holy Week.

This cross-tree was used extensively in Christian iconography. The medieval mosaic covering the east wall of the church of St. Clement in Rome depicts Christ crucified on a magnificent tree laden with flowers and fruits, animals and believers, as if all of creation and all of the church are the birds of the air that take shelter in its shade. The eighth-century Anglo-Saxon poem "The Dream of the Rood" describes a vision in which Christ the conquering warrior climbs up a tree with its red fruits, a tree that is both the bejeweled gold processional cross of liturgical processions and the cross stained with blood.

This paradoxical tree is found in the Markan and Matthean parable of the mustard bush (Pr12A, Pr6B). A mustard seed grows into a bushy annual plant, not in any way an example of the mythic tree of life with all the birds of the air making nest in its shade. The mustard seed, like the cross of crucifixion, is only paradoxically an image of the tree of life. The church honors as a tree of life a tree that is not a tree. This paradox is similar to many other Christian truths: for example, the church gives gifts to God by giving them to the needy, and the faithful encounter the divine when serving one another.

However, the church is beginning to focus also on natural trees. The ecological movement makes us aware of the necessity of forests full of healthy trees for the maintenance of life on this planet. Some contemporary theologians are investigating the concept of panentheism—that God is manifest in all that lives—as a helpful idea for our time, and the tree as an available image of the cosmos. Of course, this symbol, as is the case with all symbols, comes with a caveat. Much of New Age religion employs the tree as a dominant symbol of the life force. Oftentimes this image represents a pantheistic (as distinct from pan*en*theistic) idea that what is alive is what is divine. For pantheists, there is no God who is beyond the universe. Rather, the life of the universe, represented in the tree, is what is divine, and people who are disconnected from natural life and stunted by urbanization can honor what is natural—for example, a magnificent tree—as the source of a better existence. Christians will want their own use of tree imagery to praise God the creator, the benevolence of God before and beyond the natural order encountered in the cycles of the universe. Such praise for creation prods the church to abandon its medieval understanding of the earth as an unfortunate place to be and our existence on it a wretched one. Although many Christians have experienced earth as "a desert drear," a more appropriately Christian response to creation is to see in the magnificence of nature the divine creativity for which we give thanks. For Christians, to be under the tree is to find occasion for praise.

For the church, the tree remains also an image of the community of the faithful. Believers are united in support of one another, without which none of us will bear our fruits. The sap is shared in common. As one, nurtured by the Spirit, we help to heal the nations.

Water

exodus, flood, Jordan,
river, sea, water, well

Related chapters: CREATION, FISH

The lectionary's readings connect water with birth, death, renewal, and cleansing, with the Trinity and with the community. These water references in all their multivalence open up the many meanings of baptism and urge the liturgical assembly to plentiful use of water.

PSALM 63:1

O God, you are my God; eagerly I seek you;
my soul thirsts for you, my flesh faints for you,
as in a barren and dry land where there is no water.

BLESSING OF
THE BAPTISMAL
WATER

Holy God, mighty Lord, gracious Father: We give you thanks, for in the beginning your Spirit moved over the waters and you created heaven and earth. By the gift of water you nourish and sustain us and all living things. By the waters of the flood you condemned the wicked and saved those whom you had chosen, Noah and his family. You led Israel by the pillar of cloud and fire through the sea, out of slavery into the freedom of the promised land. In the waters of the Jordan your Son was baptized by John and anointed with the Spirit. By the baptism of his own death and resurrection your beloved Son has set us from the bondage to sin and death, and has opened the way to the joy and freedom of everlasting life. He made water a sign of the kingdom and of cleansing and rebirth.

THOMAS
HERBRANSON

This is the Spirit's entry now:
the water and the Word,
the cross of Jesus on your brow,
the seal both felt and heard.

This miracle of life reborn
comes from the Lord of breath;
the perfect man from life was torn;
our life comes through his death.

Let water be the sacred sign
that we must die each day
to rise again by his design
as followers of his way.

Renewing Spirit, hear our praise
for your baptismal pow'r
that washes us through all our days.
Lord, cleanse again this hour.

Do not despise the divine laver, nor think lightly of it, as a common thing, on account of the use of water. For the power that operates in the water is mighty, and wonderful are the things that are wrought thereby. When Hagar was in straits for the needs of life, and was herself near death, and her child yet more so, an angel unexpectedly appears, and shows her a well of living water, and drawing near, she saves Ishmael. See here a sacramental type: how from the very first it is by the means of living water—water that was not there before, but was given as a boon by an angel's means—that salvation came to one who was perishing.

GREGORY OF NYSSA, SERMON FOR EPIPHANY

"Listen to what I got to say, you people! There ain't but one river and that's the River of Life, made out of Jesus' Blood. That's the river you have to lay your pain in, in the River of Faith, in the River of Life, in the River of Love, in the rich red river of Jesus' Blood, you people! All the rivers come from that one River and go back to it like it was the ocean sea and if you believe, you can lay your pain in that River and get rid of it because that's the River that was made to carry sin. It's a River full of pain itself, pain itself, moving toward the Kingdom of Christ, to be washed away, slow, you people, slow as this here old red water river round my feet."

FLANNERY O'CONNOR, "The River"

MANY WORLD RELIGIONS CELEBRATE the symbol of water by incorporating in their ritual practice pilgrimages to holy springs, watery rites of initiation, prescribed ablutions, or burial in water. Perhaps because water is so obvious a central religious symbol, we do not give it enough attention, assuming that people readily grasp its many meanings. Yet in a society in which many people never witness childbirth, death by water is relatively rare, purified water is plentiful, and daily showers are routine grooming, it may be that we cannot fathom the multivalence of the water imagery in the lectionary. As in the texts and rituals of many world religions, Christianity uses water in four different ways: to recall birth, to evoke death, to typify renewal, and to suggest washing.

Human life begins swimming in womb waters. The mother knows birth is imminent when her waters flow out, as if the waters could swim the infant out into the world. The Bible includes many birth narratives. A good number of eminent biblical characters enjoyed a miraculous birth: Isaac, Jacob, Samuel, John the Baptist, Jesus. Moses, although born without divine intervention, is saved from infant death by once again being cradled in the water. Water plays a significant role in the creation narratives. According to Genesis 1, the waters existed before the created light; in Genesis 2, a stream arose from the earth before the Garden of Eden was made; in Job 38, God prescribed the bounds for the sea, when its waters burst out from the womb. Furthermore, the people of Israel were born in water. The exodus narrative tells of the creation of the people, who like each person must find a path through the water to emerge alive. Significant encounters are birthed at wells. Eliezer's search for a wife for Isaac and the conversation between Jesus and the Samaritan woman reinforce our sense that from water comes life.

Although humans cannot live long without water, neither can they survive long within it. If the infant does not come out of the water, it dies. Was it because of our psychological awareness of this prenatal condition, or because of memories of the receding ice age, that many ancient cultures told myths of a great flood? Genesis 6–9 interweaves two versions of this myth. The God version is more attuned to natural phenomena, and the LORD version is more indicative of ancient Israelite religion. The ambivalence of water—that which is required for life will readily kill—makes water an apt symbol for much of human experience, in which death always shadows life. Many peoples' survival is based upon an annual flood and its considerable destruction. But perhaps many Westerners do not automatically envision death when seeing water.

Water renews life. Many biblical narratives occur at wells, places where the community gathers to share life. People travel to rivers, lakes, and the sea for bodily renewal and for communal connection. Public parks and shopping malls often contain fountains to help turn artificial places into communal spaces. Some medieval Christian churches and shrines were built near or on top of pagan water sites; reidentifying the source of the water was easier than denying the renewing power of the waters. Although many people in our culture heal their psyche and their relationships by visiting bodies of water, worshipers might not automatically think of water as a symbol of renewal.

Like many other animals, humans instinctively wash themselves clean. Dirt can cause infection; odor attracts enemies and repels friends. Many religions use washing to symbolize preparation for meeting the divine. The Pentateuch details Israelite cleansing rites, and the later prophets use washing as a poetic metaphor for the repentance required of an unfaithful people. Jesus underwent a river washing that John the Baptist hoped would help prepare the people for the coming of the kingdom. According to some ritual practice, presiders are required to wash their hands directly before the eucharist, nowadays not because their hands may be genuinely dirty, but as a symbol of everyone's need to be clean before approaching God. Perhaps because many churchgoers in our culture practice an extremely high level of personal cleanliness, the image of washing may be hard to take seriously.

All these meanings of water are evoked in the Easter Vigil. Restored to the church after centuries of disuse, the Easter Vigil is once again finding its legitimate place as the preeminent liturgy for the celebration of parish baptisms and for the renewal of everyone's baptismal vows. The four, or seven, or twelve readings of the Vigil provide images of Christ's resurrection. The readings are also a sustained meditation on baptism and its connection to the death and resurrection of Christ. By the light of the Vigil candle, we see that baptism is not a charming rite for newborns, scheduled to accommodate the family get-together. Rather, baptism is the momentous ritual of the Christians' birth, death, renewal, and cleansing, occasioned by the events of Good Friday and Easter.

The first reading of the Vigil, the creation story from Genesis 1, is a liturgical poem celebrating the earth's birth. To create the world, the Spirit of God hovers over "the deep," *tehom*, the Hebrew word derived from the name of the water goddess Tiamat, out of whom the ancient Near Eastern divine hero Marduk created the world. Thus although the Israelites discarded the mythic tale of the battle between Tiamat and Marduk, they retained the idea that life comes from water. Like an infant born out of water, so the earth comes out of the primordial waters. On the second day of creation, God separated the waters above the sky from those below the sky. The sky waters provide the rain, the earth waters constitute the rivers and lakes, so that life on earth can flourish and be continually renewed. The flood story is a second creation story. Water once again covers everything, and a second time God brings a new earth out from the birthing waters. The flood story also suggests renewal and cleansing: it is as if God washed the dirt away from an evil world. The central reading of the Vigil, the story of the escape across the Red Sea, is a third creation story. The powers of death are drowned, and the new family of Israel comes to birth after passing through the water.

Other Vigil readings also refer to water. Isaiah 55 both calls the people to drink of the water from God and likens the word of God to the rain, without which the seed will not sprout. Ezekiel 36 incorporates the image of washing. God will sprinkle water on us so that our lives are clean. The reading of the dry bones from Ezekiel 37 suggests water by its absence. Because the bones are dry, with no water, they are scattered about dead and useless. Like the bones, we too are dry and need the renewing water of life.

The Jonah reading is the third chapter, in which Jonah preaches to Nineveh, the Ninevites repent, and God relents from punishing them. In one historic list of Vigil readings, the selection from Jonah was the entire book, probably chosen, not because of the Ninevites' repentance in chapter 3, but because of the water story in chapter 1. Jonah, trying to run away from God, is brought back to life through water. Matthew's gospel cites Jonah's three days in the water as an image of the resurrection. On the walls of a small burial chamber in the catacomb of St. Sebastian in Rome is painted the entire narrative of Jonah, evidence that early Christians saw in the story of Jonah's adventure in the water a metaphor for the salvation of the Christian through baptism. This imagery governs the Vigil's epistle reading from Romans 6, in which Paul likens baptism to Christ's death and the death of our sinful self.

The Vigil is not only the primary time for parish baptisms, but also for the renewal of everyone's baptismal promises. Some clergy are being approached by adults who, not remembering their infant baptism, wish to be rebaptized. However, just as persons do not remember their birth yet annually celebrate it, so at the Vigil the renewal of baptismal vows adds each year another layer of interpretation onto an event we cannot recall.

Many Easter hymns do not mention baptism, and many baptismal hymns focus on a single infant. Fortunately, many newly written hymns express the mighty connection between the waters of baptism, the entire community, and Christ's resurrection. Even when a single child is baptized some time during the church year, singing an Easter baptismal hymn connects the individual baptism to the communal resurrection so apparent during the annual Vigil.

The renewal of baptism encouraged by a revived Easter Vigil should be evident throughout the liturgical year. Churches are holding baptismal festivals on appropriate Sundays, for example the Sunday of the Baptism of Jesus. Baptism is understood as a Christian communal event, not merely a family celebration. Connection with the congregation is encouraged, for example by assigning each baptismal candidate a parish sponsor. Church design situates the font so that people regularly encounter it. The font is open and filled with clean water. Churches are replacing their small basins with much larger, even immersion, fonts. Baptizing babies naked allows for abundant water to be used. Rites of sprinkling baptismal water are part of blessings and absolutions. At a funeral, the paschal candle stands next to casket, as a reminder of the baptism of the deceased.

Many older people remember Lent as a time to trace the passion of Christ. Recalling the baptismal emphasis of the earlier church, however, the lectionary—especially in year A—presents Lent as a time to reinvigorate the community's baptismal life. In the great Johannine narratives, Jesus converses with Nicodemus about birth from above (Le2A), Jesus encounters the woman of Samaria at the well (Le3A), and Jesus heals the man born blind, who washes away his blindness in the pool of Siloam (Le4A). The lectionary's Lenten emphasis focuses not on what happened to Jesus long ago, but on what happens to Christians as they return daily to the water. The Spirit of Christ is bringing new life to the entire baptized community.

Yet another shift in baptismal practice is the rise in Western society of adult baptisms. In medieval Europe, baptism was practiced as we would inoculations: the guardian brings the infant to the practitioner for a private procedure. Because church membership was in some times and places tantamount to citizenship, medieval spirituality did not dwell on the unique gift of baptism. Some Reformation figures, for example Martin Luther and the Anabaptists, placed renewed emphasis on the power of baptism to change life utterly. In many places the contemporary church is returning to early church practice, in which baptismal waters, flowing and full, by typifying the birth, death, renewal, and cleansing, made present the death and resurrection of Christ in a community different from the surrounding culture.

The waters of baptism flow out from the Easter Vigil throughout the liturgical year. On the Sunday of the Baptism of our Lord, the gospel tells of Jesus' own immersion into the waters of the Jordan. Like the people of Israel and like Elijah on the day of his death, Jesus too begins his life by passing through the Jordan. The first reading recalls either the waters of creation (BapA, BapB) or the exodus (Bapc). An Acts reading during Easter (Ea6c) that tells of Peter baptizing new believers is held next to a reading from 1 John about birth in baptism. The imagery of the waters in Noah's flood is mentioned by the author of 1 Peter (Ea6A, Le1B). This passage states explicitly that the floodwaters evoke not cleansing from dirt, but rather the death and resurrection of Christ.

Many prophetic passages throughout the year include the imagery of water. For a desert people, water springing forth from the desert and turning its dust into a garden is a miraculous sign of God's bounty (Ad3A, Ep7B, Pr18B†, Le5c). Water is also a sign of cleansing (Pr26c†). Paul writes that God's love has been poured into our hearts (Trinc) at baptism. The lectionary includes several beloved water narratives. To complement the narrative of the woman at the well, the lectionary appoints the story of the water from the rock, Christ being the water flowing from the rock and the living water we need (Le3A). In the story of Naaman the leper, God heals through water (Pr9c°, Pr23c†). For those who use the semicontinuous first readings, year A includes the narratives of the flood (Pr4A°), Hagar's well (Pr7A°), the exodus (Pr19A°), the water from the rock (Pr21A°), and the crossing of the Jordan (Pr26A°). Jeremiah condemns those whose cisterns are empty (Pr17c°). Those who do not read the semicontinuous Old Testament readings might use Lenten Bible studies to rehearse these wonderful water stories each year.

The church can celebrate water and its many symbolic meanings in many ways. The intercessions can thank God for the gift of water, pray that the earth's waters be plentiful and clean, and plead for those suffering drought and flood. On Maundy Thursday, we wash one another's feet, the ritual juxtaposing the practical matter of cleanliness, the Christian life of service, and the baptism of Christ's death. Some congregations display banners that celebrate water with shimmering blues, greens, and silvers interwoven in long flowing streamers.

Pentecost is an appropriate time for parish baptisms, for water is closely connected with the Spirit of Christ in the world. Tertullian wrote that, like fish, we as Christians are born in water and permanently abide in water. So the water signifies not only God's creative power and Christ's cleansing death, but also the Spirit's infusion within the community. The water also functions as a symbol of one another in the church. Filled with the Spirit, we nourish one another. We are a cup of cold water for one another. The Greek of John 7:38 (Penta) is ambiguous: is the source of the living water Jesus, or the believer? The sacramental Christian responds Yes to both. Christ the water, incarnating God's water of creation, flows continuously in the Spirit, who waters the believers, who themselves become the spring of living water in the world.

Week

first day, forty days, sabbath,
seven days, three days, week

Related chapters: CREATION, DAY OF THE LORD

The sanctification of time is an important goal of much religious ritual. In Christianity, sacred time is interwoven with genuine human time, especially the seven-day week, the first day of the week, three days, and forty days.

PSALM 81:1,
3, 4

Sing with joy to God our strength
    and raise a loud shout to the God of Jacob.
Blow the ram's-horn at the new moon,
    and at the full moon, the day of our feast;
for this is a statute for Israel,
    a law of the God of Jacob.

PROPER PREFACE,
SUNDAYS AFTER
PENTECOST

It is indeed right and salutary that we should at all times
and in all places offer thanks and praise to you, O Lord,
holy Father, through Christ our Lord; who on this day
overcame death and the grave, and by his glorious resurrection opened to us the way of everlasting life.

CHRISTOPHER
WORDSWORTH

O day of rest and gladness,
O day of joy and light,
O balm for care and sadness,
most beautiful, most bright:
On you the high and lowly,
through ages joined in tune,
sing "Holy, holy, holy,"
to the great God triune.

On you, at earth's creation,
the light first had its birth;
on you, for our salvation,
Christ rose from depths of earth;
on you our Lord victorious
the Spirit sent from heav'n;
and thus on you, most glorious,
a threefold light was giv'n.

The first day was the time from Adam until Noah; the second, from Noah to Abraham; the third, from Abraham to David, as the Gospel of Matthew divides it; the fourth, from David to the transmigration into Babylon; the fifth, from the transmigration to the coming of our Lord Jesus Christ. The sixth begins with the coming of our Lord, and we are living in that sixth day. Just as in Genesis we read that the human was fashioned in the image of God on the sixth day, so in our time, as if on the sixth day of the entire era, we are born again in baptism so that we may receive the image of our Creator. But when that sixth day will have passed, rest will come after the judgment, and the holy and just ones of God will celebrate their sabbath. After the seventh day, we shall go to life and rest.

AUGUSTINE,
SERMON 259

There is one church here, and I go to it. On Sunday mornings I quit the house and wander down the hill to the white frame church in the firs. Once, in the middle of the long pastoral prayer of intercession for the whole world—for the gift of wisdom to its leaders, for hope and mercy to the grieving and pained, succor to the oppressed, and God's grace to all—in the middle of this the minister stopped, and burst out, "Lord, we bring you these same petitions every week." After a shocked pause, he continued reading the prayer. Because of this, I like him very much.

ANNIE DILLARD,
Holy the Firm

SCHOLARS OF RITUAL STUDIES distinguish between sacred time and profane time. Profane time is the everyday hours and years of the human community. Each day follows the one before, more similar than not, to the end of an individual's life or perhaps to the demise of human timekeepers. This time is marked by suffering and leads toward death. Sacred time, experienced during religious ritual, breaks out of profane time. Time-outside-of-time, it enacts the hope that the move toward death can be altered. During sacred time, the community rehearses a primordial event, such as the creation of the world or the victory over the demons. By reenacting the beginning, the community redeems time, making it new. It is as if sacred time starts things all over again.

Sacred time is characteristically communal. In the Western world, however, time is increasingly experienced as a personal commodity, the space within which the self realizes a life. Many people go for years without any religious experience of the communal renewal of time. The closest such event for many persons is a New Year's celebration. Yet even this communal partying has the private dimension of New Year's resolutions.

Like other religions, Christianity has its regularly recurring communal rituals of renewal. For Christians, sacred time is not as much time-outside-of-time as it is time-within-time: the power of the divine is made available within regular human time. Each week on Sunday morning, or each year on Easter Eve, Christians do not return to some primordial sacred time. Rather, God comes into the present time to save us. The Spirit of Christ brings the transformative power of that prior sacred time to be concurrent with us here and now. The incarnation did not happen only in perhaps 4 B.C.E. Rather, Christ is born anew in each baptized believer. Ash Wednesday's reading proclaims, "Now is the acceptable time; now is the day of salvation" (AshWABC, Pr7B). Christian ritual always weaves together sacred and profane time, primordial event and contemporary reality, Bible story characters and these people gathered here, then and now. If either the biblical past or the contemporary present overwhelms the other, a loss of Christian meaning results.

The ritual at the reading of the gospel illustrates this pattern. In the medieval church, the lector began the gospel reading with the Latin phrase *in illo tempore*, "at that time": for example, "At that time Jesus said." The scholar of religion Mircea Eliade theorized that sacred time always brought the community back *in illo tempore*, into the timeless past when salvation was available. However, the eucharistic community stands for the reading of gospel because Christ is speaking now, in this lector's words. The *that* time of Jesus' lifetime is now the *this* time of the eucharistic community, within which lives the Spirit of the risen Christ. In the Jewish seder, the family retells the story of the exodus because this very night, this very family is being saved. We do not beam back to some holy past: rather, the salvation we seek comes to us here and now. Eucharistic doctrine uses the Greek word *anamnesis* to articulate this remembering that is more than remembering, a communal recollection that makes present the past event. God saves us in this time just as God saved our ancestors in the past.

The triennial weekly lectionary exemplifies how Christians keep sacred time within profane time. The liturgical year coincides with the natural cycle of earth's Northern Hemisphere. We say Christ is born at the solstice and raised with the new life of springtime. But the lectionary does not merely retell the story of Christ. As the second readings oftentimes make clear, the Spirit of Christ is not back there, but here in this assembly, and we attend to this present community in the real time of life together. Christians further-more acknowledge a third dimension of time we call the eschaton. This mea-ger assembly is not the white-robed multitudes rejoicing in the heavenly city. Full salvation is in the future, in God's final re-creation of all time, at the last day of the LORD. Christian liturgy builds the future upon this present, for during sacred time we practice the meal, the community, the justice, the peace, the perfection of time for which we long.

The ancient world was obsessed with numbers, in ways quite different from our own. Various numbers possessed symbolic significance and nearly magical power. That some modern buildings skip thirteen when numbering their floors is a contemporary holdover of the ancient dread of some num-bers. In the Bible, the numbers with positive symbolic meaning are three, seven, twelve, forty, and a thousand. For units of time, three, seven, and forty recur most often. In the lectionary, seven days, the week, is most important in conceptualizing sacred time.

In most of the Mediterranean world, as far back as records show, calen-dars were set by the phases of moon, its waxing and waning a natural symbol that death is followed by rebirth. Historians do not agree how, when, and why lunar calendars were devised. Neither do historians agree on the origin of the week, one-fourth of the moon's cycle. Yet just as the number seven is common in world religions, the week existed in many ancient cultures, although variously explained: each of the seven visible heavenly bodies has dominion over one day of human activity (the sun over Sunday, the moon over Monday, and so forth); or, the four phases of the moon dictate human patterns, in order to keep human life synchronized with the heavens; or, the number three, associated with heavenly things, added to four, the number of the corners of the earth, equals the perfect number seven. Usually one day of the week was communally celebrated, as market day or religious observance. Even the Pentateuch provides four different explanations for the sabbath day: it recalls God's creation of the world (Exodus 20:11); it celebrates the origin of the people (Deuteronomy 5:15); it typifies the continuing religious covenant (Exodus 21:13); and it exemplifies humane life within the community (Exodus 23:12).

Sabbath became increasingly important for biblical Judaism. The seventh day of the week, the sabbath concluded a cycle of human labor, interrupting life's tasks with a different use of time. Some biblical passages that describe sabbath indicate a day for religious activity, for example, the sacrifice of the lambs. Third Isaiah speaks of the sabbath as a delight. Later, rigorous sabbath regulations helped Israel recall its identity and distinguish itself from its neighbors and oppressors, and breaking the sabbath's proscriptions came to signify apostasy. By the time of the New Testament, synagogue meetings were one of the few approved sabbath activities for Jewish men.

Without a sense of sabbath as a sign of God's holiness among a holy people, we underestimate the significance of Jesus' controversial actions on the sabbath. In Mark 2 (Pr4B), Jesus both picks grain and heals the man with the withered hand on the sabbath. The second activity sets up a debate, but the first activity was expressly forbidden (Exodus 34:21). God did not even provide manna to be gathered on the sabbath. In Luke 13 (Pr16c), Jesus heals a woman with osteoporosis on the sabbath. This reading suggests that God's salvation is greater than religious observances. In God's time, on the sabbath, and in the midst of the praying community, the Spirit of Christ can heal. Judaism teaches that before God rested on the sabbath, God had to create rest: God continually creates, even if what is created is sabbath. Christians teach that the Son does the Father's work by healing on the sabbath. Watching the Son heal, we see the Father creating: in the Spirit of the community, we encounter the Trinity.

The Jewish practice of a weekly meeting around the presence of God continued in Christianity. As John's gospel suggests, it is on the first day of the week and a week later (Ea2ABC) that the risen Christ appears to the disciples. A meeting on the first day of the week characterized Christians, no matter what culture, regardless of whether the day was a workday. The church fathers speak of three Sunday events alive in the community each week: the creation of light at the beginning of time, the resurrection of Christ, and the gift of the Spirit on Pentecost. According to the preface for Sundays of the year, on this day Christ rose from the dead: not a Sunday two millennia ago, not on Easter Day, but today on this first day of the week.

Western consumer culture multiplies options for everything. So churches also are providing weekly worship on Saturday evening, on Thursday night, or via television or Internet to accommodate those for whom Sunday is impossible or inconvenient. The church, however, needs to teach the meaning of Sunday worship, both to enrich the understanding of Sunday and to inform any substitute times the assembly might judge necessary. Christians meet on Sunday, not because it is the society's free day—Sunday is not sabbath—but because God created light, Christ rose from the death, and the Spirit enlivened the community. On each Sunday, baptism assembles the community together, to welcome one another as Christ, to eat together, and to pray for all the needy of the world.

Although *seven days* functions as both literal and symbolic time, *three days* is more wholly symbolic. Any good storyteller knows the technique of three. (1) The story narrates an event; (2) the story establishes an expected pattern by repeating the event; and (3) then it surprises the hearer by altering the pattern the third time. On the third day, relief will come. God comes down onto the mountaintop on the third day. Jesus is found in the temple after three days (Ch1c). At his trial, Jesus is accused of threatening to destroy the temple and rebuild it in three days (PasA, PasB). In Luke 13 (Le2c), Jesus states that on the first and second day he casts out demons and heals, and on the third day finishes his work. That we say Jesus rose on the third day repeats the symbolism that on the third day comes new life. Just as Jonah was released by the fish on the third day, so the poem in Hosea (Pr5A[†]) promises that, despite our current condition of despair, on the third day the LORD will raise us up to live before him.

The time between Jesus' burial on Friday afternoon and his resurrection at dawn on Sunday is not so much three days as it is forty hours. Forty, perhaps originally thought of as the time of one generation, is the most recurring biblical number for religiously significant time. It is forty days or years that numbers the rains of the flood, Moses on Mount Sinai, Israel in the wilderness, the spies scouting out Canaan, Israel in the hands of the Philistines, the taunting by Goliath, the duration of the reigns of Saul, David, and Solomon, Ezekiel lying on his right side, the threat of the destruction of Nineveh, Jesus' temptation, Jesus' days of appearing after the resurrection. A woman's seclusion after birthing a boy was forty days; it went up to eighty after a girl. The word *quarantine* arose during the fourteenth century's outbreak of plague, when a Venetian ruler isolated voyagers for forty days upon their arrival, forty chosen to reiterate Israel's time in the wilderness. Forty is a waiting time, waiting for God, waiting for salvation, waiting for the testing to be completed.

In Luke, Jesus appeared alive after his resurrection for forty days (AscABC). Granted contemporary scientific cosmology, little good is achieved by suggesting that after forty days Jesus rose up into the sky. Instead, forty denotes a waiting time. The forty days of Easter mark the condition of waiting for the Spirit of the risen Christ to be shared amongst all believers, rather than seen by a privileged few. Forty as waiting time can be more fully explored, especially in a culture that prizes instant gratification. Many people spend their lives waiting for food, health, liberty, happiness. Those fortunate enough to have good things are called by the gospel to accompany those who wait. To learn waiting, the church offers Lent. A time of forty days—you don't count the Sundays, since the day of the resurrection cannot be of the forty—Lent enacts waiting, testing, growing time. Previously, much Lenten devotion sought personal improvement through introspection on the passion of Christ. Recently in their use of the three-year lectionary, many churches are returning to the early church practice, in which Lent became the time for both catechumens and longtime believers to immerse themselves into the meaning of baptism. The forty days symbolizes all our waiting for Christ's resurrection to reenliven the whole world.

Another instance of forty days in the lectionary is the forty days of Christmas. The Christmas season concludes on February 2, the presentation of the infant Jesus in the temple. Anciently called Candlemas because its rituals continued to celebrate the light of Christ arriving at the winter solstice, February 2 invites us to join Simeon as he praises God for light. Because our society views Christmas over on December 26, many churches omit a forty-day Christmas celebration. Attention to these forty days, by for example scheduling Christmas events during the six weeks of Christmas, may heighten by contrast the observance of the forty days of Lent.

At the Easter Vigil, the paschal candle is marked both with an Alpha and Omega, the name of God who is beyond time, and with the numerals of this calendar year. The biblical stories about sacred time and the reality of profane time are interwoven, redeeming the present moment with grace. The good news is that the baptized community need not wait for a life after death for time to be redeemed. Redemption is already here, aligned with its past, preparing for its future. We are saved by the resurrection already each week, as we find life in the community that awaits a yet more complete resurrection.

Wind

cloud, earthquake,
rainbow, storm, wind

Related chapters: CREATION, DAY OF THE LORD, JUDGE

Because we think of wind, waves, cloud, and storm as natural events of weather, we miss most of the meaning of such imagery in the lectionary. In the scriptures, wind is a messenger from God, bringing down upon the earth judgment or blessing. Wind is the breath of God, the voice of God's word, a sign of God's Spirit.

PSALM 104:1,
3, 4

O LORD my God, how excellent is your greatness!
    You are clothed with majesty and splendor.
You lay the beams of your chambers in the waters above;
    you make the clouds your chariot;
    you ride on the wings of the wind.
You make the winds your messengers
    and flames of fire your servants.

BENEDICITE,
OMNIA OPERA

All you powers of the Lord, bless the Lord:
    praise and magnify God forever!
You winds of God, bless the Lord;
    you fire and heat, bless the Lord;
You lightnings and clouds, bless the Lord;
    praise and magnify God forever!

JAMES K.
MANLEY

Spirit, Spirit of gentleness,
blow through the wilderness
calling and free;
Spirit, Spirit of restlessness,
stir me from placidness,
wind, wind on the sea.

You moved on the waters,
you called to the deep,
then you coaxed up the mountains
from the valleys of sleep;
and over the eons
you called to each thing:
"Awake from your slumbers
and rise on your wings."

You sang in a stable,
you cried from a hill,
then you whispered in silence
when the whole world was still;
and down in the city
you called once again,
when you blew through your people
on the rush of the wind.

The Lord shows yet greater wonders, that he might make plain to all that he was master both of the sea and the land. Entering into the little boat he causes a storm to arise upon the sea, and causes the winds to blow and the waves to swell up. This storm arose not of its own accord, but in obedience to his power, "who brings forth winds out of his stores." He commands the winds and the sea as their Lord, and upon a sea tossed about and swollen by a great wind and a great tempest, there comes a great calm. By these happenings the Lord gave us a figure and image of his teaching, that we might be patient in the face of every storm.

ORIGEN,
*The Testing
of the Apostles*

I laid down and slept. When I woke the wind was blowing as if it would seize the house into the air. I prayed to the Lord to give me strength. And in a few minutes, I was brought into the shower of flowers, and I seen the blessed saints come through the flowers. These saints came until they filled the house, and the wind was ablowing as if it would destroy everything on the earth. The saints told me that they came to comfort me, and to give me understanding. The wind was the way God made known his power to his little ones in these last days. For this wind could not hurt his saints, for the Holy Ghost carried them over all danger. The wind was to me like a shower of glory. When I found myself again, I woke out of a sweet sleep. It was morning, and the wind was not unusual for a high wind.

REBECCA
JACKSON,
AUTOBIOGRAPHY

≈⟩

To a child's question "Why is there wind?" a newspaper published this meteorologist's answer: "The basic cause of all winds can be traced to contrasts in temperature. Surrounding cooler air rushes in to replace the rising warmer air. This movement of air, from cooler to warmer, is wind." This explanation of wind illustrates how differently contemporary people think from how the ancients did. Many polytheistic religions designate a deity, perhaps the chief deity, as the weather god. Usually imaged as male, this deity was responsible for wind and for all wild weather associated with the wind. Such wind might be beneficial or destructive for the community. The voice of the god was heard as sound of wind, and divine rage as crashes of thunder and strikes of lightning.

The weather god most important for biblical studies is Baal. Although the religion of Canaan honored El as its high god, Baal was more actively involved in the lives of the people and thus the more popular object of worship. The name *Baal* means owner, or lord, the name indicating the supreme importance of weather for the community. Baal, called "the rider of the clouds" and thought to reside on top of the highest mountain in Syria, was depicted as holding two clubs, one thunder and one lightning, with which he had defeated the sea monster Yam. The story in 1 Kings 18 of the contest between the prophets on Mt. Carmel indicates that Baal, as lord of the sky, was recognized as able to send fire down from heaven.

Although the Hebrew Scriptures were given their final shape by strict Yahwist worshipers, considerable borrowing from the imagery of Baal is present in the imagery of YHWH. The wind from God is the voice of God's creative power. The Hebrew noun *ruah* can mean wind, breath, or spirit, and translations of the Bible must choose one noun to describe God's movement over the waters in Genesis 1:2 (VigilABC, TrinA, BapB). This ruah is the spirit or breath of God infusing order into chaos. In the story of the exodus (VigilABC, Pr19A°), the east wind sent by God causes the water to divide so the Israelites can cross over. In Psalm 29, perhaps originally a hymn to Baal, the wind is identified with the voice of God. Psalm 18 (repeated in 2 Samuel 22) describes God as manifested through earthquake, smoke, a devouring fire, volcanic coals, darkness, wind, clouds, rain, hailstones, thunder, and lightning. In Nahum 1, God's anger against Nineveh will take the form of whirlwind, storm, clouds, earthquake, fire, and flood, and will "rebuke the sea and make it dry." In the story of Noah's flood, a wind from God made the waters subside. Daniel 7 indicates that the coming Son-of-man will arrive riding on the clouds of heaven. A name listed in 1 Chronicles 12:6, *Bealiah*, means "Yahweh is Baal." Perhaps for some period of time syncretism was the commonly held belief.

Although the Old Testament contains many references to the wild wind of God's rage, such passages are rare in the lectionary. The poem from Isaiah 64 (Ad1B) asks God to come down to earth in earthquake and fire, but this time with forgiveness. Some ancient myths describe the rainbow as the bridge between the realms of heaven and earth. This idea of covenant, as well as the idea that God's weapon, the bow, has been transformed into a beauteous phenomenon in the sky, concludes one of the two biblical versions of Noah's ark (Le1B).

The Jewish day of Pentecost celebrated the giving of the law on Mt. Sinai. The story in the book of Exodus of the giving of the law is marked by characteristic Baal imagery: God appears on top of a mountain, with thunder, lightning, cloud, and earthquake. Exodus 19:19 says that when Moses talked to God, "God would answer him in thunder." So in Acts 2 (PentABC), God arrives in "a sound like the rush of a violent wind," and fire appears, not on the top of a holy mountain, but on the top of each believer's head. In the Gospel of John, the Christian Pentecost occurs on Easter day when Jesus breathes on the disciples his spirit (Ea2ABC), that same spirit that was released as he died (GFrABC).

Several narratives from the life of Christ use the imagery of the cloud, that phenomenon of weather that the Old Testament identifies with the presence of God. A pillar of cloud was seen as the presence of God leading the people of Israel through the wilderness, and a cloud rested over the tabernacle and later filled the temple in Jerusalem. From this cloud God speaks at Jesus' baptism and transfiguration. Weather imagery is found in the passion and the resurrection accounts in Matthew: at the death of Christ an earthquake rocks Jerusalem (PasA), and on Easter morning an angel (EaA) who resembles lightning descends from heaven, effecting an earthquake. The theophany from Job is paired with the story in Mark of the stilling of the storm (Pr7B†). Like Baal and YHWH of old, Jesus is able to speak his voice over the storm and bring peace to chaos.

The biblical imagery borrowed from the weather god is balanced by the paradoxical imagery in the story of Elijah in the cave (Pr14A†, Pr7c°). Elijah hears the voice of God not in the wind, earthquake, or fire. Rather, God "speaks" in "a sound of sheer silence" (NRSV). This story contains an example of how the Bible first uses, and then rejects, classic religious imagery. Although Elijah's cultural and religious milieu led him to expect that God will speak through the forces of nature, in his greatest despair Elijah encounters a wholly other voice, a voice of silence. This story may be the most helpful of all the Bible's weather stories for contemporary Christians. Although people want to hear God loud and clear—the divine voice tearing open the sky, God's breath like wind blowing seeds to new soil and knocking over dead trees— God's voice is instead often heard as a sound of silence.

Dangers are inherent in using the ancient imagery of the weather god. It suggests an equation between natural disasters and God's anger, as if a tornado signified that God was furious with the victims. The Bible incorporates this ancient worldview, and church history offers many examples of Christians assigning guilt to victims of catastrophic weather. "Who sinned?" asked the disciples, when disaster strikes; but Jesus indicated that such thinking missed the point.

In nearly every case in the lectionary, wind and its effects are vehicles of God's grace. The wind from God creates a good world; God's voice adopting Jesus sounds from a cloud; a whirlwind brings Elijah to heaven; the storm becomes a sign of Christ's mastery over all; the rainbow bridges us from Ash Wednesday toward Easter; and an earthquake accompanies the resurrection. Wind is no terror, but the movement of God's mercy. Even though we think of wind scientifically, as a change in the temperature of air, not as a change in the temperature of God's emotions, some Christians who reject imagery of God's anger still speak of the rain as blessing from God. Because Christians are not deists, the church tries to avoid a wholly secular worldview that divorces God completely from nature.

Perhaps we might think of God, who created the world, as being in the creation, a created universe experienced not only as exhilarating winds, nourishing rains, and picturesque clouds, but also as terrifying tempests and typhoons. The mystery of God, imaged in nature, is both lightning and rainbow, both wild wind and wonderful weather. For some contemporary believers, the language of wind, whirlwind, storm, and earthquake can function as useful imagery for the power of God, which is itself unseen, yet can mightily change what it encounters.

Wisdom

magi, teacher, Torah,
wisdom, Wisdom

Related chapters: PROPHET

In Judaism, God's wisdom is made known through the Torah. In the New Testament, God's wisdom is found in the mystery of Christ's cross and is enacted by the Spirit of God in the Christian community. Some Jewish poems personify Wisdom as a semidivine woman, and some Christians incorporate this female figure into their spirituality.

PSALM 111:10

The fear of the LORD is the beginning of wisdom;
  those who act accordingly have a good understanding.
The praise of the LORD endures forever.

O ANTIPHON,
DECEMBER 17

O Wisdom, proceeding from the mouth of the Most High,
pervading and permeating all creation,
mightily ordering all things:
Come and teach us the way of prudence.

WILLARD F.
JABUSCH

Open your ears, O faithful people,
open your ears and hear God's word.
Open your hearts, O royal priesthood,
God has come to you.
God has spoken to the people,
  hallelujah!
God has spoken words of wisdom,
  hallelujah!

They who have ears to hear the message,
they who have ears, now let them hear;
they who would learn the way of wisdom,
let them hear God's word.
God has spoken to the people,
  hallelujah!
God has spoken words of wisdom,
  hallelujah!

I said, "What did our reasoning convince us of?" Trygetius answered, "That a man who lacks wisdom is in need." "What, then, is being in need?" I asked. "Not to have wisdom," he replied. "But what should be called wisdom except the wisdom of God? We have received on divine authority that the Son of God is none other than the wisdom of God, and the Son of God is truly God. Therefore, whoever possesses God is happy."

AUGUSTINE,
The Happy Life

On top of this dome you see a very beautiful figure standing. She is the great ornament of God and the broad stairway of all the other virtues that live in God, joined to God in sweet embrace in a dance of ardent love. This figure represents the Wisdom of God, for through her all things are created and ruled by God. She is adorned with the holy and just commandments, which are green like the first sprouts of the patriarchs and prophets, and white like the virginity of Mary, and red like the faith of the martyrs, and brilliant blue like the lucent love of contemplation which, by the ardor of the Holy Spirit, mandates love for God and one's neighbor.

HILDEGARD
OF BINGEN,
Scivias

Because religion is one way that a people cope with the problems of nature and society, religion usually makes claims of wisdom. Perhaps the earliest stage of the wisdom genre is aphorisms, short memorable sayings that convey knowledge of the created world, the values of human experience, and the moral traditions of that society. Truths are passed down in what are pejoratively called old wives' tales. Organizing lists of wisdom sayings later becomes an art or science, and cultures evolve systems of theology or philosophy. The philosopher Plato considered wisdom to be the supreme virtue. Ancient courts maintained schools of advisers who taught everything from table manners to political savvy. Only by everyone heeding such wisdom would the state function properly. In Aeschylus's play *The Eumenides*, it is Athena, the goddess of wisdom, whose judgment ensures orderly life in the civilized city of Athens.

Within religious systems, wisdom is described as one manifestation of the divine. Some polytheistic religions have a deity identified as wisdom who is venerated in hopes that the suppliants will receive the wisdom to survive and thrive. One example is the Egyptian goddess Maat, who represented an ideal resembling the Confucian Way: wisdom entails knowing and living according to the order we see in creation; embodying such wisdom will ensure an orderly life in society. Some scholars claim that Maat was the precursor of the biblical figure of Wisdom.

The Hebrew word *hokmah* implies that wisdom entails skill and ability. Bezalel, famed for his wisdom, was the builder of Moses' tabernacle. The Israelite tradition developed an entire literary genre that includes aphorisms about nature and table manners (e.g., in the book of Proverbs), alphabetical acrostics (e.g., Psalm 25), essays from the sage (e.g., Baruch), reflections of the skeptic (e.g., Ecclesiastes), and praises of Wisdom's reign over the universe (e.g., Sirach 24). Although little connection is made between this genre and Israel's remembrance of salvation history, some wisdom literature, for example Psalm 119, affirms that true wisdom is found in the Torah. The poems that laud Wisdom as a female figure indicate influence by neighboring wisdom goddesses and Greek philosophy. Scholars do not agree whether the sages of the late wisdom school employed the image of heavenly woman as a poetic device or actually venerated Sophia as a goddess. In either case, glorification of the female Wisdom coincided with a period of intensified androcentrism in Israelite society. Often in religion, the higher the goddess, the lower the women. History does not offer many examples of the contemporary assertion that goddess veneration ensures women's equality and self-esteem.

Several New Testament epistles continue the language of the wisdom literature. The Christian writers describe the difference between the world's wisdom and the wisdom that comes from the Spirit of Christ. In most of the New Testament, the feminine noun *sophia*, "wisdom," gives way to the masculine noun *logos*, "word." Perhaps the early church was distancing itself from gnosticism, which celebrated the presence and power of Sophia. Perhaps the move away from sophia reflected that century's intellectual misogyny. Philo, for example, wrote that because what is feminine cannot possibly indicate eminence, the highest religious value must be expressed in masculine terms.

Yet Christians continued some evocation of wisdom in their descriptions of Christ. Today some churches use the seven ninth-century "O" antiphons during Advent, and many more are familiar with the hymn based on the antiphons, "O come, O come, Emmanuel." These antiphons, each of which invokes a name or an image for the coming Christ, begin on December 17 with the image of Christ as Wisdom, whose arrival will ensure a renewed creation. The antiphon relies for its imagery on the biblical poems in which at the beginning of time God created Wisdom first (e.g., Proverbs 8:22) or, even, Wisdom herself "makes all things new" (Wisdom 7:27). The Eastern church makes considerable use of the term *Hagia Sophia* in its liturgical language and in the naming of its churches. A sculpture popular in early medieval times called The Throne of Wisdom depicted Mary seated as if to evoke a chair and holding on her lap the child Jesus.

The lectionary uses the wisdom genre in several different ways. Passages from the epistles discuss the wisdom that comes from the Spirit of Christ, a wisdom unlike that of the world. The wisdom of Christ is manifest in the cross and through the Spirit within the community, argues Paul in 1 Corinthians (Ep4A, Ep5A, Le3B). The letter to the Ephesians carries the same message. The wisdom of God has been made known through the mystery of Christ (Pr10B). Ephesians 3 uses parallel terms: believers will come "to comprehend" and "to know" the love of Christ that surpasses knowledge (Pr12B). To know Christ is to have wisdom.

By extension, wisdom is now expressed within the life of the Christian community. We are to live wisely (Pr15B). As the book of James says, wisdom will govern everything the community does, both within itself and outside in the world (Pr20B). The complaints of the Teacher in Ecclesiastes (Pr13c†) indicate that the wisdom of the world finally ends in death and affords nothing. The famous chapter on love from 1 Corinthians seems influenced by the wisdom genre (Ep4c). The Christian lives in love as the manner of knowing in part and moving on toward knowing fully.

In the Epiphany narrative, the magi, those who read the stars and understand the orderly ways of the universe, come to acknowledge the mystery of Christ. Their lives will be shaped in wisdom by Wisdom (EpABC). Some Christians continue the annual custom of marking the lintel of their outside doorway each Epiphany with the numerals of the year and the letters C, M, and B. The letters stand both for the traditional names of the magi, Caspar, Melchior, and Balthasar, and for the Latin phrase *Christe mansionem benedica,* "Christ, bless this house." The ritual is accompanied with a prayer for wisdom.

As the book of Baruch makes clear, the wisdom that God gives the chosen people is manifest in the Torah. Far more than a genre dealing with etiquette, the Torah is the wisdom of God. The New Testament depicts Christ as the ultimate manifestation of the Torah. At the beginning of Jesus' ministry, people inquire into the source of this wisdom (Pr9B). In Matthew 11 (Pr9A), Jesus cites wisdom and describes God's truth as other than what is normally known by the wise. Some biblical translations use the feminine pronoun *her* in verse 19, indicating that the wisdom Jesus cites is Wisdom herself. The wisdom encountered in Christ is a paradoxical wisdom, an illogical truth. In an evocation of Sirach 51:23-26, Jesus calls to the wise and promises an easy yoke. The picture of Jesus as the new teacher of divine wisdom undergirds the sermon on the mount in Matthew's gospel (Ep5A, Ep6A, Ep7A, Pr3A, Pr4A) and the Lucan parallels (Ep6c, Ep7c).

The lectionary includes several biblical passages that personify wisdom as a regal woman. Wisdom herself invites the people into the wholesome life she grants (VigilABC, Trinc, Pr15B†, Pr19B°). The passage from Proverbs 9 is particularly useful for Christians. The foolish woman offers stolen water and bread eaten in secret, but the church, following Wisdom who serves up bread and wine, offers water flowing freely in baptism and bread shared in the weekly meal. The narrative of King Solomon choosing wisdom over riches (Pr12A†, Pr15B°) is perhaps a refined version of ancient Near Eastern stories in which the king unites with the goddess of wisdom to ensure an upright reign. The christological descriptions in Colossians 1 (Pr11c, Lastc) and in Hebrews 1 (ChDyABC, Pr22B) appropriated Sophia poetry for Christian use.

Much medieval Christianity, still influential in the popular understanding of the church's beliefs, connects Christ mainly with salvation after death.

But as the epistles teach, the body of Christ is to live out God's wisdom in this world, and we do so by honoring God's created order and helping one another to live a moral life. The church is called to embody the wisdom of Christ. Yet knowledge of church history and awareness of contemporary Christian practices demonstrate that wisdom in daily life remains an elusive goal.

Still, Christ is not a Confucius, an old wise man teaching that by adhering strictly to a preordained order, the society will live in peace. Christianity teaches that humans will not be able to follow any natural order and that, thanks to the paradoxical surprise we term *gospel*, the resurrection is God's sign that divine wisdom is creating all things new. The Bible's eschatology proclaims that the creation that fully manifests God's wisdom is still in the future. Christ as Wisdom is more than the ecological interdependence of the universe, other than the logical conclusions of the philosopher. Christ is a wisdom beyond the world, a wisdom of grace and mercy.

As the church reincorporates wisdom into its vocabulary, it will see how useful for contemporary consciousness is the depiction of Wisdom. Some theologians judge that the Sophia image offers a necessary balance to the church's male soteriological imagery. Although early theologians taught that Christ became human and took into himself all humanity, much church language and policy has suggested that in some way males are more fully redeemed than females. Let Wisdom, the magnificent wise woman who creates, thinks, orders, judges, and as an emissary of God serves up a meal of bread and wine, take her place along with other images of Christ. Some images are objective (Door), others masculine (King), others nongender-specific (Shepherd), still others abstract (Truth). The goal is not to revive an ancient Near Eastern goddess but to bring all our treasures into the liturgy. Each treasure glistens in its own way. Perhaps Wisdom can radiate for contemporary believers the beneficent mercy of the community of Christ.

Afterword

You, O Christ, are the kingdom of heaven;
You, the land promised to the gentle;
You, the grazing lands of paradise;
You, the ineffable marriage chamber;
You, the bread of life, the unheard of drink;
You, both the urn for the water and the life-giving water;
You, the inextinguishable lamp for each one of the saints;
You, the garment and the crown,
You, inaccessible sun, will shine in our midst,
and all will shine brightly,
to the degree of their illumination by your Spirit. . . .
SYMEON

IMAGINE YOURSELF STANDING in the center of the nave of the fif-teenth-century Lutheran church in Lohja, Finland. You are looking toward the altar. On the right front wall, at, say, one o'clock, is a twelve-foot-high painting of creation. At two o'clock is the fall, and at three, over the door most often used, is the birth of Christ. Next comes a Jesse tree, and then the ministry of Christ. Along the back wall is Christ's passion and death, and up the left side of the nave are the resurrection appearances. At nine o'clock, opposite the main door, is an enormous Saint Christopher. At ten and eleven o'clock are the last judgment and images of heaven and hell, and above the altar a classic depiction of the Trinity.

But the images of the life of Christ are only the beginning. On all the vaults of the ceiling are images from Old Testament stories, sometimes, like cartoons, with each episode of the narrative shown. Above the altar are scenes of the exodus and the manna in the wilderness. And in between all the biblical scenes are pictures from the lives of the saints. There is Queen Helena finding the True Cross, and there Catherine of Alexandria, with her wheel, and as in many Scandinavian churches, on each side of each pillar is a saint, holding up the church.

But there is more. The tree of Jesse extends its swirling branches through-out the entire church building. Each episode in the life of Christ, each of the Old Testament narratives, each depiction of a saint is bordered by the cir-cling branches of an encompassing vine that entwines everything back to the Jesse tree. The small tendrils of the branches reach down to you, and you discover that you too have a place on the tree. It is as if 500 years ago the painter illustrated the recent hymn:[1]

Christ, holy Vine, Christ, living Tree,
be praised for this blest mystery:
that Word and water thus revive
and join us to your Tree of Life.

During the liturgy, you are in the images, so that, after the liturgy, the images can be in you.

That is the hope for this book.

Appendixes
and Indexes

Revised Common Lectionary Images

Advent, Christmas, Epiphany

Advent 1	day of the LORD; light, mountain
Advent 2	prophet; fire, tree
Advent 3	prophet; harvest, journey, water
Advent 4	name of God; mother, prophet
Christmas Eve	poor; kingdom, light, mother
Christmas Day	emanation; creation, kingdom, light
Christmas 1	family; prophet, sacrifice
Christmas 2	light; family, Israel
Epiphany	kingdom; light, prophet, wisdom
Baptism of the Lord	water; creation, judge, servant
Epiphany 2	name of God; Israel, sacrifice, servant
Epiphany 3	fish; cross, light
Epiphany 4	poor; mountain, sacrifice, wisdom
Epiphany 5	light; food, wisdom
Epiphany 6	judge; covenant, harvest, heaven-earth-hell
Epiphany 7	outsider; Israel, temple
Transfiguration	light; mountain, wind

Lent, Easter

Ash Wednesday	treasure; day of the LORD, Israel
Lent 1	week; food, judge, tree
Lent 2	mother; judge, heaven-earth-hell, Israel
Lent 3	water; judge, outsider
Lent 4	light; judge, kingdom
Lent 5	Spirit; light, Israel
Passion Sunday	kingdom; judge, servant
Maundy Thursday	servant; food, sacrifice
Good Friday	name of God; servant, temple
Easter Vigil	resurrection;
	Gen 1 creation, Gen 7-9 water, Gen 22 sacrifice,
	Exod 14 battle, Isa 55 food, Prov 8 wisdom,
	Ezek 36 body, Ezek 37 Spirit, Zeph 3 city,
	Jonah 3 prophet, Deut 31 covenant, Dan 3 fire

A primary image for the day is listed first; secondary images are listed after the semicolon. Images related to the semicontinuous readings in the season after Pentecost are indicated by °.

Easter Day	resurrection; garden, heaven-earth-hell, Israel
Easter 2	body; family, kingdom
Easter 3	food; prophet, sacrifice
Easter 4	shepherd; judge, food
Easter 5	journey; heaven-earth-hell, mother, temple
Easter 6	Spirit; judge, water
Ascension	heaven-earth-hell; body, week
Easter 7	name of God; battle, Israel
Pentecost	Spirit; body, day of the LORD, prophet
Trinity	name of God; creation, family

Sundays after Pentecost

Proper 3	food; judge, mother
Proper 4	name of God; covenant, judge °water
Proper 5	body; family, judge °journey
Proper 6	shepherd; covenant, sacrifice °mother
Proper 7	family; prophet, resurrection °water
Proper 8	name of God; prophet, servant °sacrifice
Proper 9	wisdom; battle, kingdom °marriage
Proper 10	harvest; garden, judge, Spirit °family
Proper 11	harvest; day, name of God, Spirit °heaven-earth-hell
Proper 12	treasure; family, wisdom °covenant
Proper 13	food; covenant, Israel °battle
Proper 14	wind; mountain, prophet °clothing
Proper 15	outsider; Israel, temple °food
Proper 16	city; body, Israel °mother
Proper 17	cross; battle, prophet °name of God
Proper 18	Israel; light, prophet °sacrifice
Proper 19	servant; family, judge °water
Proper 20	harvest; body, outsider °food
Proper 21	outsider; judge, servant °water
Proper 22	servant; harvest, treasure, tree °judge
Proper 23	food; city, mountain °sacrifice
Proper 24	kingdom; name of God, prophet °name of God
Proper 25	kingdom; judge, mother °prophet
Proper 26	servant; city, family °water
Proper 27	light; day, resurrection, marriage °covenant
Proper 28	servant; battle, day, light °prophet
Last	judge; body, kingdom, shepherd

RCL YEAR B

Advent, Christmas, Epiphany

Advent 1	day of the LORD; servant, treasure, wind
Advent 2	journey; city, day of the LORD
Advent 3	prophet; clothing, water
Advent 4	mother; kingdom, prophet
Christmas Eve	poor; kingdom, light, mother
Christmas Day	emanation; creation, kingdom, light
Christmas 1	sacrifice; family, light
Christmas 2	light; family, Israel
Epiphany	kingdom; light, prophet, wisdom
Baptism of the Lord	water; Spirit, creation
Epiphany 2	name of God; body, prophet
Epiphany 3	fish; day of the LORD, week
Epiphany 4	prophet; name of God, sacrifice
Epiphany 5	body; creation, journey, servant
Epiphany 6	outsider; body, journey, prophet
Epiphany 7	body; Spirit, water
Transfiguration	mountain; heaven-earth-hell, light, wind

Lent, Easter

Ash Wednesday	treasure; day of the LORD, Israel
Lent 1	journey; covenant, week, water
Lent 2	cross; family, mother
Lent 3	temple; covenant, wisdom
Lent 4	cross; body, light, treasure
Lent 5	harvest; marriage, temple
Passion Sunday	kingdom; judge, servant
Maundy Thursday	servant; food, sacrifice
Good Friday	name of God; servant, temple
Easter Vigil	resurrection;
	Gen 1 creation, Gen 7-9 water, Gen 22 sacrifice,
	Exod 14 battle, Isa 55 food, Prov 8 wisdom,
	Ezek 36 body, Ezek 37 Spirit, Zeph 3 city,
	Jonah 3 prophet, Deut 31 covenant, Dan 3 fire
Easter Day	resurrection; food, garden, judge, prophet
Easter 2	body; Israel, prophet
Easter 3	body; family, name of God
Easter 4	shepherd; covenant, name of God
Easter 5	tree; sacrifice, prophet

Easter 6	covenant; mother, water
Ascension	heaven-earth-hell; body, week
Easter 7	emanation; name of God, Israel
Pentecost	judge; day of the LORD, mother, Spirit
Trinity	mother; family, Spirit, temple

Sundays after Pentecost

Proper 3	food; covenant, marriage
Proper 4	week; light, servant °prophet
Proper 5	battle; family, garden, heaven-earth-hell, °kingdom
Proper 6	tree; harvest, judge °shepherd
Proper 7	wind; creation, week °covenant
Proper 8	body; battle, poor °battle
Proper 9	journey; heaven-earth-hell, Israel °kingdom
Proper 10	prophet; family, kingdom °temple
Proper 11	shepherd; battle, kingdom, temple °kingdom
Proper 12	food; name of God, wisdom °marriage
Proper 13	food; body, heaven-earth-hell °prophet
Proper 14	food; emanation, sacrifice °family
Proper 15	food; body, wisdom °wisdom
Proper 16	food; battle, covenant °temple
Proper 17	body; covenant, harvest, poor °marriage
Proper 18	body; outsider, poor, water °poor
Proper 19	cross; fire, judge °wisdom
Proper 20	servant; judge, wisdom °family
Proper 21	name; heaven-earth-hell, mother, Spirit °battle
Proper 22	marriage; emanation, kingdom °heaven-earth-hell
Proper 23	treasure; judge, poor °judge
Proper 24	servant; sacrifice, temple °creation
Proper 25	light; Israel, sacrifice °family
Proper 26	covenant; sacrifice, temple °family
Proper 27	poor; food, sacrifice °mother
Proper 28	day of the LORD; battle, temple °mother
Last	kingdom; day of the LORD, name °kingdom

RCL YEAR C

Advent, Christmas, Epiphany

Advent 1	day of the LORD; kingdom, tree
Advent 2	journey; prophet, temple
Advent 3	fire; city, Israel
Advent 4	mother; kingdom, sacrifice
Christmas Eve	poor; kingdom, light, mother
Christmas Day	emanation; creation, kingdom, light
Christmas 1	temple; clothing, family
Christmas 2	light; family, Israel
Epiphany	kingdom; light, prophet, wisdom
Baptism of the Lord	Spirit; heaven-earth-hell, name of God, Israel
Epiphany 2	food; marriage, Spirit
Epiphany 3	prophet; body, Israel
Epiphany 4	outsider; prophet, wisdom
Epiphany 5	fish; judge, temple
Epiphany 6	poor; resurrection, tree
Epiphany 7	covenant; creation, food, harvest
Transfiguration	mountain; light, wind

Lent, Easter

Ash Wednesday	treasure; day of the LORD, Israel
Lent 1	week; food, harvest, name of God
Lent 2	mother; covenant, fire, heaven-earth-hell
Lent 3	judge; food, harvest, journey
Lent 4	food; family, judge
Lent 5	body; treasure, water
Passion Sunday	kingdom; judge, servant
Maundy Thursday	servant; food, sacrifice
Good Friday	name of God; servant, temple
Easter Vigil	resurrection;
	Gen 1 creation, Gen 7-9 water, Gen 22 sacrifice, Exod 14 battle, Isa 55 food, Prov 8 wisdom, Ezek 36 body, Ezek 37 Spirit, Zeph 3 city, Jonah 3 prophet, Deut 31 covenant, Dan 3 fire
Easter Day	resurrection; garden, judge, mountain
Easter 2	body; kingdom, name of God, week
Easter 3	fish; light, shepherd
Easter 4	shepherd; body, clothing
Easter 5	emanation; marriage, outsider, water

Easter 6	judge (water); Israel, tree
Ascension	heaven-earth-hell; body, week
Easter 7	Israel; day of the LORD, name of God
Pentecost	emanation; city, day of the LORD, family
Trinity	emanation; creation, water, wisdom

Sundays after Pentecost

Proper 3	wisdom; harvest, resurrection
Proper 4	outsider; family, temple °sacrifice
Proper 5	poor; body, prophet °food
Proper 6	servant; judge, kingdom °kingdom
Proper 7	body; clothing, outsider °wind
Proper 8	journey; prophet, servant, Spirit °heaven-earth-hell
Proper 9	journey; harvest, mother °outsider
Proper 10	outsider; covenant, harvest °prophet
Proper 11	food; body, creation, mother °food
Proper 12	family; body, judge °marriage
Proper 13	treasure; clothing, wisdom °family
Proper 14	day of the LORD; city, family °sacrifice
Proper 15	day of the LORD; journey, prophet °tree
Proper 16	week; fire, mountain °prophet
Proper 17	food; kingdom, outsider, sacrifice °water
Proper 18	cross; covenant, family °creation
Proper 19	treasure; fire, judge, shepherd °creation
Proper 20	servant; battle, poor °body
Proper 21	heaven-earth-hell; poor, treasure °kingdom
Proper 22	servant; family, judge °city
Proper 23	outsider; prophet, water °city
Proper 24	judge; battle, prophet °covenant
Proper 25	outsider; battle, Israel °food, day
Proper 26	outsider; sacrifice, water °judge
Proper 27	resurrection; day of the LORD, family °temple
Proper 28	day of the LORD; fire, name of God °city
Last	kingdom; body, light, shepherd

January 1
Holy Name of Jesus   name of God; family, mother, sacrifice

January 1
New Year's Day   judge; week, kingdom

February 2
Presentation   light; family, sacrifice

March 25
Annunciation   mother; prophet, sacrifice

May 31
Visitation   poor; mother, Israel

September 14
Holy Cross   cross; body, wisdom

November 1
All Saints, A   poor; kingdom, shepherd, family
All Saints, B   body; food, mountain, marriage
All Saints, C   poor; kingdom, Spirit

Thanksgiving, A   body; covenant, harvest
Thanksgiving, B   clothing; harvest, battle
Thanksgiving, C   food; journey, sacrifice

Roman Lectionary (Revised) Images

Advent Season, Christmas Season

Advent 1	day of the LORD; light, mountain
Advent 2	prophet; fire, tree
Advent 3	prophet; harvest, water
Advent 4	name of God; mother, prophet
Christmas Midnight	poor; kingdom, light, mother
Christmas Day	emanation; creation, kingdom, light
Holy Family	family; prophet, body
Christmas 2	light; family, wisdom
Epiphany	kingdom; light, prophet, wisdom
Baptism of the Lord	water; judge, servant

Lenten Season, Easter Triduum, Easter Season

Ash Wednesday	treasure; day of the LORD, Israel
Lent 1	week; food, judge, tree
Lent 2	light; mountain, journey
Lent 3	water; judge, outsider
Lent 4	light; judge, kingdom
Lent 5	Spirit; light, Israel
Passion Sunday	kingdom; judge, servant
Holy Thursday	servant; food, sacrifice
Good Friday	name of God; servant, sacrifice
Easter Vigil	resurrection;
	Gen 1 creation, Gen 22 sacrifice,
	Exod 14 battle, Isa 54 marriage,
	Isa 55 food, Bar 3 wisdom,
	Ezek 36 body
Easter Day	resurrection; garden, heaven-earth-hell, Israel
Easter 2	body; family, food
Easter 3	food; prophet, sacrifice, kingdom
Easter 4	shepherd; judge, Spirit
Easter 5	journey; food, temple
Easter 6	Spirit; water, covenant

A primary image for the day is listed first; secondary images are listed after the semicolon.

445

Ascension	mountain; body, week
Easter 7	name of God; Spirit, Israel
Pentecost Sunday	Spirit; body, day of the LORD, prophet
Trinity Sunday	name of God; mountain, family
Body and Blood	food; body, journey

Ordinary Time

2 ordinary	name of God; Israel, sacrifice, servant
3 ordinary	fish; cross, light
4 ordinary	poor; mountain, Israel, wisdom
5 ordinary	light; food, wisdom
6 ordinary	judge; covenant, wisdom, heaven-earth-hell
7 ordinary	outsider; Israel, temple
8 ordinary	food; judge, mother
9 ordinary	name of God; covenant, judge
10 ordinary	body; judge, wind
11 ordinary	shepherd; covenant, sacrifice
12 ordinary	family; prophet, covenant
13 ordinary	name of God; prophet, resurrection, family
14 ordinary	wisdom; resurrection, kingdom
15 ordinary	harvest; servant, Spirit
16 ordinary	harvest; day of the LORD, judge, Spirit
17 ordinary	treasure; family, wisdom
18 ordinary	food; covenant, battle
19 ordinary	wind; mountain, Israel
20 ordinary	outsider; Israel, temple
21 ordinary	city; wisdom, kingdom
22 ordinary	cross; sacrifice, prophet
23 ordinary	Israel; covenant, prophet
24 ordinary	servant; covenant, judge
25 ordinary	harvest; body, heaven-earth-hell
26 ordinary	outsider; judge, servant
27 ordinary	servant; harvest, tree
28 ordinary	food; mountain, treasure
29 ordinary	kingdom; name of God, prophet
30 ordinary	kingdom; poor, prophet
31 ordinary	servant; covenant, mother
32 ordinary	light; wisdom, resurrection, marriage
33 ordinary	servant; family, day of the LORD, light
Last	judge; resurrection, kingdom, shepherd

RL YEAR B

Advent Season, Christmas Season

Advent 1	day of the LORD; servant, treasure, wind
Advent 2	journey; city, day of the LORD
Advent 3	prophet; clothing, water
Advent 4	mother; kingdom, prophet
Christmas Midnight	poor; kingdom, light, mother
Christmas Day	emanation; creation, kingdom, light
Holy Family	sacrifice; family, mother
Christmas 2	light; family, wisdom
Epiphany	kingdom; light, prophet, wisdom
Baptism of the Lord	water; Spirit, covenant

Lenten Season, Easter Triduum, Easter Season

Ash Wednesday	treasure; day of the LORD, Israel
Lent 1	journey; covenant, week, water
Lent 2	light; sacrifice, judge
Lent 3	temple; covenant, wisdom
Lent 4	cross; temple, light, treasure
Lent 5	harvest; marriage, temple
Passion Sunday	kingdom; judge, servant
Holy Thursday	servant; food, sacrifice
Good Friday	name of God; servant, temple
Easter Vigil	resurrection;
	Gen 1 creation, Gen 22 sacrifice,
	Exod 14 battle, Isa 54 marriage,
	Isa 55 food, Bar 3 wisdom,
	Ezek 36 body
Easter Day	resurrection; garden, judge, prophet,
	heaven-earth-hell
Easter 2	body; Israel, prophet
Easter 3	body; covenant, name of God
Easter 4	shepherd; family, name of God
Easter 5	tree; covenant, prophet
Easter 6	covenant; mother, water
Ascension	heaven-earth-hell; body, week
Easter 7	emanation; Spirit, Israel
Pentecost Sunday	judge; day of the LORD, tree, Spirit
Trinity Sunday	name of God; family, Spirit, covenant
Body and Blood	food; sacrifice, covenant

Ordinary Time

2 ordinary	name of God; body, prophet
3 ordinary	fish; day of the LORD, week
4 ordinary	prophet; name of God, family
5 ordinary	body; prophet, journey, servant
6 ordinary	outsider; body, prophet
7 ordinary	body; Spirit, water
8 ordinary	food; covenant, marriage
9 ordinary	week; light, servant
10 ordinary	battle; family, garden, heaven-earth-hell
11 ordinary	tree; harvest, judge
12 ordinary	wind; creation, water
13 ordinary	body; creation, poor
14 ordinary	journey; heaven-earth-hell, Israel
15 ordinary	prophet; family, kingdom
16 ordinary	shepherd; battle, kingdom
17 ordinary	food; name of God, body
18 ordinary	food; Spirit, clothing
19 ordinary	food; emanation, sacrifice
20 ordinary	food; body, wisdom
21 ordinary	food; family, covenant
22 ordinary	body; covenant, harvest, poor
23 ordinary	body; outsider, poor, water
24 ordinary	cross; food, judge
25 ordinary	servant; prophet, wisdom
26 ordinary	name of God; heaven-earth-hell, prophet, poor
27 ordinary	marriage; heaven-earth-hell, family
28 ordinary	treasure; judge, wisdom
29 ordinary	servant; sacrifice, kingdom
30 ordinary	light; Israel, sacrifice
31 ordinary	covenant; sacrifice, temple
32 ordinary	poor; food, sacrifice
33 ordinary	day of the LORD; battle, temple
Last	kingdom; day of the LORD, name of God

RL YEAR C

Advent Season, Christmas Season

Advent 1	day of the LORD; kingdom, tree
Advent 2	journey; prophet, clothing
Advent 3	fire; city, Israel
Advent 4	mother; kingdom, sacrifice
Christmas Midnight	poor; kingdom, light, mother
Christmas Day	emanation; creation, kingdom, light
Holy Family	temple; family, mother, covenant
Christmas 2	light; family, wisdom
Epiphany	kingdom; light, prophet, wisdom
Baptism of the Lord	Spirit; heaven-earth-hell, shepherd, judge

Lenten Season, Easter Triduum, Easter Season

Ash Wednesday	treasure; day of the LORD, Israel
Lent 1	week; food, harvest, name of God
Lent 2	mountain; light, sacrifice, journey
Lent 3	judge; name of God, harvest, journey
Lent 4	food; family, judge
Lent 5	marriage; treasure, water
Passion Sunday	kingdom; judge, servant
Holy Thursday	servant; food, sacrifice
Good Friday	name of God; servant, temple
Easter Vigil	resurrection; Gen 1 creation, Gen 22 sacrifice, Exod 14 battle, Isa 54 marriage, Isa 55 food, Bar 3 wisdom, Ezek 36 body
Easter Day	resurrection; garden, judge, heaven-earth-hell
Easter 2	body; day of the LORD, name of God, week
Easter 3	fish; name of God, shepherd
Easter 4	shepherd; prophet, clothing
Easter 5	emanation; marriage, prophet, water
Easter 6	judge; prophet, city
Ascension	heaven-earth-hell; body, week, light
Easter 7	Israel; day of the LORD, heaven-earth-hell
Pentecost Sunday	emanation; city, day of the LORD, family
Trinity Sunday	emanation; creation, water, wisdom
Body and Blood	food; prophet, temple

Ordinary Time

2 ordinary	food; marriage, Spirit
3 ordinary	prophet; body, Israel
4 ordinary	outsider; prophet, wisdom
5 ordinary	fish; judge, temple
6 ordinary	poor; resurrection, tree
7 ordinary	covenant; creation, food
8 ordinary	wisdom; harvest, resurrection
9 ordinary	outsider; family, temple
10 ordinary	poor; body, prophet
11 ordinary	servant; judge, kingdom
12 ordinary	cross; clothing, family
13 ordinary	journey; prophet, servant, Spirit
14 ordinary	journey; body, mother
15 ordinary	outsider; covenant, creation
16 ordinary	food; prophet, creation, mother
17 ordinary	family; body, judge
18 ordinary	treasure; clothing, wisdom
19 ordinary	day of the LORD; city, battle
20 ordinary	day of the LORD; journey, prophet
21 ordinary	outsider; kingdom, temple, family
22 ordinary	food; wisdom, mountain
23 ordinary	cross; wisdom, family
24 ordinary	treasure; fire, judge, shepherd
25 ordinary	servant; battle, poor
26 ordinary	heaven-earth-hell; poor, battle
27 ordinary	servant; treasure, judge
28 ordinary	outsider; prophet, water
29 ordinary	judge; battle, prophet
30 ordinary	outsider; battle, poor
31 ordinary	outsider; name of God, creation
32 ordinary	resurrection; battle, family
33 ordinary	day of the LORD; fire, name of God
Last	kingdom; body, light, shepherd

January 1
Mary, Mother of God   mother; name of God, family

February 2
Presentation   light; family, sacrifice

March 25
Annunciation   mother; prophet, sacrifice

May 31
Visitation   poor; mother, Israel, city

August 15
Assumption   mother; temple, battle

September 14
Holy Cross   cross; servant, wisdom

November 1
All Saints   poor; kingdom, shepherd, family

Biographical Appendix and Index

Acknowledgments and Endnotes

The psalms and their versification are from *The Book of Common Prayer* (1979), adapted by the author.

INTRODUCTION

1. Egeria, "Diary of a Pilgrimage," trans. George E. Gingras, *Ancient Christian Writers*, vol. 38 (New York: Newman Press, 1970), 104.

2. Augustine, *Confessions*, III. v. 9, trans. Henry Chadwick (Oxford: Oxford University Press, 1991), 40.

3. The most thorough is Fritz West, *Scripture and Memory: The Ecumenical Hermeneutic of the Three-Year Lectionaries* (Collegeville, MN: The Liturgical Press, 1997).

4. For a fuller history, see Hughes Oliphant Old, *The Reading and Preaching of the Scriptures in the Worship of the Christian Church*, vol. 3 (Grand Rapids, MI: William B. Eerdmans, 1999) 143–84; John Reumann, "A History of Lectionaries: From the Synagogue at Nazareth to Post-Vatican II," *Interpretation* 21 (1977): 116–30; and West, *Scripture and Memory*, 11–19.

5. The one-year list is printed in Martin Connell, *Guide to the Revised Lectionary* (Chicago: Liturgy Training Publications, 1998), 14–16.

6. *Lectionary for Mass* (Collegeville: The Liturgical Press, 1986).

7. See *The Book of Common Prayer* (New York: Church Publishing, 1979), 889–931, and *Lutheran Book of Worship* (Minneapolis: Augsburg Publishing House and Philadelphia: Board of Publication, Lutheran Church in America, 1978), 13–41.

8. *Common Lectionary: The Lectionary Proposed by the Consultation on Common Texts* (New York: The Church Hymnal Corporation, n.d.).

9. Consultation on Common Texts, *The Revised Common Lectionary* (Nashville: Abingdon Press, 1992).

10. Adrian Nocent, a member of the original Roman Catholic design committee, published *The Liturgical Year*, trans. Matthew J. O'Connell (Collegeville: The Liturgical Press, 1982). Perhaps his analysis represents the design committee's intentions.

11. Gail Ramshaw, "The First Testament in Christian Lectionaries," *Worship* 64 (1990): 494–510.

12. Each week also stipulates a psalm that relates to the first reading. This volume does not consider the psalms.

13. West, *Scripture and Memory*, 28–30.

14. Ibid, 183.

15. Lawrence A. Hoffman, ed., *My People's Prayer Book*, vol. 4, *Seder K'riat Hatorah* (The Torah Service) (Woodstock, VT: Jewish Lights Publishing, 2000), 67.

16. Melito of Sardis, *On Pascha*, trans. Stuart George Hall (Oxford: Clarendon Press, 1979), 37, 43.

17. See for example G. W. H. Lampe and K. J. Woollcombe, "Essays in Typology," *Studies in Biblical Theology* 22 (London: SCM Press, 1957). 42–47.

18. Leonhard Goppelt, *Typos: The Typological Interpretation of the Old Testament in the New*, trans. Donald H. Madvig (Grand Rapids, MI: William B. Eerdmans, 1982).

19. See the section title page in the New Revised Standard Version of the Bible.

20. See for example Paul M. van Buren, *According to the Scriptures: The Origins of the Gospel and of the Church's New Testament* (Grand Rapids, MI: William B. Eerdmans, 1998).

21. Bible Moralisee, Codex Vindobonensis 2554, Reihe Codices Selecti XL. Facsimiles are available at the Pierpont Morgan Library, New York, and at the Hill Monastic Manuscript Library, St. John's University, Collegeville, MN.

22. See West, *Scripture and Memory*, 16, 148. Also *Common Lectionary*, 21–22.

23. See *Biblia Pauperum: A Facsimile and Edition*, ed. Avril Henry (Ithaca, NY: Cornell University Press, 1987); or *The Bible of the Poor*, eds. Albert C. Labriola and John W. Smeltz (Pittsburgh: Duquesne University Press, 1990).

24. Gail Ramshaw, "The Gift of Three Readings," *Worship* 73 (1999): 2–12.

25. Julian of Norwich, *The Revelations of Divine Love*, trans. James Walsh, S.J. (Trabuco Canyon, CA: Source Books, 1961), 143.

26. Gregory of Nyssa, "On the Baptism of Christ," *Baptism: Ancient Liturgies and Patristic Texts*, ed. Andre Hamman, O.F.M. (Staten Island, NY: Alba House, 1967), 133.

27. Augustine, "The Meaning of Pentecost," *The Sunday Sermons of the Great Fathers*, trans. M. F. Toal, vol. 3 (Chicago: Henry Regnery, 1959), 34.

28. See Paul Scott Wilson, *A Concise History of Preaching* (Nashville: Abingdon Press, 1992); or Hughes Oliphant Old, *The Reading and Preaching of the Scritures in the Worship of the Christian Church*, vols. 1, 2, 3 (Grand Rapids, MI: William B. Eerdmans, 1998, 1999, 1999).

29. Augustine, "The Three Whom Jesus Raised to Life," *The Sunday Sermons of the Great Fathers*, vol. 3: 119.

30. Augustine, *Confessions*, VI. iii. 3-4.

31. William Butler Yeats, "The Second Coming," *Selected Poems and Two Plays*, ed. M. L. Rosenthal (New York: Macmillan Company, 1962), 91.

32. For a discussion of yes-no-yes, see Gail Ramshaw, *Reviving Sacred Speech* (Akron, OH: OSL Publications, 2000), 32–36.

33. George Lakoff and Mark Johnson, *Metaphors We Live By* (Chicago: University of Chicago Press, 1980), 3–6.

34. Paul Ricoeur, *The Rule of Metaphor*, trans. Robert Czerny (Toronto: University of Toronto Press, 1977), 224.

35. Ibid, 33.

36. Roy A. Rappaport, *Ritual and Religion in the Making of Humanity* (Cambridge: Cambridge University Press, 1999), 70–74.

37. Ibid, 393.

38. Paul S. Minear, *Images of the Church in the New Testament* (Philadelphia: Westminster Press, 1960), 19–27.

39. West, *Scripture and Memory*, 31, 39.

40. Jean Danielou, S.J., *The Bible and the Liturgy* (Notre Dame, IN: University of Notre Dame Press, 1956), 177–90.

41. *The Prayers of Catherine of Siena*, ed. Suzanne Noffke, O.P. (New York: Paulist Press, 1983), 187, 189. © 1983 Paulist Press, New York. Used by permission of Paulist Press.

42. Daniel B. Stevick, "The Language of Prayer," *Response* 3 (1976): 9.

43. Teresa of Avila, *The Interior Castle*, trans. Kieran Kavanaugh, O.C.D. and Otilio Rodriguez, O.C.D. (New York: Paulist Press, 1979), 172.

BATTLE

John Arthur, "This is the feast of victory," *Lutheran Book of Worship*, 60.

Martin Luther, trans. *Lutheran Book of Worship*, "A mighty fortress is our God." © 1978 *Lutheran Book of Worship*. Revised version from *Congregational Song: Proposals for Renewal* (Minneapolis: Augsburg Fortress, 2001), 1.

"The Trial of Joan of Arc," *Joan of Arc: Fact, Legend, and Literature*, ed. Wilfred T. Jewkes and Jerome B. Landfield (New York: Harcourt, Brace and World, 1964), 6–7.

Ignatius Loyola, *The Spiritual Exercises of Saint Ignatius*, trans. Anthony Mottola (New York: Doubleday Image Books, 1964), 132.

1. C. S. Lewis, *The Lion, the Witch, and the Wardrobe* (New York: Macmillan, 1950), 1.

BODY

Words at the communion, Holy Communion, *Lutheran Book of Worship*, 71.

Fred Pratt Green, "O Christ, the healer, we have come," words © 1969 Hope Publishing Co., Carol Stream, IL 60188. All rights reserved. Used by permission. In *Lutheran Book of Worship*, #360.

Augustine, sermon 272, *Sermons*, trans. Edmund Hill, O.P., *The Works of Saint Augustine: A Translation for the 21st Century*, vol. 7 (New Rochelle, NY: New City Press, 1993), 300.

Caryll Houselander, *The Risen Christ* (London: Sheed and Ward, 1958), 64–65.

CITY

Easter psalm antiphon, *Lutheran Book of Worship*, 177.

Erik Routley, "All who love and serve your city," words © 1969 Stainer & Bell Ltd., admin. Hope Publishing Co., Carol Stream, IL 60188. All rights reserved. Used by permission. In *Lutheran Book of Worship*, #436.

Augustine, *The City of God*, trans. Marcus Dods (New York: The Modern Library, 1950), 477, 478.

Kathleen Norris, "The New Jerusalem," *Amazing Grace: A Vocabulary of Faith* (New York: Riverhead Books, 1998), 383–84.

CLOTHING

Words at the clothing, Holy Baptism, *Lutheran Book of Worship* Ministers Edition, 31.

Joel W. Lundeen, "Now we join in celebration," © Joel W. Lundeen, admin. Augsburg Fortress. In *Lutheran Book of Worship*, #203.

Cyril of Jerusalem, *Lectures on the Christian Sacraments*, ed. F. L. Cross (Crestwood, NY: St. Vladimir's Seminary Press, 1977), 59.

Julian of Norwich, *The Revelations of Divine Love*, trans. James Walsh, 53.

1. Julian of Norwich, *The Revelations of Divine Love*, trans. James Walsh, 138, 143.

COVENANT

Canticle of Zechariah, translation prepared by the English Language Liturgical Consultation, *Praying Together* (Nashville: Abingdon Press, 1988), 46.

Marty Haugen, "Praise to you, O God of mercy," © 1990 GIA Publications, Inc. All rights reserved. In *With One Voice* (Minneapolis: Augsburg Fortress, 1995), #790.

Irenaeus, "Against Heresies," *Early Christian Fathers*, ed. Cyril C. Richardson (New York: Macmillan Co., 1970), 383.

Phoebe Palmer, "Entire Devotion to God," *Phoebe Palmer: Selected Writings*, ed. Thomas C. Oden (New York: Paulist Press, 1988), 198–200.

1. "Wesley's Covenant Service," *The United Methodist Book of Worship* (Nashville: The United Methodist Publishing House, 1992), 293.

CREATION

Nicene Creed, translation prepared by the English Language Liturgical Consultation, *Praying Together*, 23.

Catherine Cameron, "God, who stretched the spangled heavens," words © 1967 Hope Publishing Co., Carol Stream, IL 60188. All rights reserved. Used by permission. In *Lutheran Book of Worship*, #463.

St. Symeon the New Theologian, *Hymns of Divine Love*, trans. George A. Maloney, S.J. (Denville, NJ: Dimension Books, n.d.), 52–53.

Julian of Norwich, *The Revelations of Divine Love*, trans. James Walsh, 53.

1. "Mahapurana," *Sources of Indian Tradition*, ed. W. Theodore de Bary (New York: Columbia University Press, 1958), 79–80.

CROSS

Good Friday liturgy, *Lutheran Book of Worship* Ministers Edition, 142.

Thomas Kelly, "We sing the praise of him who died," *Lutheran Book of Worship*, #344.

"The Pasch History," *The Paschal Mystery: Ancient Liturgies and Patristic Texts*, ed. A. Hamman, O.F.M. (Staten Island: Alba House, 1969), 64–65.

Mercy Amba Oduyoye, *With Passion and Compassion*, eds. Virginia Fabella, M.M., and Mercy Amba Oduyoye (Maryknoll, NY: Orbis Books, 1988), 41–43.

1. Translated by Gail Ramshaw, "When the Cross Tells the Story," *Liturgy* 1 (1980): 12.

2. Martin Luther, *A Contemporary Translation of Luther's Small Catechism*, Study Edition, trans. Timothy T. Wengert (Minneapolis: Augsburg Fortress, 1994), 51.

DAY OF THE LORD
Prayer of the day, proper 27, *Readings and Prayers: The Revised Common Lectionary* (Minneapolis: Augsburg Fortress, 1995), 18.

Wilhelm A. Wexels, trans. Gracia Grindal, "Oh, happy day when we shall stand." © 1978 *Lutheran Book of Worship*, admin. Augsburg Fortress. In *Lutheran Book of Worship*, #351.

Ephraem, sermon 13, *The Sunday Sermons of the Great Fathers*, vol. 4, trans. M. F. Toal, 348–49.

Frances R. Havergal, "Thou art coming," *Book of Worship with Hymns and Tunes* (Philadelphia: United Lutheran Publication House, 1899), #579.

EMANATION OF THE DIVINE
Nicene Creed, translation prepared by the English Language Liturgical Consultation, *Praying Together*, 23.

Ambrose of Milan, trans. composite, "Savior of the nations, come." St. 2 © 1969 Concordia Publishing House. Used by permission. In *Lutheran Book of Worship*, #28.

Pseudo-Dionysius, "The Celestial Hierarchy," *Pseudo-Dionysius: The Complete Works*, trans. Colm Luibheid (New York: Paulist Press, 1987), 145.

Beatrice of Nazareth, "Vision of the World as a Wheel," *Women Mystics in Medieval Europe*, eds. Emilie Zum Brunn and Georgette Epiney-Bungard, trans. Sheila Hughes (New York: Paragon House, 1989), 90.

1. Augustine, *Confessions*, VII. ix. 13.

FAMILY
Introduction, Holy Baptism, *Lutheran Book of Worship*, 121.

F. Bland Tucker, alt., "Our Father, by whose name," © Church Pension Fund. Used by permission. In *Lutheran Book of Worship*, #357.

"The Rule of St. Clare," *Francis and Clare: The Complete Works*, trans. Regis J. Armstrong, O.F.M.Cap. and Ignatius C. Brady, O.F.M. (New York: Paulist Press, 1982), 130, 132, 133–34.

Martin Luther, *Small Catechism*, trans. Timothy T. Wengert, 32.

FIRE
Exsultet (Easter Proclamation), *Lutheran Book of Worship* Ministers Edition, 145.

Bianco da Siena, trans. Richard F. Littledale, "Come down, O Love divine," *Lutheran Book of Worship*, #508.

Pseudo-Dionysius, "The Celestial Hierarchy," *Pseudo-Dionysius: The Complete Works*, trans. Colm Luibheid, 183.

Hildegard of Bingen, *Scivias*, trans. Columba Hart and Jane Bishop (New York: Paulist Press, 1990), 163–64.

FISH

Cesáreo Gabarain, trans. Madeleine Forell Marshall, "You have come down to the lakeshore." Tr. © Editorial Avance Luterano. In *With One Voice*, #784.

Tertullian, "Treatise on Baptism," trans. S. Thelwall, *Baptism: Ancient Liturgies and Patristic Texts*, 30.

Marguerite d'Oingt, "The Mirror of St. Marguerite d'Oingt," *Medieval Women's Visionary Literature*, ed. Elizabeth Alvilda Petroff, trans. Richard J. Pioli (New York: Oxford University Press, 1986), 292.

FOOD

Eucharistic prayer III, *Lutheran Book of Worship* Ministers Edition, 297.

Seventeenth-century Latin hymn, trans. composite, "O Bread of life from heaven," *Lutheran Book of Worship*, #222.

Cyril of Alexandria, homily 10, *The Sunday Sermons of the Great Fathers*, vol. 3, trans. M. F. Toal, 155–56.

Catherine of Siena, prayer #12, *The Prayers of Catherine of Siena*, ed. Suzanne Noffke, 102. © 1983 Paulist Press, New York. Used by permission of Paulist Press.

GARDEN

Offertory verse, twelfth Sunday after Pentecost (proper 14), *Lutheran Book of Worship* Ministers Edition, 164.

Jaroslav J. Vajda, "God, you made this world a garden," *So Much to Sing About* (St. Louis: MorningStar, 1991), 120. © 1989 Jaroslav J. Vajda. Used by permission of Concordia Publishing House.

Gertrude of Helfta, *The Herald of Divine Love*, trans. Margaret Winkworth (New York: Paulist Press, 1993), 97.

Isaac Watts, "We are a garden walled around," *The Psalms, Hymns and Spiritual Songs* (Boston: Crocker & Brewster, 1849), 328–29.

HARVEST

John Arthur, "Let the vineyards be fruitful," *Lutheran Book of Worship*, 66.

Henry Alford, "Come, you thankful people, come," *Lutheran Book of Worship*, #407.

"The Didache," *Springtime of the Liturgy*, ed. Lucien Deiss, C.S.Sp., trans. Matthew J. O'Connell (Collegeville, MN: The Liturgical Press, 1979), 75.

Julia A. J. Foote, "A Brand Plucked from the Fire: An autobiographical sketch, by Mrs. Julia A. J. Foote." Printed for the author by Lauer & Yost, Cleveland, Ohio, 1879. Reprinted in *Spiritual Narratives* (New York: Oxford University Press, 1988), 104–106.

HEAVEN-EARTH-HELL

Apostles' Creed, translation prepared by the English Language Liturgical Consultation, *Praying Together*, 29.

Venantius Honorius Fortunatus, trans. John Ellerton, "Welcome, happy morning," *Lutheran Book of Worship*, #153.

Romanos, *Kontakia of Romanos, Byzantine Melodist*, trans. Marjorie Carpenter, vol. 1 (Columbia, MO: University of Missouri Press, 1970), 275, 278–79. © 1970 Curators of the University of Missouri. Reprinted by permission of the University of Missouri Press.

Catherine of Genoa, *Purgation and Purgatory*, trans. Serge Hughes (New York: Paulist Press, 1979), 77.

ISRAEL

Prayer at Easter Vigil (after the Exodus reading), *Lutheran Book of Worship* Ministers Edition, 148.

John Mason Neale, after twelfth-century Latin hymn, "Oh, come, oh, come, Emmanuel," *Lutheran Book of Worship*, #34.

Hadewijch, "The Jacob Letter," *The Complete Works of Hadewijch*, ed. Columba Hart, O.S.B. (New York: Paulist Press, 1980), 73.

Thomas Merton, *Bread in the Wilderness* (Collegeville, MN: The Liturgical Press, 1953), 112–13.

1. *Book of Common Worship* (Louisville: Westminster/John Knox Press, 1993), 289-290.

JOURNEY

Traditional prayer before travel, *Lutheran Book of Worship*, 167.

William Williams, trans. Peter Williams et al., "Guide me ever, great Redeemer," *Lutheran Book of Worship*, #343.

Egeria, "Diary of a Pilgrimage," trans. George E. Gingras, 56, 57, 59.

John of the Cross, "The Ascent of Mount Carmel," *John of the Cross: Selected Writings*, ed. Kieran Kavanaugh, O.C.D. (New York: Paulist Press, 1987), 93, 94.

JUDGE

Bernard of Cluny, trans. *Lutheran Book of Worship*, "The clouds of judgment gather." © 1978 *Lutheran Book of Worship*, admin. Augsburg Fortress. In *Lutheran Book of Worship*, #322.

Hildegard of Bingen, *Scivias*, trans. Columba Hart and Jane Bishop, 467.

Martin Luther, *The Bondage of the Will*, *Luther's Works*, vol. 33, ed. Philip S. Watson (Philadelphia: Fortress Press, 1972), 291, 292.

KINGDOM

Isaac Watts, "Jesus shall reign," *Lutheran Book of Worship*, #530.

Patrick, sermon for Advent, *The Sunday Sermons of the Great Fathers*, vol. 1, trans. M. F. Toal, 45.

Rosemary Radford Ruether, *Sexism and God-Talk: Toward a Feminist Theology* (Boston: Beacon Press, 1993), 119–20.

LIGHT

Easter Vigil, opening versicle and Exsultet (Easter Proclamation), *Lutheran Book of Worship* Ministers Edition, 143-45.

Ambrose, trans. Gracia Grindal, "O Splendor of the Father's light." © 1978 *Lutheran Book of Worship*, admin. Augsburg Fortress. In *Lutheran Book of Worship*, #271.

Teresa of Avila, *The Interior Castle*, trans. Kieran Kavanaugh and Otilio Rodriguez, 45.

John Bunyan, *The Pilgrim's Progress*, ed. Roger Sharrock (London: Penguin Books, 1965), 58–59.

MARRIAGE

Prayer in marriage rite, *Lutheran Book of Worship*, 204.

Johann Franck, trans. *Lutheran Book of Worship*, "Soul, adorn yourself with gladness." © 1978 *Lutheran Book of Worship*, admin. Augsburg Fortress. In *Lutheran Book of Worship*, #224.

Bernard of Clairvaux, sermon 83, *On the Song of Songs*, trans. Irene Edmonds, vol. 4 (Kalamazoo, MI: Cistercian Publications, 1980), 183, 185.

Mechthild of Magdeburg, *The Flowing Light of the Godhead*, trans. Frank Tobin (New York: Paulist Press, 1998), 49–50.

MOTHER

Eucharistic prayer B, *With One Voice* Leaders Edition, 66.

Jean Janzen, after Julian of Norwich, "Mothering God." © 1991 Jean Janzen, admin. Augsburg Fortress. In *With One Voice*, #769.

Zeno of Verona, "Seven Invitations to the Baptismal Font," *Baptism: Ancient Liturgies and Patristic Texts*, 64–66.

Sallie McFague, *Models of God: Theology for an Ecological, Nuclear Age* (Philadelphia: Fortress Press, 1987), 113.

MOUNTAIN

Prayer of the day, Transfiguration, *Lutheran Book of Worship* Ministers Edition, 128.

Susan Palo Cherwien, "In the desert, on God's mountain," *O Blessed Spring* (Minneapolis: Augsburg Fortress, 1997), 28–29. © 1989 Susan Palo Cherwien, admin. Augsburg Fortress.

Ephraem, sermon on the Transfiguration, *The Sunday Sermons of the Great Fathers*, vol. 2, trans. M. F. Toal, 46–47. Reprinted by permission of Ignatius Press, San Francisco.

Elisabeth of Schoenau, "Visions—Book Two," trans. Thalia A. Pandiri, *Medieval Women's Visionary Literature*, 164.

NAME OF GOD

Thomas Olivers, "The God of Abraham praise," *Lutheran Book of Worship*, #544.

Augustine, "Teaching Christianity," trans. Edmund Hill, O.P., ed. John E. Rotelle, O.S.A., *The Works of Saint Augustine: A Translation for the 21st Century*, vol. 11 (Hyde Park, NY: New City Press, 1996), 107, 108.

Catherine of Siena, prayer #20, *The Prayers of Catherine of Siena*, ed. Suzanne Noffke, 186. © 1983 Paulist Press, New York. Used by permission of Paulist Press.

OUTSIDER

Bidding prayer, Good Friday liturgy, *Lutheran Book of Worship* Ministers Edition, 140-41.

Koh Yuki, trans. *Lutheran Book of Worship*, "In a lowly manger born." © 1978 *Lutheran Book of Worship*, admin. Augsburg Fortress. In *Lutheran Book of Worship*, #417.

"Some Tales of St. Bridget," *Mystics, Visionaries, and Prophets: A Historical Anthology of Women's Spiritual Writings*, ed. Shawn Madigan, C.S.J. (Minneapolis: Fortress Press, 1998), 50.

The Little Flowers of St. Francis, ed. Raphael Brown (Garden City, NJ: Doubleday Image Books, 1958), 96.

THE POOR

Canticle of Mary, translation prepared by the English Language Liturgical Consultation, *Praying Together*, 50.

Harry E. Fosdick, "God of grace and God of glory," *Lutheran Book of Worship*, #415.

St. Francis of Assisi, "Legend of the Three Companions," *Writings and Early Biographies: English Omnibus of the Sources for the Life of St. Francis*, ed. Marion A. Habig, 3rd rev. ed. (Chicago: Franciscan Herald Press, 1973), 896–897.

Dorothy Day, *By Little and By Little*, ed. Robert Ellsberg (New York: Alfred A. Knopf, 1983), 114.

PROPHET

Canticle of Zechariah, translation prepared by the English Language Liturgical Consultation, *Praying Together*, 46.

Sarah E. Taylor, "O God of Light," words © 1952, ren. 1980 by The Hymn Society of America, admin. Hope Publishing Co., Carol Stream, IL 60188. All rights reserved. Used by permission. In *Lutheran Book of Worship*, #237.

Jarena Lee, "The Religious Experience and Journal of Jarena Lee," *Spiritual Narratives*, 17, 18.

Martin Luther King Jr., "I See the Promised Land," *A Testament of Hope: The Essential Writings of Martin Luther King Jr.*, ed. James Melvin Washington (San Francisco: Harper & Row, 1986), 282, 286.

RESURRECTION OF THE BODY

Proper preface, Sundays after Pentecost, *Lutheran Book of Worship* Ministers Edition, 217.

John of Damascus, trans. John M. Neale, "Come, you faithful, raise the strain," *Lutheran Book of Worship*, #132.

The teachings of Macrina, in Gregory of Nyssa, "On the Soul and the Resurrection," *Nicene and Post-Nicene Fathers*, Second Series, vol. v, ed. Philip Schaff and Henry Wace (Grand Rapids, MI: William B. Eerdmans, 1972), 467.

Niceta, "The Names and Titles of Our Saviour," *Writings of Niceta of Remesiana*, trans. Gerald G. Walsh, S.J., *The Fathers of the Church*, vol. 7 (Washington, DC: Catholic University of America Press, 1949), 9–12.

SACRIFICE
Prayer after communion, *Lutheran Book of Worship*, 229.

Charles Wesley, "Victim Divine, your grace we claim," *Lutheran Book of Worship*, #202.

Irenaeus, "Against Heresies," *The Mass: Ancient Liturgies and Patristic Texts*, ed. Adalbert Hamman, O.F.M. (Staten Island, NY: Alba House, 1967), 177–78.

Rose Hawthorne Lathrop, "Sacrifices for the Poor—A Difficulty Challenged," *Rose Hawthorne Lathrop: Selected Writings*, ed. Diana Culbertson, O.P. (New York: Paulist Press, 1993), 204.

SERVANT
Installation of a Lay Professional Leader, *Occasional Services* (Minneapolis: Augsburg Publishing House and Philadelphia: Board of Publication, Lutheran Church in America, 1982), 136.

Tom Colvin, "Jesu, Jesu," words © 1969 Hope Publishing Co., Carol Stream, IL 60188. All rights reserved. Used by permission. In *With One Voice*, #765.

Martin Luther, "The Freedom of a Christian," *Luther's Works*, vol. 31, ed. Harold J. Grimm (Philadelphia: Muhlenberg Press, 1957), 344.

Letty Russell, "The Impossible Possibility," *Women and the Word: Sermons*, ed. Helen Gray Crotwell (Philadelphia: Fortress Press, 1978), 87–88.

SHEPHERD
Commendation, Burial of the Dead, *Lutheran Book of Worship*, 211.

Edinburgh *Psalter*, "The Lord's my shepherd," *Lutheran Book of Worship*, #451.

Melito of Sardis, *On Pascha*, trans. Stuart George Hall, 3, 17.

Perpetua, "The Martyrdom of Saints Perpetua and Felicitas," *Maenads, Martyrs, Matrons, Monastics: A Sourcebook on Women's Religions in the Greco-Roman World*, ed. Ross S. Kraemer (Philadelphia: Fortress Press, 1988), 98–99.

SPIRIT
Holy Baptism, *Lutheran Book of Worship*, 124.

Jean Janzen, after Hildegard of Bingen, "O Holy Spirit, root of life." © 1991 Jean Janzen, admin. Augsburg Fortress. In *With One Voice*, #688.

Ambrose, "The Holy Spirit," *Saint Ambrose: Theological and Dogmatic Works*, trans. Roy J. Defarrari, *The Fathers of the Church*, vol. 44 (Washington, DC: Catholic University of America Press, 1963), 66–67.

Edwina Gateley, "Prophetic Mission: Sniffing Out the Kingdom," *Mystics, Visionaries, and Prophets*, 492.

TEMPLE
Dedication of a Church Building, *Occasional Services*, 169.

Nikolai F. S. Grundtvig, trans. Carl Doving and Fred. C. M. Hansen, "Built on a rock." © 1958 *Service Book and Hymnal*. In *Lutheran Book of Worship*, #365.

Gregory the Great, homily 39, *The Sunday Sermons of the Great Fathers*, vol. 3, trans. M. F. Toal, 351–52.

Evelyn Underhill, *The Ways of the Spirit*, ed. Grace Adolphsen Brame (New York: Crossroad, 1990), 196, 198.

TREASURE
Prayer of the Church, *Lutheran Book of Worship*, 52.

Eleanor Hull, "Be thou my vision," *With One Voice*, #776.

Jacob of Voragine, *The Golden Legend*, trans. William Granger Ryan (Princeton: Princeton University Press, 1993), 64–66.

Teresa of Avila, *The Interior Castle*, trans. Kieran Kavanaugh and Otilio Rodriguez, 86.

TREE
Proper preface, Passion Sunday, *Lutheran Book of Worship* Ministers Edition, 212, alt.

Delores Dufner, "Faithful cross, O tree of beauty." © 1993, Delores Dufner, O.S.B. Published by OCP Publications, 5536 NE Hassalo, Portland OR 97213. All rights reserved. Used with permission.

Bonaventure, "The Tree of Life," *Bonaventure: The Soul's Journey into God, The Tree of Life, The Life of St. Francis*, trans. and ed. Ewert Cousins (New York: Paulist Press, 1978), 120–21.

Catherine of Siena, *The Prayers of Catherine of Siena*, ed. Suzanne Noffke, 147–48. © 1983 Paulist Press, New York. Used by permission of Paulist Press.

WATER
Holy Baptism, *Lutheran Book of Worship*, 122.

Thomas Herbranson, "This is the Spirit's entry now," © Thomas Herbranson. In *Lutheran Book of Worship*, #195.

Gregory of Nyssa, "A Sermon for the Feast of the Lights," *Baptism: Ancient Liturgies and Patristic Texts*, 126, 130.

Flannery O'Connor, "The River," *The Complete Stories of Flannery O'Connor* (New York: Farrar, Straus and Giroux, 1971), 165.

WEEK
Proper preface, Sundays after Pentecost, *Lutheran Book of Worship* Ministers Edition, 217.

Christopher Wordsworth, "O day of rest and gladness," *Lutheran Book of Worship*, #251.

Augustine, sermon 259, *Saint Augustine: Sermons on the Liturgical Seasons*, trans. Mary Sarah Muldowney, R.S.M., *The Fathers of the Church*, vol. 38 (Washington, DC: Catholic University of American Press, 1959), 370.

Annie Dillard, *Holy the Firm* (New York: Bantam, 1977), 58–59.

WIND

James K. Manley, "Spirit, Spirit of gentleness," © 1978 James K. Manley. In *With One Voice*, #684.

Origen, "The Testing of the Apostles," *The Sunday Sermons of the Great Fathers*, vol. 1, trans. M. F. Toal, 318–20.

Rebecca Jackson, *Gifts of Power*, ed. Jean McMahon Humez (Amhurst, MA: University of Massachusetts Press, 1981), 182.

WISDOM

O Antiphon for December 17, *Lutheran Book of Worship*, 174.

Willard F. Jabusch, "Open your ears, O faithful people." © 1966, 1982, Willard F. Jabusch. Administered by OCP Publications, 5536 NE Hassalo, Portland OR 97213. All rights reserved. Used with permission. In *With One Voice*, #715.

Augustine, "The Happy Life," *Augustine of Hippo: Selected Writings*, ed. Mary T. Clark (New York: Paulist Press, 1984), 188, 192.

Hildegard of Bingen, *Scivias*, trans. Columba Hart and Jane Bishop, 465–66.

AFTERWORD

St. Symeon the New Theologian, *Hymns of Divine Love* trans. George A. Maloney, 14.

1. Susan Palo Cherwien, "O blessed spring." © 1993 Susan Palo Cherwien, admin. Augsburg Fortress. In *With One Voice*, #695.

Bibliography

REFERENCE WORKS

The Anchor Bible Dictionary. Edited by David Noel Freeman. New York: Doubleday, 1992.

Chevalier, Jean, and Alain Gheerbrant. *A Dictionary of Symbols*. Translated by John Buchanan-Brown. New York: Penguin, 1994.

Day, A. Colin. *Roget's Thesaurus of the Bible*. San Francisco: Harper, 1992.

Dictionary of Biblical Imagery. Edited by Leland Ryken, James C. Wilhoit, and Tremper Longman III. Downers Grove, IL: InterVarsity Press, 1998.

The Encyclopedia of Philosophy. Edited by Paul Edwards. New York: Macmillan, 1967.

The Encyclopedia of Religion. Edited by Mircea Eliade. New York: Macmillan, 1987.

Gaster, Theodor H. *Myth, Legend and Custom in the Old Testament*. New York: Harper & Row, 1969.

The Jerome Biblical Commentary. Edited by Raymond E. Brown, Joseph A. Fitzmyer, and Roland E. Murphy. Englewood Cliffs, NJ: Prentice Hall, 1968. (The first edition is more useful for images than the second edition, *The New Jerome Biblical Commentary*, 1990.)

LECTIONARY

Connell, Martin. *Guide to the Revised Lectionary*. Chicago: Liturgy Training Publications, 1998.

Consultation on Common Texts. *The Revised Common Lectionary*. Nashville: Abingdon Press, 1992.

van Buren, Paul M. *According to the Scriptures: The Origins of the Gospel and of the Church's Old Testament*. Grand Rapids, MI: William B. Eerdmans, 1998.

West, Fritz. *Scripture and Memory: The Ecumenical Hermeneutic of the Three-Year Lectionaries*. Collegeville, MN: The Liturgical Press, 1997.

LANGUAGE

Lakoff, George, and Mark Johnson. *Metaphors We Live By*. Chicago: University of Chicago Press, 1980.

Miller, Casey, and Kate Swift. *Words and Women: New Language in New Times*, 2nd ed. New York: HarperCollins, 1991.

Ramsey, Ian T. *Religious Language*. New York: Macmillan, 1963.

Ricoeur, Paul. *The Rule of Metaphor*. Translated by Robert Czerny. Toronto: University of Toronto Press, 1977.

Wheelwright, Philip. *Metaphor and Reality*. Bloomington, IN: Indiana University Press, 1962.

BIBLICAL IMAGES

Ambrose. *Theological and Dogmatic Works*. Translated by Roy J. Deferrari. *The Fathers of the Church*, vol. 44. Washington, DC: Catholic University Press, 1963.

Brown, Raymond E. *The Gospel According to John. The Anchor Bible*, vols. 29 and 29A. Garden City, NJ: Doubleday, 1966, 1970.

Catherine of Siena. *The Prayers of Catherine of Siena*. Edited by Suzanne Noffke, O.P. New York: Paulist Press, 1983.

Danielou, Jean, S.J. *The Bible and the Liturgy*. Notre Dame, IN: University of Notre Dame Press, 1956.

Frye, Northrop. *The Great Code: The Bible and Literature*. New York: Harcourt Brace Jovanovich, 1982.

Henry, Avril, editor. *Biblia Pauperum*. Ithaca, NY: Cornell University Press, 1987.

Jeremias, Joachim. *The Parables of Jesus*, revised edition. New York: Charles Scribner's Sons, 1963.

Keel, Othmar. *The Symbolism of the Biblical World*. Translated by Timothy J. Hallett. New York: Crossroad, 1985.

Keel, Othmar, and Christoph Uehlinger. *Gods, Goddesses, and Images of God in Ancient Israel*. Translated by Thomas H. Trapp. Minneapolis: Fortress Press, 1998.

Toal, M. F. *The Sunday Sermons of the Great Fathers*. 4 vols. Chicago: Henry Regnery Company, 1958.

Wilder, Amos. *Theopoetic: Theology and the Religious Imagination*. Philadelphia: Fortress Press, 1976.

BATTLE

van Rad, Gerhard. *Holy War in Ancient Israel*. Translated by Marva J. Dawn. Grand Rapids, MI: William B. Eerdmans, 1991.

BODY

Chauvet, Louis, and Francois Kabasele Lumbala. *Liturgy and the Body. Concilium* 1995, 3. Maryknoll, NY: Orbis Books, 1995.

Minear, Paul S. *Images of the Church in the New Testament*. Philadelphia: Westminster Press, 1960.

CITY

Ellul, Jacques. *The Meaning of the City*. Grand Rapids, MI: William B. Eerdmans, 1970.

Hoppe, Leslie J., O.F.M. *The Holy City: Jerusalem in the Theology of the Old Testament*. Collegeville, MN: Liturgical Press, 2000.

CLOTHING

Hines, Dick. *Dressing for Worship*. Grove Worship Series 138. Cambridge, UK: Grove Books Limited, 1996.

COVENANT

Dumbrell, William J. *Covenant and Creation: A Theology of Old Testament Covenants*. Nashville: Thomas Nelson, 1984.

Ralph, Margaret Nutting. *Plain Words about Biblical Images*. New York: Paulist Press, 1989.

CREATION

Clifford, Richard J., and John J. Collins, editors. *Creation in the Biblical Traditions*. The Catholic Biblical Quarterly Monograph Series 24. Washington, DC: Catholic Biblical Association of America, 1992.

McFague, Sallie. *The Body of God: An Ecological Theology*. Minneapolis: Fortress Press, 1993.

Sproul, Barbara C. *Primal Myths: Creating the World*. San Francisco: Harper & Row, 1979.

CROSS

Seymour, William Wood. *The Cross: In Tradition, History, and Art*. New York: G.P. Putnam's Sons, 1898.

DAY OF THE LORD

Minear, Paul S. *New Testament Apocalyptic*. Nashville: Abingdon Press, 1981.

Rowland, Christopher. *The Open Heaven: A Study of Apocalyptic in Judaism and Early Christianity*. New York: Crossroad, 1982.

EMANATION OF THE DIVINE

Armstrong, A. H., and R. A. Markus. *Christian Faith and Greek Philosophy*. New York: Sheed and Ward, 1960.

FAMILY

Moxnes, Halvor, editor. *Constructing Christian Families: Family as Social Reality and Metaphor*. New York: Routledge, 1997.

Perdue, Leo G., et al. *Families in Ancient Israel*. Louisville, KY: Westminster John Knox Press, 1997.

FIRE

Fleming, David A., S.M., editor. *The Fire and the Cloud: An Anthology of Catholic Spirituality*. New York: Paulist Press, 1978.

Morgenstern, Julian. *The Fire Upon the Altar*. Chicago: Quadrangle Books, 1963.

FISH

Goodenough, Erwin R. *Jewish Symbols in the Greco-Roman Period*, vol. 5. New York: Pantheon Books, 1956.

Wuellner, Wilhelm H. *The Meaning of "Fishers of Men."* Philadelphia: Westminster Press, 1967.

FOOD

Davison, Gary P., editor. *Banquet of Praise*. Washington, DC: Bread for the World, 1990.

Feeley-Harnik, Gillian. *The Lord's Table: Eucharist and Passover in Early Christianity*. Philadelphia: University of Pennsylvania Press, 1981.

GARDEN

Barr, James. *The Garden of Eden and the Hope of Immortality*. Minneapolis: Fortress Press, 1992.

HARVEST

Borowski, Oded. *Agriculture in Iron Age Israel*. Winona Lake, IN: Eisenbrauns, 1987.

HEAVEN-EARTH-HELL

Bernstein, Alan E. *The Formation of Hell: Death and Retribution in the Ancient and Early Christian Worlds*. Ithaca, NY: Cornell University Press, 1993.

McDonnell, Colleen, and Bernhard Lang. *Heaven: A History*. New Haven, CT: Yale University Press, 1988.

Stadelmann, Luis I. J., S.J. *The Hebrew Conception of the World: A Philological and Literary Study*. Rome: Pontifical Bibical Institute, 1970.

ISRAEL

Goppelt, Leonhard. *Typos: The Typological Interpretation of the Old Testament in the New*. Translated by Donald H. Madvig. Grand Rapids, MI: William B. Eerdmans, 1982.

JOURNEY

Crabtree, Harriet. *The Christian Life: Traditional Metaphors and Contemporary Theologies*. Minneapolis: Fortress Press, 1991.

Fowler, Jim, and Sam Keen. *Life Maps: Conversations on the Journey of Faith*. Edited by Jerome Berryman. Waco, TX: Waco Books, 1978.

JUDGE

Griffiths, J. Gwyn. T*he Divine Verdict: A Study of Divine Judgement in the Ancient Religions*. Studies in the History of Religions, vol. 52. New York: E. J. Brill, 1991.

Reiser, Marius. *Jesus and Judgment*. Translated by Linda M. Maloney. Minneapolis: Fortress Press, 1997.

KINGDOM

Lerner, Gerda. *The Creation of Patriarchy*. New York: Oxford University Press, 1986.

Perrin, Norman. *Jesus and the Language of the Kingdom*. Philadelphia: Fortress Press, 1976.

LIGHT

Eliade, Mircea. *The Two and the One*. Translated by J. M. Cohen. London: Harvill Press, 1965.

Pelikan, Jaroslav. *The Light of the World: A Basic Image in Early Christian Thought*. New York: Harper & Brothers, 1962.

MARRIAGE

Matter, E. Ann. *The Voice of My Beloved: The Song of Songs in Western Medieval Christiainity*. Philadelphia: University of Pennsylvania Press, 1990.

MOTHER

McFague, Sallie. *Models of God: Theology for an Ecological, Nuclear Age*. Philadelphia: Fortress Press, 1982.

Neumann, Erich. *The Great Mother: An Analysis of the Archetype*. Princeton, NJ: Princeton University Press, 1955.

MOUNTAIN

Donaldson, Terence L. *Jesus on the Mountain*. Journal for the Study of the New Testament Supplement Series 8. Sheffield, UK: JSOT Press, 1985.

NAME OF GOD

Mettinger, Tryggve N. D. *In Search of God: The Meaning and Message of the Everlasting Name*. Translated by Frederick H. Cryer. Philadelphia: Fortress Press, 1987.

Smith, Mark S. *The Early History of God: Yahweh and the Other Deities in Ancient Israel*. San Francisco: Harper & Row, 1990.

OUTSIDER

Douglas, Mary. *Purity and Danger*. London: Routledge & Kegan Paul, 1966.

Reynolds, Vernon, et al., editors. *The Sociobiology of Ethnocentrism*. Athens, GA: University of Georgia Press, 1986.

THE POOR

Boff, Leonardo, and Virgil Elizondo, editors. *The People of God Amidst the Poor*. Concilium 176. Edinburgh: T. & T. Clark, 1984.

Hoppe, Leslie J., O.F.M. *Being Poor: A Biblical Study*. Wilmington, DE: Michael Glazier, 1987.

PROPHET

Crowe, Frederick E., S.J. *Theology of the Christian Word*. New York: Paulist Press, 1978.

Heschel, Abraham J. *The Prophets*. New York: Harper & Row, 1962.

Lee, Bernard J., S.M. *Jesus and the Metaphors of God*. New York: Paulist Press, 1993.

RESURRECTION OF THE BODY

Charles, R. H. *Eschatology: The Doctrine of a Future Life in Israel, Judaism, and Christianity*. New York: Schocken Books, 1963.

SACRIFICE

Daly, Robert J., S.J. *Christian Sacrifice: The Judeo-Christian Background before Origen*. Washington, DC: Catholic University of America Press, 1978.

SERVANT

Combes, J. A. H. "The Metaphor of Slavery in the Writings of the Early Church." *Journal for the Study of the New Testament Supplement Series* 156. Sheffield, UK: Sheffield Academic Press, 1998.

SHEPHERD

Luther, Martin. *God My Shepherd: Meditations on Psalm* 23. Translated by W. M. Miller. St. Louis: Concordia Publishing House, 1955.

SPIRIT

Lampe, G. W. H. *God as Spirit*. Oxford: Clarendon Press, 1977.

Moltmann, Jürgen. *The Spirit of Life*. Minneapolis: Fortress Press, 1992.

TEMPLE

Clements, R. E. *God and Temple*. Philadelphia: Fortress Press, 1965.

McKelvey, R. J. *The New Temple of the Church in the New Testament*. New York: Oxford University Press, 1969.

Mazar, Benjamin. *The Mountain of the Lord*. Garden City, NY: Doubleday & Company, 1975.

TREASURE

Crossan, John Dominic. *Finding Is the First Act: Trove Folktales and Jesus' Treasure Parable*. Philadelphia: Fortress Press, 1979.

TREE OF LIFE

Altman, Nathaniel. *Sacred Trees*. San Francisco: Sierra Club Books, 1994.

Cook, Roger. *The Tree of Life: Image for the Cosmos*. New York: Thames and Hudson, 1974.

WATER

Batto, Bernard F. *Slaying the Dragon: Mythmaking in the Biblical Tradition*. Louisville: Westminster John Knox Press, 1992.

Propp, William Henry. *Water in the Wilderness*. Atlanta, GA: Scholars Press, 1987.

WEEK

Herrmann, Siegfried. *Time and History*. Translated by James L. Blevins. Nashville: Abingdon Press, 1981.

Rordorf, Willy. *Sunday: The History of the Day of Rest and Worship*. Philadelphia: Westminster Press, 1968.

WIND

Eliade, Mircea. *Patterns in Comparative Religion*. Translated by Rosemary Sheed. New York: Sheed & Ward, 1958.

Henry, A. M., O.P. *The Holy Spirit*. Translated by J. Lundberg and M. Bell. New York: Hawthorn Books, 1960.

WISDOM

Johnson, Elizabeth A. *She Who Is: The Mystery of God in Feminist Theological Discourse*. New York: Crossroad, 1992.

Murphy, Roland E. *Tree of Life: An Exploration of Biblical Wisdom Literature*. New York: Anchor Doubleday, 1990.

CHILDREN'S PICTURE BOOKS WITH RELIGIOUS IMAGERY

Berger, Barbara Helen. *The Donkey's Dream*. New York: Philomel Books, 1985.

dePaola, Tomie. *The Garden of the Good Shepherd*. Chicago: Liturgy Training Publications, 2000.

Eisenberg, Ann. *Bible Heroes I Can Be*. Illustrated by Rosalyn Schanzer. Rockville, MD: Kar-Ben Copies, 1990.

Hoffman, Mary. *Earth, Fire, Water, Air*. Illustrated by Jane Ray. New York: Dutton Children's Books, 1995.

Hunkin, Oliver. *Dangerous Journey*. London: Marshall Morgan & Scott, 1985.

Leichman, Seymour. *The Boy Who Could Sing Pictures*. New York: Holt, Rinehart & Winston, 1973.

Mitchell, Stephen. *The Creation*. Illustrated by Ori Sherman. New York: Dial Books, 1990.

Sasso, Sandy Eisenberg. *In God's Name*. Illustrated by Phoebe Stone. Woodstock, VT: Jewish Lights Publishing, 1994.

Spier, Peter. *Noah's Ark*. Garden City, NJ: Doubleday & Company, 1977.

Wildsmith, Brian. *Exodus*. Grand Rapids, MI: Eerdmans Books for Young Readers, 1999.

Wildsmith, Brian. *The True Cross*. New York: Oxford University Press, 1977.

Wood, Douglas. *Old Turtle*. Illustrated by Cheng-Khee Chee. Duluth, MN: Pfeifer-Hamilton Publishers, 1992.

Index of Images and Liturgical Terms